The Open Adoption Experience

Also by the Authors

Lois Ruskai Melina

Raising Adopted Children

Making Sense of Adoption

*Adoption: An Annotated
Bibliography and Guide*

Sharon Kaplan Roszia

Cooperative Adoption
(with Mary Jo Rillera)

The Open Adoption Experience

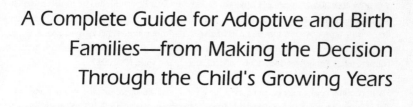

A Complete Guide for Adoptive and Birth Families—from Making the Decision Through the Child's Growing Years

Lois Ruskai Melina and Sharon Kaplan Roszia

HarperPerennial
A Division of HarperCollins*Publishers*

HarperCollins books may be purchased for educational, business, or sales promotional use. For information please write: Special Markets Department, HarperCollins Publishers, Inc., 10 East 53rd Street, New York, NY 10022.

FIRST EDITION

Designed by Barbara DuPree Knowles

Library of Congress Cataloging-in-Publication Data
Melina, Lois Ruskai.
  The open adoption experience : a complete guide for adoptive and birth families—from making the decision through the child's growing years / by Lois Ruskai Melina, Sharon Kaplan Roszia. — 1st ed.
    p. cm.
  Includes bibliographical references and index.
  ISBN 0-06-096957-1 (pbk.)
  1. Open adoption. 2. Birthparents. 3. Adoptive parents. 4. Children, Adopted—Family relationships. I. Roszia, Sharon Kaplan, 1942–   II. Title.
HV875.M369   1993
362.7´34—dc20   92-56254

00 01 02   RRD(H) 20 19 18 17 16 15 14 13 12

Contents

Acknowledgments

We wish to thank the many hundreds of families with open adoptions all over the world who have shared their questions, concerns, feelings, and solutions with us, and whose experiences form the basis for this book: people who have raised issues at conferences where we have spoken, who have written to us, who have participated in the Cooperative Adoption Support Group at Parenting Resources, who agreed to be interviewed personally, and who responded thoroughly and thoughtfully to our questionnaire. We are aware that sharing their stories with us often was emotionally exhausting and we want them to know how much they helped us clarify many of the issues and reach conclusions about the necessary attitudes and approaches to open adoptions.

We would like to acknowledge the contributions of those people who have "pioneered" the modern idea of open adoptions, especially Annette Baran, the staff of Catholic Social Services in Green Bay, Wisconsin, Patricia Martinez Dorner, Jeanne Etter, Vera Fahlberg, James Gritter, Mary Iwanek, Reuben Pannor, Mary Jo Rillera, Kathleen Silber, Phylis Speedlin, and Barbara Tremitiere. Many of them, along with other professionals, agreed to be interviewed for this book, and we would like to thank them for sharing their expertise with us: Anne Brodzinsky, Ellen Roseman-Curtis, Carol Demuth, Pamela DeMan, Jeanne Etter, Mary Fleischman, James Gritter, Hillary Hanafin, Randall Hicks, Mary Mason, Linda Nunez, Cheryl Reber, Patricia Roles, Kathleen Silber, Terry Winterberg, and Candace Kunz.

Despite their busy schedules, several people, including professionals, adult adoptees, birth parents, and adoptive parents, read parts or all of this manuscript in its early stages. We would like to thank them for their time, attention, and thoughtful advice: Annette Baran, Toni Bryant, James

Gritter, Lori Horlacher, Connie Hornyak, Lynn Lape, Betty Jean Lifton, Mary Mason, Reuben Pannor, Marlene Piasecki, Cindy Johnson Rodriquez, Pat Sanders, Kathleen Silber, Deborah Silverstein, and Linda Yellin. Special thanks to Patricia Irwin Johnston and Randolph W. Severson who repeatedly offered us valuable suggestions and who kept us on track.

We would like to thank our editors at HarperCollins: Janet Goldstein, for her enthusiasm for this book, and Peternelle van Arsdale, for her careful reading of the manuscript and good humor throughout. Mary Schierman made sense out of the revised manuscript and made corrections with the same kind of care that she took with Lois Melina's two other books. Without her help we would not have made our deadline.

In addition, we each have some thanks to give:

LOIS RUSKAI MELINA

As someone who always hated group projects at school, I surprised myself by wanting to collaborate on a book with someone. Sharon Kaplan Roszia proved to be everything I hoped for in a coauthor. She was available, thoughtful, cooperative, understanding, and fun to work with, and I learned much from her. Furthermore, I now know from personal experience that there is no one I'd rather be with during a major earthquake.

I would like to thank Pat Sanders, Carol Land, and Barry Slobin for their hospitality.

I am also grateful to Stephanie Crosswhite, my exceptional assistant, who signed on in the midst of this project but never lost her sense of humor, even when my deadlines meant canceling her own plans.

Throughout the writing of this book I was sustained and nourished by my friends, including my running partners and fellow swim team parents. Their understanding and support is deeply appreciated. I feel especially blessed to have the friendship of Lynn Baird, who was always there to listen, help me sort out the important from the unimportant, or give me a hug, no matter how chaotic her own day.

Finally, my husband, Carl, and my children, Emily and Galen, were again remarkably patient and compassionate, no matter how preoccupied I became with writing this book. The concrete things they did stand out, like making dinner, giving me some quiet time, helping me at the office, or feeding my horse, but what I really value is the love shown by those actions.

SHARON KAPLAN ROSZIA

Professionally, I'd like to thank the following people who gave me voice, encouragement, and shared wisdom: Linda Nunez, Mary Jo Rillera, Deborah Silverstein, Carol Land, Barry Slobin, Annette Baran, the staff of Children's Services Center of Monterey, my colleagues at Parenting Resources, and all the children and families who taught me by sharing their journeys with me. My special thanks to Lois Ruskai Melina, whose humor, friendship, and skills I have grown to love.

Personally, I thank Rena, Robert, Gloria, Arnie, Buddy, Adrienne, Tom, and Connie L. for sustaining and loving me. I send prayers and thanks to Leonard, May, Aaron, Selma, and Kathy, whom I miss. And to my source: Baruch Ashem!

Introduction

Like many adoptive parents, Maddie and Jeff met their daughter's birth mother before their daughter's birth, and kept in contact with her during and after the pregnancy. One of the things they found they had in common with Susan, the birth mother, was their love of animals. Maddie and Jeff had even included a picture of their collie in their resume photograph. So when little Jenny's first word was "dog," Maddie's first thought was how much Susan would enjoy hearing the story.

Looking back, Maddie says it was then that she truly understood what it meant to be involved in an open adoption. Telling Susan was not an obligation but a joy, because Maddie knew Susan would appreciate the story in a special way. Maddie realized that the connection between each member of this family circle was like no other bond.

The relationship between the birth family and the adoptive family of a child placed for adoption is unique. In adoption, new families are created by law, reflecting a social agreement that a nonbiologic parent or set of parents completely replaces a child's birth parents,[1] assuming all rights and responsibilities formerly held by them.

Yet there is an awareness among everyone involved that regardless of the way adoption changes parental roles, both legally and in practice, the

1. Many writers spell *birth parents* as one word. We have chosen to spell it as two words to be consistent with *adoptive parents*.

genetic and historical link between the child and the birth family cannot be abolished. Children reflect both *nature* and *nurture,* though the exact interplay between those factors is still a mystery. Consequently, the child has a connection to both the birth parents and the adoptive parents, because each has made a significant contribution to the child's development. This dual responsibility for who a child is and who he becomes also creates a connection between birth parents and adoptive parents (and their entire extended families[2]). Through them, a human life is created and nurtured into someone who will become an adult, influence others, and connect previous generations to the future.

This connection has not always been acknowledged. Information about the birth parents was kept secret from the adoptive family, and vice versa. The birth parents and the adoptive family didn't communicate with each other, either directly or indirectly. These adoptions have been called "closed," "confidential," or "traditional."

In recent years, however, the practice of adoption has changed to acknowledge the connection between birth families and adoptive families. In adoptions referred to as "open" or "fully disclosed," birth parents, the adopted child, and the adoptive parents know each other and interact directly at their own discretion. Their contact may be in person, or through correspondence and phone calls. In their book by the same name, Sharon Kaplan (Roszia) and Mary Jo Rillera named this kind of arrangement a "cooperative adoption."

There are myriad alternatives between these two extremes. There are adoptions called "semiopen" in which the birth parents and the adoptive parents communicate through the adoption agency or facilitator,[3] but do not reveal their complete names or addresses. In addition, a study of open adoptions by Ruth McRoy, Ph.D., of the University of Texas at Austin, Harold Grotevant, Ph.D., of the University of Minnesota, and Susan Ayers-Lopez, M.A., of the University of Texas at Austin has identified two other types of adoption: those in which the adoptive parents and birth parents exchanged information through an intermediary at one time, but later

2. Much of what we say about birth parents and adoptive parents applies to their extended families as well. For simplicity sake, however, we refer to birth parents and adoptive parents unless addressing issues unique to their extended families.

3. For the sake of brevity, we use the term *facilitator* to mean anyone who arranges an adoption, including a licensed adoption agency, social worker, adoption service or independent adoption practitioner, lawyer, or physician.

stopped, and those in which families had direct contact with each other at one time but terminated that contact at some point after placement. These researchers found so much variation in the amount and type of contact birth parents and adoptive parents have with each other that among their major categories of adoption they identified more than thirty-seven "subcategories." Clearly, there is as much variety in the relationships between birth and adoptive parents as any other kind of relationship.

Donor insemination, surrogacy, in vitro fertilization with a donor egg or donor embryo, and other forms of assisted reproductive technologies in which the legal parents of a child are not both the biologic parents are also forms of adoption, even though a legal adoption process does not always take place. These forms of adoption are "open" if the biologic and legal parents meet or have contact with each other (see Chapter 15).

If you've been confused by what is meant by an "open" adoption, it is because not everyone agrees on the definition. Further complicating the issue is that adoption professionals often speak of "openness" in adoption when they mean "truthfulness." So when people talk about being "open" about their adoption, they may simply mean they are honest in acknowledging that their child was adopted.

Some adoption agencies and adoption facilitators offer birth and adoptive parents a full range of choices concerning openness, whereas others have restricted their practices to a particular level of openness. Most adoption practices appear to be moving to increased degrees of contact between birth and adoptive families.

These changes are happening because many people believe open adoption offers birth parents, adoptive parents, and adoptees of all ages advantages that confidential adoptions do not. By staying in touch with each other, children do not have to lose people who have a significant connection to them. They can see that they are valued by their birth family and that their adoptive placement wasn't a rejection. They can have access to reliable information about their origins and the reasons for the adoption plan.

Birth parents do not have to lose touch with their children to ensure that they will find permanent parents and can be reassured that they made a good choice as they observe their children growing and thriving. Adoptive parents feel more secure in their role as parents when they receive direct permission from the birth parents to be their child's parents, and when they see that the birth parents' presence in their lives does not diminish their genuine parent–child relationship. Finally, families benefit from open adoptions because they eliminate some of the long-term family secrets that led to frightening fantasies and shame.

Despite what many see as benefits, you may have some questions and concerns about open adoption because it probably is different than the adoptions you knew about as you grew up. This book addresses your doubts and apprehensions in a realistic and balanced way. We believe open adoptions have much to offer birth parents, adoptive parents, and especially adopted children, but these benefits are not realized simply by meeting each other and exchanging names and addresses. Nor are they achieved if you mistrust or mislead each other out of fear.

We believe open adoption is more a relationship than an institution or a process. When open adoptions are successful, it is not because the institution is well designed but because the people involved have worked hard at the relationships. It is our belief that the relationships in adoption are dynamic; they change over time. Encounters that begin tentatively may blossom into close relationships, whereas others that are entered into eagerly become limited by time and distance. Your adoption may not be as open as many of the examples we discuss in this book. However, you can still benefit from seeing how fully disclosed adoptions can work. Yours may be one of those that evolves into a more open adoption—either because you decide to increase the level of contact with each other or because your child wants more contact—and you need to be prepared for that.

But even if your adoption never becomes fully disclosed, you can apply much of what we say to your own situation. You will need the same skills and attitudes to negotiate the exchange of pictures or gifts that you will need to negotiate visits, for we believe open adoption is as much an attitude as a practice: to work well, it must be felt in your heart. There are adoptions in which birth families and adoptive families have direct contact with each other out of a sense of obligation rather than desire, adoptions in which the birth families and adoptive families are mistrustful of each other, and adoptions in which one family wishes the other would disappear. But there are many adoptions in which adoptive parents and birth parents are finding a deep, emotionally intimate bond due to the love they share for the same human being. Some of these families have direct contact with each other and some do not. These families, many of whom were initially resistant to contact of any kind, can't imagine not having each other in their lives.

This book is about the connection between birth families and adoptive families, what happens when that connection is acknowledged openly,

and how to nurture the relationship that develops over time
This book will help you develop realistic expectations of this unique re-
tionship and will show how you can nurture it by utilizing the interpersonal skills you already have.

Most important, though, this book will help you understand the relationship between you and your child. It will help you understand how
your child benefits from seeing the healthy adult relationships around him
or her. And when you finish this book, you will have a better idea of what
your child needs from each relationship, and how you can help provide
for your child's emotional health and well-being.

In preparing this book, we have drawn on the experiences of real people to help you know what to expect as your relationship unfolds and how
other people have handled the unexpected. Sharon Kaplan Roszia, M.S.,
was among the first professionals to advocate for open adoption and has
counseled more than a thousand families in open adoption. And as the
mother of children by birth, adoption, and long-term foster care, she has
had a great deal of experience in her own family with children who have
contact with birth relatives.

Lois Ruskai Melina has listened to the concerns of hundreds of families
in open adoption as she has traveled and lectured throughout the country,
and is the mother of two children by adoption.

The Open Adoption Experience also reflects our interviews with adoption
professionals working in open adoptions as well as our extensive surveys
of adoptive and birth families involved in open adoptions all over the
United States. The responses to our questionnaires reflected a wide degree
of comfort with openness, and as we compared research results, observations of adoption professionals, psychological theories, interviews with
adoptees and birth parents, and our own experiences, we were able to
identify many of the common concerns about open adoptions, as well as
the attitudes, approaches, parenting techniques, and interpersonal skills
that contribute to the happiest, most successful open adoptions.

The examples given in this book are drawn from those questionnaires
and personal interviews with families. In all cases, names have been
changed, and in many cases, identifying details have been altered. Some
examples are composites of several different families. However, they all
reflect real situations and feelings.

As we wrote this book, we deliberately did not separate material dealing
with birth parents from that pertaining to adoptive parents. We believe
your relationship will benefit if you each have an understanding of the

other's concerns. Furthermore, you have many issues in common. Consequently, when we address the reader directly, the information is pertinent to both birth and adoptive families. In other situations, we clearly state whether we are referring to the birth or adoptive family.

How to Use This Book

As you read *The Open Adoption Experience,* particularly the first few chapters, you will learn about many of the losses that are inherent in adoption and the fears that people have about open adoption. This is likely to bring a lot of feelings to the surface as you face your own fears and losses. You will be tempted to ignore statements that make you feel uncomfortable, focusing instead on those statements that reinforce the feelings you *want* to have. We encourage you to take your time reading this book. Discuss the issues raised with people who are involved with you in the adoption, including your adoption facilitator. Put the book down when it seems overwhelming and think about it for a while before moving on. Nevertheless, we encourage you to read through the entire book and not just focus on the sections that reflect where you are now in your open adoption. Prospective adoptive parents and birth parents considering an adoption plan will benefit from learning about the lifelong relationships of other families. And families who have been involved in open adoptions for some time may gain insight from learning how initial interactions can affect long-term relationships. We also encourage you to keep a journal of your thoughts and feelings as you read this book and move through the adoption process.

You may begin to feel that adoption in general, and open adoption in particular, is fraught with potential problems. It is not our intention to frighten people away from adoption. We are both adoptive parents and are both personally and professionally committed to the practice of adoption. But we believe in being honest and realistic, which means approaching adoption with an understanding of how it really affects people, and all the potential problems. No relationship is trouble-free, but *The Open Adoption Experience* will help you understand and work with the unique dynamics of your individual relationship so that it can become as meaningful and mutually satisfying as possible.

The advice we have to offer is similar to the advice a couple might receive before deciding to get married. No matter how deeply two people love each other, there will be conflict in a lifelong relationship. This shouldn't deter anyone from marriage, but it helps to know how the relationship will develop—what the "honeymoon period" will be like, and how the relationship is affected by stress, children, and middle age. It helps to know what topics should be discussed, such as finances, children, fidelity, communication, careers, division of labor, and what you expect from each other and from the relationship. Finally, it helps to know that other people have had similar experiences to yours. By being just as honest and realistic, we hope we can reconcile the opposing sides of the open adoption controversy, acknowledging that there are risks but pointing out ways to minimize those risks so that the many priceless benefits can be realized.

part one

A Realistic Look at Open Adoption

The Reasons for Open Adoption

Most of us grew up during the "clean break" period of adoption. Birth parents were to remain unknown to the adoptive parents and to the children who were adopted, and the adoptive parents and the children they adopted were to be unknown to the birth parents. Even when the adopted children became adults, or when everyone involved requested that their sealed adoption records be opened, identifying information remained confidential. Today's practice of birth and adoptive parents meeting, corresponding, exchanging identifying information, and having direct contact with each other seems like a radical change in adoption practice. If you are new to adoption, it is. But those who have followed changes in the field of adoption recognize that open adoptions represent an evolution in adoption thought and practice. They are the result of a growing belief that:

- Children have a connection to their birth parents that begins even before birth and cannot be changed or denied by legal documents;
- Children need information about their origins to help form a personal identity, and it is better for children to deal with reality—even harsh reality—than with a variety of fantasies;
- Children need to know that their birth families care about them and that the adoption didn't represent a rejection;
- Birth families need not represent a threat to their children or to the attachment between the children and their adoptive parents;
- Birth parents need to know the outcome of their pregnancy and adoption plan to feel at peace about it;
- Adoptive parents feel more authentic when they receive permission from the birth parents to be their child's parents and see that the birth par-

ents' involvement with their family does not diminish their parent–child relationship.

▪ Family relationships are healthier in an atmosphere of openness and honesty.

To accept open adoption, it may be necessary for you to understand why adoptions became confidential and the limitations of confidential adoption, and how confidential adoption evolved into open adoption.

Why Confidential Adoptions Began

Throughout history, there have been various practices designed to provide infertile parents with heirs and to care for children whose parents were dead or unable to provide for them. During much of history and in many cultures, a child's move from one family to another was done openly and his original identity remained known.

In the United States, the first law "closing" adoptions was passed in Minnesota in 1917. By the 1930s, virtually all states had followed suit. With these confidential adoptions, new birth certificates were issued listing the adoptive parents, and documents pertaining to the adoption were forever sealed, including the child's original birth certificate. The primary reason for keeping the child's original identity a secret was to allow the child and her birth parents a fresh start. The birth mother, who was often young and unmarried, would be spared the stigma of being considered promiscuous and could be sure the child would never appear to call her past into question. The child would be spared the stigma of being born to parents who were assumed to be promiscuous or poor—conditions thought to be virtually inheritable—and would be given a more "desirable" identity.

This change in adoption practice occurred in a cultural climate that supported the idea of people making a clean break with their past and starting over. America was settled originally by outcasts who were unwanted in their homelands because of their religious beliefs or criminal pasts. Later, immigrants came to America because this was a place where it didn't matter who you were or where you came from—what mattered was what you made of yourself. In the United States, the ownership of property was determined less by inheritance than by hard work. Furthermore, by the 1930s, social scientists were stressing the importance of environmental factors in the development of children. It is not surprising that in this atmosphere we developed adoption practices in which adoptees were urged to leave the past behind and start over; in which birth parents were considered unimportant; in which adoptive parents required a "free and clear" claim to their children; and in which children "belonged" to the parents who did the work to raise them, regardless of any historical or cultural ties they may have had to other people.

In addition, confidential adoptions benefitted the growing field of social work. By serving as the intermediary between the birth parents and the adoptive parents, social workers became "providers" of children to families, giving social workers emotional rewards that were often lacking in other aspects of their professional service. Furthermore, as sociologist Harriet E. Gross, Ph.D., of Governors State University in Illinois, suggests, social workers promoted secrecy to ensure that their role wouldn't become obsolete. What distinguished adoption agencies from other professionals who were arranging adoptions independently was their offer of complete secrecy.

Confidential adoptions appeared to be a practice that benefitted everyone. The birth mother found a solution to her untimely pregnancy and could return to her life confident that the past would not come back to haunt her. The adoptee could get parents who were not only capable of raising her but who were probably more "respectable" and could provide her with a more advantageous environment. The adoptive parents could gain the child they wanted and raise the child as though she had been born to them, without fear that the birth parents would interfere with their parent–child attachment.

THE UNEXPECTED COST OF CONFIDENTIAL ADOPTIONS

What was not understood was that these gains did not come without a price. Because of the limited understanding at the time of loss and grief, adoption practitioners did not realize that by breaking with their pasts, adoptees and birth parents were experiencing significant losses. Birth parents lost a chance to know their offspring, to raise them, and to know what became of them. Adoptees lost the chance to know their ancestors, lost access to vital information about themselves or an opportunity to have that information updated, and lost the opportunity to know that the people who gave them life cared about them. And by pretending that these pasts didn't exist, they were not being given a chance to resolve those losses. Nor were the losses of adoptive parents recognized and resolved when they could pretend their child had been born to them. Adoptive parents lost the fantasy child to whom they would have given birth and they lost the hope of being biologically connected to the child they were raising.

Over the years confidential adoptions were widely practiced, it gradually became apparent through research, personal accounts, and case histories that the failure to recognize and grieve for these losses had long-term effects. Some adoptees had impaired self-esteem because they were unable to shake the belief that they were rejected by their mothers. Some had difficulty forming an identity because they did not have information about who they were. Some had difficulty forming relationships because they did not understand why they had lost a primary relationship with their birth parents. Birth parents felt a lasting sense of shame at having placed a child for adoption. Some had a hard time maintaining relationships. Adoptive parents sometimes felt insecure about their parenting role because they were not the child's biologic parents.

Certainly not all confidential adoptions were failures, nor did all adoptees, birth parents, and adoptive parents suffer serious psychological problems. Some did, but there were also many who managed to grieve for their losses without any guidance and lived their lives as emotionally healthy individuals. In between these extremes, however, were many people who found that their experience with adoption provided them with emotional challenges that they didn't expect and didn't always know how to conquer. The different individual responses to the adoption experience may be explained by the different personalities, temperaments, and life experiences of those involved. For example, those who experienced a lot of other losses in their lives, or who had stress factors in addition to adoption, may have had more difficulty dealing with their adoption issues than someone else. Those who had emotionally healthy upbringings may have had an easier time dealing with feelings of shame or rejection brought on by adoption because they weren't being reinforced in other ways. Those who grew up in families where feelings were hidden probably had more difficulty resolving their grief than those raised in families where feelings were identified and expressed in appropriate ways.

Unfortunately, most of the research into the psychological effects of adoption has not looked at the individual differences between people or families. Most of the studies have investigated whether a particular group of people in adoption have more psychological problems than would be statistically expected. If the adoption sample showed more problems, the cause was assumed to be adoption. The results of such research have yielded a range of findings.

Personal accounts of adoption, beginning with Jean Paton's *Orphan Voyage* and Florence Fisher's *The Search for Anna Fisher,* contributed to the discussion of the merits of confidential adoption and encouraged birth parents and adoptees to search for those genetic relatives from whom they had been separated. As more birth mothers spoke out about their personal experiences, it became increasingly clear that they were not "undesirable" people at all, but often people who loved their children and thought about them forever. Furthermore, the reunions that resulted from these searches generally did not yield birth parents who intruded physically or emotionally on the relationship between the adoptee and her adoptive parents.

Gradually, many adoption professionals began to believe that the benefits of adoptees and their birth parents having a clean break were either nonexistent or were outweighed by the potential costs. This belief was supported by gradual changes in the social climate in which adoptions were practiced along with new information about the long-term effects of grief.

The Evolution to Open Adoption

During the 1960s and 1970s—roughly the same time that adoptees and birth parents began to speak openly about their experiences—changes in sexual practices reduced the stigma to unmarried women who gave birth. And the emphasis that social scientists had placed on environmental influences began to be replaced with a renewed emphasis on the power of genetic influences.

At the same time, psychiatrists John Bowlby, M.D., and Elisabeth Kübler-Ross, M.D., separately published information about death and dying. They said that people feel grief whenever they experience loss—even when the loss has beneficial results—and that people go through specific stages of grief. Bowlby added that children have the same feelings of grief as adults, although they may be expressed differently. In addition, these experts said that failure to grieve can lead to both short-term and long-term emotional discomfort, and in some cases, serious emotional problems.

Also during the 1970s, Barbara Eck Menning's book *Infertility: A Guide for the Childless Couple,* and Resolve, Inc., the organization she founded to provide education and support about infertility, demonstrated that infertile couples experience grief that can have a long-term impact on them as parents if it is not resolved. Among adoption professionals the awareness grew that many of the problems they were seeing in adoptees, birth parents, and adoptive parents could be due to the losses they had experienced but had not adequately mourned.

Initially, the response of professionals was to keep adoptions confidential, but to help adoptees, birth parents, and adoptive parents grieve for their losses. Rather than perpetuating a pretense that their family was not affected by adoption once the child had arrived, adoptive parents were encouraged to "acknowledge the differences" in their families due to adoption. It gradually became clear that the fears adoptive parents harbored of birth parents were due more to insecurity resulting from their infertility than from any real danger. It also became apparent that children's grief at the loss of their birth parents was unrelated to their feelings about their adoptive parents. Once they understood their children's interest in their birth parents, some adoptive parents not only felt less threatened by it but wanted to help their children get answers to their questions.

Professionals' new understanding of the way people grieve also changed the way birth parents were treated. It was evident that adoption practices inhibited the normal grief process for birth mothers because the ending was so ambiguous. Hospital practices changed to allow a birth mother to be treated as any other mother who had just given birth, recognizing her need to see her child after birth, both to know the outcome of her pregnancy and to say "good-bye."

In 1983, the book *Dear Birthmother* by Kathleen Silber and Phylis Speedlin described how birth mothers at one adoption agency were writing letters to the children they were placing for adoption, explaining their reasons for making adoption plans. A major reason for the letters was to allow the birth mothers to say "good-bye" to the children they were losing through adoption so they could move on in their mourning.

However, it soon became clear that the letters served another purpose. The letters communicated to children that the birth mothers did love and want their children, but were in situations that made it too difficult for them to parent. As a result, they helped children sort out their feelings of rejection and inferiority as they grew up and helped them see their birth parents as real, valuable human beings.

Silber and Speedlin also described their agency's commitment to exchanging correspondence on behalf of birth families and adoptive families. This practice gave birth parents the opportunity to know the outcome of their decision to place their children for adoption and gave the adoptees access to information about their origins as they grew up. In addition, it provided a mechanism for sharing important medical developments in the birth family and adoptee as conditions changed or became known.

Though a startling idea at the time, because it allowed birth and adoptive families to communicate without affecting confidentiality, the practice caught on. As adoptive parents read the letters from their children's birth mothers, they began to be less fearful of the birth parents and less convinced that they were untrustworthy or unreliable people who should be shut out of their lives and their children's lives. They also began to see the benefits to their children of this minimal contact with their birth families.

It also became clear that birth parents couldn't feel responsible for their adoption decision unless they were in control of the decision. They were therefore allowed more choices in planning for their adoption, including being allowed to choose the adoptive parents for their children—often as a result of reading "resumes" with identifying information removed. Tentative meetings began to take place between birth parents and prospective adoptive parents either shortly before placement or at the time of placement. Some of the families who met at the time of placement developed a relationship that they wanted to continue after placement. Some of them corresponded for a time, maintaining confidentiality, until they became comfortable enough with one another to communicate directly. (The book *Children of Open Adoption,* by Kathleen Silber and Patricia Martinez Dorner, chronicles the outcome of many of the relationships initially described in *Dear Birthmother.*)

It would be incorrect to suggest that the move from confidential to open adoptions happened solely because social workers became convinced that adoption practice needed improvement. The 1960s had changed unmarried, pregnant young women from compliant individuals willing to do whatever they were told to save their reputations to women mistrustful of authority and unashamed of their sexual activity. Those who became pregnant seldom hid their pregnancies, so they no longer needed confidentiality to protect their reputations. Consequently, more women with an untimely pregnancy chose abortion or single motherhood than adoption. As a result of this, plus an increase in infertility in the baby boom generation, the 1970s saw a decline in the availability of infants for adoption that seemed to reach crisis proportions around the beginning of the 1980s.

Faced with waits of up to ten years at agencies, prospective adoptive looked at ways to circumvent the agency process and were willing to give up the confidentiality of agency adoptions if necessary. Birth mothers gradually learned that babies for adoption were needed so desperately that they could demand more control than ever before over the adoption process. And what many birth mothers wanted was to choose the people who would be raising their children, to meet them, and to stay in touch with them indefinitely.

Adoption agencies that didn't respond to the changes birth parents wanted soon found that birth parents were turning instead to attorneys and doctors, as well as to the direct advertisements by prospective adoptive parents—none of whom were as invested in the idea of confidentiality as agencies had been. These agencies realized that if they were to continue to offer adoption services, they would have to offer birth mothers the same kind of control and openness that other agencies, independent adoption facilitators, and adoptive parents themselves were offering.

So, just as adoption had first become confidential as a reflection of the social climate of the time, because secrecy was thought to best serve birth parents and adoptees, and because it served the needs of those in the adoption profession, so did adoption return to openness to reflect changes in the social climate, a new awareness of the needs of birth parents and adoptees, as well as the needs of the adoption institution.

THE EMOTIONAL COSTS OF OPEN ADOPTION

Open adoptions have sometimes been portrayed as adoptions without loss. After all, the birth parents do not lose their child and the adoptee does not lose her birth parents. But there are losses in open adoption. The birth parents still lose their role as the child's day-to-day parents, with all the joy that role entails. Adoptees still lose the opportunity to grow up in their families of origin and may still feel insecure or rejected. Adoptive parents still lose their fantasy biologic child and the chance to be genetically connected to the child they rear.

But these losses are not as extreme as they are in confidential adoptions. And the lack of pretense about where the child came from allows people to face their losses and grieve for them so that their grief doesn't fester and interfere with their psychological and social development.

The benefits of open adoption have not been empirically proven. Although there have been some preliminary studies of open adoption, these studies have not looked at individual differences. We do not believe open adoption automatically results in birth parents, adoptive parents, or adoptees who are emotionally healthier than those in confidential adoptions, any more than we believe confidentiality doomed people to psychological problems. We do believe, however, that when people are committed to the relationships that form in open adoption, and when they work hard at them, the benefits of open adoption are more likely to outweigh the risks.

You may believe there are still high emotional risks to open adoption. We would be less than candid if we did not acknowledge these or that your concerns are shared by many professionals. The actual and perceived risks of open adoption are addressed in the next chapter and throughout this book. However, we believe the risks of open adoption are seldom so great that children are better served by confidential adoption. We believe there are equally effective ways to minimize the risks that do not entail the emotional costs of confidential adoption.

Understanding
Open Adoption

Carolyn and Kevin, prospective adoptive parents, wanted a confidential adoption, but agreed to listen to a presentation on open adoption because they knew they were more likely to be chosen by birth parents if they agreed to openness. Carolyn expressed her reservations cautiously: "I'm not sure I want the birth parents to know where we are because they might want the child back," she said. Kevin was blunt: "We're going to be the ones paying the bills, getting up in the middle of the night when he's sick, and making the tough decisions. The birth parents will be like fairy-tale parents—giving him presents and showing up on special occasions. It's going to be too easy for him to turn to the birth parents when he's mad at us. It's not fair for them to get all the glory when we've done all the work."

Chelan, a birth mother, said little during her initial interview with the adoption worker. But she nodded in agreement when her mother said that they didn't want to have any contact with the child after birth. "It will be too hard for Chelan to get back to being a typical teenager if she keeps seeing the baby. She might even want him back."

If you have reservations about open adoption, you are not alone. Furthermore, your concerns are normal, especially since you have grown up believing adoption should be confidential. Coming around to the benefits of open adoption requires an emotional change—not just a change in your thinking. Moreover, you may be intellectually convinced that open adoption is the best way long before you feel that conviction in your heart. However, through open adoption you can gradually gain a powerful sense of comfort. It is a feeling of relief that comes from grieving for the losses you have experienced as well as for those you are afraid you may experience, and from accepting that these losses are what make adoption different from other ways of forming families.

As we outlined in Chapter 1, all adoptions entail actual losses. Some, like the loss of a parent–child relationship for the birth parents and adoptee, are obvious. Others, like the loss of being considered "normal" because you have chosen not to raise your child or you have chosen to raise someone else's child, are more subtle. It's natural and healthy to take time to assess whether you want to proceed with a plan that will involve loss. In addition, there are also fears about adoption, and about open adoption in particular. These are fears of what we *think* we might lose. They represent the unknown risks of open adoption.

Adoptive parents fear they will lose their child—either physically, if the birth parent reclaims or abducts a child the adoptive parents have come to think of as a member of their family, or emotionally, if the child loves the birth parents more than the adoptive parents. Adoptive parents also fear they will lose their privacy and a sense of control over their lives if they are involved with birth parents, especially if the birth parents are intrusive or dysfunctional.

Birth parents are afraid they will lose the ability to move forward with their lives if they stay connected to their child—that they won't be able to heal from the loss of the child if they keep seeing him. They are also afraid that they will lose their child completely if the adoptive parents don't live up to the open adoption agreement.

There are additional concerns, such as that the child will feel insecure or confused if the birth parents have contact with him. Some of these are major concerns, whereas some are minor, but they occasionally take on an importance beyond their actual consequence.

Many of these fears are present in confidential adoptions, too. But such worries can be suppressed more easily in confidential adoption because the birth parents are not physically present, and the risk therefore seems farther away. In fact, this failure to directly confront the source of one's fears often intensifies these feelings. They become an invisible threat that is frightening.

In open adoption, the discomfort level these fears create is almost impossible to ignore. As a result, worries can be dealt with at the start and are not allowed to simmer and build. For this reason, many people who were most resistant to open adoption have found themselves becoming the greatest converts to the process, proselytizing about its benefits.

By understanding that risks of certain losses are present to some degree in any adoption, you will come to realize that open adoption doesn't necessarily represent greater risks; it just brings the risks into the open. However, by recognizing that they exist, you can assess the actual threat they pose, decide whether the potential benefits of open adoption outweigh the risks, and determine whether you can live with the losses you may experience. This chapter may help you resolve these issues. This chapter may also help you see that you do not have to be a passive "victim" of the losses of adoption or the risks of additional losses. By healthy grieving, you can move beyond the losses. Furthermore, when you grieve for some of the losses you do experience in adoption, the fear of other losses is often reduced. And by utilizing skills you already have, or can develop, for interacting with people in healthy ways, you can minimize some of the risks that may seem daunting. In addition to becoming more comfortable with open adoption, through this process you will realize incredible personal growth.

Competition with Birth Parents

One of the primary fears adoptive parents have of open adoption is that the birth parents will abduct their child. Even in confidential adoptions, where there is no information available to help birth parents locate their children, some adoptive parents find themselves worrying about the possibility. They still look suspiciously at any stranger who seems too curious about their child or who resembles their child.

It's possible for birth parents to abduct their children if they know where they are, and it's true that confidential adoptions make it more difficult for birth parents to know their children's whereabouts. But experience has shown that birth parents are not likely to abduct their children in either confidential or open adoptions. For instance, in their study, Ruth McRoy, Ph.D., of the University of Texas at Austin, Harold Grotevant, Ph.D., of the University of Minnesota, and Susan Ayers-Lopez, M.A., of the University of Texas at Austin, found that four to twelve years after placement, most adoptive parents in open adoptions said they felt secure in their parenting role and had little fear that the birth parents would try to abduct their children. Those that were still concerned based their fears on actual knowledge of their child's birth parents, for example, threats by the birth parents, whereas those in confidential and semiopen adoptions based their fears on stereotypes of birth parents. Furthermore, birth parents themselves were not found to have a desire to abduct their children.

Of course, it doesn't matter how seldom this happens if it happens to you. Yet most people are willing to risk loss if the chances of it happening are small and if the rewards of risk taking are very great. It is also important to remember that open adoption provides adoptive parents with ample opportunity to assess the risk they are undertaking by getting to know the birth parents and developing a relationship with them.

The spectre of birth parents abducting the child really represents a deeper fear. Adoptive parents are afraid they will lose their child because they secretly worry that he doesn't really belong to them. They think maybe their child won't love them as much as any child loves his birth parents. They fear their child will not give them the loyalty, love, affection, and respect that they have always hoped to receive as parents. They worry about whether they will be able to effectively set limits or discipline the child if he has another set of parents to turn to. Because they didn't give birth to the child, they wonder if their attachment will be strong enough to sustain them through times of parent–child conflict, through the independence of adolescence, or after the child leaves home. These are fears that adoptive parents have in confidential adoptions as well, but as long as the birth parents aren't around, it is thought, these concerns are moot. However, in all adoptions, no matter the degree of openness, this fear, if not dealt with, can leave adoptive parents feeling insecure about their relationship with their child and constantly looking to be reassured of their child's love for them.

These fears are often intensified in infertile adoptive parents who have already experienced losing a child over and over. Each month, as they tried to conceive, they felt the joy of expectation followed by disappointment. Sometimes they became pregnant only to suffer miscarriage or stillbirth. They are conditioned to believe they will lose their child.

To believe that children will love their adoptive parents as much as if they had been born to them, regardless of whether the birth parents are accessible, it is necessary to understand how parents and children bond and how they form attachments. It's also important to understand what the day-to-day relationship will be between the adoptive parents and the child compared to that of the birth parents and the child.

BONDING AND ATTACHMENT

Because the birth mother carried the child for nine months and gave birth to her, their bond is thought by some people to be stronger than that between the child and the people who raise her. If this were true, then when birth parents have contact with their child, the bond that developed between them at birth would emerge as stronger than that which exists between the adoptive parents and the child. In other words, the only way adoptive parents and their children could feel like a family is if the people with the "real" parent–child relationship are kept apart.

In his book *When Bonding Fails,* Frank G. Bolton Jr. describes bonding as the parent's instinctive desire to protect the infant, which begins in the mother during pregnancy and continues through birth and the first few days of life. Attachment takes more time and more interaction between parent and child. It develops intensely during the first year they are together as the child learns that she can depend on *these people* to meet her physical and emotional needs, and as parents discover they are willing to make sacrifices to meet their child's needs. Attachment is solidified during the next two years, and reinforced throughout the child's life, as his needs become increasingly complex and parents continue to meet those needs.

There is a bond between children and their birth parents, but it isn't solely what accounts for the close feeling between parents and child. That feeling is a direct result of what we all think of as the nuts and bolts of parenting—getting up in the middle of the night to feed your child, bandaging him after he scrapes his knee, and comforting him when he's in emotional pain. Regardless of the bond that exists at birth, a child is going to form the close parent–child attachment with his adoptive parents because he can depend on them to meet his needs on a day-to-day basis. The birth parent who writes, calls, visits, or even cares for the child in the parent's absence is not going to interfere with that attachment process.

What families in open adoptions have discovered is that the birth parents, the child, and the adoptive parents are all clear about who the parents are. They are the ones who live with the child day after day, who know the difference between a cry of anger, a cry of frustration, and a cry of pain, and who are ultimately responsible for meeting all of their child's needs. It is the adoptive mom and dad who will know the way their child prefers to be held, and when thunder strikes in an electrical storm, it is the adoptive parents to whom the child will run for comfort.

Long before the child understands adoption, he will have lived for several years with his adoptive parents. Although he will know his birth parents and will be able to relate his adoption story, he won't really understand his biologic relationship to them until he is about six years old. That new awareness will not change his feelings about his adoptive parents any more than it does in confidential adoptions. In fact, open adoptions might actually foster a greater sense of security in adoptive parents since they are able to see, firsthand, that the existence of birth parents in no way alters their child's primary attachment.

Most families involved in open adoptions describe the relationship between the birth parent and the family as that of a good friend—a special friend or even an aunt—but not a "coparent" or someone who in any way tries to usurp the role of the adoptive parents. In fact, many adoptive parents feel a greater sense of entitlement in open adoption because they have been chosen by the birth parents, and they receive validation from the birth parents in many small ways. Some birth parents send a Mother's Day or Father's Day card to the adoptive parents. Some say things such as "I like how you take care of the baby," or "I don't know how you can be so patient with him."

Some people still worry that the birth parent will be jealous of the adoptive parents and will try to interfere with the arrangement. They also worry that the child will try to capitalize on any competition or jealousy between the two sets of parents. It is true that birth and adoptive parents sometimes do feel jealous of each other. After all, you each have a special relationship with your child that the other cannot have. Again, this is true in confidential adoptions as well, for the special relationship each of you has with the child exists whether or not you choose to recognize it.

In confidential adoptions, however, your fantasies about the other parents can actually intensify any feelings of jealousy you might have. In open adoption, you will grieve for the loss of a more typical parent–child relationship, but you will also come to accept and treasure the special relationship you have with your child. And once the loss is accepted, it will no longer be a constant discomfort. Still, nearly every adoptee will try at one time or another to play birth parents against adoptive parents with comments such as "I don't have to listen to you—you're not my real mother." This kind of comment is only effective when adoptive parents are hypersensitive to the issues it raises because they haven't confronted and grieved for that loss. Furthermore, many of the birth parents we have talked to indicated their commitment to backing up the adoptive parents so that the child couldn't use this "divide and conquer" method effectively. Such teamwork isn't an option in confidential adoption.

Fear of Intrusion

Some adoptive parents worry that the birth parents will intrude into their daily life. They think that the birth parents will want more contact than they originally indicated and hope they won't be unreasonable people with whom to negotiate. They are afraid they will lose their independence and privacy. The old image of the birth parents as undesirable people from whom they need to be protected reemerges as adoptive parents imagine all the ways birth parents could be annoying, demanding, or even dangerous. Adoptive parents may be surprised to know that birth parents also worry about the adoptive family intruding into *their* lives. Birth parents worry that adoptive parents will take advantage of them by assuming they will act as no-cost babysitters, or will try to give the child back if there are problems. They are concerned about whether the child's presence in their life will be an intrusion in the future, especially when they marry and have children.

One of the reasons open adoption is frightening to many prospective adoptive parents is that they fear the relationship gives the birth parents permission to enter their lives in an emotionally intimate way, and they are reluctant to give this kind of permission on the basis of what is often just a brief acquaintance. In many respects, open adoption is a unique way of forming a relationship. Most of the time, relationships develop gradually. We meet people with little expectation of forming a deep or lasting connection. As we get to know each other, we may discover similarities and develop some familiarity. We tentatively seek out a closer association, revealing ourselves increasingly as we build trust. Sometimes we find that someone who initially seemed like someone we'd want to be close to is not as likeable or as trustworthy as we expected and the relationship is stunted or deteriorates. We certainly don't make a commitment to be intimately involved with another person for the rest of our lives until we know the person well enough and have enough interactions with that person to feel confident that we can pledge our faithfulness to that relationship.

In adoption, however, we make a commitment to be intimately connected to people when we agree to adopt their child or choose them to raise our child. And as that commitment is made, birth parents simultaneously select an intimate relationship for their child and adoptive parents simultaneously agree to raise a child with an intimate connection to someone else. We often make this commitment without having the luxury of allowing the relationships to grow to their natural level of intimacy and stand the test of time.

In confidential adoption, in which the birth parents never meet or communicate in any way with the adoptee or adoptive parents, the relationship gets stunted at a peculiar point: people have an intimate connection to each other, but are never given the opportunity to explore the relationships or allow them to develop.

In semiopen adoption, in which birth parents and adoptive parents meet without revealing their full identities and communicate with each other through a third party, the relationships have the opportunity of growing gradually, but may become arrested at the point where further development is not possible without direct access to each other, unless people take the next step to a fully disclosed adoption.

In open adoption, in which the birth parents and adoptive parents communicate directly with each other, the relationships have an opportunity to grow and develop, but first you must make a commitment to be involved with each other. To be committed to being deeply connected to each other before we feel completely comfortable in the relationship is highly unusual, but it is not without parallels. For example, in time of war, men and women in a military unit entrust their lives to their comrades without first building individual relationships. Typically, they emerge from the experience feeling a deep bond despite differences in backgrounds or values. Even if they see each other only occasionally in subsequent years, there is a depth to their relationship that time and distance will not erase.

Nevertheless, it probably feels awkward and artificial at best to meet someone for the purpose of assessing whether you want to enter into a close, long-term relationship with them. It's similar to applying to a dating service hoping to find a mate on the first one or two .ches. Indeed, open adoptions have been compared to the old-fashioned arranged marriage. But although there are parallels between how your relationship will develop in open adoption and the courtship and dating that precedes a marital commitment, the two relationships really aren't comparable. You will not be living together or interacting on a daily basis. You will not need to be consulting with one another before making important decisions.

Your relationship will not be equal. The *power* in the relationship is directly related to the legal issues in adoption. Whoever is the child's legal parent will have more power and control in the relationship. Since the child's legal parent will change during the course of your relationship, the power balance in the relationship will also shift. Eventually the child, too, will exert some control in the relationship.

In practice, the relationship in open adoption is more comparable to that between in-laws. Very often, people don't meet their in-laws until after they have decided to get married. They meet with the understanding that they will be entering into a long-term relationship primarily because they both love and are concerned for the well-being of the same person. They may have different values. They may have different lifestyles. They are probably different ages. But often, even before getting to know each other very well, they make a commitment to making the relationship work because doing so is in the best interest of someone else, to whom their commitment is firmly established.

As in-laws get to know each other, they may find their relationship deepening to the point where it exists outside of their common commitment to the other person. They may take vacations together not out of obligation but because they genuinely enjoy each other's company. They plan to be together on holidays because they want to be, not because they are expected to be.

Others may find their relationship with their in-laws cordial, but not as deep as they might like it to be, just because something doesn't "click." And some may have a less than ideal relationship—a jealous mother-in-law, an alcoholic father-in-law, a manipulative daughter-in-law, a self-centered son-in-law. But even in those situations, there is often an understanding that we have to make an effort at least to stay connected. There is a common belief that it is terribly tragic when relationships within a family break down—even when those relationships are established by law rather than genetics.

BOUNDARIES IN OPEN ADOPTION

Fear of intrusion may also be the result of some negative associations people have with the term *open*. To some people, *open* means that there are no barriers, no rules. An open marriage is one in which the partners do not honor the accepted rule that they will not have other sexual relationships. An open meeting is one in which anyone can attend. When someone reads you like an open book, it means you have no privacy.

Adoptive parents are skeptical of an arrangement in which it sounds like the birth parents can come and go from their lives at will. After having to reveal details of their intimate lives to fertility specialists and social workers, they understandably want to have as "normal" a life as possible, with the privacy that all families expect to have. Not only do they not want to share parenting, they don't want to have their plans disrupted by unexpected visits from birth parents or be forced to invite them to family gatherings.

However, open adoptions do not require that you live without rules or by someone else's set of rules. It is not an arrangement whereby the front door of the adoptive parents' home is always unlocked to the birth family. An adoptive family can and should have appropriate boundaries about its relationship with the birth family. The difference between open adoption and confidential adoption is not that there are no longer boundaries but that there are boundaries where there used to be walls. Walls, like the old Berlin Wall, are impenetrable. Boundaries, like border crossings, allow for decisions to be made about when they can be crossed. Walls are put up by fearful people, willing to sacrifice some possible good to be sure that all the bad will be kept out. Boundaries are put up by people who are confident of their ability to differentiate the positive from the negative and willing to take the chance that occasionally something adverse might cross the boundary in order to assure that the boundary will be accessible to all the positive things that might be available.

Establishing boundaries may be more difficult for you because the adoption process (as well as the infertility process for adoptive parents) involves such a loss of privacy that you may be out of practice in setting limits. It's important to remember that you have the right to set boundaries in this relationship and to begin the relationship with that idea in mind. The tone you set with each other during the preplacement period is likely to continue for some time after the placement. Furthermore, remember that you can choose whether you want to be in a relationship with the other person. If, prior to the placement, this seems like someone who doesn't respect boundaries, you don't have to remain in the relationship, or you can set stronger boundaries.

Birth Parents' Feelings

One of the biggest fears of birth parents, adoptive parents, and their extended families is that birth parents will find it too painful to see their child but not be his parents. They are afraid that each time they see the child it will reopen an emotional wound that will never fully heal. For a long time adoption functioned on the premise that if birth parents didn't see their child they could put the child, and their loss, out of their minds. Eventually, it became clear that this wasn't realistic—out of sight *doesn't* mean out of mind.

Open adoption is predicated on the belief that by choosing adoptive parents for their child and observing that their child is thriving in his new family, birth parents can resolve their grief more easily than when they knew nothing about the child's welfare. By seeing their child in his adoptive family, the birth parents can openly deal with the sacrifice of their child. Assured of their child's health and security, they can begin their own healing process. But this is not automatic—it is a choice they must make.

Birth parents who are reluctant to "let go" of their parenting role may indeed have a difficult time seeing their child. This situation is similar to seeing a former boyfriend or girlfriend—it's painful if you haven't accepted that the relationship is over. You can avoid the pain by avoiding the person, but it doesn't help you heal. By confronting the source of the pain, birth parents realize they will have to work through their loss if they are to continue to have contact with their child. Birth parents who are able to work through their feelings and move beyond the loss find another role they can play in their child's life. They can still nurture the child, although not on a daily basis and not in the same way they would if they were raising the child. They can share family stories and a sense of family or ethnic heritage with the child. Their feelings of inadequacy can be lessened and even erased as a special relationship develops between them.

Finally, it's important to understand that the child the birth parents visualize as they grieve is the baby they relinquished at birth. The child that they see growing before them seems part of his adoptive family—not as much a part of them. Just as it seems "right" to the adoptive parents for this child to be in their family, it seems "right" to the birth parents, as well.

Once again, this point has not been empirically proven. Research has yielded a variety of findings and not everyone agrees on how to measure healthy grief resolution. Surely there will be individual responses by birth parents to seeing their children after placement. But these will be influenced not only by the openness of the adoption but by other factors, including the kind of preparation and counseling the birth parents received prior to placement as well as afterward.

Many birth parents worry that the adoptive parents will renege on the open adoption agreement by not maintaining contact. Unfortunately, in some cases this concern is founded. Adoptive parents go along with an open adoption plan because they recognize it is the only way some birth parents will place a child for adoption, and after the adoption is finalized, they change their phone number, move, or stop communicating with the birth parents. However, this doesn't happen in most cases.

Birth parents can take some steps to minimize the risk of losing contact with the adoptive family by getting to know the adoptive parents well so that they can assess whether these are trustworthy people. Chapters 3 and 4 contain some guidelines birth parents can follow in evaluating whether particular adoptive parents make good "risks" for an open adoption. Exchanging Social Security numbers is also a good idea. With that information, you will have a better chance of being able to find each other, and the willingness of everyone to provide that information is a powerful statement of their intentions. Birth parents can also behave in a trustworthy manner themselves so that adoptive parents don't have an excuse to break off contact. In addition, birth parents who work with a skilled facilitator who is as committed to the needs of the birth parents as to those of the adoptive parents are more likely to encounter adoptive parents who understand the importance of maintaining communication.

You may have other concerns about open adoption as well. Adoptive parents may worry that their child will be confused or feel insecure if his birth parents are involved in his life. They may be concerned that their child will feel doubly rejected if his birth parents don't exercise their option to have contact with him. Rather than seeing value in the child having access to information about his origins, the adoptive parents may wonder how they will handle information about the birth parents that might be disturbing to the child. These apprehensions are addressed later in this book as problems to be solved rather than as risks.

Concerns of the Extended Family

Extended family members may also express fears about open adoption. Their concerns are twofold. Because they care about you, they may be concerned you will be hurt and they will share many of your worries. Your families want to protect you, and their concerns are compounded by the lack of control they have in adoption. You are making decisions that will affect your entire families, and they have no control over the results. Their decision may have been different. They may feel cultural pressures that you do not feel or may have had experiences with loss or adoption that you have not had.

But the fears and concerns of the extended family reflect their own fears of loss, too. If the birth parents reclaim or abduct the child, the entire extended adoptive family will experience a loss—not just the adoptive parents. Just as adoptive parents worry about whether their attachment to the child will be the same as it would have with a child born to them, the extended family wonders if the child will fit in and be accepted in the adoptive family. Birth families are also concerned that the birth parents will be hurt by seeing the child or by adoptive parents who renege on their agreement. The entire birth family must confront their loss of the opportunity to nurture this child the way they would have if the child had remained in the family. Birth relatives as well as adoptive relatives wonder whether they will be considered grandparents, aunts, and uncles.

You can help your families by letting them know that you are aware of the risks and that you feel the risks are minimal or that you believe you'll be okay if the worst happens. You can provide them with opportunities to become more comfortable with adoption in the same ways you have—by reading books or attending educational sessions to learn more about it, and by grieving for their losses.

Semiopen Adoptions

To many people, semiopen adoptions, in which the birth parents and adoptive parents communicate anonymously with one another through an intermediary, seem to offer all the advantages of fully disclosed adoptions without any of the risks. Semiopen adoptions offer the possibility of birth families and adoptive families exchanging information, but they don't have the emotional risks that come with personal relationships. Semiopen adoptions also appear to offer the same "safety" that confidential adoptions were designed to offer—adoptive parents could feel certain the birth parents would not abduct their child, challenge their role as parents, or compete for their child's love.

Your fears about having contact with each other are natural. But semiopen adoptions don't eliminate the things you're worried about any more than confidential adoptions did. There is as much need to work through your fears if you're planning a semiopen adoption as there is if you are planning a fully disclosed adoption. In the study of open adoptions referred to earlier, four to twelve years after placement, adoptive parents in semiopen adoption were more fearful of the birth parents, had less sense of entitlement, and had less satisfaction about the amount of control they had than parents in either confidential or fully disclosed adoptions.

Semiopen adoptions have disadvantages that are often overlooked because they may not be immediately apparent. In a semiopen adoption, all the communication may be between the birth family and the adoptive parents—eliminating the child's involvement. In the University of Texas–University of Minnesota study, about half of the adoptive families involved in semiopen adoptions had not yet shared the letters from the birth mothers with their children. Parents who did not share the correspondence with their children said their children were too young, or were concerned for siblings who had confidential adoptions.

When children don't participate personally in the relationship with their birth parents, they don't realize the benefits. They don't have the opportunity to get their questions answered directly and concretely. Birth parents remain mysterious phantoms who must be "bad" because they are being kept away from them. They don't have the opportunity to feel the birth parents' love for them, which can counter the feelings of rejection that adoptees often have. Nor do they have a chance to grow up with the relationship and integrate it into their lives as their understanding of adoption and of relationships grows. When the child is older and learns of the correspondence from his birth mother, he may be angry that this communication went on behind his back and may feel a loss of control.

But even when children are aware of the communication with their birth parents, it's not the same as it would be if the adoptees and birth parents are communicating directly. When communication goes through an intermediary, there is always the question of whether it is being censored—perhaps not to the adults but to the child. When you don't get information from the original source, it feels diluted. Furthermore, the more people who are involved, the more opportunities there are for a breakdown in communication.

Semiopen adoptions may become fully disclosed before the adoptive parents are prepared for it. The child may choose to reveal his name and address to his birth parents. The intermediary may deliberately or inadvertently reveal identifying information. If that happens, you may be forced into a close relationship without being clear about what your roles should be or what the rules will be. There may be an urgency to the relationship as everyone attempts to make up for lost time, rather than a chance for the relationship to grow at its natural pace. Thus, prior to placement it is important to get to know each other as well as you can. Should your semiopen adoption become fully disclosed, it will be easier if you already have some basis for a relationship.

You may be feeling pulled to semiopen adoption because you aren't sure you can trust the other parents enough to do an open adoption. Ask yourself if you have solid reasons to be cautious, or if your feelings have more to do with your fears about losses.

If you chose semiopen adoption, continue to work on grieving for your losses and on building trust with the other family through your correspondence. Think of the semiopen adoption as an intermediary step on the way toward open adoption, even though you may never take the final step. Be prepared for the natural growth and evolution of the relationship.

Working Through Your Fears

While the factual information you receive about the risks of open adoption may help alleviate some of your anxieties, you are unlikely to feel comfortable taking the risk of future losses until you resolve the losses you have already experienced or that you know you will have through adoption. The losses of adoption generally come on the heels of other losses. The adoptive parents have the losses of infertility, including loss of control, loss of privacy, loss of a fantasy child, and perhaps loss of self-esteem. Birth parents have the losses associated with an untimely pregnancy, which include a loss of status or reputation, the change of plans for nine months or perhaps the rest of their lives, the loss of control, and sometimes the loss of youth. These losses can leave you feeling fragile—unable to bear any new losses. So you may shy away from situations that even hint of loss. The slightest possibility of misfortune may seem unbearable.

In addition, some of these losses may leave you particularly vulnerable to the threat of other losses. The unfounded fear adoptive parents have about their children emotionally rejecting them in favor of their birth parents arises out of the feelings of loss they have at not having given birth to their children, as well as to feelings of inferiority and inadequacy resulting from infertility. The fear that the birth parents will intrude in their lives is due in part to the feeling of being out of control that is inherent in infertility and adoption. Adoptive parents may also wonder what right they have to control interactions between a child and his birth parents—a feeling that is the direct legacy of their awareness that they have lost something significant in not giving birth to this child. You must grieve for these losses to have the courage to face new challenges in your life.

The Grieving Process

Grieving is a natural, normal, and healthy emotional response to loss. Smaller injuries, either physical or emotional, heal faster than bigger injuries. And just as your body heals faster from physical trauma if you are in otherwise good shape, you will recover faster from emotional wounds if you are emotionally healthy. If you've had a lot of losses in your life, especially those losses for which you haven't properly grieved, it can take longer to heal from a new emotional wound. But no matter how healthy you are, if you don't take care of yourself when you're injured, you won't heal.

Unresolved grief isn't emotionally fatal—it doesn't immobilize you, but it may leave you with some vague emotional discomfort that prevents you from experiencing life as fully as you otherwise might. You might think of it as a low-grade infection. You don't feel sick enough to stay in bed, and you may not even have any specific symptoms—you just don't feel quite well or have very much energy. And your weakened condition leaves you susceptible to further injury. When grief is allowed to surface, it is similar to having a full-blown infection that prohibits you from functioning until you treat it effectively.

Throughout the adoption process, you will experience both minor losses, such as the loss of privacy, and major losses, such as the pain the birth parents will feel after they relinquish their child. The process of grieving for these losses is the same, though the feelings are much stronger with more significant losses. Refer to this section whenever you are experiencing loss in the adoption process and need to be reminded that your feelings are normal and will eventually diminish.

As you grieve, you gradually progress from saying, "I can't live with this pain," to "I can go on living *despite* this pain," to "I can go on living *with* this pain." As you live with the pain, it diminishes until you can finally say, "I can enjoy life even though I've had pain and may sometimes feel the pain again." You will never feel that you didn't have the loss or that the loss wasn't important. But you will be able to get on with your life uninhibited by the loss.

There is a variety of descriptions of the grief process and different names for the stages of grief. You may work with a counselor who describes the process a little differently. But the feelings are the same. You may not experience the feelings in the same order that we present them. You probably will experience some stages of grief more acutely than others. But you will experience them at some time.

The first stage of grief is sometimes called *denial.* You feel numb. You tell yourself the dent is so small that it isn't even noticeable; that your loved one really hasn't died but will walk through the door any minute. "I can't be pregnant." "I can't be infertile."

Crying is one of many ways your feelings are manifested at this time. You may feel nauseous, weak, "foggy," or confused. You may have difficulty concentrating or holding a conversation. You may have difficulty eating or sleeping. You may feel actual physical pain, like you've been kicked in the stomach. Or you may feel nothing at all.

The next stage is *bargaining* or *protest.* You resist the loss, saying, "I won't let this happen." This is the stage when you list what "might have been" and tell yourself "if only." "If only I hadn't been in such a rush, I would have seen the other car." "If only I'd been home when he had his heart attack—I could have saved him." You still believe the loss is reversible if you can find the right thing to bargain. "Please don't let me be pregnant and I'll never have sex again." "Please let me get pregnant and I'll give up my job." One reason you tend to blame yourself for the loss is to feel in control of it. If you can figure out what you did to cause the loss, you can possibly reverse it, or at least make sure it never happens again.

"Searching" behavior may be common at this time. You keep expecting whatever was lost to reappear. You see people who physically resemble the person who was lost. You wait for a call saying the loss didn't happen. You may feel energized during this stage, calling adoption facilitators or taking other actions to try to feel in control. You may also feel anguish.

When you begin to realize that nothing can change the loss, you experience *anger* or *anxiety*. You're angry at yourself for denting the car, or at the other driver for being in your way. You may have irrational fears that you will lose something else or someone else important to you. You may continue to have difficulty eating, sleeping, and thinking. Anger and anxiety often need to be expressed in physical ways. You may feel agitated. You may have physical complaints such as headache, backache, diarrhea, or blurred vision. You may feel like you're going to explode and may want a lot of physical or sexual activity. You may be tempted to use substances to calm yourself. People may seem silly to you.

This is the stage when you ask yourself why this had to happen to you and when you perhaps feel that you did something wrong to deserve this kind of punishment. It's also the point at which you look for someone you can blame for the loss. Maybe you are angry at the car or at whomever you think was responsible for people being in the car at that time. When someone dies, you often get angry at the person for dying. You may get angry at the doctor who couldn't save the one you love, or at yourself for being unable to save him. "He told me I wouldn't get pregnant." "Why do we have to go through so much to get a child?" It isn't unusual for people to lose their faith in God at this time as they question why this happened to them. You may feel anxious about additional losses, becoming overly protective of other children or others whom you care about.

When you reach the point at which you know the loss can't be reversed, you experience *sadness*. "My whole life will be changed by this pregnancy." "I'll never know what it's like to have a biologic child." Your sense of despair at what has been lost may be heightened if you made the choice. "I did this to myself. I could have not done it. But there's no way to undo it now."

You may feel indifferent or apathetic or have a lack of energy. "There's nothing I can do about it—why bother." You may have difficulty getting dressed in the morning or going to work or school. You may feel a loss of interest in things that previously had been very important to you. You may not want to talk to anybody. You may feel helpless and hopeless—that you have no future. You may feel desperately alone—that nobody knows how you are feeling.

You may find it hard to laugh as well as hard to cry. "I'm all cried out," people frequently say. Some people find that rather than their emotions spilling over at this time, they "leak" their emotions. They may be teary, have oily hair, bad breath, or body odor. It's important to make a point of taking care of yourself at this time.

Eventually you reach a point at which you can move beyond the loss and get on with your life. The pain doesn't disappear completely, but it diminishes, and the loss doesn't preoccupy your thoughts anymore. You feel better. You look better. You have more energy. You have a sense of the future. You recognize what you have gained from your loss and you acknowledge new skills or relationships that you have acquired. This stage is called *acceptance, recovery,* or *resolution.*

Although everyone is unique, men often experience anger more readily than women, and women experience anxiety. The anger/anxiety stage of grief is often more difficult for women to work through than men, whereas the sadness stage can be difficult for men who have been raised to be "tough."

When you grieve, the stages of grief aren't always experienced in order. You may move back and forth from denial to anger and back to denial again, for example. Furthermore, although you may reach a point at which you accept the loss and can move beyond it, it doesn't mean that from time to time the loss won't resurface with a new intensity. That doesn't mean you haven't grieved for your loss, but perhaps that something triggered your memory of the loss, such as a song, a time of year, or a place. Sometimes new losses bring up feelings of previous losses—especially if you haven't grieved completely for the old losses. Adoptees who become birth parents or adoptive parents, as well as birth parents who adopt or who place another child for adoption, may find their earlier losses revisiting them as they grieve for the losses they are currently experiencing in adoption.

COPING WITH GRIEF

As you grieve, you must keep reminding yourself that you will feel better eventually. You won't believe that in your heart, but your mind must keep repeating it. It's a good idea to talk to others who have experienced the same kind of loss so that you can hear from them that the pain eventually diminishes.

Many people find it helpful to keep a journal at this time. When the loss seems overwhelming, or when they lack energy, they can refer to their journal to remind them what their reasoning was in making their plan. They can also see that even though they are still feeling pain, they are progressing—something hard to see on a day-to-day basis. Identify people you can be with who will be supportive when you're feeling sad or angry. Let people know specifically what you need from them. Trust that you will only let out your emotions when it is safe to do so and that you will be able to stop when you want to.

Although it may be difficult, take care of yourself in whatever way you can so that your emotional pain is not worsened by factors such as fatigue or poor nutrition. Make an attempt to eat well and get enough rest. This is particularly important for birth mothers because the way you take care of your body directly affects your child's mental and physical development.

Remember that grieving takes time. You can't grieve if you are overly busy.

Meeting New Challenges

As you grieve for your losses, you will find that you will regain a sense of control over your life and will have renewed energy, hope, and self-confidence. With that sense of control and vitality comes the ability to draw on the skills you have or to develop new skills to guide you in your open adoption relationship.

Because open adoption involves relationships, we believe the more skillful you are at relationships, the more successful you can be in open adoption. No matter what your age or educational background, you have some experience with people. Think about important relationships you have had and the skills you have used in those relationships. Identify what you believe to be your strengths in a relationship as well as your weaknesses. Think about the kind of people with whom you have had successful relationships.

Open adoption is likely to be successful if you can be *assertive* (but not aggressive) about taking care of your needs as well as be sensitive to the needs of others. You will need to establish, maintain, and respect interpersonal *boundaries*. This is one way of saying that you need to be able to "mind your own business" as well as respectfully communicate to other people when you think they aren't minding theirs. It means being honest, kind, and polite and following the Golden Rule. It means respecting the generally understood rules about privacy, as well as specific rules that individuals may have. For example, you probably know people who are comfortable having you walk into their homes without knocking. Others require a knock, whereas others prefer that you telephone before going to their homes.

You will also need good *communication* skills, which include being able to express your own preferences without being demanding as well as being able to listen to others when they express theirs. You may need to learn to communicate with someone for whom English is not a first language, or with someone whose style of communicating is different than what you are used to. For example, one birth mother was frequently concerned by reports from the adoptive mother about the health of her son until she understood that the adoptive mother tended to overdramatize things. Once the birth mother learned that situations were seldom as serious as the adoptive mother indicated, she was more comfortable talking with her.

You also need *problem-solving skills.* This includes knowing when a conflict can be solved through compromise, in which each person gives up something until some middle ground can be found; when a conflict needs to be solved through consensus building, in which you work toward a solution that you can all embrace without giving up something important; and when it's time to say, "We'll do this your way, and maybe next time we can do it my way."

TAKING THE NEXT STEP

As you begin the adoption process you may see adoption as the best choice under the circumstances, but not what you would choose for yourself if you had ultimate control over your life. It's hard to deliberately embark on a journey that you know will result in losses and to continue on that journey as you experience them—no matter how much benefit you can also see in your choice. You have to constantly remind yourself that the risk of some of the losses you fear is minor, that certain risks can be minimized, and that the benefits are worth the losses.

Thinking about open adoption is a little like making a commitment to marry someone and remain faithful to them for the rest of your life without knowing who that person will be. The idea of a permanent, monogamous relationship in such a case may seem filled with sacrifices. You fear giving up your independence and privacy. You worry that your partner will be too demanding or that you'll relinquish your identity. You're afraid you won't be compatible forever, and worry you're passing up all the other partners you could have had. But once you meet the right person, you realize that you can handle any losses there are and that the benefits of the relationship will far outweigh the sacrifices you'll make. As with finding the right mate, you won't be able to let go of a lot of your concerns about open adoption until you meet the right family.

part two

Moving Toward Open Adoption

Readiness for Open Adoption

Your basic belief system, philosophy of life, experiences, and attitudes all contribute to your feelings about adoption. You may have had personal experience with adoption, fostering, or stepparenting in which you could see that biologic ties are only one way to bind a family. But you have had other experiences as well, perhaps not as obviously connected to adoption, that have shaped your views as you consider adoption. Think about your beliefs about human beings, your religious upbringing, significant events in your life, and movies and books that have made impressions on you, and consider how they might contribute to your attitudes toward adoption and open adoption. For example, in some families, the attitude that "blood is thicker than water" is a core belief that the family uses to measure acceptable and unacceptable behavior. In those families, it may be more difficult to take in an adopted child as a full member of the family or to allow a child to leave the family to be adopted. On the other hand, those families may be more accepting of the need adoptees have to remain connected in some way to their birth families.

The following questions may help you understand how you have developed certain beliefs and attitudes. There are no right or wrong answers to these questions. In some cases you may find that you have developed attitudes radically different from those you grew up with. After you've thought about these questions, compare your beliefs to the list on pages 39–40.

- Were there a lot of secrets in your family—topics that could not be discussed, events or people never mentioned? Do you know about all your relatives, what they were like, where they lived, and how they died?

If there are relatives you do not know or do not know about, do you know why?

▪ In your family, were new family members, such as those who married into the family, easily integrated into the family or looked on as outsiders? Did your family believe in taking care of problems within the family or were they willing to go outside of the family for help?

▪ How did your family view people who were different, had different backgrounds, different educations, or different beliefs? How were family members viewed who were different?

▪ How were beliefs changed in your family—through education, by obeying an authority, through prayer, through personal experience?

▪ What are your religious beliefs and how do they contribute to your interactions with other people? What is the attitude of your faith group toward people who engage in premarital sex? toward infertility? toward adoption? Do you have faith in yourself, in God, or in a higher power?

▪ What are your beliefs about other people? Do you think people are basically good and trustworthy? Do you tend to trust people until they prove themselves untrustworthy, or are you suspicious of people until they earn your trust?

▪ In what ways have you grown and changed and seen relationships grow and change?

▪ What experience have you had with adoption, foster care, and stepfamilies? What was your family's view of biologic connections? ethnic heritage? heredity and environment? Whom do you know who has been involved in adoption, foster care, or stepparenting? How have their experiences shaped your attitudes?

▪ Is there anyone who doesn't like you? How do you deal with that? How do you deal with people whom you do not like? Do you know people whose lifestyle or values conflict with your own? How do you deal with them? Are any of them your friends? Can you love someone without approving of everything they do?

▪ How do you cope with fear and uncertainty? How do you deal with risks? How important is it to you to be in control?

▪ How strong is your self-esteem? Can you withstand scrutiny and disapproval if you feel you have made the right decision? Do you need to have other people's agreement or approval to feel good about a decision you've made? Do you trust your instincts and your ability to appraise other people's characters?

▪ What is your view of families? What builds and maintains closeness between people? What can destroy family relationships?

One adoptive mother said she grew up in a family that emphasized openness and honesty. She couldn't imagine raising her child with secrets—including secrets about the birth parents. Another adoptive mother said the religious upbringing of her and her husband emphasized that justice and doing what was right was more important than feeling comfortable or getting what you want. Another adoptive parent said he believed he could enter into a relationship with the birth parents because he was confident of his ability to get along with people. Several people have told us that their belief that God has a plan for them enabled them to proceed with adoption.

The following attitudes and beliefs contribute in positive ways to people's ability to embrace adoption in general, and open adoption in particular. Compare them to your attitudes and beliefs, keeping in mind that there is no "score" that indicates whether you're likely to succeed in open adoption. This list is offered only as a guide:

▪ People are inherently good, although they sometimes behave in unacceptable ways.

▪ All relationships have risks. People are capable of dealing with risks in relationships.

▪ Long-term secrets usually involve shame and are unhealthy ways of dealing with information.

▪ Honesty is the best policy.

▪ Judge not.

▪ Differences do not make people inferior. People can learn a lot from people with different abilities, philosophies, values, or beliefs.

▪ Parents do not "own" their children.

▪ Both environment and genetics contribute to the development of individuals.

▪ People can interact with others even though they may not like them or approve of their behavior.

▪ People need other people and sometimes need to ask for help.

▪ People can grow and change.

▪ It is unhealthy for people to have to control every aspect of their lives or the lives of those they love.

- Direct communication is more effective than indirect communication.
- Discomfort often leads to personal growth.
- A healthy sense of humor is helpful in difficult relationships.
- There is no limit to the amount of love a person can give or receive. Loving someone does not dilute that person's love for other people. Parents can love more than one child; children can love more than one parent.
- People have a moral responsibility to the life they bring onto this planet.

ATTITUDES TOWARD ADOPTION

In addition, healthy attitudes toward adoption enhance the likelihood of the adoption being successful:

- Children have a right to know who they are and how they joined their families and to grow up knowing the truth.
- Children do not cease to have a connection with their birth family because they are adopted. They have a right to information about their birth family and to maintain a connection with them.
- Children have a right to be recognized by society as full and equal members of their adoptive families.
- Children have a right to freely ask questions and express their feelings about being adopted.
- Children have the right to be accepted as individuals with a unique genetic heritage that is modified, enhanced, and developed by the environment in which they are raised.
- Children have a right to a positive sense of racial identity as well as a positive sense of family identity.
- Families have the right to choose the circumstances under which they disclose to others their involvement in adoption. Information about a child's origins is private information that belongs to the child. The child has the right to choose the circumstances under which that information is disclosed.
- Being placed for adoption is a separate issue from being adopted. Being infertile is a separate issue from being an adoptive parent. Having an unwanted pregnancy is not the same as not wanting the child. Each has a separate emotional reaction.

Accepting and Understanding Adoption

Once you decide that you want to consider adoption seriously, you need to be able to articulate why you have chosen adoption. If you are considering adoption primarily because someone else wants you to, you need to spend more time thinking about adoption as well as your other options.

BIRTH PARENTS

Birth parents can evaluate their own readiness by asking themselves if they truly accept and understand the following:

▪ Open adoption means permanently terminating parental rights; having no legal rights to the child and perhaps no legal guarantee that contact with the child will be maintained; forever giving up their role as parents to the child; realizing that the child's adoptive parents will probably raise the child differently from the way the birth parents would.

▪ Understanding that while adoption may solve some immediate problems, it will involve intense, permanent losses for which they will grieve; deciding to suffer these losses because it is the best decision for the child, even though it may not feel like the best decision for the birth parents; being prepared and willing to experience the grief that will follow.

▪ Recognizing that their child will have another family, which includes other parents, siblings, grandparents, and extended family members; understanding that the child may feel closer to these people than to her biologic relatives, and that she will develop differently than she would have if she remained with her birth family.

▪ Accepting that by losing their role as parents to this child, they may also lose their role as grandparents to her children; understanding that adoption affects all generations in a family, including birth grandparents and the siblings or half-siblings of the child placed for adoption.

▪ Understanding that children are not interchangeable or replaceable; that even though they may have another child someday, that child will not be the same as this child—if this is their first child, they will never again experience having a "first" child.

▪ Believing that the adoptive parents will not be "second-best" parents, but will love the child as much as if she had been born to them and will raise her as well as they would have raised children born to them.

▪ Believing that they have worth as human beings and worth in their child's life.

▪ Accepting that they cannot know or be expected to know the outcome of their decision. They cannot know for certain that their decision will be the best one for the child or for themselves—they can only make what appears to be the best choice based on what they know at the time.

▪ Recognizing that their lives will be changed by whatever decision they make.

▪ Recognizing that their child will suffer losses as well as gains, but believing the gains to the child will outweigh the losses.

▪ Understanding and honoring that relinquishing their parenting rights does not relieve them of certain responsibilities to the life they helped create.

▪ Feeling both apprehensive about the difficult time ahead and confident about the rightness of the plan.

▪ Being willing to tell other people about the adoption plan.

ADOPTIVE PARENTS

Readiness to become a parent through open adoption means:

▪ Understanding that a child they adopt will come with genetic traits from another family and will be different from a child who might have been born to them; being willing to acknowledge the permanent connection this makes between the child and her birth family and to accept the importance of the birth mother, birth father, and their families to the child.

▪ Believing that adopting a child may be a second choice, but is not a second-best alternative—that having a child by adoption is an equally acceptable way to build a family as having a child by birth.

▪ Agreeing to suspend infertility treatment temporarily and concentrate their time, energy, and financial resources on adoption (see Chapter 4).

▪ Understanding that being adopted carries losses of its own and that children deserve an opportunity to express their feelings about being adopted, including their feelings of grief; not expecting their children to feel "grateful" to them for adopting them.

▪ Understanding that no one "owns" their children; that the responsibility of parents is not to bind their children to them but to raise them to be competent, confident, independent individuals.

▪ Recognizing that because their family was formed in a unique way, they will have different experiences than other families—experiences that are normal for adoptive families, but may present challenges for parents and children alike.

▪ Understanding that adopting a child will not solve their infertility problems, take away all their hurt, or fulfill all their dreams, but will be a joyous experience in its own way.

▪ Realizing that while they can choose to whom they want to disclose their child's adoptive status, it is not a secret to be hidden from people, nor is it something everyone needs to know. (This subject is discussed in more detail in Chapter 8.)

▪ Deciding what kind of child they feel they can best parent. (See Chapter 15 for information on open adoptions with older children and children of a different race or ethnic background than their adoptive parents.)

▪ Letting go of the need for a child to meet certain criteria to be acceptable, such as IQ, physical characteristics, abilities; feeling that they have worth as human beings regardless of whether or not they have children, whether those children are biologically related to them, and regardless of how their children turn out.

▪ Accepting that they cannot know or be expected to know the outcome of their decision. They cannot know for certain that their decision will be the best one for the child or for themselves—they can only make what appears to be the best choice based on what they know at the time.

▪ Recognizing that their child will suffer losses as well as gains, but believing the gains to the child will outweigh the losses.

▪ Feeling both apprehensive about the adoption plan and enthusiastic about it.

At this point you are ready to look for a program or facilitator who meets your needs and whose philosophy fits with yours. At first, the process of finding any adoption program, much less one that offers the kinds of services you want, may seem daunting. Begin by finding out what is available locally. Look in the yellow pages of the telephone book under "adoption agencies," "attorneys," and "pregnancy counseling." Talk to others who have adopted or placed a child for adoption. Contact an adoption support group. But keep in mind that you needn't restrict yourself to programs in your own community. Consult books and directories for lists of programs and organizations outside your community. Don't be afraid to ask questions to see if a program will work for you.

As you obtain information about different programs, keep in mind that you may be tempted to select a program or facilitator that seems to protect you from the risks of open adoption. Evaluate such programs carefully. We believe a good adoption program:

▪ Focuses primarily on the needs of the child, while also trying to meet the needs of the adoptive parents and birth parents;

▪ Has a variety of professionals available to you, either on staff or as referrals, including attorneys, social workers, counselors, and health-care professionals;

▪ Offers extensive opportunities for education, counseling, and support for everyone connected to the adoption before, during, and after the placement;

▪ Provides accurate, relevant information about the legal and financial issues involved;

▪ Is not threatened if clients find resources outside of the program;

▪ Sees adoption as involving both losses and gains for everyone involved;

▪ Encourages participation by birth fathers and the extended family members of birth parents and adoptive parents;

▪ Offers options and empowers birth parents and adoptive parents to make informed choices;

▪ Offers birth parents and adoptive parents the flexibility to build the kind of relationship that is right for them.

Once you decide you're ready to proceed with adoption and have chosen a facilitator, it is time to find your match.

Choosing
Each Other

Choosing birth or adoptive parents is a process that involves both your mind and your heart. You will have some specific ideas of what you are looking for, such as age, race, or educational background. But subjective factors, such as how at ease you feel around each other, are also important. Because there are so many more prospective adoptive parents than birth parents who make adoption plans, you may question whether you actually choose each other or whether birth parents choose adoptive parents. This is a mutual decision. While birth parents may have more adoptive parents to choose from, adoptive parents must be active participants in the selection process if the relationship is going to work long-term.

You can begin to get an idea of the kind of birth or adoptive parents you want to find by thinking about the kinds of people with whom you feel comfortable, as well as by visualizing your child and the open adoption relationship. Think about the people with whom you get along well. What do they have in common with each other? What are their personalities like? How do they communicate? What makes you trust them or want to spend time with them?

Birth parents should imagine the rest of their pregnancy, the birth of the child, and the moment when they give their child to the adoptive parents. They should imagine the kind of parents they want their child to have—their religious preference, their recreational activities, their occupation, whether they have other children, whether they enjoy pets, sports, music, outdoor activities, or artistic endeavors. Do they want parents who are liberal or conservative in their thinking? How do they envision their parenting style, such as how they discipline, show affection, and express their feelings? Do they want parents who are outgoing or quiet; practical jokers or serious? Will they consider unmarried couples, single parents, gay or lesbian parents? They should consider the racial or ethnic background they want the parents to have. Furthermore, they should think about why these characteristics are important to them.

It's also important for them to imagine their child growing up, how they expect to be part of the child's life, how their extended family will be part of the child's life, and how the other birth parent's family will participate in the child's life. Do they want to communicate by phone and mail or do they want to have visits, too? How frequently will they want to have contact? How do the extended family members expect to be involved in the open adoption? Are they comfortable letting their family and the other birth parent's family develop relationships with the adoptive family?

Stacy, a birth mother, was opposed to her family interacting with the adoptive family unless she was present. Her family felt they should respect her wishes, but it held them back from having as full a relationship as they wanted—and as the adoptive parents wanted. Eventually, Stacy was able to let go of her need to control the open adoption relationships, but before that happened, the difference between her expectations and those of the rest of her family and the adoptive parents caused some tension.

Adoptive parents should imagine the time leading up to their child's birth, whether they expect to attend the birth, and how they will take the baby home. They should also imagine the child as a teenager or young adult, especially when adopting a child of a different race or ethnic background. Adoptive parents should think about their own experience growing up and what their parenting style is likely to be. They can envision in what ways the birth family will be part of the child's life and part of their life.

Like the birth parents, adoptive parents should imagine how they will communicate with the birth parents, and how frequently, in what ways the birth parents will be part of their life, and how the extended birth family will be involved with the child. Again, visualizing this in concrete terms, such as how they will celebrate the child's fifth birthday, is helpful. However, keep in mind that your ideas about the amount and kind of contact you both want are likely to change dramatically over the course of the adoption.

As part of this exercise, develop a sense of what in your vision is essential and what is negotiable. Visualizing the way you expect things to be will not guarantee that they will turn out as you want them to, but it will help you assess whether a particular birth or adoptive family is right for you, and will otherwise help you make choices that will increase your chances of being satisfied with the open adoption.

Your adoption facilitator may include a visualization session as part of your adoption preparation. Adoption facilitators can bring up possibilities for you to consider, point out requests that are unusual or unrealistic, and tell you when requests that seem unreasonable are really sensible. You may feel more secure knowing that your facilitator will bring you back to reality if your visualization starts to take you off track, or that your facilitator will push you to consider alternatives that you might not otherwise allow yourself to hope for.

When the time comes for birth parents to select the adoptive parents they would like to consider, they or their adoption facilitator will be able to screen applicants on the basis of criteria such as religious preferences, marital status, and the existence of other children in the family. But social worker James Gritter, M.S.W., of CFCS—Catholic Charities in Michigan, suggests that philosophic compatibility, similarity of values, and harmonious tone are equally important. Cheri wanted adoptive parents who would raise her child in the Catholic faith. But she was drawn to a couple who practice no organized religion. Nor were the lifestyles or educational backgrounds of Cheri and the adoptive parents at all alike. What they had in common was the way they expressed themselves physically. They moved their bodies a lot when they spoke. They touched each other a lot. None of them could sit still for more than ten minutes without getting up and moving about. The tone of their families was the same, and Cheri felt comfortable having her child raised in this environment.

It is vitally important to the success of open adoption to have a match in which the adoptive parents are willing to grant more openness than the birth family initially wants. As we see in Chapter 8, birth parents typically want more contact after placement than they expected to want, and adoptive parents often want less—at least at first. If the maximum the adoptive parents are willing to give in the way of openness only covers the birth parents' minimum requirements, it's likely they will soon have serious conflict because there is no room to negotiate.

A birth mother who selects adoptive parents early on in her pregnancy may still be denying the pregnancy, and may think she will not want much contact with her child. As the baby becomes real for her, however, and she becomes more in touch with her feelings about the child, she may want more contact than she originally thought. If she has selected adoptive parents who do not want much contact, this could become a source of conflict. The adoptive parents might think the birth mother is changing the rules in the middle of the game, and may be angry at having invested time, energy, and money in this relationship, perhaps passing over other opportunities. The birth mother may think the adoptive parents are being too rigid. She may want to choose other adoptive parents but may worry that it's too late.

Of course, neither of you may be sure of what you're willing to put into an open adoption relationship until you meet the people you'll be having the relationship with. For example, many people might think they would be unwilling to marry someone with a severe physical handicap, thinking that they aren't able to make the sacrifices that would be required. Once they meet someone and fall in love, however, they may find that they are willing to give more to a relationship than they thought.

But there is a difference between allowing yourself to grow in a relationship and compromising yourself. Adoption mediator Jeanne Etter, Ph.D., points out that the value of having a clear idea about the level of openness you want before a meeting takes place is that you will not be tempted to give up too much for the sake of a match. Once you get to know someone and have at least the beginning of a relationship, you are likely to want to please that person. But if you surrender too much, you may feel cheated and dissatisfied later. Although an open adoption is a lifelong commitment, and the relationship is fluid and will change over time, the starting point does affect the future relationship.

Etter recommends that birth parents request a minimum of one visit with the child and adoptive family each year, even if they don't think they'll ever want to visit. Most of her clients request a minimum of two visits each year. Etter believes even reluctant adoptive parents can agree to one or two visits each year if they know further visits will only take place by mutual consent.

Once you have some specific ideas of what you want and expect in a relationship, you have a basis for assessing individuals and arrangements. Birth parents can proceed to select a pool of prospective adoptive parents, and adoptive parents can feel empowered to make some decisions themselves about whether to get involved with particular birth parents, rather than being passive participants in the matching process.

Finding Each Other

Birth parents and adoptive parents discover each other in many ways. Some know each other before they are faced with the decision of whether to become involved in adoption and find that they naturally turn to each other at this time, such as a young woman who looks to a family member to adopt her child. Others have a casual acquaintance, perhaps from attending the same church. Some find each other when a birth parent responds to a newspaper advertisement placed by the adoptive parents or through word of mouth. Birth parents may select adoptive parents from a limited number of adoptive parents chosen for review by the adoption facilitator or by looking through a photo album or stack of "resumes."

It is important for both the birth and the adoptive parents to feel some control over a choice that will have a profound impact on them for the rest of their lives. Much of the conflict in open adoption is actually a struggle for control. Both the birth and the adoptive parents enter the selection process feeling out of control. They may respond to this by demanding more control or by not exercising the control they have, thereby setting themselves up for an unsatisfactory relationship.

A birth mother may feel out of control of her body as the child she didn't expect to conceive grows and changes her physically and emotionally. Birth parents may feel out of control of their lives in general as an unplanned pregnancy causes them to change their plans for school, work, or marriage.

Adoptive parents who are infertile or who have experienced difficulty carrying a child to term may also feel out of control of their bodies. As they enter the adoption process, they may feel that they have to answer questions that other people don't have to answer and satisfy people in ways other people don't have to before they will be able to be parents. Because there are so many people seeking to adopt compared to the number of infants placed for adoption, they may feel that all they can do is wait to be chosen by the birth parents. Once chosen, they may feel they have to proceed with a match whether it seems ideal or not because they don't know if they will be chosen again.

During the process of open adoption, you will probably discover that you cannot have as much control as you would like. When that happens, allow yourself to experience and express your feelings about the loss of this control in an appropriate way, by talking about it, working it out through exercise, or finding other areas of your life where more control is both possible and reasonable.

As long as you are fighting for control that you will not be able to have, you're not progressing in confronting your losses, and you will probably find it difficult to move on with the process of adoption, or with any open adoption relationship you're trying to build. If you suppress your feelings about your loss of control, they may come out suddenly and with more intensity than they need to have, which could prove a setback to a fragile new relationship. For example, you might choose not to negotiate about an issue simply to assert your right to be in control, rather than because the issue is really nonnegotiable.

Adoptive parents need to understand how important it is for birth parents to be able to select the parents who will be raising their child. One illustration often repeated in discussing open adoption is that parents would be unlikely to leave their child with a babysitter they hadn't met, just because they had the word of a reputable agency that the babysitter would do a good job. For them to feel that they have made a responsible decision in planning for the future of their child, birth parents need to select the adoptive parents. Some birth parents will need to review all the available resumes, whereas others will be content to know that other choices are available if they care to review them. Birth parents should work with an adoption facilitator whose adoption process meets their needs. Those who need to see all the possibilities before narrowing their choices will want to work with an adoption facilitator who is comfortable presenting them with all the adoptive parents who meet their minimum requirements rather than a facilitator who screens the adoptive parents himself, selecting a handful for birth parents to examine. Birth parents who need help narrowing their choices should work with a facilitator who is prepared to do that.

One birth mother sent a descriptive letter about herself to dozens of physicians, attorneys, and adoption agencies, asking if they knew of any adoptive parents who might be suitable for her child. Another birth mother, who was a prostitute, interviewed more than fifty couples from one coast of the United States to the other. Although several couples met her initial criteria, none of them seemed suitable. The facilitators she worked with thought she was being excessively critical because she really wanted to keep the baby. But she maintained that none of the couples she had met really approved of her, and she suspected that if she chose one of them, they would not maintain contact with her after a few years.

Eventually, however, she met a lesbian couple whose own experience having a lifestyle that was not approved of by many people made them more tolerant of the birth mother's lifestyle. The adoption has been highly successful.

Adoptive parents who feel that the birth parents are in charge of the selection process should remember that they have the right to say "yes" or "no" to a match. They can say "no" to birth parents who do not seem like people they want to be closely involved with, who seem ambivalent, who live too close or too far away, who have a high-risk pregnancy, or who, for whatever reason, do not seem like a suitable match.

THE MAGIC MATCH

Those who have observed the process of birth parents selecting adoptive parents for their children describe it identically: it's "magic." Whether they are responding to a newspaper advertisement or choosing from among photographs and letters of dozens of adoptive parents, something about the adoptive parents catches the attention of the birth parents.

While birth parents often have criteria for their child's adoptive parents, there are hundreds of adoptive parents who could fit those requirements. What is magical about the match is the intuitive way birth parents look at a photograph or read a letter from adoptive parents and find instant familiarity. Social workers who placed children for adoption in the days when they carefully selected the adoptive parents for the birth parents are often amazed at the way birth parents will select adoptive parents who seem completely different from them, only to have them develop immediate rapport with each other. Adoption facilitators see birth parents pass over adoptive parents who appear to present themselves well, but who actually have reservations about adoption. Somehow, that reserve is apparent to the birth parents. They see adoptive parents who are overweight or plain selected over those who look like magazine cover models. One young birth mother explained her choice saying, "These people have an inner beauty."

One birth mother, who was a construction worker with a bawdy sense of humor, selected adoptive parents who hadn't seemed unusual in any way in their preadoption interviews. After the three of them met, however, the birth mother and the adoptive father were engaging in earthy banter, slapping each other on the knees as they enjoyed some hearty belly laughs. "I like her because we can go out and have a beer together," the adoptive father said. Something in this couple's photograph indicated subconsciously to the birth mother that she would feel comfortable with them.

Birth parents should make sure they feel a sense of familiarity when they look at a photograph of prospective adoptive parents who seem appealing. They may feel it with the first adoptive parents they see, or they may need to look through many photographs and letters before they find someone who "clicks." This is an important step. They are selecting the people who will raise their child. They are also selecting someone they hope to have a long-term relationship with.

Because you probably don't have a lot of time to get to know each other, you are going to want to begin a relationship having as much in common as possible. If birth parents aren't finding any adoptive parents who seem right, they should look at more possibilities. However, if after looking at many possible adoptive parents, the birth parents still can't find anyone who they could imagine raising their child, perhaps it's because they can't imagine anyone else raising their child. They may want to reconsider the adoption plan and talk to a counselor about other alternatives.

Adoptive parents who have been waiting a long time to be chosen should be careful not to give way to feelings of inadequacy and inferiority. Birth parents aren't looking for the most attractive parents— they're looking for people they consider to be the best parents for their child based on who is most like the parents they had or wished they had. While waiting to be chosen by birth parents, adoptive parents should keep in mind that there is a child meant for them. It just may not have been conceived yet.

When birth and adoptive parents don't have a chance to get to know each other, there is less chance that there will be the magical "click." Although this might not seem important if you don't expect to have a lot of contact, if the relationship becomes more open—as many do—it could make the development of that relationship a little more difficult. Even if you do not plan now to have a fully disclosed adoption or visitation, take the time to get to know each other and make sure you could get along if the level of openness ever changes.

If your adoption is going to be between family members, you already have some common factors, even though you may think of yourselves as very different. You are familiar to each other because you already know one another. But you may also have some family baggage that can inhibit your relationship. This issue is discussed in more detail in Chapter 15.

Part of the value of finding familiarity in each other is that you feel comfortable together and respect each other, which will help you sustain a long-term relationship. This benefits you, but it also helps your child when your relationship is satisfying because he doesn't feel caught between two antagonistic families. In addition, children may feel less "abandoned" when they know their birth and adoptive parents took time to carefully choose each other. Finally, adoptees sometimes feel that they just don't belong in their adoptive families. They feel loved and valued, but sometimes "out of sync." There may be some obvious differences, such as a child who loves the out-of-doors being adopted by book lovers, or a musical child being adopted by a family of athletes. Or the differences may be more subtle, such as a "night owl" being adopted by earlier risers. Like a shoe that is the right size but still doesn't feel comfortable, adoptees sometimes feel that the nonverbal language spoken in the family is a foreign language that they've had to learn rather than their mother tongue.

Years ago, social workers tried to match a child to adoptive parents based on the IQs, talents, interests, and physical features of the birth parents and the adoptive parents. But this didn't always guarantee a good fit. No one has researched this issue among families in open adoption, but it's very possible that the more familiarity the birth parents and the adoptive parents find in each other—the more comfortable they are with each other—the more likely the child will feel like the adoptive family is one that "fits."

However, there is a potential disadvantage to the practice of having birth parents select adoptive parents for their child. Just as people sometimes select life partners with the same negative qualities as their parents, the familiarity the birth parents feel with the adoptive parents may be based on undesirable qualities. The adoptive father may turn out to have a hot temper similar to that of the birth mother's father. The adoptive mother may be excessively critical, just as the birth mother's mother was. As you get to know each other, birth parents should pay attention to any signs that the adoptive parents may not be suitable as their child's parents. One birth mother, whose mother was an alcoholic, eventually was able to express to her counselor that she thought the adoptive mother was an alcoholic. The initial familiarity she had felt with the couple was due to the similarity in behavior between the adoptive mother and the birth mother's own mother. By verbalizing this realization, the birth mother learned to watch for signs of dysfunctional behavior in other adoptive couples that attracted her, and the adoptive parents learned that the wife's drinking problem could not be ignored. Your counselor may have some techniques to help you identify unhealthy patterns of relationships that you might want to be alert for in choosing parents.

Meeting Each Other

How you first have contact with each other will be determined to some extent by the approach you have taken to finding each other. You may be working with a facilitator who structures your first phone call or meeting for you, or you may find each other without the aid of a facilitator.

Your first direct contact with each other is likely to be a telephone call. You'll probably feel nervous because you want to make a good impression. You're also likely to be a little wary—afraid to reveal too much about yourself to someone you haven't met. You'll probably have a lot of questions, but feel unsure of how many to ask right away.

Keep in mind that this is an introductory phone call, and not the time to investigate each other. If you try to get a lot of information from each other during this initial telephone call you'll probably be told what you want to hear rather than what you need to know. Although it may feel like you have to hurry to get to know each other well enough to decide if you want to be involved in an open adoption, you'll learn more about each other if you let the relationship take its own course over the first few encounters.

The most successful first phone calls are those in which you allow yourselves to relax and have a casual discussion about things that probably seem trivial, such as what you enjoy doing in your free time and what kinds of movies you've seen recently. One birth mother talked with the adoptive family for three hours about horses. Nothing they said was essential to making a match, but the ease with which they communicated was.

What's important in this first encounter is not what you talk about but how you communicate: where in the conversation you laugh, who is loud and who is quiet, who leads the conversation, whether the choice of language and rhythm of the conversation is conducive to communicating with each other. Be sure to be polite, warm, concerned, and honest. Before hanging up, discuss what the next step will be, so that you both have the same understanding. You wouldn't want the relationship to fall apart because each of you was waiting for the other to make the next call.

THE FIRST MEETING

Before you meet, imagine what it will be like. Think about a blind date you might have had. Where did you feel comfortable going on that first date? What put you at ease? Did you like being in public or did you prefer privacy? Were you comfortable meeting during the evening or did you prefer to meet during the day? How did you begin to converse and get to know each other? How did you separate? What did you say if you wanted to see each other again? What did you say if you didn't? Imagine how your upcoming meeting will be like this blind date and how you can use your experience to make the meeting more successful for you.

Like the initial telephone call, the first meeting should be a casual opportunity to get acquainted. Although you may have many questions, you won't want to appear to be conducting a census interview. Just chat about yourselves. When in doubt, talk about the one common interest you can be sure of—the baby. Adoptive parents should be aware, however, that the birth mother may be uncomfortable if she feels her growing belly is the focus of their attention.

Keep in mind that not everyone has an easy time talking to people whom they just met. If you find yourself having trouble talking to one another, it doesn't mean it isn't a good match. It may mean someone is quiet or shy, or that you're all feeling awkward. Bring something to do when you meet, such as a photo album to look at, or plan an activity, like a trip to the zoo. When the conversation lags, suggest taking a walk together. Perhaps you will find that you feel comfortable just being together.

Sometimes the adoptive father feels like a "fifth wheel" at these meetings, especially when the birth father isn't present. Indeed, he may feel left out throughout the adoption process, which often seems more geared toward women than men. Birth and adoptive mothers should make an effort to include the birth and adoptive fathers in planning and preparing for the open adoption.

While you will probably be anxious about whether you are pleasing to the other person, keep in mind that you probably want to like each other. Adoptive parents want to like the birth parents because they want to have a baby and they want to like the people their child came from. They are also flattered to have been chosen and therefore already have a warm feeling about the birth parents. Once they have been chosen, they tend to look for the positive qualities in the birth parents and minimize their negative characteristics. Birth mothers often find that the adoptive parents are the first people they've met who have been excited about their pregnancy. They often respond positively to the warmth and acceptance they feel from the adoptive parents.

Even though it's hard to be open with someone you've just met, and whom you want to impress, remember that nobody wants to get into a relationship with someone who seems "too perfect" or who seems to be hiding something. Be yourself, which means being imperfect. Allow yourself to be vulnerable, to express your emotions. Remember that someone has to be the first one to go beyond superficial conversation. Once you do that, others are free to reveal themselves, too. Be willing to use humor, when it's appropriate. It will not only "break the ice" and enable you all to feel more comfortable with each other but it tells the other person something about who you are. And people who can laugh together are more likely to sustain a relationship than people who can't.

When it's time to end the first meeting, try to give each other an honest reflection of your feelings at that point, to the best of your ability. Remember how it felt at the end of that blind date. You weren't sure how the other person felt about you. You wanted the other person to know whether you wanted to go out with him again or not. Remember how it felt when the other person indicated an interest that you knew wasn't sincere—or worse, that you thought was sincere and found out later was not.

It's helpful to be as specific as you can be with each other about why you like each other or don't like each other, or how you plan to proceed. Birth parents can say, "I really like you, but I feel like I have to talk to some other people, too, just so I'm sure I've found the right ones." Adoptive parents can say, "We seem to have hit it off. I think we'd like to get to know you better." Or they might say, "I don't know if we're the right parents for your child. I think you should keep looking." However, you may want to reflect on the meeting or talk it over with your partner or support person before making even a tentative commitment. In that case, you can say, "I enjoyed meeting you. I want to think about this a little. I'll call you Friday." Be sure to discuss what the next step will be.

After the meeting, reflect on what you learned. Talk it over with your partner or whomever you brought to the meeting as your support person. You might start, as one adoption facilitator suggests, by asking yourself whether you feel better or worse having met the other parents. If you feel better, it's probably a good sign. If you feel worse, it may be a sign that the match isn't good, or that you aren't ready for adoption. Don't underestimate your impressions—they are probably closer to the truth than you might think.

Only you can decide whether you want to proceed with the relationship despite some negative feelings. But don't go ahead just because you don't want to hurt the other person. You will most likely decide not to continue the relationship later because the closer you get to placement, the more need you will have to feel good about the relationship. Birth mothers who are feeling a lot of pain at the time of placement will find it easy to use their vague dislike of the adoptive parents as an excuse to parent their children themselves. Adoptive parents will find it easy to terminate contact after placement with a birth mother they don't like. When birth parents decide to raise their child themselves for the wrong reasons, or adoptive parents discontinue contact without good cause, everyone loses—especially the child.

Also keep in mind that when you meet for the first time, you will find that the adoption possibilities you have been discussing become real. The birth mother will no longer be a fuzzy image but a real person with a personality, a future, and a family. Adoptive parents may see that the birth parents are confused and vulnerable rather than irresponsible, arrogant, or powerful. When face-to-face with the birth parents, adoptive parents may realize that their child will not be a blank slate that they can form into the child of their dreams but will come with a set of genes inherited from the people sitting across from them. If this is a new realization for them, they may experience the loss of their fantasy adopted child, just as they experienced the loss of their fantasy biologic child when they accepted their diagnosis of infertility or decided to adopt rather than conceive a child. They may have to step back from the adoption process for a bit while they experience their feelings about this realization and adjust their expectations to fit the reality.

When faced with the realities of the birth family, some adoptive parents may decide against adoption or decide that they have to do more preparation before they adopt. They may not be ready to raise a child who comes with another family. They may not be ready to accept the fact that another set of genes will determine much of who their child is. Or they may decide to be more selective about the child they are going to adopt and the birth family they will be involved with. Adoptive parents who have these reservations should pay attention to them. No matter how much they want a child, they should not adopt a child if they cannot accept that the child has *this* birth family who will be a part of him biologically and a part of their family forever.

Similarly, for the birth family, the adoptive parents will no longer be a vague concept but real people with an extended family and perhaps other children, a parenting style, and a way of interacting with other people. Birth parents may see that the adoptive parents are needy and powerless rather than people who have everything and are going to get their child, too. When face-to-face with the adoptive parents, birth parents may realize that their child will be different growing up with these people than he would be if he grew up with them. They may have to reconsider whether this particular parent or set of parents is what they want for their child. They may realize for the first time what it will mean to continue to have contact with their child but not be a mother or father to him. As a result, they may start to grieve for their anticipated loss of the parenting role. They, too, may have to step back from the adoption process at this point while they experience their feelings and come to grips with the reality of adoption.

When these realities set in, some birth parents decide they cannot place their child for adoption. The first indication that they may decide to parent their child may be that they are exceptionally critical of every adoptive parent they meet. It's important for birth parents to be discriminating—to look for the adoptive parents they think will do the best job of raising their child and with whom they want to be involved forever. But if the birth parents are finding something wrong with every adoptive parent, that may be the birth family's way of saying, "We're not going to find someone acceptable. It's time to talk about parenting this child ourselves."

If you decide not to proceed with the relationship, try to give a specific reason. You can let the other people know that they are fine people, but they are not what you are looking for, and perhaps you can lessen their feelings of rejection. For example, birth parents could say, "You know, I wanted my baby to go to a family that didn't have any other children, but I didn't realize that he might never have any brothers or sisters if you aren't able to adopt again. I think I want to look at some parents who already have a child so that I'm sure he'll have a brother or a sister." Adoptive parents might say, "We're not sure our personalities mesh with yours well enough for us to have the kind of closeness we both want."

Of course, it's kind of like your blind date saying, "You're a really nice person, but I'd like us to just be friends." It still hurts to not be chosen. You will experience the anger and the sadness that have become familiar to you with the other losses of adoption. You'll go over all the "if onlys": "If only I'd suggested the park instead of the restaurant." "If only I hadn't asked about other children." Eventually you'll be able to say this match wasn't meant to be, and move on in the adoption process, either to another match, or to an alternative to adoption.

If you are told that the other parents do not want to proceed with the relationship, accept the decision gracefully. Resist the temptation to plead or to offer something, such as money (which may be illegal) or a different level of openness (which you may not want) to try to restore the relationship. And even though your relationship may dissolve, be prepared to remain interested in each other. It is natural for birth parents to want to know if the adoptive parents they didn't choose ever got a baby, or for adoptive parents to wonder about the baby the birth parents had. You have shared your vulnerability with another human being and it's natural to feel a certain intimacy even after only one meeting.

Learning More About Each Other

Even if you feel good about each other after your first meeting, give yourself time to get to know each other better—if you have the time to do so—before making a decision about the match. Put as much time and energy as you can into getting to know each other, building trust, and establishing communication. We can't emphasize enough that you are embarking on a lifelong relationship that will be seriously stressed in its early stages. Your relationship must move beyond your common interest in your child for it to be the kind of relationship your child can benefit from.

Try to talk to each other as often as possible. If you live close enough to get together, take the opportunity to spend time together in a variety of settings and activities. If you do not live near each other, think about any long-distance relationships you have had, such as pen pals, friends who have moved away, or extended separations from loved ones. What helped maintain those relationships or contributed to the demise of the relationships? You may want to talk on the phone, exchange videos, write letters, or send cards. Especially during the early stages of your relationship, be sure to end each letter or phone call by discussing how you will next contact each other.

Getting to know each other will involve a gradual process of revealing yourselves. You'll be tempted to only reveal your best qualities because you want to be liked; you want to be chosen. Furthermore, the path you've traveled to this point may have already made you feel inadequate and damaged your self-esteem. You're likely to be very protective of yourself. But even though you may want to only show your best self, you'll only develop a superficial relationship if you can't be more open. Once again, use your past relationships as models. Friends aren't "best friends" until they are willing to let each other know they have weaknesses or imperfections. Maybe the class beauty tells you she worries that people won't like her if she doesn't change her nail polish every day to match her outfit. Or perhaps a co-worker confides in you that his "perfect" marriage is having problems. Those kinds of revelations bring you closer together. Furthermore, it's often the "quirks" you have in common that make a relationship work.

After Laura met Adrienne, the birth mother, and found that Adrienne's easygoing style matched her own, Laura was nervous about having Adrienne meet her husband, who tended to be organized almost to a fault. She was surprised to find the birth father just as well organized as her husband. The occasional frustration each woman felt at dealing with her partner gave them some common ground, and their partners' occasional frustration with the easygoing women in their lives gave them a common bond. Entering into what is expected to be a close relationship without revealing your flaws is like never letting your lover see you without makeup or a shave. You're never sure if that person would love you as you are. But if someone sees you at your worst, and still accepts you, then you feel more secure that the relationship is solid.

We're not suggesting that you attempt to be as obnoxious or unkempt as possible. But think about what is least likeable about you and the ways you try to hide that. Perhaps you have a weight problem so you make it a point to eat very small portions of food in public. When you have the opportunity, mention your weight problem and how you've struggled with it. As you do that, you free the other people to acknowledge problems they've struggled with. You may find that you share a common problem, but at the very least, you will undoubtedly find that you share the human struggle against imperfection.

It feels risky, but expressing honest emotions in appropriate ways will bring you closer together. For example, if you say, "I have to confess, I'm feeling a little nervous about meeting the rest of your family. I really want them to like me," you've shown you're vulnerable. The other parent might then say, "I'm a little nervous about having you meet the rest of my family, too. My father isn't really excited about this plan. He may be pretty critical. But I've learned not to pay much attention to his criticism. And my mom is real enthusiastic. I know she'll like you." You now have formed an alliance against the potential criticism of the baby's grandfather.

However, whenever you feel vulnerable in this relationship you are building, remember that you are building the relationship for your child. Part of being a parent involves sacrificing your own comfort when doing so would benefit your child.

Although it's important to simply spend time with each other to learn about each other's personality, interests, and temperament, you also have some specific information to share with each other, and you probably have a limited amount of time in which to share this information before each of you must make a decision about whether to proceed with this adoption. It may be difficult to move beyond casual conversations to discussing such vital information. You don't want to appear to be interrogating each other. And you also may be worried that if you go beyond casual conversations, one of you will find out something that will make the adoption less likely. The fact is, however, if one of you learns something that makes you want to end the relationship, it's better to learn that sooner rather than later. It may be easier to begin a serious talk if you set up a meeting by expressing that as its purpose. You may find it helpful to read through the rest of this book before having serious discussions with each other so that you have some idea of the issues that need to be discussed, how your relationship is likely to proceed, and the areas that might give you conflict.

If you don't have a lot of time to get to know each other, you will have to compress the process of learning about each other and sharing vital information. Again, your counselor may have some techniques that will help you do that.

Caution Signs

No one can predict whether what appears to be a promising match will actually result in a successful open adoption. However, some matches are riskier than others.

Birth parents are less likely to place for adoption if:

- They are married, have other children, and plan to stay together;
- They are very young, because they tend to be self-centered and unable to project into the future, or may be rebelling against parents who want them to place;
- They are having their first child in their late thirties or forties, because they often don't realize what they are denying themselves until the baby is born;

- The birth mother's mother is not in favor of adoption and the birth mother needs her approval;
- They have not had education and counseling about their adoption decision;
- They seem confused or evasive about their histories or their plans, or the information they provide is vague, inconsistent, or just doesn't make sense;
- They have had a lot of losses in their lives;
- They have no plans for the future;
- They have no emotional support;
- They come from a culture in which there is pressure to raise the baby themselves or pressure for their family to raise the baby;
- Their families would be willing to help them raise the baby.

Adoptive parents may not be ready for adoption if:

- They are unwilling to put their infertility treatment on hold temporarily while they pursue adoption;
- They have no experience with openness in their lives;
- They are exceptionally private and don't allow a lot of people into their lives;
- They are still very angry;
- They are deeply depressed;
- They don't want to invest much time, money, or emotional energy in the relationship;
- They have moved quickly from fertility treatments to adoption;
- They have not had adequate adoption preparation or counseling;
- One partner is pursuing adoption to please the other;
- They have recently had an adoption fall through or have had another significant loss, and they have not adequately grieved for the loss;
- They are intolerant of differences.

Think seriously before proceeding with a relationship under these circumstances. This is not to say these birth parents or adoptive parents should be avoided, but working with them will take extra effort. You may be the kind of person who can take such risks. But if, for example, you're an adoptive parent who has recently had an adoption fall through, you might not be willing to start a relationship with a birth parent who is less likely than most to continue with an adoption plan.

Whatever the risks, you might find yourself so badly wanting to make the adoption work that you're willing to overlook the bad and only see the good qualities in each other. You should force yourself to carefully evaluate the relationship and to consider changing your mind about these other parents. Fantasize about what it would be like not to choose each other. If you still feel this is a good match, you will have the sense of having actively chosen each other rather than having just gone along with events as they have occurred.

Making a Commitment

If the relationship looks promising, or if you decide you're willing to continue despite your doubts, it's time to make a commitment to each other. You may not feel completely sure about each other, but that is because you can't predict the future. Although you might like to take more time to get to know each other, you have to balance your need to feel secure in your choice with the need to make a decision quickly.

When you're ready to make a commitment, the birth mother needs to say to the adoptive parents: "If I decide to place, I will place with you." And the adoptive parents need to say: "If you decide to place, we would like to raise your child." This is an exciting moment and you should celebrate it together. Brenda, a birth mother, treated the moment as she would an engagement, inviting the adoptive parents out to dinner and presenting them with a wrapped package containing a baby rattle.

Nevertheless, it is important to realize that no matter how committed she may feel, the birth mother cannot make a legal or even a full emotional commitment to the adoption until after the child is born. She will have to look at her child as separate from her before she can be sure of her plan. Adoptive parents, too, cannot be completely sure of their commitment until after the child is born and is real to them, although they often feel more certain of their decision prior to the child's birth than the birth mother does. For example, if the child is born with birth defects, some adoptive parents may decide against the adoption. (Making the final decision is discussed in Chapter 6.)

Once you have made this preliminary commitment, you should focus your attention on this relationship. Just as you don't continue to date others after you are engaged, birth parents should not be working with other prospective adoptive parents, and adoptive parents should not be working with other birth parents, or continuing with infertility treatments. Many professionals believe adoptive parents should suspend infertility treatment for at least one year while they are trying to adopt and during the first year after placement. Both adoption and infertility treatment require a great deal of time, energy, and money, and although it's understandable that adoptive parents want to pursue all avenues of obtaining a child, it's important that they have enough energy to devote to identifying and meeting their own needs and working through whatever adoption issues they may have.

Most importantly, you need to devote as much time and energy as possible to getting to know each other well. You are making a commitment to be involved with each other forever, and even though you have a good feeling about each other, you want to be sure that this is the right match and you want to plan how the adoption will proceed to minimize the risks of any conflicts.

5

Getting to Know
Each Other

Some birth and adoptive parents have little opportunity to get to know each other well prior to placement, or must develop a relationship long distance. Some are able to develop a relationship deeper than they expected to have and become closely involved in each other's lives on a daily basis. How your relationship develops will be determined by the time and energy you have available for the relationship, your proximity to one another, the guidance you receive from your facilitator, and your own individual personalities and ways of interacting.

Often the birth mother and the adoptive mother form a close relationship during the time prior to the placement. This isn't surprising. They share a maternal interest in the child. Furthermore, of all those involved in the adoption, the birth mother and adoptive mother are given the most permission to express their feelings. And expressing your feelings is one way of becoming close to someone.

Sometimes the adoptive mother feels maternal toward the birth mother, especially if she is very young. The adoptive mother takes her to the doctor, inquires about her nutrition, goes shopping with her, listens as she talks about her feelings about the birth father. The adoptive mother may be able to give her the kind of support that her own mother isn't able to give for whatever reason—grief, disapproval, or other issues between them unrelated to the adoption.

If the birth mother is a teenager, she is at a point in her life when she is trying to become more independent of her parents, yet the untimeliness of the pregnancy also creates some needs. She may be torn between her desire to be treated as an adult, because she is growing up and expecting a child, and her desire to be taken care of and allowed to finish her own childhood. A birth mother who is rebelling against her own parents may welcome nurturing from the adoptive parents, and it's only natural for the adoptive mother to want to nurture the birth mother. At an unconscious level, though, the adoptive mother may know that if she takes care of the birth mother at a time when she feels needy and abandoned, a strong attachment is likely to form between them, and the birth mother will therefore be more likely to place her child with the adoptive parents. The adoptive mother should make sure her desire to take care of the birth mother is sincere rather than an attempt to influence her. However, even sincere intentions can place undue pressure on the birth mother, and the adoptive mother should consider how she might feel about all the attention she paid if the placement were to fall through.

There are other hidden dangers when the adoptive mother acts too maternally toward the birth mother. The birth grandmother may become jealous, seeing the adoptive mother as not only taking away her grandchild but her daughter as well. It can be a source of conflict, and the birth mother may feel caught in the middle, forced to choose between her mother and the adoptive mother. There is also a risk that the birth mother will become dependent on the adoptive parents and expect to receive the same kind of nurturing after placement that she did before. If the adoptive parents are not as available to her after placement, the birth mother may feel that the caring shown to her prior to her delivery was manipulative. She is likely to feel abandoned—that she's not only lost her child but her substitute parents as well.

Adoptive parents need to ask themselves how they plan to interact with the birth mother after the placement. Will they still be willing to meet with her at any hour of the night to discuss her boyfriend? Will they still want her to use their beach house? Will they still take her shopping? They shouldn't get more involved with her prior to the placement than they are willing to be after the placement, when they will have their own child to nurture. When they do things for her that are specifically related to the pregnancy and placement, that should be made clear. For example, they can say, "It's important for your baby to have good prenatal care, so we want you to see our family doctor (or obstetrician). We'll pay for it just as we'd pay for quality medical care if we were pregnant." Adoptive parents who can't justify their nurturing actions in terms of the welfare of their child or their genuine concern for the birth mother as a person, and not just as the woman who is carrying their child, should think twice about their motives. It's always possible to give more later; it's very difficult to give less without hurting someone.

For similar reasons, adoptive parents should think carefully before inviting the birth mother to move in with them during her pregnancy. While they may genuinely care about the birth mother, this takes their nurturing to another level and increases the pressure on the birth mother. Adoptive parents should ask themselves where they expect the birth mother to go after the baby's birth. Will they be comfortable having her at home with them? It's asking a lot to expect a birth mother to move out of their home at the same time that she is grieving for the child she will never parent. It is possible for open adoption relationships to work with the birth mother living with the adoptive parents, but it's doubly important that everyone understand what to expect after placement.

Brianna lived with the adoptive parents for several months prior to the baby's birth because her parents were so upset by her pregnancy that they refused to allow her to live at home. Brianna understandably did not want to return home after the baby's birth, but she also didn't want to remain with the adoptive parents and be that close to her baby during that emotionally and physically difficult time. Fortunately, another member of the adoptive family offered to let Brianna live with her after the baby's birth. She moved in with the relative about a week before the baby was due so that the change would not seem as sudden.

The level of involvement of the adoptive father is strongly influenced by the personalities of those involved, but also by the birth mother's history of relationships with men. For example, if she is feeling angry toward men because of some behavior by the birth father, she may not find it easy to trust the adoptive father or become close to him. If she has never had a consistent male role model in her life, she may respond eagerly to the nurturing of the adoptive father, or it may make her uncomfortable.

Karyn, a sixteen-year-old birth mother with a defiant air and a preference for heavy metal music, developed a strong bond with Doug, an adoptive father who was a high school social studies teacher. Doug knew how to talk to Karyn and understood that her attitude reflected her age rather than her feelings for the adoptive parents. Karyn had never had a reliable man in her life, so dealings with Doug were difficult for her at first, but once she found she could trust him, the relationship blossomed.

Eileen, a motorcycle-loving birth mother, was drawn to a couple by a photograph of Dan, the adoptive father, taken with his motorcycle. She joined him on Saturday trips until her pregnancy made riding a motorcycle uncomfortable, then spent time with him working on their bikes. Not only did they build a relationship together but she began to see that this was how Dan would spend time with her child and this cemented her confidence in the placement.

However, it's easy for the birth and adoptive fathers to be left out simply because the birth and adoptive mothers have become close. Mothers may need to make an effort to show the fathers that their participation in the open adoption is valued.

The Birth Father and the Adoptive Parents

Birth fathers are often not involved in the adoption decision, but birth fathers and their extended families are important people to the child, and they deserve more attention than they are usually given. Birth fathers are often ignored because doing so makes the already difficult adoption process a little easier. Frequently the birth mother and the birth father are no longer together by the time she is making adoption plans. The birth mother may feel abandoned, betrayed, or used by the birth father. She may feel angry that she is suffering more than he is from the pregnancy that they are equally responsible for. She may feel jealous that he's still in school having fun while she's dealing with the physical demands of the pregnancy and having to drastically change her plans.

The birth mother's family may share her feelings about the birth father, blaming him for the untimely pregnancy. As a result, they may resent having him play any further role in their daughter's life. If the birth mother didn't know the birth father well, she may be particularly embarrassed to have contact with him during this intensely personal and emotional period of her life. If she hasn't worked through all her feelings about him and their lost relationship, she probably won't want him around to bring those feelings to the surface. Part of her counselor's job is to help her face her feelings about the birth father, as well as about the baby.

Adoptive parents may want information about the birth father, but they, too, sometimes prefer that he remain in the background during the pregnancy. They may see him as one more person who must approve of them. In addition, he's one more person they must like before they can feel comfortable proceeding with the adoption. It was scary enough for them to meet the birth mother, hoping she would like them and they would like her. Now they have to start over again with the birth father.

Furthermore, there's a stereotype of birth fathers that may keep the adoptive parents from treating him respectfully. Birth fathers are sometimes viewed as callous, uncaring men who lost interest in the birth mother once they'd gotten what they wanted or who abandoned the birth mother after learning about the pregnancy. This isn't much different than the stereotype of the birth mother as a promiscuous woman too selfish to let a child interfere with her life, who easily forgets about the child she gave birth to. Fortunately, we now have a much more realistic view of birth mothers, recognizing them as women who, many times, got involved in a sexual situation without fully acknowledging the possible ramifications—women who, despite their desire to raise their children, were able to put their children's needs above theirs, and who never forget about their children. Of course, not all birth mothers fit that profile, but it is far more consistent with the majority of birth mothers than the old stereotype. And the image of birth fathers that is accurate more often than the stereotyped image is that of a young man who got involved in a sexual situation unprepared for the outcome. Once faced with the outcome, he was confused and uncertain about his proper role and unable to express his feelings about the situation in a culture that discourages young men from being nurturers or showing vulnerability.

The birth mother, the adoptive parents, and the adoption facilitator also may worry that the birth father could complicate matters by not agreeing to the adoption. If the birth mother is married, her husband must agree to the adoption. (If the birth mother's husband is not the birth father, the situation is more complicated and a lawyer should be consulted.) If the birth parents are not married, the birth father is legally required to be notified if his child is to be placed for adoption. But the law does not cover all possible scenarios. The birth father may object to the adoption, but may not be willing to raise the child himself. Or he or his family may be willing to raise the child, but the birth mother objects. He may want different adoptive parents or a different level of openness than the birth mother. It isn't clear how much say he can have in the adoption plan, but if he objects to the birth mother's plan, there may be a court battle or the birth mother may decide to keep the baby to avoid the possibility of the birth father getting custody. Unfortunately, the legal process of adoption is often much easier if the birth mother says she doesn't know who the birth father is or that she was raped.

Regardless of the birth mother's relationship with the birth father, how she perceives she was treated by him, his rights or needs as a father, his interest (or lack of interest) in the pregnancy, or his preference for the outcome of the pregnancy, he is the biologic father of the child. His child needs to have him involved in his life and he has a moral responsibility to the life he helped create. And everyone else involved in the adoption needs to understand this and be willing to involve the birth father and negotiate a settlement that is in the best interests of the child.

In most cases, the birth father doesn't want to be a disruptive influence; he simply isn't sure what his role should be. And this shouldn't be a surprise. Our culture gives men mixed messages about their rights and responsibilities when they aren't married to the mothers of their children. We want them to take equal responsibility for the pregnancy, but we aren't sure they should have the right to prevent the birth mother from placing a child for adoption. We indicate to the birth father that if he doesn't intend to marry the birth mother, he has no right to tell her what to do, and then we criticize him for abandoning her to deal with the pregnancy herself. So it's not surprising that the birth father who wants to take some responsibility for the pregnancy or be somehow involved in the child's life might express that desire in unskilled ways.

The birth father needs to be invited into the adoption process and given some direction as to how he can be involved in appropriate ways. Often, says one adoption worker, when the birth father realizes he can have a responsible role without having the ultimate responsibility of raising the child, he is eager to play an active part. He can be helped to see how important it is for him to be available to provide information about himself and his family to the child, to let her know in concrete ways that he cares about her even though he is not in a position to parent her, and perhaps to be a male role model as the child grows up.

Furthermore, some of the birth father's behavior is due to the grief he is feeling with regard to the adoption. He may appear to be uninterested in the pregnancy or the child, but frequently that attitude masks his real interest in the child he's helped to create. He may be embarrassed to show his concern for the birth mother or their child, especially if their relationship has ended, or he may think demonstrating an interest isn't "cool" or "macho." More likely, though, he is experiencing grief that he will not be able to be a father to this child—even though he realizes it's impossible at this point in his life. It's similar to the loss the birth mother experiences, and yet he may feel that she's getting all the attention—that no one recognizes his suffering.

More often, he thinks that he doesn't have a right to expect sympathy when he isn't having to go through the pregnancy and birth. He probably feels a loss of control because he is given very little say in what happens to the child. Threatening to withhold his consent or trying to manipulate the birth mother into raising the child herself are just awkward, "chest-beating" kinds of ways for the birth father to get attention, to gain some control, or to acquire the status that comes in some ethnic groups or groups of young males as the result of fathering a child. Sometimes the most effective way to deal with a birth father who is behaving in this way is to treat him with the deference he is demanding. If the birth father is treated as an adversary, he'll behave like one, fighting the adoption all the way. But if he is respected, he may be more reasonable to work with.

Lucas, a birth father, resisted all the adoptive parents' efforts to get to know him. Finally the adoptive father went to Lucas's place of business, introduced himself, and offered to wait until he got off work so that the two of them could go to dinner and talk. Once Lucas saw that the adoptive parents were sincere about wanting his participation, he became more involved in the plan.

Like everyone involved in adoption, the birth father needs help sorting out his feelings and grieving for his losses. He, too, needs to understand that just because he feels the loss of this child deeply, it doesn't mean that the child shouldn't be placed for adoption. Once he learns what he has lost and is given the opportunity to express his feelings, he will be more likely to participate in an appropriate and meaningful way in both the adoption plan and the open adoption. As we see in Chapter 6, the birth father who doesn't sort out his emotional reactions to the pregnancy and the adoption plan prior to the time of placement is often thrown into confusion when the baby is born, possibly disrupting the careful plans of the birth mother and adoptive parents.

If the birth father is married to someone other than the birth mother, he may resist the plan for openness, fearing that it will someday threaten the security of his marriage. Sometimes the right of a child to have information about her birth parents and access to them conflicts with a birth parent's right to privacy. Adoptive parents can discuss with the birth father the importance of the child having access to information about him and contact with him in a way that respects his privacy. However, they cannot guarantee that their child will fulfill any agreement they make with the birth father. Furthermore, they are not obligated to be a party to his infidelity by maintaining secrets. He made choices, and the consequence of those choices may be that his wife may learn about his child.

It can be valuable for both men if the adoptive father reaches out to the birth father at this time, especially if the birth mother and adoptive mother are very close. By developing a relationship with the birth father, the adoptive father can begin to feel that he is an active participant in the adoption. Furthermore, he may have more time and energy to spend helping the birth father clarify his role than other people. One adoptive father met with the birth father at a local sports bar every Monday night to watch football and share a pizza while the adoptive mother and birth mother went shopping. In this casual atmosphere, they could talk about what was to happen and the role each of them would play.

Extended Family

While it's tempting to keep your relationship simple by involving as few people as possible, don't wait too long to introduce members of your extended family to each other. You may be reluctant to do this if they are not in favor of the open adoption plan; however, by involving them you give them the opportunity to become more educated about open adoption, confront and grieve for their losses, and get to know the other parents as real people rather than as stereotypes or vague phantoms. When this happens, they are likely to be more enthusiastic about the plan.

You may also find that involving members of the two extended families helps the two sets of parents learn more about each other. Your family members not only have stories about you to relate but they may be willing to ask questions or provide information that you are reluctant to mention. And remember, extended family members sometimes become key players in the success of the adoption and the life of the child. Birth grandparents may be prepared to assume their roles as grandparents even though the birth parents are not ready to become parents. While the birth parents organize their lives or finish growing up, birth relatives can be consistent, loving figures in the child's life. Adoptive grandparents may have more time than the adoptive parents to interact with the birth parents, especially after the baby arrives, and they can take the birth mother to the doctor, take her shopping, or give her a place to live.

Occasionally, if the extended family is unsure of how they should participate, they may wait to be invited into the relationship. Virginia felt she was a failure as a mother because her teenage daughter was pregnant with her second child. Because she didn't feel she was a good mother, she didn't feel she had a right to be treated as a grandmother. She needed to be told by the adoptive parents and her daughter that she was a valued member of her grandchild's life.

Another set of birth grandparents wanted to be involved in the open adoption, but were reluctant because their son was denying paternity. They believed their son to be the birth father and wanted to know their first grandchild, but they felt that by expressing their desire to be grandparents to the child they were being disloyal to their son. They did finally choose to be involved as grandparents, and several years later, their son acknowledged his paternity.

Opal wanted to raise her daughter's baby herself, but the birth mother wanted to place the baby with adoptive parents. Opal felt inadequate—that her daughter thought the adoptive parents would make better parents than she would. However, when Opal could see the adoptive parents as real people with flaws rather than as the perfect parents she imagined them to be, she was able to let go of her jealousy.

Sometimes a strong friendship forms between the adoptive mother and birth grandmother. They are often close in age and the adoptive mother may relate better to the birth grandmother than to the teenage mother. Both women share a sincere interest in the well-being of the birth mother, and both may be determined that the birth mother follow through with the adoption plan. This is a welcome scenario, although not without complications. For instance, if the birth mother feels she is being pushed to place her child for adoption, she may either rebel against the pressure or proceed with the adoption and blame her mother for her pain. If she feels that her mother and the adoptive mother are working together to see that she places the baby for adoption, she may feel the need to assert more control. The birth mother can take responsibility for her decision as well as feel support from her parents if the birth grandparents discuss different options with her, sharing their opinions and knowledge, but leave the decision up to her. They must let go of the outcome and be willing to accept whatever the birth mother decides.

With so many complicated alliances forming, jealousy only makes things stickier. Even if the adoptive mother and birth grandmother are not pressuring the birth mother, their close relationship may leave her feeling left out. Some birth mothers may also feel threatened by the adoptive parents' relationship with the birth father and his family. Adoptive parents have to walk the fine line between nurturing certain relationships at the expense of others. It is important to keep in mind that the child will benefit from as many close relationships between the adoptive family and the birth family as possible.

EDUCATING EXTENDED FAMILY MEMBERS

Birth and adoptive grandparents have many of the same questions about their roles in an open adoption. They want to know what the child will call them, whether they can send letters or gifts, and what the other grandparents think about them. They wonder if they will be expected (or allowed) to babysit, if they will be included in family celebrations, and how they will communicate with the other family.

Birth parents and adoptive parents should discuss these issues and make them part of the open adoption agreement. (The open adoption agreement is discussed later in this chapter.) In general, children benefit from having access to as much information about their origins as possible and from having access to as many people as possible who love them. For these reasons, extended family members should be able to communicate with the child as long as they comply with any rules that are agreed upon by the two families.

Usually relationships are less likely to dissolve through neglect or misunderstanding when they are direct. Although it might seem simpler to have all communication passed through the birth parents or adoptive parents, that puts an enormous burden on them. In one situation, the adoptive parents agreed to send one set of photographs to the birth mother who would then distribute them to the birth father's family and her extended family. But the birth mother never followed through. When several months went by with the birth grandparents not receiving any photographs, they blamed the adoptive parents for not living up to their agreement. Although it took a lot of time for the adoptive parents to send everyone their own set of photographs, they decided the extra effort was worth the relationships they were preserving for their child.

Keep in mind that due to the number of children in families that have experienced divorce and remarriage, it isn't unusual for children today to have more than two sets of grandparents. Unlike the birth parents, who will not be acting as parents to the child, the birth relatives can still retain their roles as grandparents, aunts, and uncles without impinging on the roles of their counterparts in the adoptive family.

There may be some feelings of competition between grandparents, just as there sometimes is when a child has only two sets of grandparents. Just as you will find many of your anxieties put to rest as you meet and get to know each other, the extended family members will be more at ease with the plan if they have similar opportunities. At first they may experience the same kind of awkwardness as you did, but allow them to develop their own relationships. It frees you from taking responsibility for communicating between several different people.

Giving family members the opportunity to meet and get to know each other early in your relationship is especially important if they will be at the hospital together. It can be very awkward for birth grandparents and adoptive grandparents to meet for the first time as they wait for the baby to be born who will tie their families together forever.

Difficult Situations Prior to Placement

Not every open adoption relationship proceeds smoothly. Sometimes you will know from the outset that the relationship will need extra effort. But sometimes the relationship appears to be promising, only to develop tension or difficulties later on.

Think about how you have handled difficult relationships in the past, paying attention to strategies that worked or didn't work. Do you tend to end a relationship at the first sign of trouble? Do you hang on to a relationship even when it is apparent it has no future? What have you learned about productive ways to interact with people when you are having problems with them? Knowing the answers to these questions will help you assess how to proceed with this relationship if it becomes difficult.

We do not intend to give the impression that birth parents are more demanding or difficult than adoptive parents—both can be challenging to work with. However, when the adoptive parents present problems prior to placement, birth parents are less likely to stay in the relationship because there are so many other adoptive parents to choose from. Adoptive parents may stay in a relationship with difficult birth parents because they so desperately want a baby, and they hesitate to pass up the opportunity being offered to them.

THE NEEDY BIRTH MOTHER

Sometimes a birth mother can seem to make too many demands on the adoptive parents. She might call frequently needing to be taken to the doctor's office or asking for more money to make it to the end of the month.

Although the adoptive parents want to set limits on a birth mother who calls with a new crisis every other day, they may be afraid the birth mother will choose other adoptive parents if they say "no" to her. However, if the adoptive parents do not set limits before placement, they could have a difficult time setting them later, or the birth mother could feel that they've changed the rules now that they have her baby. Furthermore, just as parents often find that their children know they love them when they care enough to set limits, birth parents who look to the adoptive parents as role models may also respond positively to limits.

During the pregnancy, adoptive parents need to communicate what they are able to do and what they are not able to do. They can remind the birth parents that after the child's birth, they are going to be busy caring for the baby and may not have the time to go shopping or to the doctor with the birth mother, and they can suggest that she should find other supportive people in her life so that she isn't totally dependent on them.

Linda, a birth mother who had poor parenting and was very disorganized in her approach to life, selected Sharon and Tom, adoptive parents who were just the opposite. She told them that they were the kind of parents she would have wanted and began to treat them as such. Sharon and Tom liked Linda and wanted to help her, but taking care of her became a full-time job. In addition, Linda's inability to plan ahead presented a significant conflict with their structured lifestyle.

To relieve the crisis that was developing, Sharon and Tom put together a coupon book for Linda with a series of certificates for assistance that they were willing to give. Some coupons set clear and specific boundaries in a way that let Linda know she was cared about. One said: "We will help you balance your checkbook." Another said: "We will drive you to work if your car doesn't start." Other coupons helped Linda learn how to take care of herself. For example, one said: "We will help you look for a job." Linda understood she could not ask the adoptive parents to give her more than what was in the coupon book. They continued the practice after the baby's placement, giving her a new coupon book each year.

DESPERATE OR OVERBEARING ADOPTIVE PARENTS

It's not always the birth mothers who are needy. Sometimes adoptive parents have waited so long to become parents and have had so many losses that their desperation is apparent. When they are chosen by a birth mother and the match looks promising, the adoptive parents may become obsessed with the birth mother and her pregnancy. Not surprisingly, the more desperate they appear, the more uncomfortable birth parents often are with them.

Sometimes, in their desire to make sure their child-to-be is receiving optimal care, adoptive mothers become oppressive, frequently asking the birth mother if she's drinking enough milk and presenting her with articles about prenatal care. Adoptive parents have probably been thinking about pregnancy for several years and have definite ideas on nutrition and health care during pregnancy. Furthermore, if the child has medical conditions that could have been prevented by better prenatal care, they are the ones who will be living with the results. The adoptive parents may also think that if they are paying for the medical care of the birth mother, she should take their advice.

Although birth mothers sometimes need a lot of guidance, adoptive mothers should be sure to treat them as responsible adults. The baby is inside the birth mother, and she may not want anyone telling her how to take care of herself. Since she has not yet transferred parental rights to the adoptive parents, she may resent their acting like they have any say in the care of the child. If she feels an obligation to listen to advice from the adoptive parents because they are paying her medical bills, she could feel manipulated by the financial situation.

When there is disagreement over prenatal care, adoptive parents need to remind themselves that they are not in control of the birth mother, the child, or the pregnancy. Although the relationship might entitle the adoptive parents to make suggestions, it should be offered with the assumption that everyone is equal and responsible. Adoptive mothers might think about how they would feel if, after placement, the birth mother were to call and say, "Be sure to put the baby in her car seat," or "Remember that the baby needs her shots next week." If the birth mother is neglecting herself or actively doing something that endangers the child, adoptive parents may want to be assertive about expressing their feelings and preferences. If that approach isn't successful, they could choose to move out of the match. But in most cases, when adoptive parents' suggestions border on the intrusive, it reflects their frustration that they can't make all the decisions about their child's health and safety. This is another one of the losses that adoptive parents must learn to accept in order for the process to work.

Birth parents who are feeling uncomfortable with the level of involvement of the adoptive parents during the preplacement stage should keep in mind that the adoptive parents have had to cope with a great deal of loss in their journey to becoming parents. They may not realize their concern feels like pressure or lack of trust. Discuss this issue with them or with a counselor. The birth parents should let the adoptive parents know that they need more space or more respect. Use humor to remind them when they are becoming overbearing. Try Sharon and Tom's method and make them a coupon book with certificates good for one telephone call with nutritional advice or one reminder to wear a seat belt.

ANGRY BIRTH PARENTS

Some birth parents are just difficult to get along with. They may seem to be easily offended, demanding, or rude. They may constantly change the rules, or appear to be displeased and offended by everything the adoptive parents do or say. They may act like they don't have to give anything to the relationship because they are surrendering their child.

If they behave this way only with the adoptive parents, it can be an early sign that they will not place the baby at all or will not place with these adoptive parents. However, if they are like this with everyone, it is a reflection of their personality, temperament, or interpersonal skills. There are several reasons for this kind of unpleasantness, foremost being the enormous amount of control afforded by having something of great value that someone else wants.

Birth parents may not be used to having such strength, and may abuse the power or may want to hang onto it for as long as they can. They may also be afraid the adoptive parents will not keep in touch with them after the adoption is finalized and may be using their discouraging behavior as a test to see how much they will take before they back out. The important thing to remember is that although interacting with such difficult birth parents can require a great deal of patience, they often do go through with the placement, so persistence is rewarded.

Adoptive parents who seem to work best under these circumstances are those who have had success interacting with similar people in their families or at work, and are thus able to interact with the birth parents without taking their anger personally. It is also helpful to treat each incident separately rather than allowing them to accumulate. In many cases, the adoptive parent can apologize sincerely to the birth parent for her unintentional offense, and then let the matter go. It's often forgotten the next day.

In some cases, a birth father who opposes the adoption plan may be aggressive with the adoptive parents to the point of being threatening. A therapist may be able to assess whether his behavior reflects a pathological psychologic condition or if his aggressiveness is not as threatening as it appears. Then it's up to the adoptive parents to decide if they want to be involved in this adoption. While a semiopen adoption might appear to be the answer in a situation like this, adoptive parents must consider the possibility that the adoption may inadvertently become fully disclosed, especially if they want to have full openness with everyone but the birth father.

As with an angry birth parent, sometimes the best way to deal with a threatening birth father is to allow him to have the impact he is seeking. If he feels his minor threats are frightening the adoptive parents, he is less likely to escalate his threats. In other situations, however, the most effective way to deal with a threatening person is to let him know he's not being effective. Again, a counselor may be able to help the adoptive parents determine which is the appropriate approach.

COMMUNICATION DIFFICULTIES

Birth parents who are very young, who have never had to deal with adults or make adult decisions, and who may be far away from home and their support system may not know how to communicate with the adoptive parents. Adoptive parents may have a difficult time discerning the birth parents' needs, thoughts, or feelings. The adoptive parents may give the birth mother a new maternity outfit, but may not be able to tell if she likes it. The birth mother may respond to questions with vague statements such as "Okay" or "I don't know."

It is sometimes helpful to find someone the birth mother's own age for her to talk to, especially if she does not have any friends or family in the area. It can also facilitate communication if the adoptive parents take the birth mother to a place that feels familiar to her, such as a church or restaurant.

However, if the adoptive parents feel that they are doing everything they can to communicate with the birth mother, they must depend to a great extent on their own evaluations. They can proceed as though what they are doing is pleasing and adequate because it probably is. They can share their concerns with a counselor not in the hope of getting answers but just to share the burden.

Some birth parents may talk a lot without making sense or may have difficulty following a conversation. Sometimes they appear to be communicating well, but it's clear from later conversations that they didn't understand what was being said. They may have difficulty sitting still long enough to talk or listen. This may reflect learning disabilities, communication disorders, anxieties, or deeper psychological problems such as schizophrenia.

Although it can be frustrating to adoptive parents to try to communicate with birth parents under these circumstances, they should remember that it can be frustrating for the birth parents, too. They are not deliberately obstructing communication. They simply do not have the skills to be articulate. Adoptive parents should resist the temptation to finish the birth parents' sentences, to interrupt the birth parents, or to communicate their impatience through their body language, which will be observed by the birth parents.

Adoptive parents should try to communicate concretely, slowly, and using as few words as possible, but they may have to try alternate ways of communicating with birth parents under these circumstances. One adoptive parent found it effective to have the birth mother tape songs from the radio that were meaningful to her. When she taped "Somewhere Out There," the theme from the movie *An American Tail,* the adoptive parents knew that she understood the adoption plan. One adoptive mother made a giant calendar with appointments, important phone numbers, and the baby's prenatal developmental stages. You can also communicate using greeting cards, body language, or poetry.

Of course, not all adoptive parents have good verbal skills either. And sometimes difficulty communicating with each other can be traced to shyness. These situations may also call for creative efforts, including nonverbal expression.

LIES AND DISTORTIONS

Since the foundation of any relationship is trust, it can be difficult to work with people who do not tell the truth, who are evasive, who distort the facts, or who tell different stories at different times or to different people. You should not expect to be able to change the behavior or the thought process of people who do not tell the truth. However, you can minimize the opportunities for distortion or misrepresentation by insisting that decisions be made when everyone involved can be present. You can set boundaries so that you do not get drawn into arguments over what was said or not said, and you can decide not to care whether the other parents think they are fooling you or not. Finally, you can decide what you will or will not do in a relationship with someone you cannot completely trust. In these ways, you can feel that you have some control.

THOUGHTLESS COMMENTS BY ADOPTIVE PARENTS

Sometimes what appears to be a promising match falls apart because of thoughtlessness on the part of an adoptive parent. Perhaps the adoptive mother refers to the baby as "my baby." Or the adoptive father loses his temper, saying, "We're paying all the bills. The least you could do is . . . " Adoptive parents sometimes feel they must be sensitive to the birth parents and make allowances for their behavior, but must "walk on eggs" to avoid saying or doing something that could annoy the birth parents.

The fact is that the relationship between birth and adoptive parents is inequitable—the parents who are the legal guardians of the child have more power. That may not be fair to either birth parents or adoptive parents, but it is the nature of the relationship. In the placement stage, birth parents need to remember that the adoptive parents feel powerless and vulnerable. They want a baby desperately and feel that there's nothing they can do or say that will guarantee that they can make this happen. Naturally, they will sometimes feel angry, and occasionally they will direct that anger at the birth parents who appear to have all the power.

When adoptive parents make a thoughtless or insensitive remark, birth parents can assess whether this is consistent with everything they know about the adoptive parents. They can keep in mind the reasons they chose these adoptive parents and remind themselves of the sensitivity the adoptive parents have shown them in the past. Birth parents shouldn't assume those acts of kindness were false just because the adoptive parents made one comment that was unkind. Although it may be tempting to select other adoptive parents, remember that these adoptive parents also looked ideal at one time and that everyone has faults. Birth parents won't know whether another set of adoptive parents would be more sensitive until they have gotten to know them as well as they know these adoptive parents and until they have been stressed the way these adoptive parents have been.

Resolving Conflict

As you get to know each other, you may try to overlook incidents that annoy or anger you because you don't want to jeopardize the adoption plan. We're often reluctant to express our disfavor with someone until we are sure our relationship is secure enough to withstand the strain a confrontation might bring. But avoiding confrontation brings its own set of problems. When we bury or ignore our feelings rather than dealing with them, they aren't resolved. This can leave us feeling angry toward another person and can result in tension in the relationship. We just can't feel as comfortable around someone when there are issues between us that haven't been settled.

By avoiding confrontation you may be setting a pattern for later interactions. Eventually all the unresolved tension will result in a serious blowup or the tension will be so uncomfortable that you'll drift apart. None of that is in the child's best interests.

Furthermore, by confronting your conflicts early in your relationship, you'll learn whether this is someone with whom you can work out your problems. If not, you can choose to become involved with people who are more reasonable or whose style of resolving conflict is more in keeping with yours, or you can decide you're willing to risk the relationship anyway.

Once again, it's useful to recognize your style of dealing with conflict. Did you grow up in a family in which it was acceptable to express anger? How did your parents respond when you were angry? How did they respond to each other? If a parent left the house after a marital argument, you may have learned to fear that people leave when someone gets angry at them. When you are angry, do you prefer to get the issue settled as soon as possible, even if it means being uncomfortable, or do you prefer to wait until you've settled down to confront someone?

How did you feel when people were angry with you? Did you feel inadequate, stupid, victimized? Did you feel that you were given an opportunity to respond and be heard? Some people grew up in a family where they were expected to be perfect, or to behave with more maturity than their years. When they made a mistake—even one that wasn't their fault—they were criticized. Many people who grow up in these kinds of families feel shame when they disappoint someone or are criticized. Shame is the feeling that you are a bad person because you have broken some rules. This is different from guilt, which is the feeling we get when we know we've broken the rules. Sometimes people try to prevent this feeling of shame by becoming defensive whenever someone tries to criticize them. They tell themselves it's the other person's problem and never take responsibility for things they may have done. Other people run away when they are criticized. Sometimes they get in the car and drive off. Sometimes they just leave the room and refuse to discuss the issue. And sometimes they feel that they have to get out of the relationship.

Very few people can express anger or respond to criticism in healthy ways. So you needn't think that you won't have a successful open adoption unless you can give and take criticism with ease. You probably already have some skills at dealing with conflict even though they may not be as refined as they could be. Think about the relationships you have had in which you were able to resolve conflict. What was different about those relationships compared to those in which you were not able to resolve conflict?

You can also learn new skills. What is important is that you are committed to trying to work out your differences without them destroying your relationship. No relationship is without its conflicts, and because yours involves a lot of intense feelings and changes in roles just as you are getting to know each other and work out your relationship, there is a lot of potential for misunderstanding.

As we've mentioned, grieving for the losses in adoption will involve feeling anger and sadness. Often when we experience a negative feeling like anger or hurt, we direct those feelings at someone. That person feels attacked, and rather than being responsive to our feelings, seeks to defend herself against the attack that is most certainly going to result in negative feelings for her.

Most of the time we are sad or happy or angry about something rather than at someone. Try to express your feelings—to yourself and to others—in these terms. For example, instead of saying, "I'm so mad at Angie. She keeps making appointments with me and then breaking them," you could say, "I feel worthless when someone makes an appointment with me and doesn't keep it. And I'm scared to think I might not be able to trust Angie to keep her promises after the adoption."

When confronted with someone's feelings about your actions, use a technique that many counselors recommend. Instead of rushing into a defense of your actions, simply repeat what you've been told and ask the person if you heard her correctly. For example, in this situation, Angie might say, "You are angry because I broke my appointment with you. You felt worthless that I broke the appointment because I didn't think enough of you to keep it. You're worried that I won't keep my promises after the adoption. Is that right?" You can then say that's an accurate reflection of your feelings, or clarify them further, such as, "That's almost right. I feel worthless when you decide your other responsibilities are more important than your responsibility to me. I feel scared that after the adoption, you'll think even less of your responsibility to our relationship." And again, Angie would repeat what she had heard.

Once you have clarified your feelings, you can make a request that Angie change her behavior. You can't control Angie's behavior, or demand that she change. You can only express your preference and hope that you can work out a mutually satisfactory solution.

For example, you could say, "I would prefer that you not make an appointment with me unless you are certain you can make that commitment, and that you only cancel an appointment if there is a real emergency." Angie would repeat your request, asking if she heard you correctly, and then reply. Perhaps she would say she would try to meet your request. Perhaps she would say she doesn't know if she could meet your request. Then you can let her know what the consequences might be. Perhaps you'll decide not to arrange meetings in advance, but to be spontaneous.

In expressing your feelings, be sure to say, "I feel . . . " rather than, "You made me feel . . . " You may think that this other person caused you to feel angry or sad by her comments or actions. But we are responsible for our own feelings. No one can make us feel any way we don't choose to feel. In the example we've been using, Angie is responsible for breaking appointments and needs to know that when she breaks appointments, you feel worthless and scared. But not everyone would feel worthless because someone broke an appointment with them. Not everyone would feel scared that Angie might break other promises. Your feelings of worthlessness and fear are real, but you bring that interpretation to the interaction. Once Angie knows that the consequence of her actions is that you feel worthless and scared, and you may be unable to continue to trust her, she can decide if she wants to change her actions. You can't demand it.

Because anger is one of the stages of grief, it may help you to think about your anger not as an isolated emotion but as the result of a loss you've experienced. When someone fails to meet with you on schedule, you lose your expectations of what might have happened at that meeting. Perhaps you lose some self-esteem because you don't feel important enough to the other person. Perhaps you are feeling the loss of control involved when someone doesn't behave the way you want her to. Perhaps you need order and predictability in your life, and when you lose it due to a last-minute change of plans, you feel discomfort.

By recognizing anger as a stage of grief, you are better able to dissociate your feelings from the other person. Furthermore, by recognizing the loss that resulted in the anger, you may have an easier time getting past your anger. In the process, you may also learn something about yourself that will help you the next time.

Sexual Overtones

When men and women who haven't known each other come together by adoption, there can be unexpected and confusing sexual overtones. This relationship begins as a result of the sexual activity of the birth parents and often the infertility of the adoptive parents, and may quickly grow to a level of emotional intimacy in which there is a strong feeling of connectedness. As a result, you may feel some sexual awkwardness.

If birth parents and adoptive parents "click" because of some nonverbal familiarity, it may be the same kind of "click" that they would feel if they were meeting potential dates. Men and women who haven't had a lot of mature friendships with people of the opposite sex may slip into a pattern of flirting as a way to get to know someone. Young men and women who are emotionally vulnerable may feel physically drawn to someone who lets them know they are available to meet their needs.

A birth mother might become jealous of the attention the adoptive mother gives the birth father, or an adoptive mother might resent her husband's solicitous behavior toward the birth mother. An adoptive father might be embarrassed to be seen in public with a woman who is assumed to be pregnant with his child. An adoptive mother in her forties may be hurt if she is mistaken for the teenage birth mother's parent. An infertile adoptive mother might be jealous that the birth mother can give her husband something she cannot. The adoptive father may feel left out because the birth mother is embarrassed to have him in the delivery room, or, if the adoptive father is present, the adoptive mother may feel uncomfortable having her husband see another woman in such an intimate situation.

Brandi was alone with Charlie, the adoptive father, the first time she felt the baby kick. She asked him if he wanted to feel the baby move. Charlie froze. He was afraid that if his wife walked in while he was on the floor touching Brandi's abdomen, that she would misunderstand the situation. But he was concerned that if he indicated this to Brandi, it would destroy their comfortable relationship. He avoided the situation by saying, "Let's wait for Sally to get home. I want her to be here the first time we feel the baby move."

Of course, some birth mothers do not feel sexy at all during pregnancy. Furthermore, because they are experiencing a lot of emotional pain as a result of some imprudent sexual behavior, they may feel downright repulsed by the idea of sex. Adoptive parents who have waited a long time to become parents often feel closer to each other when they are about to receive a child than at any other time in their marriage. Generally, no one is eager to sabotage the adoption by a casual flirtation. If you do experience some confusing feelings, don't be reluctant to discuss them with your adoption counselor.

The Importance of Support

You may find it helpful to become involved with an open adoption support group. Sharon Kaplan Roszia has been facilitating such a group since 1981. Each month, she gathers birth parents, adoptive parents, and extended family members who are actively involved in open adoptions to discuss their relationships. Some of those who participate in the group have been attending meetings for several years. Others are just starting to think about open adoption. Sometimes both a birth relative and an adoptive relative of the same child will attend, but often only one side of the family is represented due to scheduling conflicts, proximity, or preference.

The meetings are an opportunity to share joys, problems, concerns, progress, and fears in the open adoption relationship. As you begin yours, you may find enormous support in meeting and hearing from people who have been through the experience. So many families that we contacted in writing this book said they felt they were sailing in uncharted waters as they entered open adoptions. You don't have to feel that way. Others have been through the process, and you can benefit from their experience.

Not all open adoption groups mix birth families and adoptive families, but it can be very helpful for each to hear the other side's perspective. For example, at one meeting, Tracy, a birth mother, and Ginger, an adoptive mother, asked the group to help them resolve a conflict they were having over breastfeeding. Both wanted the exclusive right to breastfeed the baby at the hospital. Tracy believed this was a gift she could give her child and was afraid Ginger wanted to breastfeed as a way of pretending that this was her biologic child. Ginger was afraid that if Tracy breastfed the baby she would become too attached to the child.

As the discussion progressed, both birth mothers and adoptive mothers shared their feelings about breastfeeding. It became clear to Ginger that her concern was that she wouldn't form an attachment to the child. The adoptive mothers who had breastfed their babies explained that it was a wonderful experience, but that they didn't feel it was the only way in which they formed attachments. The biologic mothers explained to Tracy how she was going to want to hang on to the baby after the birth and that breastfeeding might add to her pain. Tracy eventually decided to nurse the baby in the hospital, but was prepared for the emotional risk she was taking, and Ginger formed a strong attachment without breastfeeding.

If your adoption facilitator doesn't provide peer support as part of his services, ask to be referred to a group in your area, if there are any. If there are no support groups in your area, consider forming your own with the people you have already met as you learned about adoption.

If you find that you are having friction that can't be resolved by yourselves or through a group, don't hesitate to consider some individual or joint counseling. Make sure that you select someone experienced in open adoption relationships. If you have already been involved with therapists separately, you may want to have both therapists involved in the counseling sessions, so that each of you feels you have an advocate in the process of resolving your conflict. Discuss ahead of time who will pay for such counseling, especially if you disagree about whether counseling is necessary.

Of course, not every community has enough open adoptions for there to be therapists with extensive experience resolving conflict between birth and adoptive parents. But you can probably find a minister, counselor, family systems therapist, or physician who has done enough marriage or family counseling to help you work through the problems in your developing relationships. You can also contact your local court system, which may have a mediation counselor used to settling conflicts in custody cases. Much of the time the conflicts you have in open adoption are similar to conflicts in any relationship and the skills needed to resolve them are the same.

Evaluating the Relationship

As you get to know each other prior to placement, you will continue to assess whether the relationship will work. Most of the time you will meet, like each other, get to know each other, be able to resolve your differences, and proceed toward the birth of the child with the expectation of a successful open adoption. But occasionally, a match that initially looked promising develops insurmountable problems or tension so great that you are not comfortable proceeding. And sometimes, you just get a gut feeling that this relationship isn't going to work no matter how much effort you make. Follow these instincts even if you're scared or if dissolving the relationship creates another loss for you, especially if your instincts have been right in the past.

Although no one can predict the outcome of either the most promising or the most fragile match, the following situations are indications that the relationship may fall apart despite your best efforts, either before the birth, at the hospital, or after the placement:

- Lack of support for the adoption plan in the family;
- Adoptive parents saying all the right things but seeming insincere;
- Adoptive parents seeing the birth parents as too demanding even when they are making reasonable requests;
- Birth parents or adoptive parents being resistant to participating in a support group or counseling;
- Adoptive parents unconcerned about the future of the birth parents;
- Birth or adoptive parents who don't keep appointments or live up to agreements;
- Birth or adoptive parents who are unavailable or disappear at crucial times;
- Birth or adoptive parents who are discovered to have been repeatedly dishonest;
- Birth or adoptive parents who get angry over little things—they appear to be nitpicking or looking for ways to disagree;
- The extended birth family suddenly pulling together and expressing support for keeping the child in the family.

No one factor alone is cause for alarm, but if a pattern of risky behaviors seems to be developing, you need to seriously evaluate whether you want to continue the relationship. Although you may have invested several months in this relationship, those months will seem insignificant next to a lifetime of involvement with the wrong people. If you end the relationship now, there is still time for the birth parents to evaluate other adoptive parents and for the adoptive parents to disengage before they become any more emotionally invested. If you decide to end the relationship, try to give the other parents a specific reason. This will help both of you proceed.

You will also find it helpful in the long run to say good-bye face-to-face. Although a final exchange may be difficult, it can help heal the wounds caused by the stresses you experienced in the relationship or by its unexpected ending. Your facilitator should help you set up such a session.

But if the relationship continues to look promising, it is then time to discuss specific plans for the transfer of parental rights and how you envision your future relationship.

Making a Plan

Sometimes relationships that have been proceeding smoothly founder over misunderstanding during times of fatigue or high emotion. For example, the adoptive parents may have assumed they would be present at the birth of the child only to arrive at the hospital and be prohibited from entering the birthing room. The birth parents may have thought that when the adoptive parents agreed to send them pictures, they would send them every month, only to discover a few years after placement that they are only receiving one photo on the child's birthday. These kinds of conflicts can often be avoided if you take the time to discuss specific plans for the remainder of the pregnancy, labor, and delivery; the time after the birth before the baby goes home; and future interactions with each other as the child grows up.

You probably developed some ideas of how your open adoption would proceed before you even began looking for each other (see Chapter 4). Now it's time to reconcile your expectations with each other's. Some adoption facilitators recommend face-to-face sessions called "vision matching" in which you state your expectations about the different stages in your relationship. By doing so, you will have a chance to see potential areas of misunderstanding or conflict and your facilitator can help you resolve them. By reading through the rest of this book, you'll get a good idea of the topics you'll want to discuss. You may want to consider taping this session, both to share with your child and to use as a reference if any questions arise about your agreement.

THE OPEN ADOPTION AGREEMENT

Some facilitators have the birth and adoptive parents sign a preadoption agreement outlining their understanding of the arrangement. Among the topics to include in the agreement are:

▪ The kind of communication you will have, including whether it will be direct or through an intermediary, and whether it will include letters, telephone calls, photographs, audiotapes or videotapes, or visitation;

▪ The frequency of communication or visitation and the circumstances under which the birth family may visit, for example, whether the birth parents can take the child without supervision, and if so, at what age;

▪ How you will communicate changes in address or telephone number—you might want to give each other the name of someone who will always know your whereabouts or exchange Social Security numbers;

▪ The kind of information that will be exchanged;

▪ The type and frequency of contact between the adoptive family and other members of the birth family, including extended family members or other children of either birth parent;

▪ How information will be shared with the child (see Chapter 12);

▪ How birthdays and other special occasions will be celebrated (see Chapter 8);

▪ Who will pay for the birth parents to visit;

▪ How the agreement will be modified to meet changes in your needs and circumstances (see Chapters 8 and 10);

▪ How conflicts will be resolved, including who will pay for the costs of counseling, mediation, or legal services if they are required.

Your agreement should outline expectations rather than obligations. For example, the agreement might read, "The birth parents want to receive a letter from the adoptive parents at least once a year," rather than "The adoptive parents will send a letter at least once a year." Try not to be too specific about your expectations. If you say, for example, "The birth parents expect to receive photographs on the first of every month," the birth parents may feel that their wishes have been ignored if photographs don't arrive until the fifteenth. That could cause tension in the relationship. It's far better to say something like, "The birth parents would like to receive photographs at least three times a year."

Even though you may sign a preadoption agreement, it is more a statement of intent than a legal document binding you to the behaviors you outline. At the time of this writing, only Washington state makes open adoption agreements part of the adoption decree and requires that birth and adoptive parents maintain them. As open adoption continues, however, more states may institute legal consequences for failing to live up to the terms of an agreement. Be sure to find out what the laws are in your state regarding the legality of open adoption agreements, keeping in mind that these laws may be changing quickly.

However, there are also natural consequences in a relationship when someone doesn't respect the boundaries that have been agreed to, fails to live up to agreements, invades someone's privacy, or violates the trust that's been established. It's a good idea to discuss how you might feel and how you might respond if that happens. Think about other relationships you might have that have been tested in these ways and how you reacted. Discuss the possible effect on your relationship of behavior that is inconsistent with your expectations.

Adoption mediator Jeanne Etter, Ph.D., has found it beneficial to include in her agreements a statement that says the adoptive parents are not obligated to maintain the agreement if the birth parents become adversarial. That is, if the birth parents take legal action to reclaim the child after the adoption has been finalized, the adoptive parents are under no obligation to maintain openness. Etter says some birth parents file to reclaim their children knowing that there is no possibility of their being able to do so because they are under pressure from their family or the other birth parent. But taking such action places enormous strain on the open adoption relationship. If birth parents know that by taking legal action they risk losing contact with their child, only those birth parents who truly want to reclaim would take that significant step.

Ultimately, the real penalty for failing to live up to your open adoption agreement is that the child you both care about suffers. In addition, your relationship with the child may suffer as she discovers that you did not live up to the agreement. And remember that even when there are no other consequences, breaking your word without good reason reflects on your personal integrity.

Anticipating Feelings

Obviously there is much to talk about and prepare for prior to the baby's birth. You also need to be prepared for the feelings you will experience during labor, delivery, placement, and the first year after placement. You will experience a variety of emotions, some of them quite intense, because the losses and gains of adoption are profound. Unless you are prepared for these feelings, understand they are part of the process of grieving, and remember that they will in time diminish, you may have difficulty maintaining the open adoption agreement. Discuss these with each other, with the friends and relatives you expect to support you emotionally during this time, with your facilitator or counselor, and with your adoption support group. Talk to others who have been through the process themselves so you can learn from their experience. Read through this book, particularly the next few chapters, so that you can recognize your feelings and your experiences as part of the adoption process and can be prepared for them. Keep a journal and read through it as you proceed in the adoption process.

part three

Birth and Placement

6

Before, During, and
After the Birth

The last few weeks before the baby is born may feel like years. The birth mother feels increasingly limited physically by the changes in her body and may even be quite uncomfortable. Unlike mothers who are planning to raise their babies themselves, the birth mother does not have the fantasy that she will soon be caring for a cute, lovable baby to help her through these weeks. Instead, she may be expecting pain and sadness at the thought of separating from that baby.

The adoptive parents may feel that these last weeks are taking longer than the many years they have spent trying to become a family. They may be torn between being excited about the arrival of the baby, which they hope will mean taking the baby home and becoming his parents, and being fearful that the birth mother will decide to parent the baby herself. Their excitement is further tempered by knowing the pain and sadness that will be experienced by the birth mother if she proceeds with the adoption plan. They may be tempted to try to avoid thinking about the birth by keeping busy at work or with projects, by taking a vacation, or by detaching themselves from the process. The more prepared you are for the experience, the better able you will be to cope with the variety of intense and sometimes conflicting feelings you will have, as well as avoid problems due to misunderstandings.

The Adoptive Parents' Preparation

While the future of their role as parents is in doubt over the course of these last few weeks, it is still important for the adoptive parents to prepare for the possibility that they will soon have a child. Adoptive parents need to approach the birth of the child as they would a child born to them—with hope, realistic preparation, and an awareness that there are no guarantees. Once a baby arrives, simple things like going for a morning jog become more complicated. The pace of the parents' lives slows to accommodate a baby who cannot be rushed. The adoptive family must adapt to meet the needs of a demanding infant, which means that people in the family who previously could count on having top priority for the attention of the adoptive mother or father must now compete for that attention with the new arrival. Not only will the new child displace other children in the family but he will disrupt the relationship between the husband and wife as they learn how to share each other with the new child.

Adoptive parents can prepare emotionally for the birth of the child into their family by fantasizing about the baby and talking about the way their house, their lives, and their routine will be different. It's all right for adoptive parents to have mixed feelings about the changes that are about to take place. Sometimes adoptive parents who have put all their time, energy, and financial resources into trying to become a family are reluctant to admit that there are benefits to being childless (or having only the children that they have). They're afraid if they admit to these feelings that they are not committed to the adoption or that their ambivalent thoughts will somehow jinx the adoption. Mixed feelings are all right—they are common to nearly every experience. Adding to the family is a change and every change involves loss—the loss of what was before. For example, it is a loss to leave your family to get married, even though you are through with that part of your life and are ready to move on. Parenthood is difficult and involves a great deal of sacrifice. Acknowledging that does not mean you don't also look forward to the tremendous joy that can be found in raising children.

If this is their first child, the adoptive parents should be preparing for the arrival of the child by reading basic infant care books or taking a baby care class. Because adoptive parents don't always have the opportunity to learn about infant care during prenatal visits to the doctor or childbirth preparation classes, they are sometimes stunned to get the baby home and realize they don't have any idea how to diaper, bathe, or feed an infant. This is a particular shock after presenting themselves as more capable of parenting than the birth parents. If the adoptive mother is planning to breastfeed, she should begin to prepare for that. (Breastfeeding is discussed in more depth later in this chapter.)

Sometimes adoptive parents find it helpful to spend this last bit of free time finishing projects or cooking and freezing casseroles for later consumption. They should be sure to eat a proper diet, exercise, and get sufficient rest so that they are prepared physically for the demands of caring for an infant.

THE NURSERY AND LAYETTE

Cultural traditions will influence the way parents prepare for the arrival of the child. In some cultures it is considered bad luck to have a baby shower or otherwise accumulate items for the child before its arrival. Adoptive parents should explain their cultural ways of preparing for parenthood to the birth parents so that there is no misunderstanding. One birth mother nearly changed her mind about the adoptive parents she had chosen when they didn't want to have a baby shower. The birth mother assumed the adoptive parents were not excited about the baby's arrival; she didn't realize that in the Jewish tradition, baby showers are not held prior to the baby's birth.

If adoptive parents would normally have had a baby shower to prepare for the arrival of a child, that is an appropriate way to prepare for the child they are adopting. As with all rituals, the baby shower has multiple levels of function. It does help parents prepare materially for the arrival of a child, but it also serves to gather together people who want to share in the happiness of the parents-to-be, join their hopes together, and let the new parents know who will be there to support them as they move to this new stage in their lives. The emotional power of this event is far more important than the bibs and rattles collected by the parents-to-be.

If parents do not want to collect many baby items because the adoption is still uncertain, friends can give them personal items that would provide comfort regardless of the birth mother's decision, such as a gift certificate for a massage or an offer to prepare a dinner or picnic basket. Parents who feel embarrassed at being given baby gifts because their personal finances enable them to provide for all the baby's needs might prefer donations to a charitable organization for children.

The adoptive parents may want to look at baby furniture, perhaps even buy a rocking chair, and talk about the way they want to decorate the nursery, although actually decorating the nursery has some advantages and disadvantages. The benefit is that it helps the adoptive parents to adjust to the possibility that they will soon have a child. By making room for the baby in their home, they are reminded to make room for a child in their hearts and in their lives. The nursery provides them with a tangible daily reminder of the way their lives may soon change. It helps them prepare emotionally by expressing their hope and faith that this will happen. One prospective adoptive father built a wooden cradle that he called his "Field of Dreams" cradle, inspired by a movie popular that year. A key element of the movie expressed this father's wish: *If you build it, he will come.*

Some birth parents want to see the nursery the adoptive parents have prepared. They like being able to envision exactly where their baby will be. It confirms for them that they've chosen parents who want to provide a good environment for a child. However, others may feel pressured to proceed with the adoption plan if they know the adoptive parents have spent time and money fixing up the nursery. You may want to discuss this issue, understanding that you each have your own needs and feelings about the amount of preparation the adoptive parents are doing for the arrival of the child.

Adoptive parents may be reluctant to have a nursery ready because they don't want to be too hopeful, or they are afraid that if the adoption does not proceed as planned, the baby's room will be a daily reminder of what they have lost. It's natural to want to protect yourself from possible hurt. The fact is that if the birth parents decide to raise the baby, the adoptive parents will be hurt no matter how much, or how little, preparation they do.

However, some adoptive parents, particularly those who have had one or more planned adoptions fall through, may keep themselves emotionally detached from the birth mother, her pregnancy, and the upcoming birth of the child. Although this may protect them if the adoption does not proceed as planned, they also keep themselves from preparing emotionally for the possibility that they will be welcoming a child into their family.

Ellen, an adoptive mother who had this experience, said she didn't even refer to the child as hers for several months after the placement. The attachment process between Ellen and the child was complicated by the fact that Ellen had put so much energy into not getting her hopes up that it took several months to believe she was really a mother and could respond emotionally to her child in addition to meeting the baby's physical needs. Fortunately, Bruce, the adoptive father, had not remained as aloof as Ellen and could provide the emotional support the child needed during the months it took for the adoptive mother to make the psychological transition to being a parent.

Most adoptive parents are unable to be this detached. And if disappointment does occur, the reality of the nursery can help the adoptive parents face and express their grief. Adoptive parents can reach a middle ground by painting the nursery walls or carpeting the floors, but saving the infant motifs for later. They can shop for furniture but put it on layaway or in storage at a friend's. And from a purely practical standpoint, we strongly recommend that adoptive parents have at least a few items ready for the arrival of a baby, such as a simple layette, a car seat, and some baby bottles and formula. Having the essentials on hand means that if the baby comes home, they will be able to care for him without first stopping at the shopping center, and they will also have some tangible reminders that they are likely to become parents soon. In case the adoption does fall through, the nursery items can be packed up and put away or given to the birth mother if she decides to raise the baby herself.

Birth Parents' Readiness

Birth parents, too, should prepare for what they expect will happen to the baby after the birth. It's a good idea for the birth parents and the adoption facilitator to go over the hospital plan, run through the paperwork that will need to be taken care of, and review the legal process. Much of this may not have been discussed with the birth parents since they initially contacted the adoption facilitator.

Birth parents also need to think about their plans after the birth, beginning with the trip home. They should know where they will go when they leave the hospital and who will drive them there. If they expect to proceed with the adoption plan, it isn't necessary for them to be prepared to take care of a baby. However, they should at least prepare a "nest" for themselves—a comfortable place for them to return to. They can stock the refrigerator and pantry; purchase sanitary pads for postpartum bleeding and nursing pads to absorb any breast milk that might leak; accumulate new books to read, music to listen to, or videos to watch during their recovery. They should know whom they can call on for emotional support, even in the middle of the night. They should be thinking about what they will say about the baby to people who knew they were pregnant but might not be close enough to them to know about the adoption plan, such as people in their apartment building.

Birth parents could also begin planning for their lives after the birth, such as whether they will go to school or get a job. This helps them to focus on the future beyond placement of the child. They will not want to make any major changes in their lives while they are grieving, but it can help them function during that difficult time if they have a plan already in place.

If the birth parents are very ambivalent about their plan, or are still seriously considering keeping the baby, having some basic baby materials around may not only be practical but it may give them a concrete way to think about what it would be like to have the baby at home, and to help them make up their minds.

EMOTIONAL PREPAREDNESS

As they take care of some of the practical matters related to the placement of the baby, the birth parents' feelings may begin to surface in a way they hadn't before. It's important for the birth parents' counselor to review with them the feelings they can expect to go through after the birth and to help them develop strategies for coping. (The ways people feel when they are grieving are discussed in Chapter 2.) The counselor can ask the birth parents how they usually act when they are sad or angry, if they should plan to have a close friend or relative stay with them, and can provide them with information on when and where to go for help if they need it.

The counselor can also review with the birth parents the reasons they planned an adoption and chose these adoptive parents. Some counselors have the birth parents write down these reasons so they can refer to them later when the reasons are obscured by the emotions that accompany the birth and placement of the child. Birth parents might even want to bring this paper with them to the hospital.

The counselor can also meet with members of the birth family to discuss the feelings they might have, their expectations, and the ways they can emotionally support the birth parents. If the birth family has expectations that conflict with the birth parents' plans, this is a good time to identify those conflicts and resolve them. They could all join a support group if they have not done so already. Although they may be tempted to wait to meet with the group until after the birth, it is a good idea to attend a few meetings beforehand. Setting the groundwork early can make it easier to go back after the placement when they are in even greater turmoil.

As you get ready for the birth and placement of the child, keep in mind that you can prepare for the experience, but you can't predict completely how you will feel or react. Don't be too quick to judge or interpret each other's actions or feelings. As the time of the birth approaches, the adoptive parents often become anxious and fearful that the birth mother won't place her baby with them, and the birth mother becomes anxious and fearful because she plans to do just that. As these emotions come to the surface, your interactions with each other may change in a variety of ways. Adoptive parents may become hypervigilant for any signs that the birth mother has or has not changed her mind about the adoption plan, and may ask for statements of reassurance from her. Some adoptive parents, particularly those who have expected placements in the past only to have the birth mother decide to keep the baby, may withdraw from the birth mother as the birth approaches, trying to protect themselves from pain if this birth mother, too, decides to parent her child. As his wife becomes more anxious, the adoptive father may take on the role of protector. This can easily be misinterpreted by either the birth or the adoptive mother as denial or detachment.

The birth parents may become annoyed at the adoptive parents, easily finding fault with them. They may be feeling jealous, or they may not want the adoptive parents around as much because they remind them of what is about to happen. They may be realizing that their time with the baby is nearly over and may not want to share the baby with the adoptive parents during these final weeks. Sometimes the adoptive parents actually are annoying—hovering over the birth mother and reminding her that they are prepared to become the baby's parents.

This is a stressful time in your relationship. Continue to communicate with each other, expressing your needs in nondemanding ways and checking out your behavior with each other. For example, the adoptive parents can say, "Let us know if we are calling you too often." The birth mother could say, "I feel like you aren't interested in me anymore and I'm worried you might not want to take the baby." Such honesty can prevent a world of misunderstanding.

Final Plans for Labor and Delivery

During the last few weeks of the pregnancy it is important for you to sit down with each other and discuss your expectations about the birth of the child. Your adoption facilitator may do this routinely or you may want to ask your counselor or facilitator for assistance. The birth of a child is a highly personal experience, and most mothers have specific ideas about what they want it to be like, such as who will attend the birth and how they will interact with the infant immediately afterward. Birth mothers are no exception. Indeed, because the birth of the child may be both the first and last time the birth mother interacts with the child as that child's mother, the experience can have special meaning for her. She will carry with her forever the memory of the time she and the baby had together as mother and child.

Similarly, adoptive parents will have ideas about what the birth of their child should be like. These may be based on fantasies that go back to their expectations of giving birth to a child or may be based on stories they've heard of other open adoptions. Moreover, as they approach the moment they have been waiting for and planning for so long, their feelings, desires, and insecurities move closer to the surface than ever before. Some adoptive parents may worry that any move they make could jeopardize the placement.

Both the birth and the adoptive parents should not only articulate what they want but why they want it. Some birth parents may not know what their options are, or may think they don't have a right to express their wishes. They may think they owe the adoptive parents the experience they want since they are paying the birth mother's expenses and relieving her of an enormous responsibility.

It is important for you to clarify how and when each of you will interact with the baby during and after the birth because so many of the actions are heavy with emotion and symbolism, and the priority in which you execute those activities can symbolize your significance to the baby. It's similar to a young man who comes home from a trip and is met at the airport by his mother and his girlfriend. Both are important to him, but he can only greet one first and his choice may be interpreted as symbolic of the significance each has in his life.

At the birth of the baby and immediately afterward, those people with a close relationship to the baby will expect to participate in the more intimate interactions, such as attending the birth, holding and feeding the baby. Those with the closest relationship to the baby, that is, the parents, will expect to be the first to participate in those interactions. But because you may all think of yourselves as being the most significant person to the baby, there may be moments when desires and expectations clash. There are no rules in open adoption about who holds the baby first or decides what the baby should wear. Either the birth parents or adoptive parents can have these parental entitlements. But sometimes you cannot both have them—only one person can be first. Be cognizant of what you are asking for, especially if you want exclusive recognition of your right to interact in these ways. Be aware that given your plan, it is reasonable for each of you to think of yourself as the child's parent and to expect to interact with the baby in that way. Among the topics you will want to discuss ahead of time are:

- How and when will the adoptive parents be notified that the birth mother is in labor or has delivered?
- Who will be with her during labor and delivery? Who will be her childbirth coach? Who will cut the umbilical cord?

- Will the adoptive parents be at the hospital? What will their role be at the hospital?
- Who will hold the baby first?
- Who will feed the baby in the hospital? Does the birth mother plan to breastfeed? Does the adoptive mother plan to breastfeed?
- How long will the birth mother stay in the hospital after the birth? Will the baby room with her or be cared for in the nursery?
- Will the baby be circumcised? Will the adoptive parents be consulted about any necessary medical decisions about the baby, especially if the baby must remain in the hospital after the birth mother's release? Who will be notified if the baby develops complications after the birth or if a diagnosis of medical problems is made after the birth?
- What medical conditions might cause the adoptive parents to reconsider their decision to adopt this baby?
- Who will receive the original copies of the baby's footprints, handprints, and any official hospital photographs? Will the hospital provide duplicates? Who will take home hospital gifts and the baby's hospital bracelet?
- Who will choose the clothes the baby will wear home from the hospital?
- How will you leave the hospital? Who will leave first?
- What is your plan if the baby arrives prematurely or needs medical attention and must stay in the hospital longer? What are your plans if the birth mother has a cesarean section and must stay in the hospital longer than the baby?

Be sure to talk to your extended family members about their expectations of what will happen during labor, delivery, and in the hospital. For example, the birth grandparents may expect to be in the delivery room and may be shocked to find themselves excluded while the adoptive parents are included. You will ease tension later by working out any conflicts in advance.

In an ideal situation, everyone will have the same expectations about who holds the baby first or who is asked to cut the umbilical cord. When expectations conflict, however, it's important to realize that the birth experience belongs to the birth parents, particularly the birth mother.[1] She has the right to have her choices respected, and she may choose to include the adoptive parents in the birth experience, but she should not

---

1. We recognize that birth fathers are often involved in the birth and participate in the decision making. By referring to the birth mother in this chapter and the next, we do not mean to slight the birth father, but merely to reflect the usual scenario.

feel obligated to do so. She may allow the adoptive parents to participate in ways that validate their role as the baby's parents or she may retain those symbols for herself. And although the birth mother's choices may at times be disappointing to the adoptive parents, who wish that they could have sole and exclusive entitlement to the child, this is all part of the open adoption experience. For example, one birth mother asked the adoptive parents not to attend the birth or even visit her for a day after the birth. She wanted that time alone with her child. The adoptive parents were disappointed, for they had hoped to be in the delivery room when their child was born. But they realized they would have a lifetime with the child and could give the birth mother the one day she asked for without resentment.

Finally, keep in mind that the primary goal during the birth is a safe, gentle transition for the child from the womb to the world, and not the entitlement needs of parents.

A PRIVATE BIRTH

Sometimes a birth mother prefers to have the birth of her child be a private experience. She does not want the adoptive parents as her labor coaches, in the delivery room with her, or even at the hospital at all. After the baby's birth, she may want to breastfeed and have the baby in the hospital room with her. She may not want the adoptive parents to visit her or the baby for a while, and she may even want to take the baby home for a brief time. She may not want to sign any documents pertaining to the adoption while she is in the hospital.

Adoptive parents should not assume the birth mother intends to parent her child because she does not want to share the birth experience with them. A birth mother, especially one who is very young, may want a private birth because she is self-conscious about having people she has only recently met with her at such an intimate time. She may feel embarrassed to have the adoptive parents see her body at the time of birth. She may be afraid of the pain during labor and delivery and may not want the adoptive parents to see her if she screams or loses control. She may be afraid of the emotions she might experience and may not want an audience. One birth mother said she wanted to be around only those people who had known her a long time—those people she knew had already seen her at her worst.

For similar reasons, another birth mother was afraid she would say mean things to the adoptive parents if they were with her during labor and delivery. She was already feeling jealous of them because they would get to take the baby home and she was afraid she wouldn't be able to contain her negative feelings under stress. Not only did she not want to hurt the adoptive parents but she didn't want to risk angering them for fear they would not stay in contact with her after the adoption. It is not uncommon for women who love their husbands deeply to lash out at them verbally or physically during labor and delivery, irrationally holding them responsible for their pain and resenting them for not having to share in it. Although it isn't the birth mother's responsibility to protect the adoptive parents, it is understandable for a birth mother to worry about the effect her anger might have on the fragile open adoption relationship.

A birth mother may also be afraid that it will be awkward or contentious to have her extended family and the adoptive family at the birth. One birth mother promised the adoptive parents they could attend the birth only to have her mother say she didn't want the adoptive parents there and would refuse to be present if they were. Faced with the loss of support of her mother, the birth mother asked the adoptive parents if they would wait at home. Another birth mother knew that her mother was uncomfortable showing her emotions in front of people whom she did not know well. Rather than have her mother feel embarrassed, she asked the adoptive parents not to come to the hospital until the day after the birth.

To some birth mothers, the presence of the adoptive family may seem like pressure to make a decision when they are in emotional and physical pain. They might think they would be unable to deny the adoptive parents the child after inviting them to witness his birth. But a birth mother may want a private birth because that just seems like the natural way for her to complete the pregnancy experience. If the birth father is with her, they may feel they started the experience together, privately, and they want to finish it the same way.

DIRECT INVOLVEMENT IN THE BIRTH

Some birth parents want to have the adoptive parents as involved as possible in the birth. They may have developed a relationship with the adoptive parents so close that the needs of the adoptive parents are as important to them as their own, and they may have become dependent on the adoptive parents. They may be very social and enjoy having a lot of people supporting them during labor and delivery. Many want their baby to start his relationship with the adoptive parents right away.

The birth mother may ask the adoptive mother to be her labor coach and may ask the adoptive father to videotape the birth or cut the umbilical cord. The birth mother may give the baby to the adoptive parents to hold immediately after birth. She may want the adoptive parents to have all the new parent experiences, such as feeding and bathing the baby.

Shauna and Ray called the adoptive parents, Eric and Louise, as soon as Shauna started labor. They all met at the hospital, along with Eric and Louise's parents. Ray, Eric, and Louise were in the delivery room when Shauna gave birth. Shauna held the baby for a few minutes, then gave him to Ray. With everyone in the room shedding tears, Ray handed the baby to Louise saying, "Here's your son, mama."

The Role of Extended Family

The extended family members of the birth parents and the adoptive parents may feel awkward at the birth. Sometimes this is because they have not had the opportunity to meet the other family yet, and they feel that they are sharing a profoundly moving and important experience with virtual strangers. They may have difficulty expressing the broad range of feelings they are experiencing with people who will have an entirely different perspective on what is happening. Sometimes extended family don't agree with the adoption plan. The birth family may be hoping the birth mother will decide to raise the baby herself or will allow another family member to do so, and the adoptive family may be mistrustful of open adoption and may view the other family suspiciously. They may be afraid someone in the birth family will sabotage the adoption plan.

Like the birth parents and adoptive parents, their extended families may be overwhelmed by the miracle of life that is taking place nearby, but may not be sure whether it is appropriate to show their feelings in front of the other family. They may misinterpret each other's actions or emotional responses. The birth may bring up old or unresolved feelings about children or parents in members of the extended families, especially for those with a prior experience with adoption. Finally, everyone may feel awkward because there is nothing to do but wait.

After the birth, extended family members may not know what kind of behavior is expected of them. As extensions of the birth and adoptive parents, the extended families feel the symbolism of the various parenting and familial functions. For example, they may want to hold the baby but may not know if that is appropriate.

Just as the adoptive and birth parents benefit by going through the labor and delivery process one point at a time, expressing their visions for each step along the way, it is helpful to go through the process with the extended families. Extended family members can make their feelings known and the birth and adoptive parents can let them know what the plan is and how they fit into it. If the birth and adoptive families have not yet met, this would be a good time to get them together. Those that plan to be at the hospital may want to meet there for a cup of coffee together while the adoptive and birth parents tour the facility—almost like a rehearsal dinner the night before a wedding.

All of the attention at the hospital will be directed at the birth parents, the adoptive parents, and the baby. The emotions that the birth and adoptive parents will feel will be so intense that it will take all their energy just to cope. They cannot be expected to be available to provide emotional support to extended family. Members of the extended family could plan to have people with them at the hospital who are not as emotionally involved to provide them with emotional and practical help. This is particularly important for the birth grandmother who may feel, for example, too emotionally distraught to drive herself home from the hospital.

Working with the Hospital

Hospitals are institutions with procedures or protocols that determine how certain situations are handled. They have their own procedures for handling labor and delivery, including who may attend the birth. They may also have special procedures when the birth involves the possible placement of a child for adoption.

Years ago, standard hospital procedure did not allow birth mothers to see their children after birth—birth mothers weren't even allowed on the maternity ward so that they wouldn't see other mothers with their babies. This was thought to help the mother resolve the loss of her child, but we know now that these procedures complicated the grieving process by denying the birth mother the reality of her pregnancy and the birth.

Today, hospitals no longer insist on separating birth mothers from their children or from the maternity floor, but it doesn't mean that procedures in the hospital where the birth mother will deliver are consistent with your plans—or flexible enough to accommodate your plans with little notice. For example, hospitals might have a regulation saying that only two people other than the father of the child can attend the birth. It could be a problem if the birth mother wants her mother and the adoptive parents with her and assumes incorrectly that the hospital will treat the adoptive father as the "father."

Furthermore, hospitals are made up of individuals, each of whom brings to a situation his or her own biases, experiences, and expectations. The hospital staff might not understand or agree with your plans for the birth, especially if they haven't had experience with open adoptions before. By now you have probably discovered that many people are suspicious of open adoption, and some members of the hospital staff might share this opinion and may be unwilling to cooperate with your plan to have the adoptive parents attend the birth, hold the baby after delivery, or participate in decisions about the child's medical treatment. Some members of the hospital staff might also have strong opinions about adoption in general and attempt to influence the adoption plan.

Hospital personnel may also misinterpret the feelings they are observing because they do not fully understand the emotional reactions in adoption. For example, they may witness the birth mother's grief and mistake her feelings of sadness for regret. They might then try to convince her not to place her child for adoption, when what she needs is someone to understand that even though she is hurting, she believes her decision is the right one for her.

Hospital personnel may become involved in the interactions between the birth parents and the adoptive parents because they view the birth mother as their patient and they are trained to protect their patients. If the birth mother is in physical or emotional pain, the hospital staff wants to alleviate it. If it is adoption or the presence of the adoptive parents that appears to be causing the pain, it's natural, though not always appropriate, for the hospital staff to want to intervene to minimize the trauma to the birth mother.

It is therefore imperative that the birth mother communicate with hospital personnel in advance about her plans for the birth, outlining as many details as possible. This plan can be put in writing and sent to the hospital so that there is no question about what the birth mother wants and no question that the hospital has been notified of those plans. The adoption facilitator can help her identify the people who need to have copies of her plans, such as the doctor, the director of nursing, the supervisor of the obstetrics department, the hospital social worker, and the hospital chaplain. If hospital procedures or individual staff members have questions or concerns about the plan, these can be raised—and resolved—in advance rather than during labor or delivery. You may want to ask your adoption facilitator to assist you in providing the hospital with a copy of your plan and helping you fill out any documents the hospital might require. This role could also be assigned to the adoptive or birth father, who may be searching for a way to feel useful.

The birth mother may want to appoint one person to act as her advocate during labor and delivery. This could be an attorney, social worker, or family member. If the birth mother changes her mind at the hospital about her plans for labor and delivery, the advocate can communicate her current needs to those people who need to know about the changes. Any questions about the adoption could be channeled through this advocate, who can also protect the birth mother from untimely attempts to discuss her adoption plans with her. However, any time communication is handled by a third party, the potential for misunderstanding increases, so the birth mother will want to weigh this option carefully.

No matter how well intentioned they might be, it is not appropriate for anyone to initiate a discussion of the future of the baby during the birth mother's labor, delivery, or during the first twenty-four hours after delivery, although those close to her can let her know they are willing to listen or discuss options with her if she chooses. Even later, only those people with whom the birth mother wants to discuss her decision, such as her counselor or social worker, should attempt to discuss her plans with her.

The adoptive parents may want to let the hospital staff know that they intend to adhere to hospital protocols and defer to the birth mother's preferences, even if those are different than they originally planned. They can also reassure the staff that they intend to respect the birth mother's requests and decisions and will not attempt to pressure the birth mother into a decision she is not prepared to make. Once the hospital staff realizes that the birth parents and adoptive parents are not adversaries but are united in their desire to meet the needs of the birth mother and the baby, they are likely to be more relaxed about the adoptive parents' participation and the open adoption plan.

Putting the Plan into Effect

When the birth mother goes into labor, the doctor, the birth mother's labor coach, the person designated as the birth mother's advocate at the hospital, and anyone else who expects to be notified (such as the birth grandparents, birth father, and adoptive parents) should be called. Some adoptive parents arrange to wear beepers so that they can be reached immediately. The adoption facilitator should also be informed—even when you don't expect there to be conflict at the hospital it is important for him to be aware of the birth so that he can be available to provide counseling or mediate a dispute if necessary.

No matter how carefully the birth is planned, be prepared to have those plans change. Regardless of how much the birth parents have prepared for this experience, when faced with the reality, their needs and wants may be much different than they had expected. Their feelings may be more intense than they ever realized, and they may have underestimated the powerful symbolism of parenting, such as the desire to feed or name the baby, or the degree to which they would want to claim their roles in public. Again, the fact that the birth parents change their minds about the plan for the child's birth does not necessarily mean they intend to change their mind about the placement. They need to be allowed to take the process one step at a time without being asked to jump ahead to the next step or provide the adoptive parents with reassurance.

Noelle had planned to have the adoptive parents in the delivery room with her when her baby was born. But when she went into labor, she decided she didn't want them even in the hospital. Her mother called them to ask them to wait at home. After the baby was born, Noelle decided she wanted some special time with her baby, and her mother called the adoptive parents again and asked them not to visit the baby at the hospital. When it was time to go home, Noelle decided she couldn't leave the baby at the hospital, and her mother phoned the adoptive parents to say Noelle would be taking the baby home for a few days. Not surprisingly, with each call, the adoptive parents became more and more convinced that the birth mother had changed her mind. But after three days, Noelle's mother called the adoptive parents to say Noelle was ready to have them pick up the baby.

Although Noelle had pondered keeping the baby, in her heart she had planned all along to place the baby for adoption. Excluding the adoptive parents from the birth was not a rejection, nor was taking the baby home a trial. She simply felt that she needed some time alone with her baby to complete her pregnancy experience. Once she felt she had done all she could do, she was ready to turn over the parenting responsibilities to the adoptive parents. She didn't realize prior to the birth that she would feel that way. Indeed, she could not articulate her need for privacy at the time—she just knew she needed it. Of course, it won't always be that plans change in the direction of excluding the adoptive parents. One birth mother, who had expected to feel self-conscious during the birth, found herself so overwhelmed by the intensity of the experience that she wanted to share it with the adoptive parents, whom she had previously asked to wait outside.

Childbirth is a profoundly moving experience. It can be prepared for, but its full impact cannot be anticipated. Even people who have given birth before, and doctors and nurses who witness it several times a day, find each experience to be unique. As involved as the adoptive parents may be with the birth mother, and as invested as they may be in the child, the birth experience still belongs to the birth mother, and she has the right to make decisions about the birth, even if that means radically changing plans midstream.

CESAREAN SECTION

An emergency cesarean birth disrupts the natural flow of the birth experience and causes last-minutes changes in plans. People who expected to attend the birth may not be admitted to the operating room. The adoptive parents may have a chance to see and hold the baby before the birth mother. The birth mother may delay decisions while she deals with her physical recovery from surgery. Even plans for leaving the hospital can change because the child may be ready to be released before the birth mother. Discuss ahead of time how plans may change if a cesarean section is required, and if it happens, be prepared to be flexible.

After the Birth

The birth of the baby marks the beginning of what is often the most difficult time in an open adoption. Up until the baby's birth, the birth mother is clearly in control of the baby and his destiny. She is making all the decisions that affect the baby; she has the baby; and she is recognized as the legal parent. After finalization of the adoption, the adoptive parents are in control. They act as the baby's parents; they have the child; and they have legal authority. But between the time the baby is born and the adoption is finalized (or the birth parents make the decision to parent the child themselves), both the birth parents and the adoptive parents feel that they have some claim to the child.

Adoptive parents may want to be treated as the baby's parents as soon as the baby is born—to be in the delivery room, make decisions about the baby, dress the baby, and take the baby home. The adoptive parents may view any resistance on the part of the birth parents as a sign that they do not intend to proceed with the adoption plan. But the birth parents may not see their parenting role ending at the moment of birth or quite so abruptly. To them, the entire hospital stay may feel like the last scene in a drama that began with the conception of the child.

Birth parents who aren't prepared to immediately transfer all their parenting functions may view attempts by the adoptive parents to take on these functions as premature, intrusive, or insensitive. Some birth parents want to transfer the parenting role to the adoptive parents gradually, sharing parental functions such as feeding the baby and holding the baby before relinquishing their roles completely. Keep in mind during this time that the child cannot speak up and express his preferences, needs, and rights. While it may seem critical that everyone respect your needs and rights, remember that the most important person in this adoption is the child.

For a long time the adoption system tried to avoid the conflict that can result during this ambiguous time in the adoption process. Babies were placed in foster care until the birth parents' rights were terminated. Adoptive parents did not assume any parenting functions—often they weren't even told the child was born—until the birth parents had relinquished any legal claim. Although adoptive parents felt more secure with this system, it did not serve the birth parents, the adoptive parents, or the child well. Birth parents wondered if their children were ever adopted. Adoptive parents were often denied the time frame of the pregnancy in which they could prepare to form an attachment to a child and get ready mentally, emotionally, and physically for the significant changes that were to occur in their lives. The child was denied the opportunity to immediately begin to form an attachment to the parents who would be raising him.

Although most foster parents are loving and competent caregivers, it is far better for a child to be with parents who intend to have a permanent parent–child relationship. Furthermore, the baby is the person least able to make adjustments because of his immature neurological system, yet when babies didn't go directly from the birth parents to the adoptive parents, they had to make transitions into and out of foster care. And when adoptive parents were not in touch with the birth parents at the time of birth, they often did not learn the pregnancy and birth story to relate to the child—something many people take for granted, but which experts like Marshall Schechter, M.D., coauthor of *Being Adopted,* believes to be an important element in identity formation.

From the time the baby is born, through the time the birth parents terminate their parental rights and the adoptive parents finalize the adoption, be aware that there will be situations in which your rights conflict and your roles overlap. In resolving these, you can't necessarily look to the legal or social system to define your relationship, since the child's legal parents may not be functioning as parents. During this time, you need to try to see everyone's viewpoint; to put yourself in the place of the other parents and see that just as society has legitimized the rights you feel you have, it has also legitimized the rights the other parents feel they have. Also keep in mind that as difficult as this transition may be for you, it's better for the child. Finally, remember that adoption is the delicate process of moving a child from one family to another, and that child is totally unaware and unconcerned with legalities or rights.

Welcoming the Baby

Birth parents need to claim their children as their own before they can say good-bye to them. They need to hold the baby, welcome him, and acknowledge in some way that this child came from them. They do this by examining the baby—counting his fingers and toes and looking for signs of resemblance to themselves. No matter who is in the room or how committed the birth mother is to the adoption plan, it is important for her to have the opportunity to welcome the fruits of her labor into the world. It is also fitting and natural for other people to celebrate the birth of this child and to congratulate the birth parents on the contribution they have made to the human race. As the birth parents see that they brought forth a beautiful and, we hope, a healthy baby, they can feel an important sense of accomplishment and completion.

Some birth mothers say they don't want to see their babies. Although we believe it is important for birth mothers to make choices about their birth experience, examining and claiming the baby is so important that those working with her—the adoption facilitator, the adoptive parents, her extended family, and health-care professionals—should encourage her to see her baby. Ideally, the importance of this should be explained to her earlier when she is making a plan. But even birth mothers who have chosen not to see their babies should be given the choice again at the hospital after the birth.

Seeing the baby helps make the entire pregnancy real to them, which helps them face their grief at the loss of their parenting role. Birth mothers who do not see their babies often wonder if the babies lived or if there were any congenital medical problems. Even if they continue to have contact with their children, they may have irrational thoughts about the outcome of the pregnancy because they didn't see the child right after birth. For example, the birth mother may question whether the child she is seeing with the adoptive parents is the same child to whom she gave birth. But if for no other reason, the birth mother should see her baby because it is a powerful acknowledgment of the child's existence and the birth mother's role in the creation of the child.

After the birth parents have welcomed the baby, they can indicate their readiness to acknowledge the role the adoptive parents will be playing in the child's life by allowing them to welcome the baby and by sharing in the joy the adoptive parents are feeling. Some birth parents will want to do this soon after the birth, but some may not be ready to begin the transfer of parental roles right away. This is something they may not know until they experience the birth itself.

SPENDING TIME WITH THE BABY

In addition to welcoming their child, birth parents need to spend some time alone with their baby as the parents of the baby. The birth parents can explain to the baby why they are placing him for adoption and can give him permission to love his adoptive parents. Although the baby can't understand the words, they are important for the birth parents to say. It's also valuable to be able to tell the child later that this permission was given. Some people also believe that even though the baby can't understand the words, something important is communicated. Birth parents sometimes videotape their time together with the baby, both for themselves and for the child.

For some birth parents, a few minutes after the baby's birth is sufficient, whereas others will want to spend more time, occasionally wanting to bring the baby home from the hospital overnight or for a few days. Keep in mind that right before we say good-bye to someone we care about is the time when we most want to linger. This is especially true when we know that the next time we see them our relationship will have changed dramatically.

Adoptive parents also want to spend time alone with the baby. They often want to examine the baby and count his toes and fingers to claim or accept their child as their own. Adoptive parents may also want to feed and hold the baby. They are responding to the innate ability of babies to get adults to meet their needs, which is what brings them close to each other, thus promoting attachment. If the birth mother is willing to let the adoptive parents have contact with the baby in the hospital, a good time for the adoptive parents to do so is while the birth mother is in recovery after the birth.

Because there has been so much emphasis on the importance of immediate postnatal contact between parent and child for bonding, or the building of attachment, adoptive parents worry that if the birth parents spend a lot of time alone with the baby, they will form an attachment that they will be unable to break—either they will decide not to place the child for adoption or they will place the child for adoption but the child will have a closer relationship with them than with his adoptive parents. A birth mother feels a bond to a child she has carried for nine months. She doesn't place her child for adoption because she doesn't feel any connection but because she is strong enough to put the child's best interests ahead of her feelings.

Adoptive parents may worry that unless they spend time alone with the baby, they will have difficulty forming an attachment, and that even if they adopt the baby, their relationship will not be as close as it might have been if they had been allowed to hold the baby immediately after birth or feed the baby in the hospital. As we point out in Chapter 2, attachment is a lifelong process that takes more than a few hours or a few days. It is the feeling that grows as parents meet their child's needs. Attachment builds with adoptive parents even if they have not had contact with a child for hours, days, months, or even years immediately after the birth. Indeed, adoptive parents have formed strong attachments with children who have spent time in foster families or with their biologic families before being adopted.

Breastfeeding

Some birth mothers want to breastfeed the baby in the hospital, even though they may not have planned for this. The physical changes in the birth mother as her body begins to produce milk are telling her body to nurse the baby. The love that she feels for the baby is pulling her close to the baby and breastfeeding is the ultimate expression of closeness between mother and child. She may be aching, both physically and figuratively, to nurse her child. For this reason, some birth mothers feel that breastfeeding their babies—even if it is only once—is part of the birth experience. They need the experience to have the sense of having successfully finished what they began. Many birth mothers also feel a responsibility to nurse. Only the breast milk of biologic mothers contains colostrum, a substance that enables the mother's antibodies to disease to be transferred to the child, protecting him from many illnesses during his first few months of life when he is most vulnerable. Colostrum is also rich in protein, which gives the baby a nutritional boost.

But breastfeeding also promotes attachment between the mother and child. It can be more difficult for the birth mother to separate from her child if they have shared this level of closeness. The separation may be more difficult physically as well. While mothers experience a fullness in their breasts during pregnancy due to the preparation of the breasts for lactation, the milk doesn't actually come into the breasts until three or four days after the baby's birth. Prior to that, the breasts are producing colostrum. If the baby nurses, the milk may come in more heavily than it would if the baby hadn't nursed, and the birth mother may experience more discomfort as her milk dries up.

The birth mother should not feel guilty if she decides not to breastfeed her baby. The baby will receive good nutrition from formula or the breast milk of the adoptive mother. She can hold her baby and feel close without breastfeeding. At the same time, the birth mother should not assume that by breastfeeding she is taking the first step to keeping her baby. She can breastfeed and place her baby for adoption if she believes the physical and emotional costs are worth the gains.

Sometimes the adoptive mother wants to breastfeed even though she may not have planned on it. She, too, is feeling the emotional pull of the child and wants to be as close as she can to the child. Breastfeeding is one of the many ways an adoptive mother can get close to her child and feel that she is meeting his needs, and as the parent meets the child's needs, attachment forms. Adoptive mothers who want to breastfeed should consult their local chapter of La Leche League for assistance and support.

Those who do not want to breastfeed should not be concerned that they will be unable to form an attachment, or that by feeding formula to their child they are giving their child substandard nutrition. When properly prepared, formula provides good-quality nourishment for a baby, and there are many other ways to form attachment. Moreover, infants do not realize all the benefits of nursing from an adoptive mother that they do from a biologic mother because the milk produced by mothers without a pregnancy does not contain colostrum. In addition, adoptive mothers usually are unable to produce enough milk to meet their infant's complete nutritional needs. Most must feed their babies at least two bottles of formula each day in addition to nursing.

Some people are surprised to learn that adoptive mothers can breastfeed. The injection of hormones or drugs is not necessary. The breasts can often be stimulated to produce milk by the baby's sucking action or by manual or mechanical stimulation with a breast pump. Lactation is not immediate; it takes two to six weeks of stimulation for the breasts to begin producing milk. Some adoptive mothers begin stimulating their breasts before the baby's due date so that they are ready to begin nursing as soon as the baby is born. However, some mothers prefer not to take this approach. Not only is it inconvenient to sit down with a breast pump several times each day but adoptive mothers may be worried about the possibility of successfully achieving lactation only to have the birth mother decide against adoption.

An alternative is to use a supplemental nutritional system such as the Lact-Aid Nursing Trainer or Medela SNS after the baby is home. The baby receives a supply of formula through a thin plastic tube stationed next to the mother's nipple. As the baby sucks at the breast, the tube provides enough reward to the infant for him to continue to suck, and the sucking stimulates the breast to produce milk. Eventually the breast produces milk itself and sometimes the supplemental nutrition system can be discontinued. This method has its disadvantages as well. It can be as inconvenient to carry around and set up a supplemental nutrition system for several weeks (along with the baby, diapers, car seat, etc.) as it is to sit down with a breast pump several times a day. Furthermore, some babies learn to focus on the source of the milk and ignore the nipple. Adoptive mothers need to decide for themselves which "inconveniences" they prefer.

The question of who will breastfeed the baby can become a source of conflict between the adoptive mother and the birth mother. This may be one of the parenting functions that both the adoptive mother and the birth mother may want to claim. You will have to be sensitive to each other's feelings as you work this out, keeping in mind what is best for the child.

Emotional Reactions

During the first twenty-four hours after the birth of the baby you will feel like you are riding an emotional roller coaster—in the front seat without holding on. The birth parents will feel euphoric at bringing forth new life. They will feel incredible love for the child and satisfaction at a job well done. Kathleen Silber, M.S.W., coauthor of *Dear Birthmother* and *Children of Open Adoption,* says birth mothers may not be prepared for the overwhelming feeling of love that they have for the child at birth. Indeed, for a birth mother from a dysfunctional family, the unconditional love of a baby for his mother may be a totally new and moving experience. The birth parents may feel more competent and worthy than they have ever felt in their lives. They may be in awe at the miracle of new life.

There is also for many birth mothers a sense of relief at arriving at what appears to be the end of a difficult experience—relief at being able to get back to the size and shape they were before they became pregnant, at being able to resume their normal routine and activities, at knowing that they have made a plan for their child's future with which they can be comfortable. If they have established a good relationship with the adoptive parents, there is also joy at knowing that their dream of becoming a family is about to be realized and that they are responsible for helping the people they have come to care about fulfill their fantasies.

As the birth parents indicate their intention to transfer their parental role to the adoptive parents, they will begin to feel the pain and sadness of separating from the child. While they may be comforted by knowing that they have made a responsible decision for their child, this will not cancel out their grief. (See Chapter 2 for specific examples of how it feels to grieve.) In addition, there may be some consolation for the birth parents in knowing they will not lose contact with the child entirely if they have an open adoption, but there is also some fear that the adoptive parents will not keep in touch or that it will be too painful to see the child.

They may also feel confused about the future. The birth of a baby is an awesome experience. It isn't surprising that many birth parents wonder, if only for a moment, whether they could find a way to raise the baby themselves. The adoption plan, which may have seemed like the only reasonable or responsible decision for them to make before the birth, may not seem like such a clear choice. Even those who want to proceed with the adoption plan may realize that it will be more difficult than they imagined. They may be anxious about whether they will be able to bear the pain. If they are seriously considering raising the baby, they may feel sad as they realize how disappointed the adoptive parents will be, guilty for not proceeding with the adoption plan, and afraid of the adoptive parents' anger. They may be worried that if they keep the baby they'll lose their relationship with the adoptive parents—people who have shown they care for the birth parents during a difficult time. They may feel angry and jealous of the adoptive parents.

The birth parents may try to suppress those feelings so that they don't diminish the joy the adoptive parents are feeling. They may be afraid that by acknowledging their own joy they might weaken their resolution to place the child for adoption. They may try to focus on the adoptive parents' joy so that they can't feel the pain and sadness. Sometimes birth parents genuinely feel happy for the adoptive parents and think that if they are happy to see such joy in the eyes of the adoptive parents, they can't also be feeling sadness at their own loss. But as we've said before, adoption involves a lot of conflicting emotions, and it is important to experience them all, and not try to pick the most dominant emotion. Birth parents will have a full range of feelings about the birth of their child and they have every right to express them without being concerned about the effect they may have on the adoptive parents. Their job is not to protect the adoptive parents from the emotions connected with this event.

Not surprisingly, adoptive parents also feel euphoric at the birth of the child they hope will be theirs. For many, this joy is fed by years of disappointment—failed attempts at conception, failed pregnancies, failed attempts to adopt. At the same time, they experience fear that this latest, best, brightest hope to become parents may not be realized if the birth parents decide to parent the child themselves. They may also feel compassion for the birth parents as they realize the pain they will experience if they proceed with the adoption plan. One adoptive mother said she was not prepared to feel sadness at the moment the birth mother handed her the baby. But she realized that she could empathize with the birth mother's imminent loss of the child.

Some adoptive parents are so moved by their awareness of the sacrifice the birth parents are making for them that their pain is real to them. One adoptive mother at this moment said to the birth mother, "I can't take your baby away from you." The birth mother responded, "But I need you to." Both were crying. Both understood the feelings of the other and their own conflicting emotions. The kind of relationship these mothers had is what you are striving for in open adoption, but it is only realized in a few extraordinary situations. It is a relationship where each of you can put aside your own needs and wants and look at what is best for everyone involved: a relationship where you are as concerned about the feelings and well-being of others as you are about yourself.

Some adoptive parents feel their awareness of the birth mother's pain robs them of experiencing the pure joy they expected to feel at the time of their child's birth. They have fantasized about getting a child for so long and imagined only their happiness. Some say they regret having been a witness to the birth mother's pain.

The "old" adoption system that insulated adoptive parents from the pain of the birth parents may have made for happier placement stories, but it wasn't real. Because adoptive parents did not see the birth parents' expressions of love and sadness, the harmful myth developed that birth parents didn't care about their children, which led to feelings of rejection on the part of the children. It is important for adoptive parents to understand what the birth parents felt at the time they placed their child for adoption so that they can help their child understand that, and so they can understand the conflicting feelings their child may have later as she becomes aware of what it means to be adopted. Furthermore, it's important to remember that all birth involves pain—both physical and emotional. Adoptive parents who are insulated from the pain of childbirth not only can develop unrealistic ideas about adoption but haven't fully experienced the authenticity of birth.

Naming the Baby

Naming a child is a powerful symbol of parental entitlement and authority. Although there are other ways to claim a child, in this culture, naming is one of the most meaningful ones. In Western cultures, parents usually name their child immediately after birth. This poses some unique considerations in open adoption. Because birth parents cannot legally relinquish their parental rights until after a child is born, they are the child's legal parents at the time of birth and have the right to name him. Some do with the expectation that the adoptive parents will keep that name for the child. For many birth parents this is an important gift of themselves to their child: although their child will never carry their family name, they can at least give the child a first name.

Adoptive parents should keep in mind that if the birth parents want to choose the name it is not necessarily a sign that they intend to keep the child. However, the adoptive parents probably will want to name the baby themselves. They will have to live with the name on a daily basis, and it's natural for them to want the child to have a name they like. In addition, the choice of the name can be a powerful symbol of their parental relationship, and for some people, the name that they have carried around for years in their minds is the only remnant of the fantasy child that is left. It's hard to let go of it and call the child by the name given to him by the birth parents. Of course, not all birth parents want to give their children a name—some take the opportunity to validate the adoptive parents' rights. Some birth mothers say they want to save the names they've chosen for the children they will parent. And some name their child fully expecting the adoptive parents to change it.

Clearly you should at least discuss names as well as the expectations each of you has for your role in naming the child. Included in this discussion should be any family, religious, or cultural traditions regarding names that are important to you. For example, in the Jewish faith, children are named after deceased relatives. You should all be aware of how important it is for each of you to feel that you have made some contribution to the child's name. But you should also look at the naming process from the child's point of view. How will you explain to him how he came to be named? If you squabble over the name, will you be able to justify that to him? If you refuse to acknowledge the name given to the child by the other parent, can you explain that to the child? Finally, keep in mind that giving the child a name will not make you any more connected to that child than you are by virtue of your relationship with him. He will not be any more the biologic child of the birth parents if they name him than he is already. He will not be any more the authentic child of the adoptive parents if they name him than he already is.

One adoption agency highly recommends that the birth and adoptive parents jointly agree on a name for the child prior to the child's birth. They reason that this is one of the few opportunities parents have prior to the child's birth to test their ability to negotiate with each other. If the naming process results in a great deal of conflict, they will look at whether the birth parents are not ready to let go of their role or whether the adoptive parents are really ready to have the birth parents in their lives on a long-term basis. Other adoption facilitators say that although it is a good idea to discuss the naming process, it isn't necessary for birth and adoptive parents to agree on a name together. Birth parents may not be ready to let go of their role yet, and they may feel pressured to negotiate something that would be better left until after the baby's birth.

One open adoption that had gone smoothly suddenly hit a serious snag after the baby's birth. Amy, the birth mother, had expected to give the baby his first name, while Brian and Kathy, the adoptive parents, not only had expected to name him but hated the name Amy had selected. They could not agree on a compromise. Their adoption facilitator asked Brian and Kathy if this disagreement was a "deal breaker." With tears in her eyes, Kathy said that it was. Luckily, once Amy learned how important the issue was to Kathy, she agreed to allow her to pick a first name and she chose the middle name. When Brian and Kathy adopted a second child, the issue of naming was one of the first topics they brought up for discussion.

Years later Kathy had nearly forgotten that she was willing to let the adoption pass rather than compromise on the issue of names. But she said the issue was not the choice of names as much as it was the ability to negotiate with Amy. She did not want a long-term relationship with a birth mother with whom she couldn't work out conflicts.

Sometimes birth and adoptive parents negotiate until they can find a name they all like. The adoptive parents might choose the first name and the birth parents the middle name, or vice versa. Often birth parents will allow the adoptive parents to select the name entirely themselves, and sometimes the adoptive parents give that right to the birth parents. Occasionally a name chosen by the birth parents is combined with a name chosen by the adoptive parents, such as "Norita."

Think carefully before naming the child after someone in the family. Some adoptees strongly object to being called "junior" or named for other male relatives. Although adoptive parents often do this to indicate how much a part of the family the child is, it often feels false to the boy, particularly during adolescence when he is trying to establish his identity. It might be better to use the names of the birth parents or adoptive parents as middle names rather than first names, if it's important to the adoptive parents to use them.

Interacting After the Birth

Because the birth and hospital experience may be different from what you expected, and because you may be experiencing emotions you didn't expect to have or an intensity of emotions that you were unprepared for, you may feel unsure of yourself and unsure of how to interact with each other. The tendency in a situation like this is often for people to behave the way they think they ought to and express feelings they think people expect them to have, rather than to be themselves. You need to be honest with yourself and with each other, while maintaining a perspective broad enough to allow for the likely possibility that events and actions may have meaning other than the interpretation you are giving them. Rather than jumping to conclusions, express your feelings and check out with each other how your actions and statements are being received.

For example, you may have agreed that the baby would stay in the nursery and the adoptive parents could bring their family and friends to see the baby. However, the birth mother may have decided after the birth to keep the baby in her room with her, and she may not appreciate having the adoptive parents bring a stream of friends and relatives into her room. She may tolerate the visitors because she understands that the adoptive parents want to share their excitement with their friends, but she may resent the intrusion and eventually tell the adoptive parents that they can't bring any more visitors to see the baby. The adoptive parents may interpret this as a sign that she can't be trusted to live up to the agreements she makes, or they may think she doesn't want the adoptive parents to show the baby to their friends because she doesn't plan to let them raise the baby. The adoptive parents' resentment may grow until they say to her, "This is our baby. We should be able to decide who can visit him."

The ensuing power struggle could be avoided if the adoptive parents realize that they need to check out plans with the birth mother, such as by saying, "We know you didn't plan to have the baby in your room with you when you agreed to having visitors. How would you like us to show the baby to our family when they stop by?"

You may resist communicating with each other through the adoption facilitator or through the advocate the birth parent appointed to represent her at the hospital because you would like to believe your relationship is not in conflict. However, using a third party to help you communicate does not mean you are unable to communicate without this person; it simply recognizes that this is a time when actions, statements, and even facial expressions can be easily misinterpreted because everyone's feelings are raw and intense. Someone who is experienced in dealing with adoptive parents and birth parents at the time of the birth can help you communicate with each other so that the fragile relationship you have built up is not destroyed by a careless comment or misunderstood deed.

The Birth Father

It is not uncommon for a birth father who has perhaps denied paternity or not wanted to become involved in the pregnancy or decisions about the child to suddenly come forward after the birth and want to claim his legitimate right as the baby's father. But the sudden appearance of a birth father who is sounding like he objects to the adoption plan can cause concern for everyone involved.

The birth mother may be afraid that if she terminates her parental rights so that the adoption can proceed, the birth father will exercise his rights to the child. The adoptive parents may be worried that the birth father will not agree to the adoption or that the birth mother will keep the child hoping that the birth father will remain involved in her life.

It is necessary for everyone to slow down in this situation and allow the birth father to process the many conflicting feelings that he may not have been prepared for. This is a time for counseling and care, not coercion. Oftentimes what the birth father needs is an opportunity to get to know the adoptive parents so that he is reassured that they are capable people who will love his child. He may need the opportunity to sort through his feelings of sadness, anger, and guilt. He is no doubt feeling out of control, and a natural reaction is to grab whatever control is available to him; that means threatening to withhold his consent. He may also need help understanding what an appropriate role is for him in the current situation and how to assume that role. In addition, he may need to be told in concrete ways what he can do for the baby, such as making a gift, writing a letter, compiling a photo album, and staying in contact with the adoptive family.

The more the adoptive parents can reach out to the birth father to say, "We'd like you to get to know us better, and we'd like to get to know you better," and the more respectful they can be of his feelings and his role as birth father, the more likely it is that he will make responsible decisions rather than impulsive ones.

Gifts

It is not only appropriate but touching to send flowers to the birth mother or gifts for her personal comfort—an attractive nightgown or a basket containing hand lotion and cologne. A permanent memento, such as a piece of jewelry or a figurine, is also acceptable. A book of poetry or spiritual readings is another way for adoptive parents to express their deep feelings at this time. Whatever the adoptive parents give should be appropriate regardless of whether or not she decides to place the baby for adoption. Adoptive parents can give the birth mother a photo album. If she keeps the baby, she can fill the album herself. If she places the baby, the adoptive parents are indicating their commitment to keeping that album filled. It can be a reassuring symbol for the birth mother at that time.

Later, if the birth parents proceed with the adoption plan, you can give each other gifts that symbolize your relationship. Adoptive parents sometimes give the birth mother a locket with the baby's photograph or a *mizpah*—a piece of jewelry that has two parts; one is kept by the birth mother and the other by the adoptive mother. The birth mother frequently gives the adoptive parents a gift for the baby that she has made herself—a quilt, a sweater, or a piece of needlework—along with a letter explaining her decision and her feelings to the child. One birth mother gave the adoptive parents a ceramic figurine of parents with a new baby with a touching message that communicated that she saw them as the child's parents.

Since every state has laws governing what adoptive parents can give to a birth mother in the way of material goods, adoptive parents should be sure to check with their adoption facilitator to make sure the adoption is not jeopardized by a technicality.

Reviewing the Decision

No matter how sure the birth parents have been of their plan to place the child for adoption, they will have to make that decision anew after the birth of the baby. No matter how sure the adoptive parents have been of their plan to adopt, they will have to make that decision anew after the birth of the baby. Prior decisions have been only preliminary, based on incomplete information, even though they may have seemed like final decisions. Now that the baby is separate from the birth mother, the birth mother can see the baby as a real infant with real needs. The adoptive parents, too, can evaluate whether they are prepared to meet this child's needs now that much more is known about the baby. You need to give yourselves and each other permission to carefully consider the adoption plan and arrive at a decision that is separate from your earlier plans.

It is particularly frightening to adoptive parents to have the birth mother contemplate her options. Adoptive parents can't imagine how the birth mother could resist the beautiful baby she is holding. They can't put themselves in her place; they see the baby only from their perspective—as people who are in a position to parent that child. Furthermore, as we've pointed out, infertility and the frustrations of the adoption process often leave adoptive parents expecting loss. They find it hard to believe they will ever realize their dream because so many times the fulfillment of their expectations seemed at hand, only to vanish.

Adoptive parents need to understand that if the birth parents have been getting good counseling and not operating in denial about the pregnancy, they have understood that their child would be beautiful and lovable and that they would want to parent him. They have understood that it would hurt to be separated from the child, but they know that they are not in a position to be effective parents. There's no reason to assume they will think differently now that the child is born and they can see the child face-to-face, but they still must have the opportunity to review that decision, if only so they can feel all the more confident about the placement.

As the birth mother considers her options, adoptive parents may be tempted to hover over her, looking for reassurance that she intends to place, or even pressuring her to place. Too often, this behavior has the opposite effect. The birth mother, who believed the adoptive parents cared about her, may now wonder why they don't understand her need to feel completely sure about her decision. She may feel they are only interested in getting her baby, and may wonder if the adoptive parents can be trusted.

In many open adoptions, though, the adoptive parents become so close to the birth mother that they want what is best for her and her child. They realize that no matter how much they want to adopt the baby, they don't want to deprive the birth mother they've come to care about of the right to feel that she made a fully informed choice. They don't want a baby by trickery, default, deception, or manipulation, and because the adoptive family will continue to have contact with the birth family, the adoptive parents don't want a child whose birth parents would have kept him if they'd been allowed to make the choice that was really in their hearts. They want to be confident that they are sure of their decision. The adoptive parents should remember that they will not be the only people explaining to the child why his birth parents placed him for adoption, and if the adoptive parents and birth parents can't honestly say that this was a decision the birth parents freely made, everyone loses. The birth parents must then explain why they made the placement if they didn't really want to. The adoptive parents must explain why they accepted the placement knowing that the birth parents were unsure. And the child is left feeling the placement was made without sufficient care.

One adoptive couple was convinced that the birth mother had not allowed herself to seriously consider parenting her child. At the hospital, she wanted to sign the consent to the adoption as soon as possible. They told her, "We don't think you've given enough thought to taking this baby home yourself. We want you to do that before you sign the consent." Once she began thinking about that option seriously, the birth mother found she needed more time than she thought to consider her plans. She took the baby home for five days, then called the adoptive parents to say she had decided to place the baby with them. They felt comfortable knowing that she had made her decision thoughtfully.

As she reviews her options, the birth mother should think about the reasons she decided to place her child for adoption, why she chose the adoptive couple she did, and what factors might have changed that could affect her decision. She can ask her counselor to review this with her, or she can review the reasons that she wrote down earlier. She should allow herself to imagine what it would be like to keep the baby—where will they live, how will she support the baby, and who will support this decision.

The birth mother should then consider whether she is thinking of keeping the baby because of her intense feelings of love and her awareness of how much pain it will cause her to place the baby for adoption, or whether she has actually decided she is capable of raising the baby.

There is a tendency for adoptive parents to want to pull out of the adoption if the birth parents sound like they might change their plans. Adoptive parents need to understand that careful contemplation by the birth parents needn't result in a change of plans, and the adoptive parents should remain committed to the plan themselves, or the birth parents will have little choice but to keep the baby.

Although adoptive parents need to respect the birth parents' need to reevaluate their plans, the birth parents should understand how difficult this is for the adoptive parents and should be as honest as they can with them about where they are in their thinking process. If the birth parents want time alone with the baby, but still think they will place, they should say so. If they are seriously thinking about changing plans and parenting the baby, they should communicate that as early as possible.

For similar reasons, if the birth mother is seriously considering keeping the baby, but hasn't made a final decision, she should not send the baby home with the adoptive parents, unless they understand how tentative the placement is and are willing to take the emotional risks involved. The birth mother can take the baby home herself, with the understanding that this does not commit her to keeping the baby; she can have the baby cared for by a foster family; or she can ask the hospital to keep the baby for an extra day or so while she makes up her mind. The adoption facilitator can help decide which is the best plan. (For more about birth parents who decide to raise the baby themselves, see Chapter 14.)

The adoptive parents also need to allow themselves to review their plan now that they have more information about the baby. This review includes a reevaluation of wanting to be parents, of wanting to adopt, and of wanting to adopt this baby. More information about the baby is known now that he is born and his physical and mental conditions can be evaluated. Occasionally the racial makeup of a baby is a surprise. Sometimes adoptive parents don't realize how much they wanted a child of a particular gender until faced with the possibility of adopting a child of the opposite gender. In most cases, birth mothers who plan during their pregnancies to place their children for adoption proceed with those plans, and adoptive parents are willing to adopt even children who pose more challenges for them than they imagined themselves capable of handling.

Difficult Birth, Birth Defects, Death of a Baby

Most parents-to-be, unless medical tests have revealed abnormalities in the fetus, expect an uncomplicated birth of a healthy child. Sometimes, however, births are complicated—even life-threatening for the child or the mother. Sometimes a child is born with defects or is vulnerable due to prematurity, prenatal drug or alcohol exposure, or disease. Sometimes a baby is stillborn or dies at birth.

Often when people experience a traumatic event together, such as a natural disaster, they feel closer to each other. When a birth mother experiences a difficult birth—not just a long labor but a situation in which the baby's life or the mother's life is in jeopardy—she may find it more difficult to separate from the child. She has risked her life for this child and worked to save its life. If she does place the child for adoption, she may become pregnant again soon to fill up the emptiness caused by the loss of this child. It is essential that she work with a counselor on her feelings about this experience.

One birth mother experienced a serious uterine infection following the birth. As the birth mother's doctor pondered whether a hysterectomy would be necessary, the adoptive mother considered what her moral and ethical response should be if a hysterectomy proved necessary. The adoptive mother knew that the birth mother was not ready for children at this time in her life and the loss of her reproductive function might not have the impact that it would later. Being infertile herself, the adoptive mother wondered if she should offer to return the child. Fortunately, the birth mother recovered without surgery.

If the baby is born prematurely or with a medical condition that puts the child at risk, the birth mother may also have difficulty separating from the child. She may feel a greater urge to protect a vulnerable baby than she would a child whose physical condition is normal. The birth mother may feel she is abandoning her child if she leaves the hospital before he does. She may not be sure if the adoptive parents are willing to take the responsibility for a child with medical needs, or may feel that she can't ask them to. She may feel the child's condition is a punishment meant for her or a sign that she is to keep the baby. The same is true when the baby is born with birth defects—these can range from mild and treatable to serious. The birth mother, who may already feel guilt or shame for placing a child for adoption, may feel even greater societal disapproval if she doesn't raise this child, particularly if the adoptive parents' willingness to adopt a child with congenital abnormalities is in question.

Some birth mothers believe they owe the adoptive parents a healthy child. Even if the adoptive parents adopt the child with birth defects, the birth mother may get pregnant again soon to fulfill what she believes was her promise to the adoptive parents. Parents who give birth to a child with defects may also want to prove they are capable of producing a healthy child. In addition to consulting with a counselor about their feelings surrounding the birth of the child, the birth parents should consult with a geneticist so that they have information about the likelihood of future children having similar birth defects.

Adoptive parents will need to reevaluate their decision to adopt a child with birth defects or a serious medical condition, including a child at risk for AIDS (autoimmune deficiency syndrcme). Some parents may not be able to afford the medical care the child will require, especially if they have health insurance that gives the insurance company the option of rejecting coverage for a child being adopted. It is sometimes easier for parents to raise a child with birth defects if they aren't the biologic parents of the child because they do not feel guilty for the actions or the chromosomal anomalies that caused the medical condition. Nevertheless, some adoptive parents may not feel capable of dealing physically and emotionally with a medically challenged child.

When adoptive parents decide to adopt a child whose medical challenges were unexpected, people may question why they are proceeding with the adoption when they don't have to. They may not understand that some adoptive parents feel that the child the birth mother is carrying is theirs even before it is born and they are responding as they would if the child had been born to them. When a medically challenged child is adopted, the future that you have envisioned will be different. You may want to have another "vision matching" session with your counselor to discuss the ways your interactions with the child may be different. For example, a visit from the birth parents once a year may not seem adequate if the child's life expectancy is short. If the child is institutionalized, you may want to discuss the birth parents' rights to visit or take the child on outings.

Birth parents who feel guilty about the child's medical condition may be less likely to remain in contact with the adoptive family after the placement. Adoptive parents should be prepared for the relationship to be one-sided until the birth parents are able to work through their feelings about the child. But some adoptive parents may have difficulty maintaining a relationship with the birth parents if they are angry at them for not taking better care of themselves during the pregnancy or for not being honest about their drug or alcohol use during the pregnancy. They will need to work through their feelings.

Whenever a child is born with mental or physical abnormalities, parents experience the loss of the child they expected to have. Adoptive parents who decide against adopting a medically challenged child are sometimes criticized for wanting only perfect babies. As we've said before, it's hard to choose loss. Adoptive parents have a choice that birth parents do not always feel they have (although birth parents who would have raised a healthy child sometimes place a child with birth defects for adoption). No parent would choose for a child to be born with birth defects or mental disabilities, and adoptive parents cannot be faulted if they decide they do not want their child to have mental or physical problems.

Nevertheless, adoptive parents may feel guilty for deciding not to adopt a child with medical problems, knowing that if that child had been born to them, they would have taken on the medical problems. They may feel that they have abandoned the child and the birth mother at a time of great need. They should be encouraged to talk over the experience with a counselor. Birth parents need to be aware that there are families ready to adopt children with medical risks. Parents who have experienced medical challenges in their own families are often more willing than other parents to adopt such children because they have seen beyond the losses that medical challenges present to the joy and growth that is possible in those situations.

If new adoptive parents need to be found for the child, the adoption facilitator should help find them. Adoptive parents can ask to be involved in the process of finding new parents for the child, which lessens their feeling that they are abandoning the child or the birth parents. Like the birth father who questions his right to be involved in the adoption plan since he doesn't intend to marry the birth mother, adoptive parents may question whether it is appropriate for them to be involved in the selection of new adoptive parents. Although their right to participate is not on a par with a birth parent, they have been intimately involved with the plan for this child's future and it is fitting that they continue to be.

Adoption facilitators who do not know of families willing to accept children with medical challenges should contact the agency in their state that deals with child welfare and adoption and ask for assistance in finding parents for the child. The parents who originally planned to adopt the child should be informed about the outcome of the child's placement so that they, like the birth parents, can feel comfortable about the placement.

On rare occasions, a baby is born with a terminal medical condition. When this happens, the birth mother generally does not sign the adoption consent. The question of who is or will be the child's legal parent seems irrelevant. Nevertheless, because both the birth parents and adoptive parents may think of themselves as the child's parents, it is helpful to everyone if you make decisions about the child's care together. You will want to discuss who will make final decisions about the child's medical care and who will pay for it, who will stay with the baby in the hospital, and who will take home the baby's hospital bracelet and other mementos. However, because this is part of the birth experience, if there is disagreement that can't be worked out, the birth parents' wishes should prevail.

Just as you have planned for the future of the child together, it is helpful to jointly plan the funeral of a child who dies at birth or before leaving the hospital. All of you need to put to rest your dreams for this child and the future you had planned for him. In addition, you need to put an end to the adoption process together. The adoptive parents need to tell the birth parents that they don't owe them a child. This doesn't mean your relationship needs to end, and after going through so many critical situations together, you may want to stay connected, but it may be difficult, since seeing each other reminds you of the loss you shared.

While the death of a child is tragic to any parent, adoptive parents who have experienced so many losses are often shocked by this unexpected disappointment. The birth parents may have expected to lose their parental rights, but not their child, and they may not receive the kind of sympathy and support they need if others don't realize that they too had hopes and dreams for this child and those dreams have died. The birth parents may also feel guilty about the child's death. Many people facing an untimely pregnancy wish for a miscarriage. When the baby actually dies, they may believe their wish is responsible. Some birth parents may think that if they had taken better care of themselves during the pregnancy, the child would have lived. They may irrationally think the baby died because they planned an adoption. They need specific information about the baby's condition and the causes to relieve themselves of any undeserved sense of responsibility.

An Entrustment Ceremony

When the time comes for the baby to go home with the adoptive parents, it is essential that the transfer of parental roles from the birth parents to the adoptive parents be done formally through a placement or entrustment ceremony. In such a ceremony, the birth parents physically give the child to the adoptive parents, expressing their desire that the adoptive parents raise the child, and the adoptive parents accept the child and their responsibilities as parents.

From the exchange of wedding bands to the recitation of prayers for the dead, rituals mark transitions in family life and help families heal. They create change as well as create an awareness of change, provide a vehicle for people to express their feelings, define relationships, help arrive at solutions, and restore balance to lives that have been disrupted by change or crisis. For this reason, some experts believe rituals are essential for the mental health of families. Through prepared words, songs, scripture readings, or poems, rituals clarify change, and the participants' feelings about the change are expressed. Rituals are also ways for the community to witness change and provide emotional support.

In a wedding, for example, family members and friends of the bride and groom gather to witness the creation of a new family unit. There is sadness as everyone realizes the bride and groom will no longer be part of their families of origins in the same way that they have before, and this is symbolized by the "giving away" of the bride by her parents. The couple publicly recites their vows, and the community expresses support for this new relationship. People cry at weddings because rituals help bring emotions to the surface and give people permission to express them.

Rituals are needed in adoption because adoption creates new relationships and new family units. In open adoption, where the birth parents will remain involved with the child, the change of roles must be clearly understood by everyone. Furthermore, because adoption is often a bittersweet experience, rituals help people express their emotions and help them heal.

In adoption, the legal process ending the birth parents' parental roles happens separately from the process that makes the child a part of the adoptive family. Furthermore, the actual transfer of parental roles often happens months before the adoption is finalized, so it is important to create a ceremony that clearly defines the changes that are taking place in both the birth and the adoptive families. After an entrustment ceremony, there is no doubt that the birth parents intend to have these particular adoptive parents raise their child. Birth parents can feel that this part of their experience has ended and they are able to proceed with the process of healing. Adoptive parents can assume their parenting role with confidence.

Families need to create the entrustment ceremony that meets their needs and suits their style, and it is wise for the birth and adoptive parents to plan the ritual together so that the experience can be meaningful to everyone. However, we can give you some guidelines based on entrustment ceremonies we have learned about.

The entrustment ceremony should take place before the adoptive parents take the child home. For this reason, many are held in the hospital, often in the hospital chapel. But because some birth mothers want to take their babies home for a short time, or because they consider the hospital too impersonal, entrustment ceremonies are also held in the home of a birth relative, the adoptive parents, a church, synagogue, or park. The family of a child born in November combined an entrustment ceremony with their Thanksgiving celebration. Each year the birth and adoptive families celebrate that holiday together. Often a minister or rabbi leads the service at an entrustment ceremony, but this role can also be played by a family member, a close friend, or by the birth and adoptive parents themselves.

The ceremony might begin with an opening statement of its purpose, along with a song, prayer, or reading. The birth parents would then make a statement expressing their feelings. This could include their hopes for their child, their reasons for the placement, their reasons for choosing the adoptive couple, and how they see their ongoing role in the child's life. Other birth relatives could also speak. Their feelings can be expanded upon through songs, prayers, poems, reading, or scripture verse. At some point, the birth parents hand the child to the adoptive parents, clearly stating their wish that the adoptive parents raise their child. The adoptive parents accept the child, and make a statement expressing their feelings and defining their roles. This could include their hopes for their child, their promise to stay in contact with the birth parents, and their commitment to do their best as parents. Again, their statements can be expanded upon by other adoptive relatives or through songs or readings. Other children in the birth and adoptive families can participate in the ritual. The naming of the child could also be part of the entrustment ceremony.

As you plan the ceremony, select symbols that are meaningful. Perhaps you want to plant a tree together to signify your joint effort in bringing forth and raising new life. You may want to include symbols of your reli-

gious or ethnic heritage. There are many books that can help you plan rituals. These are listed in the Resources section at the end of this book. This
is also a time when gifts between the birth and adoptive parents can be
exchanged.

Leaving the Hospital

An entrustment ceremony avoids problems that sometimes develop when
it is time for the baby and birth mother to leave the hospital. Some hospitals will not release the infant to the adoptive parents. As a result, birth
parents have left the hospital with their babies and have handed them over
to the adoptive parents in the hospital parking lot. This often leaves birth
and adoptive parents with hollow memories or feeling that they have done
something shameful. Even when the hospital allows the child to be
released to the adoptive parents, they may feel as if they have stolen the
baby or that this important occasion was treated rather unceremoniously.
Birth parents may feel abandoned and empty.

A birth mother who leaves before the child may feel that she's abandoning the child. Adoptive parents who leave with the baby before the birth
mother sometimes feel that they are speeding away in a getaway car. If an
entrustment ceremony is held prior to leaving the hospital, the adoptive
parents are less likely to feel that they have abducted the child, and the
birth mother is less likely to feel that she has been forgotten.

If the birth mother leaves the hospital without the baby, the adoptive
parents should make sure she does not leave empty-handed. Although
flowers, a stuffed animal, or a basket of treats can in no way make up for
the baby she is not taking home, her arms at least will not feel empty.

It is often considered a thoughtful gesture for the adoptive parents to
call the birth mother as soon as they have arrived home to let her know
they have arrived safely. All the fears that the birth mother has that she
will never see her child again, despite the reassurances of the adoptive parents, are unleashed as she says good-bye to her child. A simple phone call
lets the birth mother know that the adoptive parents not only care about
her but plan to stay in touch. This can be tremendously reassuring during
the emotionally difficult time after placement.

7

Making an Adoption Plan After the Baby's Birth

Maria was sure that if her father and brother learned that she was pregnant they would kill her boyfriend. She decided to hide her pregnancy from them and place the baby for adoption. All her energy was spent keeping her family from finding out about the pregnancy. Because she was small and wore loose clothing, she was successful. But her need for secrecy kept her from getting prenatal care or arranging for the adoption. A few weeks before she thought the baby was due, Maria went to visit her sister, who understood Maria's need for secrecy. At the hospital, Maria had the nurse call an adoption agency to arrange for the baby's placement. She exchanges letters with the adoptive parents through her sister.

The idea of placing her child for adoption had never entered Paula's mind. After all, she was married and had two children at home. But two weeks after her baby was born, Paula's husband left her. With no income and two preschoolers at home, Paula felt overwhelmed. When her four-year-old son nearly had a serious accident because she was sleeping after a hard night with the baby, Paula realized she could not adequately care for all her children. She called the county office of social services and asked them to find adoptive parents for her baby. But because the baby had lived with her for nearly a month, and because her two sons knew about the baby, Paula insisted that the adoptive parents be willing to stay in direct contact with her and her sons.

Not all adoption plans are carefully considered prior to the baby's arrival. One adoption attorney estimates that in as many as one-third of all independent (nonagency) placements, the first contact between the birth mother and the adoption facilitator is made at the hospital. While those figures may not hold true for every facilitator, it is not unusual for birth parents to give adoption serious consideration only after the birth.

A decision at the hospital may not be as sudden as it appears. The birth parents may have been in contact with an adoption facilitator or adoptive parents only to decide at the last minute that they aren't happy and want to change. Perhaps, as the birth approaches, the birth mother realizes that these are not the adoptive parents she wants, or she does not believe the adoption facilitator is meeting her needs. This is one of the most important decisions she will ever have to make and she needs to be able to trust the people she is working with and feel confident about the outcome.

In one situation that is not unusual, a birth mother who had planned a confidential adoption decided shortly before the baby was due that she wanted to stay in contact with the adoptive family. The adoptive parents refused, and the birth mother returned to her home state to deliver the baby. At the hospital, she called an adoption agency and asked for adoptive parents who would agree to an open adoption. Their relationship was difficult for the first few years because they hadn't had much opportunity to get to know each other or reconcile their expectations before the placement was made, but they continue to work at maintaining their relationship.

Some birth parents do change facilitators or adoptive parents capriciously. Perhaps the relationship has run into conflict and the birth parents' way of dealing with conflict is to run away rather than confront. Perhaps the birth mother became angry at the adoptive parents or the facilitator, or she likes exercising the power she has as someone who can control the future of adoptive parents—especially if she hasn't had much control in her life already. If the birth mother is impulsively changing facilitators or adoptive parents, one option for the new facilitator who is called in at the hospital is to help the birth mother assess the benefits of reestablishing contact with the people she has worked with before, who better understand her needs and with whom she has already begun a relationship.

It's important for birth parents to realize that the more they get to know someone, the more flaws they will see in that person. Adoptive parents chosen at the hospital may look ideal compared to those the birth parents have been working with for months because they have not had enough time to get to know the new parents and discover their faults. However, no one is without weaknesses, and the birth parents must decide which imperfections they are willing to accept in adoptive parents.

Sometimes a birth mother's decision at the hospital to place her child for adoption is a sudden one. She may deny that the pregnancy poses a dilemma for her until the baby arrives, or she may not have made arrangements for an adoption because she is trying to keep the pregnancy a secret. She may be ashamed or be afraid of the reaction of her parents, the birth father, and others to the pregnancy. The birth parents may come from a cultural group that looks with disfavor on adoption, or the child may have been conceived through rape, date rape, or incest. The birth mother's family may allow themselves to be deceived because they don't want to face the ramifications of an untimely pregnancy, either.

When they learn they are pregnant, these birth mothers often react by saying to themselves, "I can't keep this baby. I'll place it for adoption." That, to them, is a plan. To explore that plan further is so emotionally painful that they do not contact an adoption facilitator until after the baby's birth. As a result, some of them may not have thought through the full implications of adoption or of how their plan might work. Fawn was able to conceal her pregnancy from her family for the full nine months. Only her boyfriend knew the truth. When the time came to deliver the baby, Fawn set up an argument with her parents and ran away. Her boyfriend called her parents to say she was well, but would be staying with him for a while. After giving birth to the baby and placing her for adoption, the boyfriend called Fawn's parents to say she was ready to come home. Her family supposedly never knew about her pregnancy.

Risks in Last-Minute Adoptions

It is difficult, though not impossible, for an open adoption to succeed when made in haste. We've emphasized throughout this book the importance of thorough preparation for the success of an open adoption relationship: both the birth parents and the adoptive parents must understand the transfer of parental roles, understand each other's concerns, and respect each other's boundaries. The major risk in last-minute adoptions is that the birth and adoptive parents have not been adequately prepared for adoption or for the open adoption relationship.

The birth mother who has not been educated about open adoption may mistakenly think that she is relinquishing the responsibilities of parenting, but not the privileges. She may think of the placement as being more like foster care. Or, she may indicate she doesn't want to remain in contact with the adoptive family because she mistakenly thinks that she will be able to forget this experience. She may also be unprepared for the feelings she will have at the time of placement. If she has been denying the pregnancy, she may not be ready for the love she'll feel for the child or the pain at being separated.

If the hospital does not call a reputable adoption facilitator, but relies instead on the personal knowledge of members of the hospital staff to find adoptive parents, the adoptive parents may not be emotionally ready to adopt. They may still be grieving their infertility and may not be aware of the importance of moving past that loss before they can fully love a child born to other parents. Adoptive parents who have not had much preadoption counseling may also have concerns about open adoption that have not been addressed and consequently may be fearful of the birth parents or uncertain about their own entitlement to parent. If she has not received adequate preparation, the birth mother may not ask for what she needs in the way of openness up front, but may later want more than she asked for. The adoptive parents may not be willing to accommodate her changing needs because some of their unresolved issues have interfered with the open relationship.

Because they have not had time to get to know each other, both the birth parents and the adoptive parents may have reservations about the other's trustworthiness. Birth mothers who have not developed a trusting relationship with a counselor or with adoptive parents may react to the pain of their loss by reclaiming the baby. Moreover, if the birth mother is choosing adoption to keep the baby's existence hidden, the secrecy becomes a condition for the placement. When she begins to hurt after the placement, she may confide in people as a way to alleviate her pain and may find that she gets the support she needs. There becomes no need for the placement, so she decides to reclaim. (Birth parents who reclaim after placement are discussed in Chapter 14.)

In a last-minute placement, there is also less possibility of obtaining a reliable medical history from the birth parents. The birth mother who has been denying her pregnancy or keeping it a secret may not have received good prenatal care and may have been careless enough about the pregnancy to have abused drugs or alcohol. There's also a risk that the birth father has not been notified of the pregnancy, and once he finds out, would object to the adoption plan.

Sometimes an adoption facilitator will make the mistake of selecting adoptive parents who have recently had an adoption fall through. The facilitator wants to alleviate the pain the adoptive parents are feeling by replacing the child they expected to parent with the child who has just become available for adoption. Although these intentions are good, adoptive parents who have not grieved for their recent loss may not be emotionally available to their new child.

If the birth mother made a last-minute decision out of impulsiveness, inability to maintain relationships, or because she was running away from confrontation, adoptive parents should expect that her style of interacting with people will continue in their open adoption relationship. The birth mother may act impulsively again by reclaiming the child, or she may prove to be a difficult person to have a relationship with: she could become unavailable for long periods of time, either because she is running away from the open adoption relationship or because she is running away from something else in her life.

Liza, a single woman who had given up hope of adopting an infant, agreed to adopt a baby born to Ariana, a birth mother with a history of mental illness who made a last-minute adoption decision. Despite many middle-of-the-night phone calls from Ariana and outrageous demands for money, Liza has managed to maintain the open relationship. To do so, though, she has had to establish strict boundaries—she has an unlisted phone number and Ariana must contact her through her attorney. They only meet under supervision.

Generally, open relationships succeed in last-minute placements when the adoptive parents are highly flexible, have been well educated about open adoption, and actively pursue a relationship with the birth parents. Many draw on the confidence they have gained in other open adoption relationships. The best adoptive parents for a hospital placement tend to be those whose attitudes strongly match those listed in Chapter 3, those who are highly compassionate and comfortable with loose arrangements, who are good at managing risk, as well as those who have faith in themselves and in a higher power.

Making the Adoption Plan at the Hospital

Birth mothers who have not made careful plans prior to the baby's birth often allow other people to manage the plan after the birth, such as a hospital staff member or a facilitator called by the hospital. However, the birth mother who decides at the hospital to place her child for adoption should take as much care in selecting a facilitator as any birth mother would (see Chapter 3). She can ask the hospital social worker, physician, or nurse for recommendations; check in the telephone book; or call a pregnancy counseling center for references. After talking to them on the telephone, she can invite those who seem to be able to meet her needs to the hospital for further assessment. She will want to ask them:

▪ What kind of counseling and preparation will they be able to provide for her both prior to the placement and after the placement? It's important to find a facilitator who realizes the education process normally used to prepare birth parents will have to be intensified, who has experience with last-minute placements, and who has staff available to provide the nearly round-the-clock work that will need to be done to facilitate this placement.

▪ How will the birth mother select the adoptive parents? Some adoption facilitators do not encourage the birth mother to select the adoptive parents in the hospital. They believe the birth mother needs to understand the adoption process, the issues in adoption, the feelings that generally accompany placement, and the realities of open adoption before deciding on adoptive parents. They recommend placing the child in foster care while the birth mother becomes more aware of what she is undertaking and has a chance to feel sure about her decision. Other facilitators vary in their approach: some will bring resumes or introductory packets of prospective adoptive parents to the hospital and encourage the birth mother to begin the selection process; some will bring a large number of resumes, whereas others will screen the applicants in their files for those willing to accept the risks of this type of placement; and some will simply present one adoptive applicant to the birth mother based on any preferences she may have stated. However, the fact that this is a last-minute placement does not alter the birth mother's need to feel in control of her decision and to place her child with people whom she feels will make the best parents. She has the right to interview as many prospective adoptive parents as she needs to before making a decision. The birth parents and the selected family should spend as much time as possible together to get to know each other and decide if they want to be involved with each other.

▪ Where will the baby be during this preparation and selection time? The baby may be able to stay in the hospital longer than usual while the birth mother makes her plans, or go into foster care, or go home with the birth mother while she makes her plans, or go home with a friend or family member. By placing the baby in foster care, the birth mother can slow down the process and reflect on her decision. However, the added move from one caretaker to another when a child is placed in foster care also puts an additional stress on the child at a vulnerable time. The birth mother who takes the baby home when she is not emotionally committed to parenting may not be able to meet the child's needs. The baby can also go home with the prospective adoptive parents, but, of course, it's very important that they understand the emotional risks of becoming attached to the baby before the birth mother has made her decision.

Adoptive parents who are asked to consider a last-minute placement should be honest with themselves about the risks such placements pose and assess whether they are able to take those risks. Under the best of circumstances they will have a chance to get to know the birth parents and their extended families and will have an opportunity to share their visions of the child's future and their future relationship. However, most of the time when the birth mother contacts an adoption facilitator at the hospital, there is little opportunity for her and the adoptive parents to get to know each other before they must decide whether to proceed with this placement or not—perhaps less than two hours. This is why it is so important for the adoptive parents to be flexible, compassionate people who can live with a wide range of possibilities.

If you have only limited contact with each other, lay the groundwork for your future relationship and try to get to the heart of issues of concern to you, perhaps through a more compressed "vision matching" session than those described in Chapters 4 and 5. Exchange as much information as you can, take a lot of pictures, and establish a mechanism for staying in touch with each other. Adoptive parents can also write out the kind and frequency of contact they are willing to offer, so that the birth parents can review it later and get in touch with them if they change their minds.

Pay attention to the impressions of other people about each other, especially the advice you are being given by your adoption facilitator or counselor. You may be so anxious to have this placement succeed—because it is so imminent—that you ignore signs for caution that you might pay more attention to in another situation. Listen to your instincts and feel free to say no to this placement if you are uncomfortable with each other— even if you can't articulate what is making you uncomfortable.

Sandy and David, an adoptive couple, met Allison, a birth mother, at the hospital. Sandy and David were pleased with what Allison told them about her history and her reasons for choosing adoption. Together they picked a name for the baby boy. Sandy and David offered to pay for individual and joint counseling and set up some sessions where the counselor could help them match their expectations. But within the first two weeks of the placement, Allison had canceled or failed to show up for several appointments, then called on short notice for visits with the baby. Sandy and David later learned that what Allison said to them about the birth father and her reasons for making an adoption plan were inconsistent with what she said to other people. They found out that she had a character disorder that rendered her capable of telling people exactly what they wanted to hear, convincing them of her sincerity.

Sandy and David, who already had two children in open adoptions, were more than willing to enter into an open relationship with Allison. However, they worried that she would never sign the consent to the adoption, but would use her power to manipulate them. They decided they could not risk becoming emotionally attached to the child any further with the prospect of finalizing the adoption at such risk, especially with other children in the home. They called Allison and their social worker to ask for a meeting and told them of their decision, adding that if the baby ever became legally available for adoption, they would want to be considered as the adoptive parents. Allison attempted to talk them out of their decision, saying exactly what she thought Sandy and David wanted to hear. Torn between what their hearts wanted and their heads were telling them, Sandy and David called their counselor to have him remind them once again that Allison's ability to convince people of her sincerity was a sign of her character disorder and that she could not be trusted. With that assistance, they reiterated their decision not to continue with the placement until the baby was legally available for adoption.

The baby was placed in foster care and Sandy and David kept in touch with his social worker. As they had suspected, Allison never signed a consent to the adoption, and each time a court date was set to involuntarily terminate her rights, she would successfully intervene. After the baby was in foster care for six months, he was placed with birth relatives.

Sandy and David grieved for more than a year for the loss of the baby they had considered their own for two weeks. But they never regretted their decision, believing that to have kept the baby longer and not been able to adopt him would have caused them even greater heartbreak.

One open adoption began with a call from the hospital to an adoption attorney. Doretta was a single thirty-five-year-old woman with a seven-year-old son. She had delivered a baby and wanted to place him for adoption. No one in her family knew about the pregnancy. The attorney suggested Ed and Kim, a couple with another child in an open adoption. Although Doretta indicated she did not want to stay in contact, Ed and Kim kept in touch, and reminded Doretta that her older son was aware of the pregnancy and had questions that needed to be addressed. They also reminded her that she could not expect her son to keep this secret for her. Doretta gradually allowed the adoptive parents to draw her into a relationship, primarily for the sake of her son. But the benefits have been realized by all.

Making a Plan Later

It is not unusual for a birth mother who is planning an adoption to want to take the baby home with her for a night or even a few days before placing the child with adoptive parents. As we discuss in Chapter 6, some birth mothers take more time than others to say good-bye to their child.

Occasionally, though, a birth mother will take her baby home with the intention of raising him only to make an adoption plan after a few weeks or even a few months. (We discuss the placement of children older than one year in Chapter 15.) Sometimes the birth mother discovers that the task is more than she is capable of at that time in her life. Perhaps she had underestimated the needs of a baby or her own ability to meet those needs, or she expected she would have more help. Often the placement of a child less than a year of age occurs because the birth mother's relationship with the birth father has fallen apart, or because the birth of the child did not cement the relationship between the birth parents in the way the birth mother had hoped it would.

Unfortunately, people are often highly critical of a birth mother who places a child for adoption after she has taken the baby home. People mistakenly assume that the birth mother is making an adoption plan because she was not able to bond or form an attachment. They don't realize that birth mothers make adoption plans *despite* the attachment they feel to the child. Birth mothers who place under these circumstances need a great deal of support, due to both the increased anguish they will feel, and the sad fact that their decision may be even less supported by their friends, family members, and society.

Rena, a birth mother, lived in shelters for the homeless for three months after the birth of her child before contacting an adoption agency. Because the shelter would not let her return without the child, Jeff and Suzanne, the adoptive parents, allowed her to move in with them while they got to know each other. Shortly after she signed the consent to adoption, she disappeared and has not been heard from since. Jeff and Suzanne feel like they were left with a child after a whirlwind romance. They treasure the time they spent with Rena, and hope to see her again, but they know that she is not a person who maintains connections.

Of course, many birth mothers who have had their children with them for a while before making plans for adoption do want direct contact with their children. They have begun to form attachments and can't imagine never seeing them again or not knowing their whereabouts. And when there are other children in the family, birth parents feel an even greater obligation to maintain the sibling ties that had begun to grow. (For more about explaining adoption to siblings, see Chapter 13.)

Adoptive parents who are interested in having a fully disclosed adoption with a great deal of contact are often the best choice for a child who has spent time with his birth mother. They should also be aware that there may be many members of the extended birth family who will also want to have contact.

Making the Transition

Although it would seem that birth parents who decide to place after taking the baby home could take more time to select adoptive parents than birth parents who decide on adoption at the hospital, in practice, once birth parents decide on adoption they begin to distance themselves emotionally from the child. Consequently, once the birth parents decide on adoption, the placement should proceed as expediently as possible. In some cases, the child may need to be placed in foster care until adoptive parents can be selected.

Don't underestimate how much even a young baby will sense about a change in environment and caretakers. Although he doesn't have the mental ability to know what is happening, he will sense a change in sights, smells, sounds, and routine. Some babies adapt quickly to such changes, but others take much longer. Psychiatrist Justin Call, M.D., believes children four to twelve weeks of age and older than six months have the most difficulty adapting to changes in environment. Children younger than one month are not as aware of their surroundings as older infants. Those children three to six months old are more adaptive to change than those one to three months of age, who notice change but are not well developed enough neurologically to adapt to changes in environment. Those children older than six months have developed a strong attachment to their caretakers, and particularly from six to twelve months of age, they are fearful of strangers.

The fewer changes the child's senses are asked to absorb, the smoother the transition will be. The birth or foster parents should not only explain the child's schedule and the ways she is used to being fed, bathed, held, and otherwise cared for but they should show the adoptive parents. Eventually, the birth or foster parents should hand the child directly to the adoptive parents to complete a feeding, diapering, or bathing, for example. This gives the adoptive parents direct permission to assume parental responsibilities, and increases their sense of entitlement. It also communicates to the child that it is all right for her to accept such care. Adoptive parents should pay attention to the sights, sounds, and smells the child is used to and replicate them as much as possible by using the same perfume and laundry detergent as the birth parents, selecting the same brands of baby food, and even playing the same kind of music if the child seems to respond positively to it.

The transition will also be easier for the child if she is called by the same name that the birth parents used. If it is necessary to make a change, perhaps because there is another child in the same family with that name or because the adoptive parents simply cannot live with the name chosen by the birth parents, they can gradually introduce that name after the child's initial transition is complete. For example, if the birth parents called the child "Kevin," the adoptive parents could use that name for several months, then begin calling the boy "Kevin Joshua," then gradually drop the original name and call the boy "Joshua."

Adoptive parents who can be flexible enough to replicate the sights, sounds, and routine to which the child is accustomed will make this traumatic change much easier for the child, and ultimately the child's welfare is what matters. And as the child settles into her new home and becomes comfortable with the adoptive parents as her caretakers, they can gradually make changes consistent with their style of parenting and beliefs about infant care.

part four

The Relationship Grows and Changes

8

The First Year
After Placement

Adoptive parents Ken and Hattie developed a trusting rela-
tionship with Magdalena during her pregnancy, and were com-
fortable planning a life that would include her. During the first
month after the placement, Magdalena would drop by without
notice to pick up the baby and take her to visit relatives. Hattie
had no doubts that Magdalena was committed to the adoption
plan, and she knew Magdalena's actions were consistent with
the way she had been raised. Nevertheless, she found herself
unable to settle in as a mother with Magdalena popping in
unexpectedly to take the baby. Magdalena became angry when
Hattie began asking her to call before coming over. She thought
this was an indication that Hattie didn't trust her, and she was
hurt that after building a strong relationship with Ken and
Hattie during her pregnancy and giving them her child, that
they would still have doubts about her. The baby is now eight
years old, and Ken, Hattie, and Magdalena continue to have
a close relationship. But the first month after the baby's place-
ment was rocky as everyone sorted out the rules and their roles
in an atmosphere of high emotion.

Their experience was not unusual. The first year after a
child is placed in an open adoption is a particularly vulnerable time for
everyone involved, and the first month is often the most difficult. No
matter how well prepared you have been for the child's placement, the
reality is always different than you expected.

Making the Transition

After the placement, the adoptive parents take on their roles as the parents of the child and the birth parents confront the loss of their parenting roles. The adoptive parents assume their roles by claiming their child as a member of the family, and by accepting that they are entitled to be his parents. All this promotes the feeling that they are inseparable from each other—the feeling that some people call bonding, but is more accurately known as attachment.

Adoptive parents are often in a state of disbelief when they finally take home their child. After all the uncertainty and waiting, they are now parents. One couple said they took turns holding the baby and rocking her. The desire each of them had to be close to the baby was so great they had to set a timer to signal when their turns were up. Like all new parents, adoptive parents typically check on the child several times during the night to make sure the child is still breathing. But the irrational fear new parents have of losing their precious child can be greater for adoptive parents if the birth mother is still able to reclaim the child or if they still fear the birth mother will abduct him.

Some adoptive parents, however, feel more distant from their new child. He just doesn't seem like *their* child. They did not give birth to him and are reminded of this when the birth parents write, call, or visit. The adoptive parents sometimes feel they are babysitting for the first few weeks or even months. A few adoptive parents may even experience something similar to postpartum depression or postpartum blues. Though not triggered by hormones as it is in a birth mother, postadoption blues may develop in adoptive parents who have built up the experience of becoming parents to the extent that they thought adoption would be the answer to all their unhappiness. When they discover that life, with its ups and downs, goes on even after adoption, that children are often demanding, and that they question whether they have the patience, energy, or ability to do the job they have been trying to do for so long, they may feel discouraged or even depressed. Working mothers who stay home may miss their jobs and feel guilty that they want more than motherhood. The old fear that infertility was a sign that they shouldn't be parents may reemerge at this time. These adoptive parents are grieving for their loss of expectations as well as the loss of their more familiar, if less desired, lifestyle.

Sometimes adoptive parents are jealous of the birth parents because it seems that they, like grandparents, get to enjoy the child without doing the work. One adoptive mother, who was exhausted caring for twin infants, said she envied the fact that the birth mother didn't have the burdens of two young children. Of course, she didn't want to change places with the birth mother. But she was experiencing the loss of freedom that a child brings. Her sadness as she looked at someone without her responsibilities was a natural part of her transition from childlessness to motherhood.

The corresponding change of roles the adults experience is not immediate. Not everyone moves in tandem during this adjustment period—something that makes the transition easier for one person might make it more difficult for the other parents. For example, the adoptive mother may assume her role as "mother" faster than the birth mother lets it go. But one of the unique aspects of open adoption is that you observe this change of roles, which can aid you in making your own transition. For instance, the birth mother may find herself more able to let go of her role as parent as she sees how capable the adoptive mother is and how easily the child responds to her.

Of course, different time frames for adjusting to new circumstances can also lead to awkward moments or conflict, and you may find that you have to renegotiate the amount or type of contact you will have with each other, or the rules surrounding that contact. Furthermore, although it may seem like the child comes into existence at the moment of birth, he has spent at least nine months with his birth mother. It may be that long or longer before his transition from the birth family to the adoptive family is complete.

During the transition, your relationship will also undergo a change. It's almost as though a new relationship forms. Trust has to build again, because you are now interacting under a new set of circumstances. Katya returned to her home town several thousand miles from the adoptive parents' home after the birth of her child. One month after the placement, she was presented with legal documents to sign that would terminate her parental rights. Katya indicated that she was willing to sign the papers because the adoptive parents had agreed to an open adoption. Her social worker, who had not been involved in the placement, reminded Katya that the adoptive parents were under no legal obligation to maintain their agreement. Was she willing to sign the papers even though there was a chance she'd never see her child again? When the situation was presented in that way, Katya had to give her decision more thought.

When they were told that Katya wanted more time, the adoptive parents worried that she was backing out of the agreement. Katya's trustworthiness

in doubt, the adoptive parents became less open with her, which she interpreted as a sign that they did indeed plan to cut her off completely once
she signed papers. Eventually, the three of them discovered the source of
the problem and proceeded with the adoption as planned. Though their
relationship was severely tested by the experience, they have struggled to
maintain openness.

Claiming the Child

Adoptive parents first claim their child as a member of their family by caring for his physical and emotional needs as though the child had been
born to them. As they get to know their child, they begin to see similarities
between themselves and the child. Sometimes these are physical similarities—adoptive parents might remark that their child looks just like the
adoptive father or mother. Others may notice that both the child and the
parents have blue eyes or dark hair. Sometimes the child's temperament,
personality, or preferences are similar to the adoptive parents'. When the
adoptive grandmother comments that the adoptive father cried every three
hours for the first two weeks after he came home from the hospital, just
like the new baby is doing, that is a way of saying that the baby belongs in
the family because her behavior is consistent with family behavior.
Sometimes the similarities between a child and his adoptive parents are
coincidental. Sometimes they are due to the birth parents' deliberate effort
to choose adoptive parents who look and act like themselves.

In an open adoption, the birth family may also make claiming statements, or the similarities between the child and the birth parents may be
obvious. One adoptive mother said every time the birth grandparents
would visit the baby they would comment on how much the child looked
like his birth mother. This offended the adoptive mother who interpreted
those comments as impeding her ability to claim the child as a member of
her family. The birth family may need to make such statements to remind
themselves why they are making an effort to stay connected to this child.
However, they don't have to make the comments within earshot of the
adoptive parents. And adoptive parents have to remember that the child
will have similarities to both families. The adoptive parent can say, for
example, "You got your blue eyes from your birth mother, but isn't it neat
that they match my eyes, too."

Although initially it may be hard for the adoptive parents to hear these kinds of statements, being reminded that their children have qualities from the birth family helps adoptive parents recognize the unique person that their child is. And there is no greater gift than for someone to be loved as the individual he is.

NAMING RIGHTS

When the child receives the family name as his last name, it is a clear way of saying that he belongs in that family. But even the conferring of the first name on the child symbolizes the authority of the parents over the child. As we see in Chapter 6, this can cause conflict between the adoptive and the birth parents if they both want to give the child the name by which he will be known.

In one adoption, the birth mother and the adoptive mother used different names for the baby for the first month. Josie, the birth mother, was not ready to let go of the child, and she communicated this by not letting go of the name she had selected. Of course, Bridget, the adoptive mother, wanted to claim the child using the name she had selected. Josie was eventually able to call the child by the name Bridget had selected, but in the meantime, Bridget's sense that she was the child's mother was undermined by Josie's inability to give her full parental authority.

Another adoptive mother was upset because the birth mother referred to the child in her correspondence by the name she had chosen, putting the name the adoptive parents had chosen in parentheses. The adoptive mother was patient, and eventually the birth mother began using the name the adoptive parents had chosen.

Of course, it's best to work out this conflict prior to the placement, but not everyone has this opportunity. Sometimes it is more difficult to execute a plan than to make one. And sometimes plans don't work out the way you intend. In one family, the adoptive and birth parents carefully negotiated before jointly choosing the baby's name. But by the time the baby was six months old, he had acquired a nickname that stuck. The birth mother was angry. She felt betrayed. But it wasn't the adoptive parents' intention to abandon the name they had chosen with the birth mother; it just happened as they interacted with him and learned more about his personality. And as the birth mother got to know the baby better, she agreed that the nickname suited him.

Regardless of expectations or plans prior to the placement, the child should be called by the name the adoptive parents ultimately confer upon him. It is their right to claim the child in this way, even if the manner in which they do so violates an agreement between the adoptive and birth parents. When members of the birth family use the name selected by the adoptive parents, they validate the child's membership in the adoptive family. Furthermore, it is important for the child to be referred to in a consistent manner. A very young child will be confused if some people call him by one name and others call him by another. Birth parents may be angry if they feel the adoptive parents have reneged on an agreement they made regarding the child's name, but they must still respect the adoptive parents' wishes.

WELCOMING CELEBRATIONS

Welcoming celebrations, such as baby showers, christenings, and naming ceremonies, also are ways of claiming a child as a member of a family, a social community, or a religious group. For this reason, some adoptive parents are anxious to have such ceremonies whereas others feel that significant claiming ceremonies, such as a baptism or conversion to Judaism, should not be done until the adoption is finalized. Other claiming rituals include sending birth or adoption announcements, getting baby photographs or family photographs taken, and passing out cigars or pencils saying "It's a boy" or "It's a girl."

Attachment

Claiming by itself is not attachment. You can look at a photograph of a nephew you have never met and note the family resemblance while not feeling emotionally attached to the child. As we note in Chapter 2, attachment develops as the child learns he can depend on certain adults to meet his needs, and the adults find themselves willing to sacrifice themselves for the child. Attachment forms quickly between some parents and children and it takes longer for others. Parents who have made an emotional commitment to sacrificing themselves for a child only to have that child reclaimed by his birth mother may be reluctant to make that emotional commitment so quickly the next time. They may meet the child's physical needs but may hold back emotionally for a little while (see Chapter 14).

Parents who are having difficulty claiming the child as a member of their family may not be able to make a commitment to sacrificing themselves for the child until they see him as belonging in their family. Although many adoptive parents feel an instant love for their child, not all do, just as parents who give birth do not always form an attachment to their child instantly. Eventually, however, parents who are reasonably healthy emotionally will be unable to resist the emotional pull of the child and will proceed to develop attachment.

Children who have been exposed to cocaine in utero are easily over-stimulated, sometimes making it difficult for parents to hold them or make eye contact with them for long. In addition, because they have difficulty expressing their needs or distinguishing between discomfort and relief, it can be hard for them to identify their parents as a source of comfort. Parents will want to seek professional advice for information on how to meet the emotional and physical needs of a child with prenatal drug exposure. (See the Resources section at the end of this book.) Children who are born blind or deaf also need special attention to attachment issues, since parents cannot use methods such as eye contact or comforting sounds to soothe or reassure their child.

As attachment builds, adoptive parents may resent the fact that the birth parents gave birth to the child and have a connection to the child that they can never have—a common genetic background, and time together prior to placement. This is a loss to them, and the sadness and anger they experience as a result is part of grieving for those losses. Parents who adopt children who were exposed to drugs or alcohol prior to birth, who were abused, or who they believe could have received better care prior to placement may feel a particularly poignant sense of loss that they were unable to protect their children. They may be angry that the birth parents didn't take their responsibility more seriously.

Entitlement

While adoptive parents generally have no difficulty claiming a child as a member of their family or forming an attachment to him, they sometimes have trouble developing a sense of entitlement. Entitlement is the belief that parents have the authority not only to *act* as the baby's parents but to *be* the baby's parents. Infertility sometimes leaves a couple believing they weren't meant to be parents. In addition, adoptive parents may question whether they have the right given that the child was born to another mother and father and that they needed to convince so many people—from the birth mother to the courts—to allow them to raise this child.

Prior to the finalization of the adoption, the authority to act as a parent is not absolute: the birth mother may be able to reclaim the child, and the social worker's ongoing assessment of the placement leads adoptive parents to feel that their child could be taken away. Although this rarely happens, adoptive parents are aware that their decisions are being observed by people who control whether they are allowed to continue to parent this child. Under such scrutiny, parents may have difficulty acting consistently or with confidence. This was certainly the experience of Hattie, mentioned at the beginning of this chapter. She couldn't feel like an authentic parent as long as the birth mother was dropping by unannounced. Her need for the birth mother to make arrangements in advance to pick up the baby was more than a request for courtesy; it was essential to her ability to parent.

We point out in Chapters 2 and 6 that open adoption can aid the adoptive parents' sense of entitlement when the birth parents choose them and give them permission to be the baby's parents, formalizing this through a symbolic entrustment ceremony at the time of placement. Adoptive parents can see that the birth parents freely give them this role and the authority that accompanies it. After the placement, the birth parents continue to validate the adoptive parents' role through their comments and gestures, such as introducing them as the child's parents. One birth mother told the adoptive parents: "You're doing such a good job with him."

Birth parents shouldn't assume the adoptive parents are so confident that they don't need to hear that they're making fine parents. In fact, many adoptive parents feel extremely insecure about their parenting skills. It may have been hard for them to attend a child-care class or to even have read a child-care book before their child arrived because of the uncertainty prospective adoptive parents feel about ever becoming parents. When they suddenly do have the child, they can be overwhelmed by the feeling that they ought to know how to care for him, particularly since the entire adoption system is predicated on the belief that the adoptive parents are in a better position to care for the child than the birth parents. It means a lot to them to hear someone, especially the birth mother and father, say how competent they are as parents.

Entitlement can be hard for adoptive parents to attain if they confuse it with ownership. One adoptive mother, who had reluctantly gone along with open adoption because it seemed the only way to get a baby, said she felt "sad, angry, and betrayed" when she realized after the placement that she would always have to share her daughter with the birth family. "She would never be mine and my husband's alone," she said. The realization prompted her to begin to educate herself about open adoption, and she eventually realized that it was not only incorrect but dehumanizing to think of children as a kind of property that belong either to their birth or to their adoptive parents. That concept undoubtedly grew out of our historical treatment of children as individuals with fewer rights than adults. It also reflected the legal framework of adoption in which a child's ties to his birth family were completely supplanted by his ties to the adoptive family. In effect, the legal system says adoptive parents can't "own" their children until the birth parents no longer "own" them. In fact, no one owns children. They are individuals who belong *in* families but not *to* families. One adoptive mother expressed her belief that children don't belong to parents, but parents belong to children. Another way to express this may be that parents own their role and the responsibilities that go with that role, but they don't own their children.

Although the appearance of ownership is realized in confidential adoptions, it does not necessarily lead to entitlement. The transfer of parental rights cannot be complete regardless of the legal system; whether or not it was acknowledged, the child will always be a part of the birth family. True entitlement comes from realizing that while the child will always be connected to both the birth and adoptive families, only the adoptive parents will be raising the child. They do so with the blessing of society through the court system, and often with the blessing of the birth parents themselves.

Coping with Grief

For the birth parents, the time after the placement is a time for letting go of their parenting roles relative to this child and grieving for that loss. This won't be easy—after all, they've had the role of parent for at least nine months. Adoptive parents who have had their child with them for even a few weeks can imagine how long they would grieve if that child were to leave them. In addition, the birth mother has had physical and emotional changes that make it difficult for her to stop thinking of herself as a mother.

The grief the birth parents experience cannot be overstated. They may feel numb or ache physically; they may be unable to function or they may cry inconsolably. They may have hallucinations that they hear the baby crying or nightmares that something dreadful has happened to the child. This is all part of the grief process, but that doesn't mean that this pain can't be alleviated. Charlene chose as adoptive parents Myra and Frank, a couple with a large house who could obviously provide for the child in ways Charlene couldn't. Charlene awakened one night after dreaming that the baby was crying and Myra and Frank couldn't hear him because he was too far away in their big house. Although it was the middle of the night, Charlene called Myra and Frank to express her concern. Myra explained that they had an intercom between the nursery and the master bedroom and held the phone to the intercom's speaker so Charlene could hear the baby breathing. Satisfied that Myra and Frank would hear the baby crying, Charlene went back to sleep.

People may expect the birth parents to recover far more quickly than is reasonable. Refer again to the discussion of grief in Chapter 2 as well as to the Resources in the back of this book on grief recovery. Among the important points to remember is that you do heal from a loss—you will feel better—but the loss is part of you forever.

Sometimes unexpected anniversaries trigger grief for the birth parents. For example, one birth mother learned she was pregnant shortly before Independence Day. Her holiday was miserable—she was nauseous and stressed from wanting to keep the pregnancy a secret from her parents. As she approached the first Independence Day after the birth of the baby, she found herself increasingly short-tempered. But it wasn't until she burst into tears while watching the fireworks that she remembered how she had used the noise of the fireworks a year earlier to drown out her sobs.

Of course, not all the birth parents' feelings just after placement are negative. One birth mother expected to be distraught the first time the couple who adopted her daughter came to her house. Instead, she was overwhelmed with a sense of pride at having brought such a wonderful child into the world, and at herself for making the right choice for her daughter. Although at times she felt the sadness she expected to feel while she grieved for the loss of her daughter, there were also times when she felt a great sense of relief, freedom, and happiness.

THE RELATIONSHIP BETWEEN BIRTH PARENTS

As they grieve, the birth mother and father sometimes find comfort in each other. Only they know what they have been through. If they aren't working through their grief in healthy ways, however, this can lead to another pregnancy to replace the child who was lost. Moreover, couples who lose a child often have a difficult time maintaining their relationship, which is due in part to the fact that all their energy is channeled into healing themselves; they have nothing left to give to each other. Adding to the strain, the other birth parent can be a reminder of the pain they've experienced, especially once healing has begun. Birth parents may be tempted to let go of the relationship without putting too much work into it if only because it is easier to justify the decision to place the child for adoption if they do. They cannot imagine a future together without their child, too. Those couples who want to remain together must put a lot of energy into their relationship at this time.

Because the birth parents may not remain a couple, it is important for each birth parent to develop a separate relationship with the adoptive parents. And the birth parents need to remember that no matter what problems may exist between them, this child will unite them forever. When the adoption is open, that could mean that they will both be invited to family gatherings, and it is their responsibility to work out their differences without involving the adoptive family.

GRIEVING AROUND CHILDREN

Birth parents who have other children may find that they want to spend a lot of time with their children as they grieve. This can be helpful as long as they don't become emotionally smothering. Others may be so withdrawn that they are unresponsive to the needs of their other children. In addition, their decision to place a child for adoption may leave birth parents feeling shamed and inadequate, which can inhibit their ability to function as parents. However, other children can also keep birth parents from giving in to their pain and motivate them to work through it. Birth parents might like to spend the day in bed or drink away their pain, but they know they have responsibilities.

Even children too young to understand what is happening in the family sense that something is different. The family pattern has been broken, the mood in the house is different, and they may feel frightened.

It can be upsetting for them to see their parents out of control, to find them unresponsive, or to hear them shouting or crying. Children may express their insecurity and fear by regressing in their behavior. They may act out as a way to get attention or because they are distracted by the turmoil in the family and can't maintain personal control. They may have problems eating or sleeping or may develop somatic complaints such as stomachaches.

Although it may seem easier to try to reassure toddlers that nothing is different, birth parents need to be honest with their children about what has happened and acknowledge that their perception that something is different in the family is correct. It's all right to tell children that mommy or daddy is sad. Children are likely to assume they are responsible, and some may think it is their duty to make their parents feel better. They need to be assured that they are not the cause of the parent's unhappiness, nor is it their job to put everything right. (For information about how to explain the adoption plan to other children in the birth family, and their emotional reaction to the placement of a sibling, see Chapter 13.)

Letting Go

The birth parents will not be able to completely let go of the child in just a matter of weeks or even months. Some birth parents find it necessary to see the child through all the milestones of infancy before letting go completely of their parenting role. Once they have been part of the child's first holidays—first birthday, first tooth, and first step—they find they can move on. (Information about celebrating holidays is discussed later in this chapter.)

One birth mother said that during the first months after placement she would fantasize that she was capable of raising her son. When she would visit the adoptive parents, however, she'd see how much better they could meet his needs. Those visits allowed her to let go of any doubts she had that maybe she would have been a better parent to him than anyone else, and they allowed for a smooth transition for her and the adoptive mother. However, another birth mother found she was unprepared for her feelings when she was unable to comfort her crying child one day while visiting him. The adoptive mother stepped in and soothed him quickly. The birth mother wasn't ready to have her child, who was with her for nine months prior to birth, find the adoptive mother more familiar and preferable after only a couple of months.

Some people think that letting go means the birth parents no longer want any contact with the child, and similarly, as long as the birth parents want contact, they have not truly let go. However, the birth parents are not letting go of the child; they are letting go of their role as parents of that child. This will take time, and they are likely to continue to want contact as they develop a new relationship with the adoptive family. Extreme behavior, such as running away, attempted suicide, or a constant need to be with the child, are signs that the birth parents are having difficulty with their grief and need counseling, but the desire for ongoing contact with the child is the nature of open adoption and does not by itself indicate maladjustment.

Extended members of the birth family may be eager to have the birth parents let go of the child emotionally. This has been a stressful time in the family and they would like things to "get back to normal" as quickly as possible, but things will never be as they were before. Perhaps the birth grandparents are afraid the birth parents will decide to keep the baby and are worried that they will reclaim the baby unless they feel better soon. They, too, need to realize that the grieving process can be facilitated but not rushed. They might also want to investigate whether their wish that the birth parents put the experience behind them is part of their own grief reaction to the adoption. They may be trying to deny their feelings in the same way that feelings were denied many years ago when adoptions were secret and no one talked about the placement after the birth mother returned from the maternity home.

People who are grieving for a loved one sometimes resist letting go because they think it appears that they don't care. They feel that they are betraying their child if they laugh, have fun, or don't think about him for an entire day. Some feel so guilty for placing the child for adoption that they punish themselves by not allowing themselves to enjoy life. And some feel guilty that they are able to let go and feel good again, wondering if this means they aren't "normal" men or women. Letting go doesn't mean forgetting about the child, and it doesn't mean not caring anymore. It only signifies that they accept that there is nothing they can do to reclaim their loss, and that it is time to find a permanent place in their heart to put that loss so they can go on with their lives.

Renegotiating Openness

It's not uncommon for the adoptive parents to withdraw from the birth parents during the first few months after placement. They want to build attachment with the child without feeling that they have to compete with the birth parents. They may find it difficult to share holidays, birthdays, and other significant events in the life of the child with the birth parents because they haven't fully accepted that they are not the child's biologic parents.

The adoptive parents may also withdraw from the birth parents because they feel inadequate or disillusioned. Nearly every new parent will at times feel fatigued by the demands of a child and wonder why they ever thought raising a child would be fun. Adoptive parents may not want to have contact with the birth parents for fear that their disillusionment with parenting will show through and their level of commitment will be questioned. One adoptive mother admitted being afraid that if her letters to the birth mother contained no hint of the sleepless nights she was experiencing, the birth mother would think parenting was easy and would reclaim the baby; at the same time she worried that if she described her difficulties in detail, the birth mother would think she didn't want to be a parent. She needed to consider the birth mother's needs and feelings, remembering how she might have felt hearing someone complain about parenting when she was childless, and recognizing that the birth mother can't be too reassured that the adoptive parents are satisfied. At the same time, on occasion it may be appropriate for the adoptive parents to share that they're tired because the baby had a difficult night.

Furthermore, though nearly all new parents have doubts about their parenting abilities, when adoptive parents find themselves in a situation in which they don't know what to do for their child, or they make a mistake, they sometimes feel additional guilt. They know they were chosen as parents for this child because the birth parents believed they were the best people to raise the child. The adoptive parents may fear that if the birth parents see any weaknesses, they will have new doubts about the adoptive parents' ability to parent. They may also be afraid that the birth parents won't approve of the way they are taking care of the child, especially if this is the adoptive parents' first child and the birth parents have raised other children. One adoptive mother said that when her daughter caught a cold from her father, she felt compelled to explain to the birth mother the precautions they had taken so that their daughter would not catch his cold and the steps they had taken to treat the symptoms of the virus. Looking back on this incident from the perspective of several years, this mother saw her defensiveness as a sign of her own insecurity—something that eased over time as she fell more naturally into her new role.

Nevertheless, some adoptive parents welcome the involvement of the birth parents even immediately after placement. They appreciate seeing the resemblance between their child and his birth family. They revel in the attention and love others want to give their child. In one open adoption, the birth mother had the beauty of a fashion model and the child inherited her good looks. They drew attention whenever they went out, and the adoptive mother thoroughly enjoyed the attention the three of them received. Adoptive parents who feel comfortable rather than threatened in a situation like this are often those who have developed a strong relationship with the birth parents during the pregnancy and can't imagine not sharing the growth of the child as well. They respect the birth parents' role in their child's life and feel comfortable about their own entitlement. Frequently, they are adoptive parents who have already experienced an open adoption or have gained a sense of entitlement to be parents through a previous child.

Birth parents occasionally withdraw from the adoptive family as a step in their grieving. They need to put some distance between themselves and the child to let go of their parenting role, just as former lovers sometimes need to grieve for their lost relationship at a distance before they can see each other as friends. Other birth parents want a lot of contact with the adoptive family right away, and find it helps them let go of their parenting role to know that the child is doing well. It confirms for them that they made the right choice in selecting the adoptive parents and making the adoption plan. They will often want more phone calls, letters, or photographs than may have been agreed on prior to placement, and some who wanted only correspondence will find they need a visit. They may need the concrete image of the child living with his adoptive parents for the placement to be real, so that when they think about the child they can visualize him sleeping in his room, eating in the kitchen, or playing in the yard. To use the analogy of former lovers again, it may be necessary for some people to see their ex-lover in a new relationship and confirm that he has moved on before they are able to let go of any hope that they can resume their earlier relationship. "When I see what they can do for my son that I can't," said one birth mother, "I know I've made the right decision."

Often, if you find the level of openness you agreed to needs to be altered, you can discuss your needs and make accommodations for each other's changing needs. But when a birth parent's need for more contact directly conflicts with an adoptive parent's need for less contact, it can cause friction. You may feel threatened, betrayed, vulnerable, or out of control if it appears the level of openness you want or agreed to prior to placement is not satisfactory and you cannot easily agree on an acceptable new level of openness. And when the adoptive parents withdraw from the birth parents during the first year, or seem to begrudge the birth parents the contact they had promised them, it feeds the birth parents' fear that the adoptive parents will renege on their voluntary agreement for openness. When the birth parents ask for more openness than they originally agreed to, it feeds the adoptive parents' fear that the birth parents will intrude in their lives. You have all probably worried about whether you could trust each other. You have all been warned by well-meaning friends or family members that the other party wouldn't live up to the agreement. Because you have only a short, intensely emotional history with each other, you may not be sure if your relationship has withstood the test of time and if you have complete faith in its strength.

Resist the temptation to jump to the conclusion that you can't trust each other. Explore the reasons that your needs may have changed and discuss them with each other. It would be nice if, while you were making your open adoption agreement, you knew exactly how you would feel and what your needs would be after the placement. But that isn't realistic. Reevaluating the agreement is a natural part of the process. You agreed to a plan based on everyone's expectations of their needs. Now you all have to evaluate whether the plan agreed upon in the abstract adequately meets the real needs you are experiencing and the actual experiences you are having.

Furthermore, you made a plan when you were experiencing very different emotions than you are now. The birth parents made a plan when they were dealing with an unplanned pregnancy; now they are dealing with their grief over the loss of a real child. The adoptive parents made a plan when they were eager—maybe even desperate—to find a child; now they have a child and desperately want to keep him. Also keep in mind that you agreed to one plan that you thought would serve you in all situations, but there will be some situations in which the plan will need modification. The needs you may have for more or less openness during the first year after the placement are due to feelings and experiences unique to this time of transition. After the adjustment is complete, the long-term plan you agreed to may once again meet your needs.

During these first few months, everyone is asked to think about some-one else's needs at a time when their own needs seem overwhelming. Because everyone's feelings are so raw, even minor discrepancies between your needs or between what you expected and what is actually happening may cause conflict. Negotiating with each other may be more difficult because everyone feels vulnerable due to changing roles, and when people feel vulnerable, it's natural for them to want tighter control over their lives. The extent to which you have all been able to successfully negotiate with each other in the past, your ability to identify and express your needs and feelings and respectfully listen to the needs and feelings of others, your willingness to be vulnerable and take emotional risks, and the degree to which you like and respect each other will all help you during this time of transition.

But the most important factor in the success of an open adoption dur-ing this critical time is everyone's commitment to doing what is best for the child. During the first few months after an infant's placement, this may be hard to remember. The ways openness will help him may not be appar-ent for a while, and openness may appear to primarily serve the birth par-ents. If they aren't exercising their right to openness, or if the adoptive parents feel less of a commitment to the birth parents, it can be easy for the adoptive parents to forget that they are making an effort to maintain a good relationship with the birth parents for the sake of their child. The birth parents may believe they don't have an obligation to remain in con-tact with the adoptive family if they find it difficult. They must also remember that while there can be advantages for them to maintaining openness, their obligation is to the child.

What is not always anticipated is that one adoptive parent might want a different level of openness than the other, because each is an individual making his or her own adjustment. For example, an adoptive mother might feel more uncomfortable about the birth mother's visits than the adoptive father, because she feels her role threatened by the birth mother in a way the adoptive father does not. Similarly, the adoptive father may not have had to face some of his concerns about open adoption if the birth father wasn't involved in the placement. However, if the birth father later becomes involved, the adoptive father may find that he has issues he did not deal with prior to the placement that are interfering with his ability to feel comfortable in an open arrangement. If you find that one of you wants less openness than you agreed on, or less than the other parents want, reread Chapter 2, which discusses some of the reasons birth and adoptive parents are reluctant to be involved in open adoption. If you are unable to work through your conflicts alone, an open adoption support group or joint counseling may help.

Sometimes conflict is not due to different needs or different ideas about how to meet those needs; rather it is due to the desire to establish or express power. As you negotiate, you will realize that the balance of power in your relationship has changed, reflecting the transfer of parental roles from the birth parents to the adoptive parents. At the hospital you experienced the beginning of this transfer of power. It is not complete even after the placement, and the ambiguity this creates only adds to the potential for conflict.

Change in Control

Prior to the placement of the child, the birth parents had the legal right to make decisions about their child and were under no legal obligation to honor any preplacement agreement they may have reached with the prospective adoptive parents. After the adoption is finalized, the adoptive parents have the legal right to make decisions about the child and generally have no legal obligation to uphold any preadoption agreement they have made.[1] No matter how committed you are to each other, and how deeply you feel a moral responsibility to upholding your agreement, the legal framework of adoption creates an imbalance of power that shifts from the birth parents to the adoptive parents.

In most states, this shift in power is not immediate. Some birth mothers place their children with the adoptive parents before signing consents. In some states there is a period of time after the child's placement when the birth parents can rescind their permission for adoption with little difficulty, and there is a waiting period before the adoptive parents can legally finalize the adoption. The legal authority still held by the birth parents and the lack of legal authority held by the adoptive parents are inconsistent with the appearance that the adoptive parents have full parental rights because they are raising the child. Yet there is an awareness among everyone involved that if the birth parents exercise their legal right to parent the

---

1. The enforceability of open adoption agreements is changing rapidly. Your facilitator will be able to tell you if the adoptive parents have a legal obligation in your state to maintain the agreement.

child after the child goes home with the adoptive parents, it will disrupt what appears to be a family and what feels like a family, even though it is not yet legally so. (Reclaiming a child after placement is discussed in more detail in Chapter 14.)

Not only does the physical transfer of the child from the arms of the birth parents to the arms of the adoptive parents affect the perception of who the child's parents now are but there are emotional changes as well. As the child spends time with the adoptive parents and has his needs met by them, the child and the adoptive parents feel irreplaceable to each other. This feeling of belonging together is influenced by the parent–child interactions, not by documents saying who the child's legal parents are. Often the adoptive parents are emotionally attached to the child long before the adoption is finalized. Yet birth parents feel a bond, too, that is not changed by the location of the child or the signing of legal documents.

LOSS OF CONTROL

Margo planned every detail of her daughter's placement: who would attend the birth, who would be the first person to hold her daughter after birth, who would hold the baby as they left the hospital, and where and when she would hand over her child to her adoptive parents. She didn't call the adoptive parents for a week after the placement. Then, when she finally dialed the number, there was no answer! She hung up and broke into tears.

Today, Margo and the adoptive parents have a close relationship, and Margo sees her daughter as often as she wants. But initially, one of the most difficult parts of the adjustment to the adoption for Margo was realizing that she wouldn't always be able to reach her daughter or her daughter's parents whenever she wanted to. She couldn't just drop by their house without calling, or expect them to be home whenever she wanted them to be. Even though the adoptive parents weren't withholding visitation or telephone contact, or even making it difficult, it was clear that she had lost control of when and where she would see her daughter. "The adoptive parents have always been accommodating to me," she says. "What was so difficult that first month, however, was having to *ask* them."

After a child is placed for adoption, the birth mother, who has controlled every substance the child was exposed to prior to birth, and who was encouraged to make all the decisions about the child, suddenly loses both physical control of the child and authority over him. The birth mother and father may have limited access to the child, or at least must make arrangements with the adoptive parents. The birth father may have had limited opportunities to make decisions about the child's future during the preplacement period, and may feel that loss even more acutely once he can see and hold the baby.

Not only did the birth parents have control of the baby prior to placement but they had a certain amount of control over the adoptive parents and perhaps the adoption facilitator, all of whom may now seem less interested in the birth parents' needs. Birth mothers and fathers may experience an additional loss of control when they find they are no longer given the deference they were prior to the placement.

Some birth parents react to the lack of control they're experiencing by becoming passive participants in the open adoption relationship. They may be reluctant to call the adoptive parents, ask questions about their child's development, or request photographs or visits. They may expect the adoptive parents to know their needs without being told, but may be hurt when the adoptive parents don't accurately interpret the birth parents' needs. Adoptive parents can help birth parents identify and express their wishes by giving them choices. For example, the adoptive parents could ask: "Would you like to visit every Sunday or would you rather call me each week and set up a specific time?"

Other birth parents try to hang onto whatever control is available to them—making new requests, ignoring the rules they had agreed to prior to the placement, or challenging parental or school authority. They may ask for loans or drop by the adoptive family's house unannounced. The coupon book mentioned in Chapter 5 is one way to put limits on a birth parent's demands. Some birth parents exercise control by delaying the signing of their consents. They don't threaten to reclaim the baby— indeed, they say they intend to sign. However, they always seem to have excuses for not setting up an appointment or for breaking an appointment. They may say they don't have time, they don't like the social worker, or they don't want to do it when it will upset them. Sometimes they want to wait until some other aspect of their life is in control again, although they may not express it that way. They may say they want to wait until they've regained their prepregnancy weight, until they've found a job, or until they've returned to school.

It's reasonable for birth parents to want to wait a few weeks before signing consents. Indeed, some professionals question whether it is even ethical to allow birth parents to sign consents sooner than that. But birth parents who wait too long to sign the consents—say, more than three months—not only risk a breakdown of the trusting relationship they've built with the adoptive parents but they leave their child and the adoptive parents in an emotional limbo, and that isn't good for the child. The adoptive parents may hold back a little emotionally while they wait for the birth parents to sign the consents, and the child loses important closeness.

Birth parents who are putting off signing consents need to discuss with a counselor whether they are seriously considering reclaiming or simply trying to hold onto control. They need to think about the child's need for emotional stability and to understand that by actively giving the adoptive parents their parenting role, they are contributing in a positive way to the child's sense of security. There is never going to be a good time to sign the consents, but it often frees birth parents to move on in their grief process. To some birth parents, the consents loom over them like a guillotine, and they resist signing the consents because it feels like when they do, the blade will fall. They find that the anticipation is often worse than the event itself.

If the adoption facilitator or adoptive parents think the birth parents are seriously considering reclaiming, they should insist on counseling for them. However, if they believe the birth parents intend to sign but are simply procrastinating, they can suggest that they pick a date for the signing of the consents six to eight weeks in the future. They can explain that the birth parents can sign before that time, but that they will plan on the birth parents signing at that time. They can anticipate objections, such as the birth parents needing a ride, and can make the necessary arrangements. Each week, they can remind the birth parents of the amount of time remaining before the signing of consents. Often the birth parents sign earlier as their way of maintaining control.

In extreme cases, birth parents who are trying to regain control of their lives may run away or threaten to reclaim the baby. One birth father denied that he was the father of the baby the birth mother was carrying until he saw the baby at three weeks of age. Suddenly, the birth father said he didn't like the adoptive parents and that he might raise the child himself. The adoptive parents were scared, but made themselves available so the birth father could get to know them and become more comfortable with the adoption. Birth fathers need their own male support system. They also need therapists who understand adoption issues and the way cultural views of adoption and masculinity may affect birth fathers as they grieve.

Adoptive parents, too, can feel powerless after the placement. Once the child is with them, it isn't surprising that they might want to have the control they haven't had to this point; however, they are very aware that nothing is definite until the adoption is legally finalized. The knowledge that even now that they've had a child placed with them they still aren't in control can be a surprising and particularly frustrating loss. Adoptive parents may react by insisting on whatever control they do have, such as refusing to renegotiate rules or procedures. Some may try to control the child by ignoring his innate temperament and personality and believing they can mold him into whatever they imagined their child might be like.

However, many adoptive parents become so accustomed to being out of control that they forget how to be assertive. They may allow birth parents to drop by without prior notification because they don't know how to express their wish that the birth parents call first, or they may be unable to enforce their decisions. They may feel angry or resentful that they are allowing such intrusions, but they feel powerless to change the situation. This anger may interfere with their relationship with the birth family.

DEALING WITH THE SHIFT IN POWER

No one can have complete control if an open adoption is going to work. But neither will open adoption be successful if anyone is left feeling completely powerless. Together, you have to discuss what kind of control is appropriate for each of you and where your needs might have conflict. Examine how important it is to you to have control, and whether that level of control is appropriate. Maybe it would be healthier to have a little more control of your life, or you realize that you are experiencing stress because you want more control than is necessary or possible. Analyze what your pattern of control is: Do you have to have a lot of control in all areas of your life, or are you fighting for control in this situation because you don't have much control elsewhere? Look specifically at the ways you have experienced a loss of control in the adoption, as well as how others have lost control, and at how you have reacted to both your own loss of control as well as someone else's.

Birth mothers and fathers will have to determine the level of control they want in their lives and are willing to take responsibility for, and negotiate in an adult manner for that authority. They have had an enormously maturing experience. Although they may still be young and immature in many ways, they have experienced a taste of authority, and it will be difficult and perhaps inappropriate to try to go back to previous ways of interacting.

Adoptive parents should understand that the birth mother and father may need to be weaned from having control of the relationship and their child. As they become comfortable with less control, the adoptive parents can assume more control. A gradual transfer of power may be easier for everyone involved. Nevertheless, it is imperative that the adoptive parents feel entitled to make decisions that affect the child's health and welfare, such as whether to put a sweater on him when they take him outside, or whether to bottle-feed or breastfeed.

Prior to placement, the birth parents had the final say in any matters that couldn't be resolved together. After the placement, the adoptive parents have the last word. Adoptive parents also have the right to expect that the birth parents will observe the same boundaries that they would request any close friend or member of their family to respect. Although under these special circumstances it may seem controlling for the adoptive parents to ask the birth parents to call before coming over, to call only during the times of day when people are generally awake, and to make requests rather than demands, these are commonly accepted rules governing interpersonal behavior in our culture.

As you understand the many losses of control in open adoption, you can better express why making a certain decision is important to you, or why you've had difficulty expressing your need for control. You may also be more willing to negotiate questions of control or to listen when someone else is explaining their needs.

If you are having difficulty negotiating a conflict, counseling may be necessary. But sometimes people reject therapy or mediation, for whatever reason. When that happens, the person who requested joint counseling can seek it as an individual. The focus of such counseling will be to deal with her frustration at the conflict, determine how she can influence the situation, and help her live with whatever remains unresolved. In some situations, counseling uncovers an underlying issue that explains why resolving the conflict was so important to one person but not the other.

Some people resist meeting with a therapist because they feel competent and rational, and they mistakenly think counseling implies some degree of mental or emotional instability. Those people may prefer to meet with someone who does not necessarily have academic credentials in resolving disputes, but who can nonetheless offer an objective, reasoned opinion, such as a family friend or minister. Keep in mind, however, that when you select an arbitrator without experience in open adoption, he may question the open adoption rather than resolve the dispute. Be clear with him that your goal is to settle a conflict, not end the relationship.

Sometimes conflicts resolve themselves or are easier to negotiate after you take a break from them. Try agreeing not to discuss a volatile topic for two weeks (or not to put yourselves in a situation where the matter would be at issue). You may find that after you've regained your composure, a mutually satisfactory solution is obvious.

EXTENDED FAMILY MEMBERS

Extended family members, too, feel a loss of control in the weeks and months immediately after placement. They might not agree with their son's or daughter's decision to place a child for adoption or to make an open adoption plan. Perhaps they wanted to raise the child themselves, or maybe they just wanted to make the decision. They may try to manipulate the situation so that it has the outcome they would choose. For example, when the birth parent is grieving for the loss of the child, they may encourage her to reclaim the child. They may talk to the other birth parent in an effort to get him to use his influence to get her to reclaim the child. Or, they may encourage the birth parents to reconsider the adoption's openness, suggesting that the birth parent move or leave the child alone. One birth grandmother carried a car seat and bag of diapers in the trunk of her car for several weeks after the placement, letting the birth mother know they were there if she decided to reclaim the child. The birth mother finally told her that her cache of baby supplies was making it too difficult for her to let go of the baby and asked her to please get rid of them.

Some birth grandparents may become overly controlling of the birth mother, birth father, or their other children so that another unexpected pregnancy doesn't happen. Their desire for more control may conflict with the birth mother's or father's need to maintain the level of control experienced during the pregnancy, to get through some difficult times by going out and having fun, or to grieve for the loss of the child by spending time with the other birth parent.

Birth grandparents may have to acknowledge that their child has become accustomed to being looked to as an adult, and in many ways has earned the right to continue to be treated as such. They may have to allow their son or daughter to have a level of freedom that they would not otherwise allow someone of that age, while still maintaining rules that would be appropriate for anyone who shares their home.

Adoptive relatives, too, may feel out of control because they fear the birth mother will reclaim the child, or because they don't agree with the decision to adopt or to participate in an open adoption. They may set up a power struggle between them and the child's birth relatives over questions such as who will babysit the child, or who will be invited to share holiday meals or other family celebrations.

Fred, an adoptive grandfather, refused to attend the child's baptism if the birth grandparents were going to attend. Although it was difficult, the adoptive parents told Fred that their decision to include the birth family in their child's life was made for the sake of their child and no one else's needs could take precedence. They told him they wanted him to be a part of the child's life, too, and that they hoped he would attend the baptism, but that they didn't intend to start choosing between grandparents.

Fred's refusal to attend functions at which the birth grandparents were present was a source of sadness to the adoptive parents, but they recognized the problem was Fred's and they tried to help him come to terms with his grief and loss of control, without allowing themselves to be manipulated. It was seven years before Fred realized the adoptive parents were not going to give in to his demands and that he was missing out on a lot of important occasions with his grandchild.

The birth mother and father will need to let go of any need they may have to control the amount of contact extended family members have with the adoptive family, and must allow them to develop and negotiate their own relationships. Otherwise, adoptive parents may feel caught between members of the birth family. For example, the birth father may not want a lot of contact and may not want his parents to have a lot of contact either. However, it isn't his right to control the amount of contact that his parents have with their birth grandchild. Nor is it his right to dictate to the adoptive parents whom they can allow to see their child.

Birth parents also must realize that the other members of the birth family do not have the same losses that they do, which may affect the kind of contact they want with the child. While the birth parents lose their parenting roles, the other members of their families can continue to act as grandparents, aunts, uncles, and cousins to the child. They lose the child as a member of their immediate circle of family, and grieve for what the loss of the child will mean to the birth parents, but it isn't the same loss that the birth parents have and they will grieve differently.

Disclosing Adoption

Although your extended family members and close friends are likely to know about your open adoption plan, you will sometimes find yourself in situations where you might have to reveal the open adoption to an acquaintance. For example, when you are all together at the park or in a restaurant, you might run into someone you know and be called upon to introduce each other. A casual acquaintance who knew the birth mother was pregnant might inquire about the child. Or someone might ask the adoptive mother about her pregnancy and delivery. After making a commitment to openness, you might be surprised to sometimes feel confused about what to say in these situations.

One adoptive mother said she didn't want to keep her child's adoption a secret, but whenever she told someone about the open adoption she was compelled to defend the practice against the concerns of other people, or she was asked personal questions about the birth parents. "I just don't want to tell anyone about the open adoption anymore," she said. Charlene Miall, Ph.D., a sociologist and adoptive parent, suggests that you may feel discomfort revealing information about your adoption because you may not receive the response you intend to receive. Birth parents may feel criticized, and adoptive parents may feel pitied or second-best. When the wisdom of the open adoption is questioned, birth and adoptive parents may feel that their good judgment is in doubt.

You can protect yourself by not revealing facts about yourself that might result in direct or indirect criticism, which doesn't mean that you tell lies but that you sometimes stop short of telling the whole truth, or just allow people to think what they want to think. For example, you can introduce each other as a member of the family, as someone very close to the family, or as a special friend. You can also choose to reveal more about your relationship, with the understanding that by doing so you are making yourself vulnerable to more inquiry and even judgment. Of course, you don't have to answer further inquiries or accept someone else's judgment about your decisions, but some people welcome the opportunity to educate others about open adoption.

Naturally, you may choose to disclose your adoption or your relationship to some people and not to others. If you are meeting someone with whom you expect to develop a greater acquaintance, you may want to be less cunning so that you don't have to later explain why you misled her. Keep in mind, though, that not all questions that appear to require an explanation about the child's origins actually do. A person who asks, "Where did that child get her red hair?" is probably not looking for details on genetics or your open adoption, but is simply remarking on the child's striking appearance. Even if the child had been born to you, an entirely appropriate reaction is, "Isn't it gorgeous?"

If the child is with you and can understand the question being asked, your responsibility is to answer the question in the way that makes the most sense to the child. For example, if the child, the birth mother, and the adoptive mother are all sitting together at the park and someone asks, "Which one of you is her mommy?" you must answer the way the child would. She has probably only heard the term *mommy* applied to her adoptive mother. Thus, the appropriate response is to indicate the adoptive mother. To respond "We both are" would be confusing. You could respond by explaining which of you is the birth mother and which is the adoptive mother, but that is probably more than the stranger wants or needs to know.

You shouldn't worry excessively that the child who hears you responding to strangers' inquiries with ambiguous or even misleading questions will conclude that open adoption is something to hide. He will no doubt see you in many situations that confirm for him that you are comfortable in open adoption and you let other people know about it. But when he observes you being selective about revealing information about his adoption, he will learn that just as you do, he has choices about the circumstances under which he can disclose his adoptive status or information about his origins.

It's a good idea to discuss the choices you have and how you will respond in these kinds of situations so that you approach them the same way and so that your intentions are not misunderstood. For example, a birth mother's feelings might be hurt when the adoptive mother didn't acknowledge her maternal role in the situation described above if she didn't understand that the reason the adoptive mother was responding that way was to avoid confusing the child.

However, you are obliged to respect the privacy of the child and of each other by not revealing personal information about them without their permission. Since the child can't give this permission for a while, you should keep the information private until she is able to do so.

To people who ask the adoptive parents about the birth parents, such as whether they were drug users or college-educated, adoptive parents can say: "I think we should give information about Jason's birth parents to

Jason before we give it to other people, and then what he reveals about his birth parents will be his choice." This holds true even with family members, because once you give away information, you can't control what is done with it. It might be shared with another child in the extended family who might not understand when it is appropriate to share that information. Even adults don't always use good judgment. Imagine what it might be like to have a family get-together and have someone remark to the birth mother: "It's too bad you couldn't figure out who the birth father was. It would've been nice to have some information about him back when Jenny was having all those medical tests done."

The point, of course, is not that someone might say something inappropriate but that you have violated a trust by providing other people with such personal information. Even positive information, such as the fact that the birth mother was a law student, is private. One adoptive mother said her husband frequently told people about the birth mother's upper-class background. The adoptive mother knew that her husband was concerned that people might think their child had been born to people in undesirable circumstances; however, she was unable to convince him that his comments about the birth mother's background not only violated the privacy of her and the child but indicated that he was reacting to the messages he had received from society that children who are adopted are second-best. Unable to persuade him to talk to a counselor or even to read a book, she finally popped an educational cassette into the tape deck of their car while they were driving to another city. After listening to the tape, the adoptive father realized he needed to be less concerned with what other people might think about his family.

Birthdays, Holidays, and Special Occasions

Birthdays, holidays, and special occasions such as baptisms and bar mitzvahs are significant events that are celebrated with rituals. As we note in Chapter 6, part of the function of rituals is to symbolically communicate the importance of events, people, and life transitions. The people invited to share in a ritual and their roles in that ritual communicate the significance of those people.

Special occasions are marked in our culture with phone calls, greeting cards, gifts, the gathering together of family and friends, special meals, religious ceremonies, and specific ethnic or family traditions. When the time comes to celebrate a special event, you will want to precisely express the relationship you have with each other. If you are unsure of that, if you are not sure that you all see the relationship the same way, or if you fear the expression of your open adoption relationship somehow diminishes another relationship that also needs to be precisely expressed, you may feel awkward.

During the first year after the placement, you will be working out ways to celebrate special occasions in the child's life—and in your families. Although the ways you celebrate important occasions may change, the first year sets the tone, to a great extent.

There are no rules of etiquette governing open adoption, but you can apply social customs to this relationship. For example, it is always acceptable for someone to wish another person well on a day of significance to her. However, open adoption can affect the significance of special occasions. Who is entitled to a card on Mother's Day or Father's Day? Do the birth parents have a significant role to play when celebrating the child's birthday? Should members of the birth family send the kind of gifts to the child that they would send to a family member or the kind they would send to a casual friend? You can, of course, worry too much about the hidden meaning in every social gesture. At the same time, the symbolism behind the gesture is what often causes conflict within families. You must let your knowledge of social customs, family and religious traditions, and your awareness of the kind of relationship you have with each other guide you. Generally, though not always, the adoptive family makes overtures to the birth family regarding celebrations. They either make plans and present them to the birth family, or ask the birth family for their input.

MOTHER'S DAY AND FATHER'S DAY

Adoptive parents are deeply touched when they are sent Mother's Day or Father's Day greetings from the birth parents or members of the birth family. In a highly symbolic way, this lets them know that the birth family acknowledges them as the parents of this child. However, adoptive parents should realize that these holidays are as difficult for the birth parents as they were for the adoptive parents during infertility treatment. Sending greetings to the birth parents is a way of acknowledging the role they had in the adoptive parents becoming a mother and father. It also acknowledges their ongoing connection to the child. Fortunately, there are now greeting cards for these holidays that acknowledge a variety of special relationships in a person's life.

BIRTHDAYS

The birth of a child is an awesome experience and birth parents commonly think about the child on his birthday. It should not be surprising or inappropriate for the birth parents to want to share in the celebration of the child's birth by sending greetings, a gift, or attending the birthday party. Many adoptive parents in open adoptions are willing to validate the birth parents' connection to their children on their birthdays. Some invite the birth parents and other members of the birth family to the birthday party. Some have one party for the child and his friends and a second party for the family, including both the extended birth family and extended adoptive family. Much depends on the adoptive parents' style of entertaining and family traditions and the adoptive parents' assessment of how much excitement the child can manage. Sometimes the birth family will want to have their own birthday celebration for the child. This isn't an appropriate symbol of the child's family situation and should be discouraged.

The birthdays of other members of the adoptive and birth families can also be acknowledged in whatever ways reflect your relationship. (For information on the birth family's responsibility to other children in the adoptive family, see Chapter 13.)

HOLIDAYS

Birth parents feel entitled to participate in the child's birthday because of the direct role they had in the birth of the child. However, holidays are times when families and close friends traditionally gather together. Birth families should only expect to be included in the adoptive family's celebrations (or expect the adoptive family to participate in theirs) if they have the kind of close relationship that resembles that between family members or close friends. Birth parents who live a great distance from the adoptive parents should not expect the adoptive parents to send the child to visit them for the holidays, as a child of divorce might spend holidays with the noncustodial parent. The child is part of the adoptive family and belongs with his family for holiday celebrations.

Not everyone needs to be included in one large gathering on a holiday unless that is how you prefer to celebrate holidays. Because holidays tend to be part of seasonal celebrations, you may be able to observe holiday festivities over many days. Keep in mind, however, that holidays tend to be times of high excitement for children and too many celebrations can be stressful for families. You may want to experiment with different ways of celebrating the holidays until you find the way that works best for you.

One adoptive family reserves Christmas Eve for just the parents and children in the family—no members of the birth family or the extended adoptive family. On Christmas Day their home is open to any friends or family members who want to come by and bring a dish for a potluck dinner. Another adoptive family spends Thanksgiving Day with members of their extended adoptive family, then has a dinner with the birth family on the weekend. That tradition has become as important to them as Thanksgiving Day itself, as it is a ritual that makes an important statement. Another adoptive family, who found they shared a love of the outdoors with several members of the birth family, celebrates the holiday season with them on an annual skiing trip. When yet another adoptive family found it too stressful to try to visit with all their birth relatives and adoptive relatives on a holiday, and impossible to entertain them all in their small house, they began a tradition of celebrating the holiday itself with friends who had no nearby family members. Throughout the holiday season, however, they would entertain or visit their birth relatives and adoptive relatives in small groups.

When the child's racial, ethnic, or religious heritage is different from that of the adoptive family's, open adoption offers the child the opportunity to learn about that heritage directly (see Chapter 15). By participating in holiday celebrations with the birth family, the child can become acquainted not only with foods, folk tales, and customs of his ethnic heritage but can experience them in a cultural context. For example, the birth grandmother who teaches the child how to make *pysanka,* the beautiful Ukrainian Easter eggs, probably will not only show the child the art but, while making the decorations, will tell tales of family members who taught her the art and will talk about how the eggs were used in family celebrations. The African-American child's birth family may invite him to attend a kwanza celebration where he learns the unique way the African-American community celebrates its African roots. Passover is a time when non-Jews are traditionally invited to share the seder supper.

Although it can be enriching to provide children with the opportunity to participate in cultural activities that they would have experienced had they remained with their birth families, it is also important to realize it is not until adolescence that children can understand that people are members of a religious group because they share common beliefs. Before that time, children believe they are members of a religious group because they attend religious services and participate in rituals common to that denomination. When a child's birth family and adoptive family belong to religious groups that are significantly different and dictate not only Sabbath observances but the way one leads his daily life, it can be confusing to the child to expect her to function as a member of both religious groups. A child born to Christian parents but adopted by Jewish parents can occasionally attend church with the birth family, but the child should be raised in the faith or faiths that are practiced or supported by the adoptive parents, and holidays should be observed according to the belief system in the adoptive family.

Although there are many marriages in which parents have two vastly different religious backgrounds and try to incorporate customs of both into family life, that is a subtly different message than the one the child receives if he is expected to be a Christian with his birth family and a Jew with his adoptive family. The birth parents can send Hanukkah gifts, and the adoptive family can send Christmas gifts to the birth parents, but it would not be appropriate for the child to celebrate Hanukkah with the adoptive family and Christmas with the birth family. However, if the adoptive family does not have strong religious beliefs, they may choose to raise their child in the birth family's denomination as a way for the child to remain connected to them.

POINTS TO REMEMBER

▪ You don't need to celebrate every special occasion created by the greeting card industry. Once you start a practice, it's difficult to stop it, so think carefully before beginning the tradition of observing occasions such as Grandparent's Day when the child has eight or more grandparents.

▪ The adoptive family can't be expected to serve as peacemaker between all the members of the birth families and adoptive families or to make adjustments on the basis of the different relationships within their open adoption family. At holiday time, adults will need to learn to get along for the sake of the child, or to make their own decisions about what they are willing to give up.

- Greetings to the birth parents can be sent by the adoptive parents or from the child. However, adoptive parents should not be too insistent on the child selecting cards or gifts for his birth parents or signing his own name. As the child gets older and understands the relationship, his interest in this practice may be affected by feelings of anger toward the birth parents or concern that he might weaken his place in his adoptive family by acknowledging his birth parents in special ways. (For more on the feelings of adoptees toward their birth parents, see Chapters 11 and 12.) Adoptive parents can approach this quandary in a similar manner to the way they might handle a relationship between the child and a godparent, grandparent, or other relative or close friend. Do they require their child to participate in the selection of cards and gifts for those people or do they make the selections and send them in the child's name? Do they insist on the child maintaining the relationship or do they maintain the relationship in trust for the child to access as he desires?

- Gifts are symbols of caring, but the value of the gift does not reflect the degree of love between individuals. Nor is gift-giving an appropriate way to attempt to increase the level of affection between people. Take care when you select gifts that you do not try to show the child how much you love him by buying him expensive things. Nor should you try to compete with other members of the child's families. If one family gives expensive gifts while another gives homemade items at holiday time, children learn the various ways people can express their love. This is one of the enriching experiences of open adoption. If there is a large economic disparity between you, the more affluent family may want to select gifts that will not embarrass the other family with their opulence without being condescending.

- Birth parents should respect the preferences of the adoptive parents regarding toys or other gifts for a child. Some parents do not want their child to have toy guns or personal telephones, for example.

- Celebrations should be among families and not just focused on one person's relationship to the child.

- When there is conflict over how special occasions will be celebrated, the adoptive parents' idea of what is best for the child and their family must prevail.

Be aware that the subtle aspects of your relationship and differences in traditions or customs may cause you to interpret special occasions differently. For example, the birth parents may feel slighted if they aren't included in a particular celebration, whereas the adoptive parents' intention was to keep the birth parents out of the limelight so as to not place them in an awkward social position. Don't be easily offended by an awkward statement or omission. Don't make assumptions—ask questions. Be quick to forgive.

Finalization and Moving On

The legal finalization of the adoption formally ends the transfer of parental roles that defines the adoption. In most states, the adoption cannot be finalized for at least six months after the child's placement or the birth parents sign their consents. You may have expected this to be the most emotionally charged event of your adoption experience. But as we've seen, the legal institution of adoption does not always reflect the emotional state of the participants.

Often, by the time the adoption is finalized, the birth parents have made significant strides toward letting go of their role as everyday parents. The adoptive parents have assumed their parenting roles and have begun to form a strong emotional attachment to the child. Their families and communities recognize and respect their new roles. One adoptive mother was hurt when her family wouldn't recognize the transfer of parental roles until they had been legalized, to the extent of not even hosting a baby shower until after the finalization. In many cases, the court action finalizing the adoption legalizes what has already taken place in the participants' hearts and minds. For that reason, it may seem more anticlimactic than you expected.

When the emotional transfer of parental roles is less complete, however, finalization may help facilitate that, just as any ritual can have an emotional impact on those participating in it. The degree to which it has this effect, however, may have to do with how the event is handled. Some finalizations are no more momentous than paying a traffic fine, whereas others are conducted more ceremoniously. You might want to discuss your wishes for the event with the judge who will be handling it.

Adoptive parents sometimes wonder whether they should invite the birth parents to the finalization ceremony. Although it feels like the birth parents are a natural part of the event, adoptive parents might be concerned that it will hurt the birth parents to attend, or potentially mar the adoptive family's enjoyment of the day. The birth parents are a part of the adoption, whether they are recognized or not. Just as the placement itself is a less euphoric but more realistic event when the birth parents' loss is recognized, so it is with the finalization. If the quality of the relationship between the birth and adoptive parents is positive and reciprocal, the adoptive parents should feel free to ask the birth parents if they would like to attend the ceremony and vice versa—the birth parents shouldn't hesitate to indicate their willingness to be involved. Nevertheless, adoptive parents may prefer the final step in creating their family to be private, just as the birth parents may have wanted a private birth, and their wishes should be respected.

As the birth parents grieve for their losses and gradually let go of their role as everyday, caretaking parents to this child, they move on or get on with their lives. They assume or resume roles other than that of parents to this child, and may return to being a son or daughter, a student, a worker, or a parent to their other children. If they are resuming roles they have held before, they may find their experience has changed them irrevocably.

It is vital that birth parents have a role to assume after the adoption. Those who do not have a goal that gives their life a purpose may turn to alcohol, drugs, or other substances to numb their pain. They may run away or attempt suicide or become severely depressed. Furthermore, if they do not have a role to assume, they fail to achieve one of their goals in making the adoption plan and, consequently, may regret their decision.

The ability of birth parents to move on and take advantage of opportunities they would have had to pass up if they had to care for an infant, such as pursuing their studies or career, can be influenced by the lack of support from their family, their peers, and society in general concerning the adoption. Some birth parents may even be ostracized by their family members, especially if they belong to a cultural group that disapproves of out-of-family placement. The family of one Hispanic birth mother didn't speak to her for three years after she placed her child for adoption. If she had not had the support of the adoptive family, who treated her as though she were their grown child, as well as her open adoption support group, she might not have been able to deal with the multiple loss of her child and her family.

Birth parents may feel that others don't approve of their actions. Worse, they may feel others don't approve of them. By participating in a support group they can receive the encouragement they need, as well as provide it to others making the same decision. Such a network can help birth parents feel strong and confident as they return to school or work or disclose the adoption to their neighbors or to new friends and colleagues. They should rehearse a response that they can use when asked about their absence, the pregnancy, or their obvious grief. As we mentioned earlier, it isn't necessary for them to disclose the adoption under all circumstances. They might want to discuss the placement with some people. To others they can simply say: "I've had a recent loss. I'd prefer not to talk about it." And in yet other situations they might want to say: "I made an adoption plan for my baby. I'd prefer not to talk about it."

Young birth mothers have special concerns as they attempt to resume roles. It isn't unusual for them to feel out of touch with their peers after placing a child for adoption. The teenage world, with its definition of crisis being an unwanted facial blemish, may seem trivial to someone who has faced one of life's most devastating losses. Unless they understand this and form a plan for dealing with it, they may drop out of school.

As you adjust to your new roles, keep in mind that no matter how much you have prepared for this transition, it will probably not proceed exactly the way you've planned. You may have different feelings than you anticipated. Some situations may not be as difficult as you thought they'd be, whereas others may be more difficult. Try to be understanding, sensitive, and compassionate. Infertile adoptive parents can remember how they felt when they were childless—how good it felt sometimes to hold a baby for even a few minutes and how sometimes the mere sight of a baby seemed too painful to be endured. Birth parents can remember that it is important for the child's well-being that his new parents develop a sense of entitlement and build attachment. Try to understand each other's needs and work out solutions that enable you all to get what you want, to whatever extent possible. Be as generous as you can without sacrificing your own needs. Finally, keep in mind that the first year after placement is just one phase of your developing relationship. As time goes on, your relationship will grow and change.

The Open Adoption Relationship Unfolds: Beyond the First Year

You began your open adoption relationship at a time when you were in the midst of emotional crisis—infertility for the adoptive parents and an untimely pregnancy for the birth parents. During the first year after placement, while your relationship was still young, you had to adjust to major changes in your relationship, again at a time of high emotion. As you heal from your losses, and become adjusted to your new role and new relationship, the actual character of your open adoption will become more apparent. How your relationship unfolds is influenced by many factors: the tone of the relationship prior to the placement, how the transfer of parental roles and rights was handled, how clear you are about the change in roles, the degree to which trust in each other has been built and challenged, the extent to which you have grieved for your losses, as well as other events in your lives unrelated to adoption.

Think about a long-term relationship you have had with someone, such as a spouse, a sibling, or a close friend. You no doubt have gone through times when you felt very warm and close to each other; times when you felt distant; times when you could barely interact without arguing. During the rough times, your history of compatibility reminds you that you can have a pleasant relationship with each other. Your belief that the relationship is important motivates you to try to preserve it.

This relationship, like every other one in your lives, will take work. Remember that the main reason you are devoting energy to it is for the benefit of the child. As one adoptive mother said, most relationships, if you let them, will move to a healthier level with time, patience, and trust. Don't lose sight of both the practical benefits that will be realized by the child and the growth you will experience as a human being.

Different Types of Relationships

There is no typical open adoption relationship. You may feel a close kinship to each other, a warm friendship, or an uncomfortable or even conflictual association, and you may contact each other by mail, by phone, or in person. The actual degree of closeness is not determined by the kind of contact you have with each other, although it may be one of the influences. There are many relationships conducted anonymously through a facilitator in which the participants nonetheless feel that they know each other intimately. There are other adoption relationships in which the birth parents and adoptive parents see each other regularly but have not progressed beyond being polite to one another. If your relationship is not like others you have heard about, don't automatically conclude that there is something wrong. As long as everyone's needs are met—especially the child's—and as long as the relationship is not based on fear, distrust, or anger, your open adoption may be fine just as it is. But by all means, if you think your relationship can be more meaningful, don't be afraid to put more energy into it.

COMPATIBLE BUT DISTANT

Many open adoptions are cordial but somewhat reserved. This could be true especially if your knowledge of each other is based primarily on correspondence. For most people, phone calls have become the preferred mode of communication, and as a result, you may find it difficult to express yourself in writing or may think you don't have sufficient time to compose a letter. You may be unsure whether the reader will understand the tone you want to convey. Say what you feel and don't worry about your writing skills, even if the recipient is someone who has a degree in English. No one is reading your letters to correct the grammar. Imagine your child reading your letters years later (and do save the correspondence). Would he learn something about you that would enable him to know you better?

Even people who telephone each other or visit sometimes feel detached. "We have nothing in common but the child," said one adoptive mother. Adoptive parents often tend to concentrate on reporting the child's milestones to the birth parents. But although the birth parents are interested in these details, your common interest in the child is not enough to allow your relationship to develop to its fullest potential. You will need to care about each other as people for that to happen.

Be open with each other about yourselves. Tell each other what's going on in your lives. If you aren't sure whether the other parent would like to hear something about you, ask yourself whether you'd want to know the information if you were in the other person's place. If you've been ill, changed jobs, gone back to school, seen a good movie—these all enable the other person to know you better and provide opportunities to find areas of common interest outside of the child. Share not only the experience but how the experience touched you.

If you find that visits with each other are awkward because you have little to talk about and you can only count on the child to entertain you for so long, find an activity to share. One adoptive mother took a craft class with the birth mother. One adoptive father joined a softball team with the birth father. In these situations, the birth parents spend time with the child before or after the activities they are sharing with the adoptive parents.

Sometimes people feel distant from each other because although they get along, one of them may not have the skills necessary to build a close relationship. Birth parents may need to grow up a bit before they can take on the role of an adult, and adoptive parents as well as birth parents may not have the self-confidence or the ability to empathize with another human being that is needed for lasting friendships. Sometimes your style of communicating keeps you from moving past politeness to a true friendship. For example, one talkative adoptive mother complained to her support group that when she was with the birth parents she had to carry the conversation. They suggested that she talk very little and see what happened. When she tried that, she realized that the birth parents had much to say, but that they paused when she expected them to continue talking. Her impulse had been to jump in and fill up those quiet spaces.

Furthermore, some people have more difficulty forming relationships because they are shy, private, or introspective. Some people prefer solitary activities or those that involve nature or animals to those involving people. Quiet people are sometimes mistakenly thought to be snobbish or rude by those who don't understand their lack of interest in people-oriented activities. But you can still find ways to relate to each other meaningfully. One adoptive father and birth father shared an interest in hunting. Both enjoyed walking through the woods alone or standing silently near a game trail. They developed a pattern of driving silently to the woods together, walking off in separate directions, and meeting back at the truck at dark. On the drive home they'd give brief reports of their days. They didn't need to say much. By walking in the same woods with the same goals, they related to each other at a level that didn't require words.

UNCOMFORTABLE RELATIONSHIPS

Some relationships are hindered by the discomfort people feel with each other. The discomfort goes beyond awkwardness, but stops short of actual conflict. Encounters may leave you angry, tense, unsettled, confused, or unsatisfied. There may be specific annoyances or issues that stand out as impediments to a good relationship.

Sometimes people tell off-color jokes or express prejudice toward minority groups that other people find offensive. It's all right to tell them that those kinds of comments are not acceptable in your presence. Similarly, if anger is being expressed in a way that is unacceptable around you, it's all right to communicate that, too.

You may have different styles of socializing. One birth father asked the adoptive father to go shoot pool with him. At the tavern, the birth father began flirting with two young women. It was clear he expected the adoptive father to join in the foursome. When he had the opportunity to speak privately to the woman the birth father was thrusting upon him, the adoptive father told her he was married and wasn't interested in anything but a game of pool. On the way home, he gave the birth father the same explanation and told him that he'd need to respect his attitude toward his marriage if they went out together in the future.

You may have different values about how money is spent, how you practice your religious beliefs, or how you discipline your children. Carla, an adoptive mother, felt increasingly uncomfortable as she spent time with her daughter's birth family. She was committed to the idea of women developing their intellect and having a sense of self-worth. She wasn't sure she wanted her daughter exposed to the birth family, who put marriage above a college education for women. Carla's support group helped her to see that her daughter would be exposed to the values of the adoptive family much more than she would the values of the birth family. But they also pointed out that should her daughter not attend college, or prefer marriage to higher education, she could find acceptance in the birth family that might be lacking in her adoptive family; being exposed to these different values would be an asset.

Sometimes your economic or educational differences can lead to feelings of jealousy or inferiority that can cause discomfort. In one situation, the birth father made repeated references to the disparity in income between him and the adoptive father, saying things like, "It must be nice to get a new car every year." Finally, the adoptive father responded, "We've worked hard to achieve what we have. Remember that one of the reasons you picked us was so we could provide for Keenan in ways that you couldn't at that time." To the birth grandmother who kept putting herself down with statements such as, "But I never went to college like you, so I guess I don't know anything," one adoptive mother said, "It sounds like you wish you'd had the chance to go to college. I hope it pleases you that your grandchild will have that opportunity." The birth grandmother responded by talking about her family situation and how that had kept her from pursuing her education. Her sharing of this personal loss brought the two of them closer together.

Sometimes contact with the other family triggers an unresolved issue for you. In one family, the adoptive father did not object to the adoptive mother visiting with the birth mother, but made it clear he didn't want to be involved. The need to always meet outside her own home eventually left the adoptive mother feeling that she was doing something shameful, and she began looking for excuses not to meet the birth mother. When the birth mother confronted her about pulling back in the relationship, the adoptive mother realized the problem was her husband's. She again began meeting regularly with the birth mother and encouraged her husband to talk over his concerns with a counselor.

Sometimes adoptive parents (especially mothers) feel their parenting ability is being scrutinized by the birth parents. One adoptive mother felt she had to justify to the birth mother every decision she made that affected her child, such as her decision to return to work and her choice of day care. Another adoptive mother spoke harshly to her child in the checkout line of the grocery store only to turn around and see the birth mother staring at her. In another situation, the birth grandmother annoyed the adoptive mother on her visits to the adoptive family's home by commenting every time she observed the child misbehaving that he didn't behave like that when he was with her. Most adoptive parents find that time resolves this issue for them. They become more confident as parents and develop a greater sense of entitlement as they function in that role and receive validation from the birth parents. They accept that they will make mistakes as parents, but that this doesn't disqualify them.

However, sometimes it may be necessary for adoptive parents to confront the birth parents. When one adoptive couple decided to have their child repeat the first grade, they received an angry and critical call from the birth grandmother, a former first-grade teacher. The adoptive mother was forceful, but not angry or defensive in her reply: "We're Hank's parents and we're going to make the decisions we feel are best for him." The birth grandmother never again criticized the adoptive parents.

Birth parents who have not faced their loss may find it troubling to be around the adoptive family. In one family, each time the birth mother would see the child, she would leave town for several weeks, ignoring her job and family members. It wasn't until she sought counseling that she could begin feeling comfortable having contact with the child. Another birth mother, whose child had serious digestive problems, was annoyed at the frequent calls from the adoptive mother asking her to gather information about her family's medical histories and the birth father's medical history. She needed to confront her feelings about not having a "perfect" child, accepting that her genetic contribution had adversely affected him, even though there was nothing she could have done to change the outcome.

Sometimes the adoptive parents' unresolved infertility keeps them from developing a sense of entitlement that would allow them to relax around the birth parents. Feeling threatened, they may be unusually sensitive to any signs that they aren't viewed as the child's authentic parents. They may look for reasons to cut off contact with the birth parents. On a visit from her birth mother, one young girl announced that she was mad at her mother for not letting her do something she wanted to do. The birth mother said to the girl, "Sometimes it's hard when people won't let us do what we want to do—especially when we can't understand why—but you have to obey your mother." Even though the birth mother had intended to be supportive, the adoptive mother misinterpreted her statement and took offense. She thought the birth mother was trying to say, "Even when your mother is wrong, you need to obey her."

If you're finding there's an issue that stands in the way of your relationship, ask yourself, a close friend, or your support group whether this issue would bother anyone or is just an annoyance to you. If it is something that is genuinely problematic, you may want to bring it out in the open in an attempt to resolve it. However, if you determine this matter is only a problem for you, try to figure out what unresolved issues are being triggered and confront them in yourself.

Your discomfort around each other may be due simply to incompatible personalities. When that is the case, think about how you deal with other people with whom you may not be entirely compatible but with whom you must interact regularly, such as members of your family or your spouse's family or co-workers. How you handle those relationships will provide you with guidance as you move from toleration to acceptance of someone in the open adoption.

CONFLICTUAL RELATIONSHIPS

Although all relationships sometimes have conflict, some relationships seem to be characterized by it. Looking back on your preplacement relationship, you may have had some clues that there would be conflict over certain issues. In one open adoption, the adoptive parents knew that the birth father could be threatening. After the adoption, the birth father violated their agreement by calling in the middle of the night and threatening to abduct the child unless his financial demands were met. The adoptive parents explained to him that they were unable to trust him under these circumstances. They arranged for an unlisted telephone number and told him they would only allow contact through their attorney. They continue to allow him to visit the child, but only in the attorney's office under supervision.

Sometimes people deliberately overlook situations that may cause conflict because they so badly want the match to work. After the placement, they find it more difficult to disregard something they don't like. You might convince yourself before the placement that a behavior or personality trait in the other parents won't be a problem, only to find it a source of aggravation after the placement.

However, sometimes potential sources of conflict are concealed. Agnes, a birth mother, learned that the adoptive parents had misled her about having other children. They told her they were afraid she wouldn't place her child with them if she knew they already had two children. Agnes already had two children herself and it was her wish that the child she was placing have the benefit of his adoptive parents' full attention—at least for a while. She was angry at being misled and found it difficult to trust the adoptive parents. Because the adoptive parents wouldn't go with her for counseling, Agnes went alone. She was able to work through her anger enough to interact with the adoptive parents reasonably. It took time, but they were eventually able to rebuild the trust that had been broken.

Fiona told the adoptive parents that she wasn't sure who the birth father was. A few months after the adoption was finalized, Fiona and her former boyfriend, Jack, resumed their relationship. Fiona told Jack and the adoptive parents that he was the child's birth father. The adoptive parents were understandably angry that Fiona had misled them. They feared Jack might object to the adoption and jeopardize its legality. And they were angry that they were not given all the information they should have had before deciding to proceed with this adoption, specifically, whether they were comfortable having an open adoption with this particular birth father.

In another situation, the birth mother's discovery that the adoptive father was a practicing alcoholic destroyed her trust in him. A recovering alcoholic herself, she had made an adoption plan specifically to get her child out of an addictive family. She had asked the adoptive parents outright if they had any alcoholism in their family and the adoptive parents had denied any such problems. Though the adoptive parents were probably denying the problem even to themselves, the birth mother felt betrayed and was concerned about the welfare of the child. While angry at the adoptive parents, she made a commitment to remain in the relationship in the hope that she could be a resource for her daughter if the father did not get into a recovery program.

When a relationship begins with deception, the revelation of that deception may result in a crisis. You may feel you can't trust each other. You may realize you wouldn't have pursued an adoption with these particular people had you known the full truth. You have had a loss of trust and loss of control, and you will probably feel angry at having been manipulated into a decision that you might not have made if you'd had all the information.

In extreme cases, the birth parents may want to revoke their consent to the placement, and in some states, depending on how the adoptive parents falsified information about themselves, they might be successful. In rare instances, the adoptive parents may also want to disrupt the adoption (i.e., relinquish their parental rights). Before either the adoptive or birth parents decide to move the child, they must seriously consider the consequences this decision may have for the child, who has been building an attachment to the adoptive parents. In most situations, you will have to find a way to accept the decision you made, as unfair as it may seem, and attempt to salvage your relationship. A counselor or support group can provide you with the important viewpoint of someone outside your situation as you attempt to rebuild trust and develop the kind of communication that was lacking earlier.

Families with a history of alcoholism, drug use, addiction, abuse, or violence are likely to be dysfunctional, and people from dysfunctional homes may not have good boundaries or be able to maintain relationships. They may bring out unhealthy ways of interacting in the people with whom they are associating, especially if they, too, had a dysfunctional upbringing. However, there are ways to remain in conflictual relationships without becoming victimized by them. You can establish firm rules and stick to them. You can also ask for help from your support group or a counselor, but you need to be realistic about the limitations of counseling. If you are trying to maintain a relationship with an addict or other dysfunctional person who is not involved in his own recovery program, counseling may help you during times of crisis but will probably not deal with the underlying problems. The focus of your individual counseling will be on trying to help yourself stay emotionally healthy rather than on trying to change the dysfunctional person. You may even want to look to programs such as Al-Anon to find support for being in such a relationship.

If your attempts to resolve a serious conflict fail, and you are considering breaking off contact, you can agree to suspend contact for four to six months. Like a trial separation, such a time-out gives you a chance to cool off and put the issues in perspective. If conflict persists, you can end the relationship. But before you do, think about whether the disadvantages of remaining in the relationship outweigh the benefits that brought you into an open adoption agreement. Consider how you will explain the end of the relationship to your child. In Chapter 10 we discuss specific circumstances that can lead to conflict even in otherwise compatible relationships.

UNHEALTHY RELATIONSHIPS

Not all dysfunctional relationships result in overt conflict. Susan Dupuis, M.S.W., of the Independent Adoption Center, points out that sometimes birth and adoptive parents bring out each other's weaknesses. This often begins when birth parents select adoptive parents who remind them of other people with whom they've had relationships. For example, a birth parent who has been accustomed to being a passive victim in a relationship may choose authoritarian adoptive parents; demanding birth parents may choose naive adoptive parents; deprived birth parents may select excessive or overwhelming adoptive parents; birth parents who are reluctant to express their needs may select adoptive parents who don't recognize the needs of others.

Sometimes the relationship appears to function smoothly because this relationship pattern is similar to other relationships the birth and adoptive parents have. The less powerful person in the relationship has learned from other associations that confrontation is ineffective and has developed coping skills for being in unsatisfactory situations. But the relationship is not really satisfying. Sometimes a crisis develops that brings the birth parents and adoptive parents into counseling, which may save the relationship. However, sometimes the relationship is so uncomfortable or unsatisfactory, and the participants are so unwilling to confront each other, that rather than seek help, they drift apart or look for reasons to end the relationship.

Occasionally, the birth parents and adoptive parents become enmeshed, or close to each other in ways that are detrimental to each person's growth as an individual. People in enmeshed relationships may be too dependent on each other. They may be unable to let go and allow the other to lead an independent life. A mother and daughter who function more like sorority sisters than like parent and child may be enmeshed. A child who serves as a surrogate spouse, protecting the parent or acting as a confidante, may also be in an enmeshed relationship. Similarly, an adoptive mother may empathize with the birth mother to the extent that the adoptive mother feels more pain than the birth mother is actually feeling, and she is unable to function effectively as a parent or enjoy parenting because of the pain she feels.

One adoptive mother was ashamed of her child's birth mother. She tried to use the trust that had developed between them to "make over" the birth mother into someone more "acceptable," until she realized she needed to accept the birth mother in order to accept her own child. Adoptive parents can act as mentors to birth parents who have not had people in their lives willing to show them ways of improving themselves. But when the adoptive parents need the birth parents to improve themselves so that the adoptive parents can feel okay about being involved with them or having their child, the relationship is taking an emotionally unhealthy turn.

As we discuss in Chapter 5, birth parents sometimes become dependent on the adoptive parents. This is particularly true of birth parents from troubled families who found unconditional acceptance in the adoptive families. Just like a teenager who needs a nudge to move out into the world, these birth parents need to know they will always be connected to the adoptive parents, but that they have the ability to take control of their lives.

Mara, an adoptive mother, said she saw Rachael, the birth mother, as a younger version of herself. She wanted Rachael to avoid the mistakes she had made and would be angry when Rachael didn't take her advice. Mara recognized that she needed to see Rachael as the person she was and not as she was imagining her. Of course, the converse is also true. Sometimes birth parents need the adoptive parents to be perfect to justify placing the child with them. They, too, need to accept the adoptive parents as the people they are and not idealize them.

In extreme cases of enmeshed relationships, one member of the adoptive couple and a member of the birth family may keep secrets from others or form alliances against them. This is not only unhealthy for the open adoption but it places other relationships at risk as well.

If your relationship with each other is warm and close but still makes you feel uncomfortable, it could be that you have become enmeshed. Again, discussing this situation with your support group or a counselor may shed some light on your relationship and how you can retain the beneficial elements of it while disentangling yourselves from each other.

FAMILIARITY IN RELATIONSHIPS

People are prone to re-creating the relationships they learned in their families of origin. If relationships in your families are healthy, the prospects of your open adoption relationship being meaningful is increased. Most people do not come from completely healthy families, however, so you will probably have some patterns of interacting that are not ideal. But by looking at your open adoption relationship and comparing it to other familial relationships, you can get an idea of why you feel comfortable, distant, or tense with each other. That can help you work through any problems you might have.

FRIENDLY RELATIONSHIPS

Many open adoption relationships have a warmth that comes from having shared a common difficulty, allowing yourself to be vulnerable to another human being and responding to that person's vulnerability, and being committed to a common goal. The birth parents may seem like good friends of the family or an aunt and uncle. There is a caring for one another. Many people in open adoption relationships gather together on holidays, on the child's birthday, and for other special occasions, just as families do. But just as all family members are not equally close, not every open adoption will produce a deep relationship. The adoptive parents might call the birth parents to babysit or allow the child to have overnight visits with the birth family, but might not expect to go on vacations together. One adoptive mother and birth mother developed the habit of going shopping together during the last weeks of the birth mother's pregnancy. They continued the practice after the baby was born, leaving the baby home with the adoptive father once a week. Although they enjoyed their excursions together, and used the time to talk about the child and important developments in each other's lives, their friendship did not go beyond that.

Sometimes emotional intimacy does not develop in a relationship because it is not an equal relationship. The adoptive parents usually have more control in the relationship than the birth parents. Unless they are able to reach out to the birth parents in ways that enable the birth parents to feel they are participating in the relationship and not at the mercy of the adoptive parents' goodwill, the relationship will not progress beyond affability. Sometimes the birth parents' immaturity results in the adoptive parents "parenting" the birth parents. The warmth that develops is similar to that between a parent and a grown child, which may have an emotional depth, but is not the same as it would be if the relationship were more balanced. Of course, some adoptive parents and birth parents begin with this kind of relationship but grow into a more satisfying one as the birth parents mature.

Some adoptive parents regret not being emotionally closer to the birth parents. "If it weren't for the distance we have to have because of the adoption, we could be close friends," said one adoptive mother. An adoptive father said, "If we'd met under different circumstances, I'm sure we'd be closer." The emotional distance these adoptive parents describe is a matter of choice, not necessity. Many adoptive parents have developed a friendship that allows the birth parents to babysit or go on vacation with the family. They do not find that this confuses the child or impairs their ability to form an attachment or effectively parent the child. It is particularly sad when someone adopts a child from a family member and insists that the birth parent no longer be as involved in family activities as she used to be or not be able to come and go as she would be entitled to as a family member. Birth parents should not have to choose between their families and their child, especially in open adoption. (For more on relative adoptions, see Chapter 15.) Not everyone in open adoption becomes best friends, but you can allow your relationship to develop to its natural level of closeness.

CLOSE RELATIONSHIPS

The relationship between some birth and adoptive families does develop a depth that may seem amazing given the differences in age, religion, background, and education that can be present. Sometimes the closeness develops during the pregnancy, but sometimes trust must grow and be tested over time before true emotional intimacy results. Tara had a congenial relationship with the adoptive mother, Beth, during the pregnancy, but had only occasional contact with her after the birth. When Tara became pregnant a second time, she called Beth and asked her to be her childbirth coach. Tara wasn't placing this baby for adoption, but she didn't have anyone close to her that she could ask to share that experience with her. Having already shared the birth of a child with Beth, she felt comfortable having her in the delivery room. When Beth responded unselfishly to her request and saw her through a difficult labor, the two became closer. A few years later Tara married. When she gave birth again, her husband was her childbirth coach, but Beth was the first person she called with the news.

Another adoptive mother said she was surprised at how frequently she thought of the birth mother. She expected to have to force herself to live up to her open adoption agreement, but she found it was natural to think about how the birth mother might enjoy hearing about an incident or seeing a particular photograph.

One birth mother, who was manic-depressive, was not able to maintain a consistent relationship with the adoptive parents. However, her parents and the adoptive parents became quite close.

Extended Family Members

Sometimes members of the birth family are highly involved with the adoptive family after the placement, regardless of whether or not they were involved in the adoption plan. While the birth parents may not have been able or ready to parent the child, the birth relatives may have been ready to assume their roles as grandparents, aunts, uncles, or cousins, and open adoption allows them to do that. In some open adoptions, members of the birth family are included in the list of people to whom the adoptive parents send letters and photographs or invite to attend special occasions.

Sometimes members of the birth family take on a more active role with the adoptive family than the birth parents, particularly in cases where the birth parent dies. Sometimes the birth parents are unable or unwilling to maintain an open relationship or are prohibited by the adoptive parents from interacting with the child because of the birth parent's choice of lifestyle. In those situations, the birth family can give the child the important sense of being biologically connected to people and accepted by his biologic relatives. Furthermore, the child can find positive role models in members of his extended birth families even though he may not be able to find them in his birth parents at a particular point in time.

In what is not an uncommon story, the birth parents in one adoption broke up shortly after the placement. Both were attending college in another state and returned to school the semester after the birth. The child was a first grandchild for both sets of birth grandparents. Evelyn, the maternal birth grandmother, lived near the adoptive parents, and had gotten to know the adoptive parents well during the pregnancy. She was thrilled when they invited her to the child's first birthday party, an experience that led to occasional visits. Since the adoptive grandparents lived in a distant state, Evelyn was the only grandparent the child had contact with on a regular basis. The adoptive parents were pleased to see that their daughter would not lack an intergenerational upbringing and encouraged the relationship. Furthermore, as the child grew, Evelyn spontaneously provided them with important information about the birth mother's childhood development, such as when she took her first step, her learning style, and the kinds of activities that used to pacify her.

Although it can be beneficial for the adoptive family to have close relations with the birth grandparents, adoptive parents may be tempted to nurture those relationships and neglect the birth parents simply because they feel more comfortable with people closer to their age. Such a situation not only deprives the birth parent and the adoptive family of meaningful associations but it can leave the birth parent feeling like a fifth wheel in an arrangement where she is actually a primary participant.

Sometimes, however, members of the birth family do not want or understand the need to maintain a relationship with the adoptive family because they have not had enough information about open adoption. They may not want to get attached to the child because they are afraid they will be hurt if the adoptive parents cut off contact with them. Birth relatives who grew up in an era of confidential adoptions may think they shouldn't have contact with the adoptive family. Like some adoptive parents, some birth relatives cling to the idea that if they don't have contact with the adoptive family, they can forget about the child. Sometimes they are ashamed that an untimely pregnancy occurred in their family or that they couldn't solve the problem it created within the family. Sometimes they are embarrassed or ashamed when a child is of mixed racial heritage. These attitudes can be signs of unresolved grief or they could just be due to lack of information. They may take time, intervention, or counseling to overcome.

Roberto, a birth grandfather, refused to allow anyone to discuss his grandchild in his presence, even though other members of the birth family saw the child regularly. One Christmas evening, Viola, the birth mother, confronted him about what she viewed as his insensitivity. Roberto told her she was the only member of the family who wanted to talk about the child, who was now nearly three years old, and that she should "stop living in the past." Viola told him other members of the family wanted her child acknowledged as part of the family. An emotional family conference followed in which Viola's sisters, brother, mother, grandparents, and two aunts told Roberto that they wanted the child recognized openly. Two weeks later, Roberto called the adoptive family and spent two hours with his grandson at a nearby park.

Younger birth relatives may not want to participate in the open adoption because they have not had enough life experience to realize the importance of maintaining biologic connections or because they have not grieved for the loss the placement has caused for them. Keith's two teenage brothers expressed total disinterest in their brother's child. They said they didn't see this child as a member of their family. Keith was hurt when his siblings didn't want to see his latest pictures of the child, but hoped that as they grew up they would at least understand why the child remained important to him.

In one unusual family, a single birth mother did not maintain contact with the adoptive family, but her thirteen-year-old daughter, Emma, did. Emma, who had always wanted a baby brother, sent the adoptive family letters and photographs, called them on the phone, and sent the child items she made at school or treats she baked at home. With her mother's permission, Emma even visited the adoptive family, taking the bus or asking the adoptive parents to pick her up after school.

Members of the birth family who become aware of the adoption plan after it is executed, or who resisted a relationship with the adoptive parents because they were in denial about the adoption plan, may not be sure how to initiate a relationship after the placement. Either the birth family or the adoptive family can reach out and let the other know they are interested in a relationship. Proceed slowly. Get to know and trust each other.

Remember that each member of the birth family will have a unique relationship with each member of the adoptive family because they are all individuals with their own needs and experiences. One adoptive couple had an excellent relationship with the birth mother, who affirmed their parenting roles in numerous ways. The birth mother's sister had an entirely different attitude. She refused to call the baby by the name the adoptive parents had chosen and was clearly hostile toward them. In discussing their concerns with the birth mother, the adoptive parents learned that the birth aunt had wanted to adopt the baby herself. The adoptive parents suggested that the birth aunt seek counseling, but she couldn't afford it and the adoptive parents did not feel it was their responsibility to pay for counseling for the entire birth family. They decided they could live with her hostility, but firmly told her that she could not visit the baby unless she called him by the name they had chosen. Another family might choose to pay for the counseling to make visits easier for everyone.

Sometimes the birth family will draw the adoptive parents into a family dispute. For example, the birth grandparents may call the adoptive parents and ask them to use their influence with the birth mother to persuade her to change boyfriends, go back to school, or move back home. At best, this leads to awkward situations and it can put relationships at risk, especially if the birth mother feels manipulated. Adoptive parents should take care not to get involved in such behind-the-scenes maneuvers by maintaining good boundaries, being honest, and resisting anything that smacks of family secrets.

Members of the extended birth family stay in contact with the adoptive family to maintain their tie to the child. No such motivation is there to encourage the extended adoptive family to maintain ties with the birth family. The child should feel a sense of unity among his birth and adoptive relatives, however, which does not always happen. A relationship between the two extended families may not seem necessary to them unless they will see each other at family gatherings. Sometimes it just takes time before the extended adoptive family accepts the open adoption relationship enough to want to develop a relationship with members of the birth family. They may have been fearful that the adoptive parents would be hurt by the open adoption. Once they see their loved ones are happy and that their roles are valued, they may be more willing to interact with the birth family.

If relatives in the adoptive family have been named as guardians in the case of the death of the adoptive parents, they should make a special effort to get to know the birth parents so they can maintain the child's ties to his birth parents if he loses his adoptive parents.

Like all relationships, your open adoption will have emotional peaks and valleys. As you overcome each hurdle, you'll learn what to expect from each other and will gain confidence in your ability to make the relationship work.

10

Changes in Lives,
Changes in Openness

During the early years of your relationship, it may have been difficult to imagine yourself and each other as growing older and changing. And you may have difficulty imagining the child as an eight-year-old or as a teenager.

Confidential adoptions froze the images that the adoptive and birth parents had of each other and that the birth parents had of the child. But open adoption allows you to witness growth and change in each other. These changes will affect how you interact with other people, including those in your open adoption. But because your agreement was based on the fact that the adoptive parents were in certain circumstances and the birth parents were in certain circumstances, you may wonder how your agreement will be affected as conditions change.

For example, the birth mother may have selected an adoptive couple because she wanted her child to have a stable, two-parent family. Years later, the adoptive parents may be divorced, or experiencing financial or emotional crisis, and the birth mother may be in a stable marriage. The adoptive parents may feel guilty that they aren't the stable couple the birth mother selected. Although they know intellectually that the adoption is permanent, they may still wonder irrationally if they have a right to continue to parent their child when their lives are unsteady and the birth mother's life is balanced. The birth mother may regret her decision, thinking, "If I hadn't made an adoption plan, my child would be better off now."

You may be different in other ways than you appeared at the time of the placement. Adoptive parents who appeared to be infertile may conceive a child later. Birth parents who consoled themselves with the thought that they could have another child when circumstances were better may have difficulty conceiving again, may find that there is never an ideal time to have a child, or may feel that they don't deserve to be a parent.

It is essential to realize that although certain circumstances led to the adoption, the adoption plan was not a contract dependent on the preservation of those conditions. The birth parents made a plan based on the information they had available about themselves and about the adoptive parents. They are not expected to be able to predict the future, nor are they responsible for circumstances beyond their control, such as actions by the adoptive parents, an economic recession, the development of mental illness, infertility, or fertility. Similarly, the adoptive parents made a plan based on the information they had available about themselves and the birth parents. They are responsible for their actions, but not everything in their lives is within their control, either.

Of course, it is important for a child to be in an environment free of stress and disruption. But it is also important for a child to have the stability that comes from having permanent parents. The birth parents traded the possibility that they would eventually become more capable and that their child would not be harmed in the meantime for the likelihood that the adoptive parents could meet their child's needs immediately as well as in the future. Child development experts agree that the first three years of a child's life are extremely important. During this time the child needs to develop trust that his needs will be consistently met by the same people. Children who experience security during infancy and early childhood can draw on those resources years later if their family is in crisis. However, children who experience erratic parenting during the first three years of life may have difficulties such as inability to identify their needs or inability to tell right from wrong—even if they later have consistent, loving parents.

When the adoptive parents have a significant change of circumstances that leaves them feeling guilty about having adopted the child, such as a divorce, they may pull away from the birth parents. They may be hoping to hide the situation until it changes. They may feel that they somehow misled the birth parents, or they may be ashamed of their situation. They need to remember that honesty is the foundation of a relationship, and by not sharing information about their change of circumstance, they may be damaging their relationship with the birth parents. The adoptive parents need to remind themselves that as long as they acted in good faith, they can't be held responsible for being unable to predict their current circumstances.

They also need to remind themselves that they have the right to make mistakes, just as all parents do, without feeling they don't deserve to have children or they should turn their child over to other people to raise (such as the birth parents). However, adoptive parents may be in such turmoil that their withdrawal is not specific to the birth parents—they may not be emotionally or physically available to anyone. Birth parents shouldn't assume the adoptive parents are pulling away from them personally or changing the open adoption agreement.

When the adoptive parents share their struggles with the birth parents, the birth parents often respond by coming to their assistance. It can help the birth parents heal and develop self-respect to be able to help someone else during a time of crisis. Karl and Jody were afraid and ashamed to tell Mio, the birth mother, that they were divorcing. Mio had made an adoption plan because she was in the middle of a divorce herself and the adoptive parents were worried she would regret not choosing another couple or not raising the child herself. When Jody finally informed Mio, her response was kind and supportive: "I really understand how things can change. If you need me, call." Another birth mother in a similar situation said to the adoptive parents: "You are both such great people. I know Felix will be all right."

Couples involved in a divorce may knowingly or unwittingly ask their friends to take sides. Adoptive parents should resist any impulse to involve the birth family in the divorce—including asking them to testify in a custody battle—but should allow them to remain friendly with both sides. The birth parents' ongoing contact with the child may depend on their ability to remain on good terms with both adoptive parents. Furthermore, the child may misinterpret the birth parents' involvement as an attempt to split up his family. It just isn't fair to put the birth parents in that position.

When you are able to share information with each other, also share your feelings. One adoptive mother felt uncomfortable around the birth mother, who had gotten married and was having difficulty conceiving a child. The birth mother finally broke the silence by saying, "You seem to be feeling guilty that you have my child and now I can't have one." She said she knew the past could not be changed, and that she felt the adoptive parents' willingness to keep their relationship open had been a special gift to her all along, but was even more cherished now that she was dealing with secondary infertility. She told the adoptive mother what was sad for her was feeling the adoptive mother pulling away at a time when she needed to know she would stay in contact with what might be her only child by birth.

In rare situations, the child may be in danger of being harmed by staying with one or both adoptive parents. Child abuse in adoptive families is not common, though such incidents are often highly publicized, making it appear so. But adoptive families are subject to the same stresses as other families, and abuse sometimes occurs. Adoption is rarely to blame. However, because of the mistaken notion that the adoptive parents are perfect, when abuse does occur, both birth and adoptive parents feel isolated. When it does happen, a plan needs to be made for the child's future that takes into consideration his need for safety as well as his need to remain connected to the people who are his family—his adoptive parents and siblings.

Even in cases of child abuse, the adoptive family deserves to be treated by child protective services like any other family, with respect for the attachment that exists between the parents and the child, with an awareness of the importance of continuity for the child, and with a presumption that reunification with the adoptive family is the goal. Such a plan should also give consideration to the importance of the child remaining in contact with other significant people, including his birth parents. But there should be no hasty moves to terminate the adoptive parents' parental rights and return the child to the birth parents just because adoption is involved.

Why Changes Occur

Sometimes changes in your lives and in your families may cause you to renegotiate changes in your level of openness. As Chapter 8 explains, during the first year after the placement you may have had to adjust your expectations of how open your relationship would be to meet the realities of your actual needs. Typically, though not always, the birth parents find they want more contact and the adoptive parents want less. As your relationship develops, you may find yourselves again adjusting the kind of contact you have with each other and the frequency with which you communicate.

Often, the birth parents move on with their lives after the child's first year or two. If they have completed a significant amount of their grief work they realize they can't hang onto the child the way they may have during the first year or so. They resume the roles they had before the birth or take on new ones. This is particularly true for young birth parents who still have much growth and development to accomplish. As they become involved with school, peers, careers, and new relationships, their focus is on themselves and not on the child. This is as it should be. One of the reasons they placed the child for adoption was because they needed to concentrate on themselves before taking on responsibility for another person, and their involvement in the open adoption may decrease as they put their attention into other areas of their lives.

If birth parents pull back from the open adoption relationship to move on with their lives, the adoptive family may still have more regular, ongoing contact with other members of the birth family. However, not all birth parents decrease their involvement with the adoptive family, and this is not necessarily a sign that they haven't grieved sufficiently. Some move on with their lives but remain committed to the level of involvement they have been having with the adoptive family.

Just as the birth parents' desire for openness changes over time, the adoptive parents may have developed a more secure sense of entitlement and may be comfortable with more contact as a result. In addition, as their child gets older and begins to be able to talk about who he is and where he came from, adoptive parents realize the benefit to their child of having contact with his birth parents. They may not only be ready for more openness but desire it.

WHEN THE BIRTH PARENT MARRIES

Some birth parents are married at the time of the adoption, and some never marry. But it is not unusual for birth parents, especially those who were teenagers or young adults at the time of the birth, to get married a few years later. Occasionally the birth mother and birth father will marry each other after the placement, but usually the birth parents take separate paths.

In some open adoptions, the birth parent's wedding provides a "coming out" for the child. Although the child's existence may not have been a secret, the child has probably not been part of the birth parent's social life. The birth parent's wedding may be the first occasion since the child's birth in which all the people important to the parent are together—immediate family, extended family, distant relatives, close friends, business colleagues, neighbors, and acquaintances. Many open adoptions have a level of closeness that make it natural for the adoptive family to fit in with this gathering.

Furthermore, the birth parent's wedding also symbolizes her movement to a new level of personal growth. It is the beginning of a new family for the birth parent—indeed, parts of the wedding ritual emphasize the transfer of family membership from the families of origin to the newly created family. Including the child placed for adoption in the marriage celebration can be a statement as simple as, "This is a person important to me." But it can also say much more. It may be the birth parent's way of saying that the child is a part of her past life, but will remain part of her future life. It may be the birth parent's way of acknowledging that the open adoption, which some may have viewed as shameful, has enriched his life.

Some birth parents want the child to be part of the wedding party, usually as ring bearer or flower girl. Think carefully about the significance of having the adoptive family attend the birth parent's wedding or having the child participate as part of the wedding party. In one situation, the adoptive parents agreed to attend the wedding but declined to allow the child to be the ring bearer. They felt his presence on the altar would draw attention away from the wedding, placing an emphasis on the birth mother's past rather than her future. Some adoptive parents have expressed concern that even as part of the congregation their child would be the focus of too much attention. However, others welcome the opportunity to wish the birth parent well and have their child meet more people in the birth parent's familial and social circle.

One adoptive family felt honored to have been seated behind the bride's mother and father when the birth mother got married. Another adoptive father felt moved to see the birth mother, who just a few years earlier had been immature and demanding, recite vows that showed her understanding of how relationships grow and prosper. This father felt the effort that he and his wife had made in developing a relationship with the birth mother and in modeling a good marital relationship played a role in her personal growth. They were pleased to be asked to witness her marriage.

Often a spouse is highly supportive of a birth parent's ongoing involvement with the child, and sees it as the sign of commitment and responsibility that it is. However, sometimes birth parents will pull back from the open adoption relationship after they marry and start a family. Like many people, the spouse of a birth parent may think the birth parent's interest in the child represents a failure to get over the experience. Because the connection between the birth mother and the child is acknowledged somewhat more than the connection between the birth father and the child, the birth father may have more difficulty getting support from his wife to maintain the open adoption. Sometimes a spouse does not like the birth parent seeing the other birth parent at gatherings at the adoptive family's home. Sometimes birth parents become so busy with their families that they neglect the open adoption relationship.

Birth parents need to educate people they love about open adoption and the importance birth parents have in a child's life. They need to explain that while open adoption provides them with benefits, its main purpose is for the child, and they have a responsibility to demonstrate their love and acceptance, as well as to remain accessible to the child.

Adoptive parents often welcome the involvement of the birth parent's spouse in the open adoption, especially when the partner appears to have had a stabilizing effect on a previously disorganized birth parent. However, adoptive parents should take care not to ignore the birth parent because they are more comfortable with her spouse.

Sometimes, however, a birth parent's new spouse or partner can cause the adoptive parents to reevaluate the open adoption arrangement. Fred and Nita genuinely cared for their child's birth mother, Cassie, and trusted her to take the child on short trips to the park, the movies, or a restaurant. But when Cassie became involved with a new boyfriend, Fred and Nita were concerned. They suspected him of drug use and felt he could be violent, although they had no proof, and they did not want him around their child. They knew that if they told Cassie their concerns she would deny that her boyfriend could possibly harm the child, and they suspected she would tell them that she'd be with the child anyway and they could trust her to take care of the child just as she had been doing. Fred and Nita worried that if they didn't let Cassie continue to take the child by herself, she would interpret that as a loss of trust in her—not a lack of trust in her boyfriend. Although they could demand that she not allow the boyfriend around the child if she took him by herself, they suspected that she would also see the rule as a lack of confidence in her judgment. Furthermore, if she didn't see the danger from the boyfriend, they were concerned she wouldn't comply with their restriction.

While they pondered what to do, Fred and Nita avoided situations in which Cassie (and possibly her new boyfriend) would have the child unsupervised. Eventually, however, they explained to Cassie that they were concerned not only for their child but for her, whom they feared was also vulnerable in the new relationship. They explained that they in no way wanted to restrict her access to the child, but they had to make decisions that they felt were best, and as long as they were concerned about this boyfriend, Cassie could only see the child under their supervision. Cassie was angry and hurt. She accused them of going back on their open adoption agreement. Fred and Nita remained firm. The incident has severely damaged their relationship, but because Cassie wants to continue to see the child, they still communicate. Fred and Nita are hoping that for her own sake, as well as for the open adoption relationship, Cassie will view the boyfriend realistically.

Birth parents may want less contact with the adoptive family after they have other children, both because they have less time for other relationships and because it can be hard to see all the children together and wonder what it would have been like to raise them together. After the birth mother grieves for this loss—one that she couldn't have grieved for at the time of the placement—she may be able to resume visits. (For more on siblings, see Chapter 13.)

OTHER REASONS FOR CHANGES

One of the more difficult changes that families may encounter is a birth parent who comes to regret her decision. When Lucille learned from the birth mother that she felt coerced by her parents into making an adoption plan, and that she had regretted the decision ever since, all the fears Lucille had about open adoption resurfaced. She was afraid the birth mother would make an attempt to kidnap the child or challenge her role as a parent. Lucille insisted that the birth mother receive further counseling and offered to pay for it. While the birth mother continued to believe she should have raised the child herself, she eventually was able to accept that she could not change her decision.

Sometimes the birth or adoptive parents move, causing them to change the frequency or type of contact they have with each other. Sometimes personal crises, such as illness in the family, leave people without any energy to maintain relationships. In one family, the adoptive mother was hospitalized for several months. All of the adoptive father's energy was spent maintaining his job, taking care of his wife, and raising their two children. He had no time to send photographs or letters to the birth mother.

If changes in circumstances or families cause you to want or need to change the level of openness you have had, actively renegotiate that change. Don't passively allow yourselves to slip out of each other's lives. Someone needs to verbalize what is happening: "It seems like we're not hearing from you as much. Is there something going on?" The other person can then explain her circumstances. Furthermore, make a commitment to staying in touch at some minimal level. More change is likely, and the time may come when you want to resume your previous level of openness.

Adoptive Parents Who Don't Honor the Agreement

Sometimes adoptive parents renege on their open adoption agreement. Some do so passively, living up to the letter of the agreement, but not its spirit. They may send blurry photographs of the child, or they may make excuses for not getting together, never actually setting a date. Some are more abrupt. They stop sending letters, move, or get an unlisted telephone number. When this happens, the birth parents have neither the access to their child nor the information about their child that they were promised, nor do they have even the sense of finality that was present in confidential adoptions. Perhaps there are things they would have said to their child in person or in a letter had they known they wouldn't have another chance. Perhaps they would have given their child a gift or memento. They have been robbed of these privileges, and so has their child. It may be especially hard to grieve for this loss because there is still the hope that they will have the contact they've been promised.

During the first two years after the placement, Tawana received letters and photographs through her attorney, as agreed upon with the adoptive parents. The third year the letters and photographs came less often. By the fourth year they had stopped completely. Tawana was fortunate to be working with a facilitator who was willing to contact the adoptive parents and arrange for joint counseling. Tawana felt the intervention was important enough to pay for her share of the counseling herself, even though it was a hardship for her.

Not every birth parent in this situation has this remedy. Sometimes the facilitator is unwilling to become involved in negotiating a resolution to such a problem. Sometimes the adoptive parents cannot be traced. Sometimes they refuse to negotiate with the birth parents or meet with the facilitator or a counselor. They may refuse to pay for joint counseling for birth parents who cannot afford it. The possibility that the adoptive parents may not live up to the open adoption agreement is one of the birth parents' deepest fears in open adoption—they enter into open adoption knowing the risk, but that doesn't make it any less painful when it happens. Adoptive parents must understand that openness is not a "gift" or "bonus" that they offer the birth parents and can take away at will. In many cases, birth parents wouldn't have chosen adoption at all if openness had not been promised. In losing contact with their child, they have lost far more than they bargained for.

We have emphasized the importance of good preparation, of choosing each other carefully, and of clearly communicating your expectations before the placement to minimize this risk. But if the worst does happen, the birth parents must grieve for losses they didn't expect to have when they chose an open adoption. They will grieve for the loss of knowing their child, of watching him grow, of being able to share experiences with him and provide him with information. These losses are the same ones that birth parents experienced in confidential adoptions, but the difference is that birth parents in open adoption had different expectations. As a result, they also feel a sense of betrayal and a deep sense of anger. They may experience fear and panic as they realize the vision they had of the future will not be realized. Their faith in the basic goodness of human beings may even be shaken. They will probably want professional help coping with their reactions.

As we write this book, Washington state has given legal standing to open adoption agreements and other states are considering similar legislation. The rationale is that if birth parents place their child with adoptive parents with the understanding that they will be able to have contact with that child, they have the right to expect that such a promise will be honored. Advocates of legalized open adoption agreements argue that although no one is obligated to make an open adoption agreement, those who do so should be legally obligated to live up to it. They hope that by legalizing the open adoption agreement, adoptive parents who are not committed to open adoption will not become involved in it.

While we believe adoptive parents have an obligation to honor their promises to the birth parents, we believe this is a moral responsibility and not a legal one. We believe open adoptions are relationships more than agreements and we are not in favor of the court system being used to negotiate relationships. More importantly, we believe it is necessary for the adoptive parents' sense of entitlement for them to have the same authority that other parents have, including the right to decide with whom their child will associate. We strongly encourage adoptive parents to find some way to maintain the open adoption, even when birth parents are troubled, but we believe this should be their choice and not a court directive. To do otherwise defines open adoptions as guardianship rather than parenting.

Furthermore, as we've stated throughout this book, we believe open adoptions work best when birth and adoptive parents take the time and commit the energy to building successful relationships, and we are concerned that people might feel less of a need to develop a strong, trusting relationship with each other if they can look to the courts to enforce the agreement when it founders. The child's needs in open adoption are better met by a good relationship between birth parents and adoptive parents than by court-mandated letters, phone calls, and visits. And even though there may not be any legal penalties for adoptive parents who do not live up to their open adoption agreements, there are consequences. When their children learn that they were denied an opportunity to keep in touch with their birth families, it may seriously damage the relationship between them and their adoptive parents. More importantly, whenever we fail to keep our word, we are not living up to our potential as human beings.

Opening a Confidential or Semiopen Adoption

Sometimes people who became involved in a confidential or semiopen adoption want to increase the level of openness. Adoptive parents who adopted a second child in a more open arrangement than their first child may feel comfortable with the increased openness and see how it has benefitted the child. They may want those same benefits for their first child and look for ways to have more contact with that child's birth parents. Similarly, birth parents who placed more than one child in different levels of openness may want to increase the amount of openness in their confidential or semiopen adoption after seeing the benefits.

Sometimes people who correspond for years in a semiopen adoption develop such a level of intimacy and trust that they begin to feel the intermediary is no longer necessary, and they find they are ready for direct contact with each other. In addition, as children grow up, take on their own identities, and begin to ask questions about their origins, adoptive parents often see the value in their children having more direct contact with their birth families. Although they might have been threatened by the presence of the birth parents at the time of the placement, years later adoptive parents are often secure enough in their role as parents and their child's attachment to them that they are no longer fearful of the birth parents. Birth parents who said they didn't want contact or wanted only limited contact with their child at the time of the placement may be ready for it years later when they realize they cannot forget about the child or completely put the adoption behind them.

You may be reluctant to initiate more contact with each other even though you may desire it or see how it could benefit the child. You may not know anyone who has opened up their adoptions and may feel that you are taking unknown risks. You may even be advised against greater openness by a facilitator committed to anonymous contact or by well-meaning relatives or friends. Keep in mind that open adoptions are relationships and are not static. They grow and change, and evolving from little or no contact to increased contact may reflect the natural development of your relationship.

Sometimes, of course, the change in your relationship is abrupt rather than gradual—you unexpectedly learn each other's identities or run into each other at the mall. You may not have made a decision to increase the level of openness, but find yourself faced with that result. Often the impetus to open the adoption comes from the child himself. He asks why he can't write to the birth mother, call her, or see her. The answers adoptive parents give the child may not satisfy him.

However, psychologist Randolph W. Severson, Ph.D., of Hope Cottage in Texas, advises adoptive parents that opening a semiopen or confidential adoption simply because they cannot deny a request from their child may be a mistake at that time. He asks parents in this situation whether they can ordinarily say no to their child. If one or both cannot, he suggests that they postpone opening the adoption until they are able to set firm limits with the child. Otherwise, they will have difficulty setting limits when the adoption is open.

Adoptive parents with a child asking for more openness may want to consider the benefits of moving to a greater level of openness when the child is still young, rather than waiting until the child is more mature. As we see in Chapter 12, much of the information and the reassurance that children obtain from direct contact with their birth parents is needed between approximately ages seven and eleven. By delaying what may be an inevitable opening of the semiopen adoption, adoptive parents may be asking the child to struggle with issues that might be much easier to understand with direct contact with the birth parents. They are also allowing the child to grow up in the open adoption rather than having to suddenly develop a relationship during the child's adolescence, when opening up the adoption could become a volatile issue between the teenager and the adoptive parents.

In such cases, the adoptive parents may be forced into direct contact without the luxury of allowing their relationship with the birth parents to evolve, to get education or counseling for everyone, to ascertain that everyone understands their roles, and to set rules for contact that take everyone's needs into consideration. The teenager may control the opening of the adoption and may do so awkwardly. Furthermore, adoptive parents may feel more threatened by the sudden appearance of the birth parents during the child's adolescence, when he is rebelling and testing them, than they would during the middle childhood years.

In what is not an unusual situation, Stacy, a birth mother, and adoptive parents Gwen and Craig had been exchanging letters and pictures for several years. Stacy was now married with two children born since the adoption. Gwen and Craig felt far more certain that their parent–child relationship could survive any test. When their eight-year-old daughter Chloe said to them one day, shortly after receiving a letter from Stacy, "Why don't we ever see her?" the adoptive parents weren't sure how to answer. They realized they felt comfortable moving to the next level of openness with Stacy. Their only hesitancy was that everything was going so smoothly—by changing their level of openness would they be asking for trouble? Would Stacy abduct Chloe once she knew where she was? Would Chloe want to live with her?

At the same time, they couldn't think of a reasonable answer to Chloe's question. They couldn't say, "We're afraid she'll kidnap you," because they didn't actually believe it—it was just a fear. They couldn't say, "We're afraid you'll want to live with her if you knew her," because they knew they were a family. They also realized that any excuse they could come up with at this time might be convincing to an eight-year-old, but would never convince a fifteen-year-old. They were concerned that the question of why Stacy didn't visit would become an issue with Chloe, and that when she reached adolescence, it could become a source of tension between them.

Gwen and Craig realized that although they knew the risks of opening up their adoption were minimal, emotionally they were still fearful. Because their adoption facilitator was in another state, they contacted a local agency specializing in open adoption and asked about counseling or education services that might help them resolve their fears. Even though the agency only offered preadoption education in a group setting, and this wasn't what they were looking for, Gwen and Craig decided to attend the group sessions anyway. To their surprise, they found they had a lot in common with couples who were considering fully disclosed adoptions. They were able to address a lot of their fears about having direct contact with the birth mother, but they also found that they were much further ahead than many of the others in the group in feeling secure about their parenting and trusting the birth mother.

After the group sessions ended, Gwen and Craig wrote a letter to Stacy telling her they would like to have more direct contact. They suggested that she contact an agency in her area to receive some education about what it would be like to have a fully disclosed adoption. They specifically discussed the need for everyone to understand what their roles would be—and would not be—and the need to have a written agreement about the rules for the new openness. Stacy replied immediately that she would like to have more contact and promised to get in touch with the counselor she had seen after the placement. With her counselor she explored her fears—that her child would be angry with her and that it would be too painful to see the child after not seeing her for eight years.

When Stacy and Gwen and Craig felt they were ready, Gwen and Craig sent Stacy their phone number. It didn't take Stacy long to call. Though everyone was tentative at first, soon they were chatting like old friends. And, indeed, they had been developing a friendship through their correspondence. After they had talked by phone several times, Gwen and Craig waited for an opportunity to tell Chloe about the new level of openness they had arranged. When Chloe asked again one day why they never saw Stacy, her adoptive parents told her that although they had not met Stacy, they did know her telephone number, and that if Chloe wanted to, she could talk to her birth mother on the phone. Chloe was excited, and a phone call was arranged for the same week.

After talking on the phone several times, Stacy and Gwen and Craig decided they were comfortable enough to meet each other. They waited for Chloe to indicate she was interested in a meeting. When she did, her parents said that a meeting would be possible, but first they wanted her to talk with a counselor about it. The counselor explored Chloe's expectations of her birth mother and of the meeting, such as what she expected Stacy to act like and how she expected to interact with her. The counselor was trying to identify any anxieties Chloe might have, for instance, that she might be returned to her birth mother. She also wanted the child to fully understand that Stacy would not be another mother but would be another concerned adult in her life. The counselor also wanted the girl to feel that she had some control over the relationship. When everyone was ready, the birth mother, the adoptive parents, and their daughter met for the first time. It was much like the first meeting described in Chapter 4. Other members of the family met later.

Stacy and Gwen and Craig could have met before Chloe became involved so that they could get to know each other personally and develop a trusting relationship. They might have arranged for their first meeting to be with a counselor who could have the same kind of "vision matching" session described in Chapter 5. However, location made this impractical. Another family might have arranged a conference call with a counselor, but these parents talked a lot on the telephone with each other about their expectations, their roles, and the rules they would follow. The adoptive parents wrote up their verbal agreement, signed it, and mailed it to the birth mother for her signature.

Gwen and Craig chose to proceed cautiously in opening up their adoption, re-creating as much as possible the process they would have used if they had planned a fully disclosed adoption from the beginning. Not everyone may feel the need to proceed that cautiously, especially if they have been communicating in such a way that they trust each other and feel certain that everyone understands their roles.

Joyce, an adoptive mother, was preparing to send a stack of photographs to Kelly, the birth mother, through the intermediary they'd used for six years when she realized she had inadvertently written the child's full name on the back of the photos. She asked herself whether the sense of safety the anonymity gave her was worth spending the time to obliterate the name on the back of all the photos. She realized that she no longer felt threatened by the possibility that Kelly might be able to find her. Six years of communication with Kelly had convinced her that she was a trustworthy person. Six years of being a parent had convinced Joyce that no one could come between her and her child. She sent the photos, along with a note suggesting that Kelly contact her directly. After two long telephone calls, they arranged a meeting.

In another adoptive family, the agency that had placed their first child in a confidential adoption had moved to fully disclosed adoptions by the time the couple adopted a second time. The education they received at the agency, along with the satisfactory experience they had with the birth mother, convinced the couple that their older child would benefit from an open adoption. They asked the agency to contact the birth mother and see if she would like to have contact with them. A social worker at the agency met with the birth mother to be sure that she understood what it would mean to have a fully disclosed adoption. Then they arranged a meeting between the birth parents and the adoptive parents to get to know each other and discuss their expectations.

In opening a confidential or semiopen adoption, the following suggestions may be helpful:

- Reread the early chapters of this book that discuss the fears people have of openness and how to begin an open adoption relationship. They are applicable even if the adoption took place years ago.

- Take advantage of other educational sources available to you, such as support groups, counseling, preadoption or postadoption education classes. You don't need to use the same facilitator who arranged your adoption if that person is not available or does not provide the necessary services. Nor do you have to limit yourself to educational materials about open adoption. Learning more about issues pertinent to all types of adoption will also help you. If the child is old enough to understand what is going on, make sure he has the opportunity to have his fears or anxieties addressed in a counseling session.

- Try to have a "vision matching" session either with an open adoption facilitator, through a conference call on the telephone with a counselor, or just among yourselves. You want to be clear about your roles and how opening the adoption will and will not change your relationships. You want to all have an understanding of the rules for contact. You also want to have an idea of how conflicts will be settled, including who will participate in counseling or mediation sessions, who will pay for them, and how the counselor or mediator will be chosen.

- Proceed at your own pace and respect the need of the other parents to proceed at their pace, which may be different from yours. Assess how comfortable you feel as the relationship changes and allow yourself to reach a level of comfort before moving to the next stage in your relationship. However, make sure you are not looking for ways to delay the evolution of the relationship because you are fearful. If you proceed too slowly, the child will not have the kind of access to his birth parents that he may need during the middle childhood years. However, if you proceed too quickly, you may not get beyond your fear, which can hamper your relationship and send the child the message that open adoption is something that makes his birth or adoptive parents uncomfortable.

▪ If the child is old enough to express an opinion, respect that opinion. If he is not ready to proceed with direct contact when the birth and adoptive parents are, spend some time exploring what his fears or anxieties might be, allowing *his* relationship with the birth parents to develop at his pace. The birth and adoptive parents can continue to develop their own relationship, including meeting each other, but they should not press a relationship on the child until he is ready. Adoptees historically have not been allowed control of their own destiny—allow the child some say in this relationship.

▪ Be aware that siblings in the adoptive and birth families may have concerns about the increasing openness of the adoption that also need to be addressed (see Chapter 13).

▪ The child's first meeting with the birth parents will be similar to the first meeting between the adoptive parents and the birth parents. Make sure the meeting takes place in a setting where the child feels safe—with the adoptive parents close at hand for reassurance and not so many birth relatives around that the child feels overwhelmed.

▪ If you did not have one at the time of the placement, consider developing a ritual to mark the importance of the new relationships that have developed and validate the transfer of parental roles that occurred years ago—much like a wedding ceremony for people who eloped or a reaffirmation of vows for a couple who have been estranged. The ceremony could include images in which a circle is completed or connected. Plan the ceremony together, allowing the child to participate, and record the event.

Changing the Open Adoption Relationship

If you entered into an open adoption without the benefit of good preparation, ongoing support, or professional guidance, your relationship has probably developed somewhat differently than we have described. If you are wishing you had done things differently, remember that you are not locked into the patterns of your past interactions, although changing them may require a lot of effort. You can still have a "vision matching" session to see what your expectations were, how they might have affected your relationships, what your expectations are now, and how you can develop a better relationship. You can still have an entrustment ceremony in which the birth parents formally let go of their parenting role and the adoptive parents assume theirs.

You can resume contact with each other even though you may have let the relationship die. You can establish boundaries where there have been walls or inadequate boundaries. You can join a support group, start writing in a journal, or set up sessions with a counselor. You can meet new relatives, make amends, take the step you've been wanting to take, or say something that has been left unsaid. You can devise a ritual to help you make the changes you'd like to make in your relationship. Changing relationships takes courage and commitment. But it is often well worth the effort, especially for the child.

part five

Children in Open Adoption

11

Growing Up in
Open Adoption

As the child grows, her need for access to her birth parents becomes more evident. The child begins to take on a distinct appearance and personality and develop abilities and interests that reflect her genetic background. Furthermore, the child becomes aware of what it means to be adopted, asks questions about her origins, and struggles to understand why she was adopted and who she is.

During the preplacement period and perhaps even the first year after placement, you may have lost sight of the benefits that may be realized by children who have contact with their birth relatives. The needs of the adults, especially the birth parents, may have seemed paramount. But as the child grows, meeting her needs becomes the main reason for you to maintain the open adoption. This will not happen just because you have each other's names or addresses. The birth and adoptive parents will have to understand how the open adoption can benefit the child and help her build the kind of relationship with the birth family that will allow the child's needs to be met.

As the child becomes more involved in the open adoption, keep in mind the probable benefits:

- Children do not need to lose the connection between themselves and their birth relatives to gain permanent parents able to meet their needs in a consistent way.
- Children can have more people in their lives who love them and care about them. They see that they can have both birth parents and adoptive parents in their lives without having to choose between them.
- Children can obtain up-to-date medical, social, and historical information about their families of origin.

▪ Children can have access to valuable information as they develop a personal identity, such as who they look like, what kinds of abilities might be genetically influenced, and how people in their birth families grow and develop.

▪ Children can learn about their ethnic or racial heritage and have contact with people who share that heritage. They can have the opportunity to learn about their ethnicity within that heritage rather than apart from it.

▪ Children can channel their energy into other aspects of personal development when they do not have to struggle to obtain information about themselves as they grow up.

▪ Children can feel a greater sense of control because they have access to answers to their questions.

▪ Information children receive may be more credible because it comes directly from the birth parents. Children can observe the birth parents themselves and draw their own conclusions about who they are and what they are like. Children have fewer missing pieces about who they are. They can deal with reality rather than fantasy.

▪ Children may feel less rejected or abandoned. The birth parents can communicate to the children that the adoption plan was made because of the birth parents' circumstances rather than any qualities or lack of qualities in the children. The birth parents can demonstrate their love and concern for their children, and take responsibility for the adoption plan so that children don't have to feel they were to blame.

▪ Adoptive parents may be better able to meet their children's emotional needs because they have had to work through their feelings about the birth parents to develop a long-term relationship with them. This can leave them feeling more secure in their parenting role and in their relationships with their children.

Obviously, these benefits cannot be realized unless the birth parents remain in contact with the child. Birth parents have an obligation to do so not only because they may have made a commitment but because they have a responsibility to the life they helped create—a responsibility not affected by the adoption decree that indicates they no longer have any parental responsibilities or rights. But just staying in contact with each other isn't enough. As we've emphasized, it is not the open adoption institution that benefits people but the relationships that open adoption makes possible. A child is not going to feel more secure, have greater self-esteem, or have a better sense of identity just because she has her birth parents' address or telephone number. Children will only fully realize the possible benefits of open adoption if the birth parents meet the needs of the child as only the birth parents can, which will require that they build a relationship with the child.

Eight-year-old Kimberly lives only 50 miles from her birth mother, Anna. They talk frequently on the phone and Anna visits often. Kimberly enjoys their visits, and Anna always has a new song to play for Kimberly on her guitar. Once, after Kimberly had told a family friend that Anna was coming to visit, she noticed the astonished look on the person's face. She asked her mother, "Mommy, why are people surprised that my birth mother visits me?" To her, visits from her birth mother were natural. She didn't know her adoption was unusual. As her awareness of adoption has grown, Kimberly has not hesitated to ask questions about what Anna was like during the pregnancy and why Anna didn't keep her. Sometimes she asks her adoptive parents these questions and sometimes she asks Anna. She feels equally comfortable talking to each of them, and they are happy to have her talk openly.

Lacey's open adoption is somewhat different. Her birth mother, Shawna, probably would not have stayed in contact with her if it hadn't been for the adoptive parents' tenacity. They wrote to her and sent her photographs even when they didn't get a response. Shawna visits sometimes, but there are more times when she doesn't follow through on her plan to come to see Lacey. Lacey knows Shawna cares about her, but she can also see that her birth mother is somewhat disorganized and unreliable and that helps Lacey understand why Shawna couldn't parent her. Lacey has asked Shawna questions about her birth father and her birth grandparents, none of whom know about her existence, but Lacey doesn't feel comfortable revealing her emotions to her birth mother. "She doesn't really understand me," she told her adoptive mother once.

Nine-year-old Chad only has contact with his birth grandmother. She visits once a year, near his birthday. It is a difficult visit for her. Reluctant to show her emotions, she avoids talking about Chad's birth parents. Chad is polite to her, but he sees the visits as an unpleasant obligation. He's happy when she leaves and he can go back to playing with his friends. Chad would benefit more from the contact with his birth grandmother if she could be more open, and someday she may be.

As we'll see in this chapter and Chapter 12, to meet the needs of the child placed for adoption:

▪ Birth parents must be willing to share information with children. They must be aware of the kinds of questions children have and must answer those questions honestly in ways that enhance a child's self-esteem.

▪ Birth parents must honor the child's existence. Reuben Pannor, M.S.W., and Annette Baran, M.S.W., who have each worked in the field of adoption for more than forty years, believe birth parents have an obligation to help the child overcome any feelings of abandonment by demonstrating their caring, and acknowledging the child on her birthday and on holidays.

▪ Birth parents must communicate that they love and care about the child. Furthermore, birth parents must demonstrate that they accept and cherish the child as she is, with her unique blend of genetics and environment. They must be accepting of the differences between them as well as the similarities.

▪ Birth parents must be able to explain the reasons for the adoption plan in ways that take responsibility for the circumstances so that the child doesn't feel responsible.

▪ Birth parents must validate the child's permanent place in the adoptive family and must give the child their blessing to love the adoptive parents without feeling disloyal to the birth parents.

▪ Birth parents must acknowledge and accept the child's variety of feelings about the adoption, which may include anger, sadness, and love, and which will change as the child grows.

The Child's Relationship with the Birth Parents

The relationship between the child and the birth parents is likely to be more successful if all the adults involved have a good relationship. The relationship between the birth and adoptive parents is likely to be more consistent than the birth parent's relationship with the child, and you can't depend on a child to know why her relationship with her birthparents is important. You can't expect her to nurture it just because someone tells her it's valuable. Adoptive parents maintain a relationship with the birth parents just as they make the effort to keep alive a child's relationships with grandparents, cousins, and other familymembers—because they see the value for the child in having these relationships.

Furthermore, even if they understand why a relationship is meaningful, children may not have the skills necessary to maintain it. Children are self-centered—if they can't see what they are gaining from the relationship, they have difficulty sustaining it. The attention span of young children is particularly short, and if they don't hear from the birth parents often, they may have difficulty remembering who the birth parents are. They may not connect the birth parent who visited them last fall with the birth parent who is sending a card on their birthday.

If the birth and adoptive parents have a good relationship, the adoptive parents can be resources for the birth parents, especially if the birth parents do not have a lot of experience with children. From the adoptive parents, the birth parents can learn about the child's likes and dislikes as well as her physical and intellectual abilities. The adoptive parents can suggest ways for the birth parents to approach the child or interact with her. The adoptive parents can help the birth parents interpret the child's language, behavior, or moods.

Perhaps more importantly, the child will model her relationship with the birth parents after her adoptive parents' relationship with them. If the adoptive parents are fearful and tentative with the birth parents, the child is likely to approach the birth parents the same way. If the adoptive parents are relaxed and open with the birth parents, the child is likely to be. The child will observe whether the adoptive parents feel comfortable expressing their feelings to the birth parents, setting limits, and asking questions. This will give her permission to voice her feelings, set her own limits, and ask for information.

Mike met his birth father when he was two years old. His adoptive parents, who had been told the birth father's identity was unknown, had only met the birth father once before themselves, and they were a little unsure of what to expect when they picked him up at his apartment. He hopped into the back seat where Mike was sitting in his car seat. "Hello, buddy!" the birth father said loudly, and the child started to cry. He was a quiet boy who needed to be approached gently, and he felt overwhelmed. On subsequent visits with his birth father, Mike avoided him, due to his own discomfort and to his adoptive parents' uncertainty. The adoptive parents and the birth father will have to bring their relationship to a more trusting level, and the birth father will have to be more sensitive to Mike's temperament if they are to be close.

As we've pointed out, every relationship in open adoption is unique, and the relationship between each birth relative and the child will be different. The various connections that will form often resemble the kinds of relationships children have with different members of their extended family. Sometimes children and extended family members have exceptionally close relationships—some families live close to each other, grandparents may be responsible for after-school care, and a child may feel as comfortable walking into his aunt's house as she would her own. In other families, the relationship between a child and her extended family members is warm and special, even though relatives are seen only occasionally. Of course, many families feel distant from each other, no matter how close together they live.

Think back on your own childhood. Perhaps you had a relative you barely knew who expected a hug and kiss when she came to visit—you may have felt uncomfortable or even fearful of this person. You may also have had a relative you saw only occasionally but whose visits, letters, or phone calls were nonetheless eagerly anticipated. Birth parents can think about why they felt closer to some relatives than to others, and how they can re-create the positive relationships with the children they have placed for adoption.

But like extended family members, birth parents have a relationship with the child within the context of the adoptive family. Birth parents do not have a relationship just with the child, apart from the adoptive family. It is not like a relationship between a child and a noncustodial parent in which the noncustodial parent removes the child from the custodial family for weekly or annual visits. Whatever their degree of closeness, birth parents will necessarily be involved with members of the adoptive family other than just their child, and they should express an interest in other children in the family and include them in their activities (see Chapter 13). It is equally important to maintain their relationship with the adoptive parents, who might feel insulted if birth relatives ignore them.

Hank's birth mother, Rhonda, lived several hundred miles away, so they didn't see each other often. Each year, though, after he was old enough to be away from home, Hank went to visit Rhonda. His older sister, Heidi, would accompany him on these visits even though she was not related to Rhonda. Not knowing Rhonda that well, Hank liked the security of having his sister with him. Heidi also made a good companion, since Rhonda's other children were several years younger than he. Had Rhonda not been willing to include Heidi in the annual visits, Hank might not have gone alone, and he and Rhonda would have lost a valuable opportunity to know each other.

BUILDING THE RELATIONSHIP

Birth parents who want to develop a strong relationship with the child and have not parented children themselves will benefit from having a basic understanding of what children are like at different ages. They should know what kind of activities will interest the children, how to talk to them, and what kind of behavior to expect. Some good basic child development books are listed in the Resources section at the end of this book.

In addition to learning about children in general, birth parents can learn a lot about their child from watching the adoptive parents interact with the child and from asking the adoptive parents for guidance. Birth parents shouldn't assume that the child will be like other children they have parented or have known. It's always best for birth parents to ask permission if they are unsure whether a child is allowed to engage in certain activities or to eat certain foods.

Most important, as in all relationships, trust between the adult and the child is essential. Trust is built by being consistent, honest, respectful, and making the child feel safe. When the birth parents fulfill their promises and follow through when they tell a child they will write, call, or visit, the child develops confidence that she can believe what they say. When birth parents behave predictably, that is, when their behavior is consistent rather than erratic, children know what to expect and they feel comfortable.

Children are also more comfortable when rules and limits are clear and when they know they will be enforced. Birth parents should find out what the rules of the adoptive family are and use them when with the child, even if they don't completely agree with them. This lets children know that being with the birth parents is not going to be a whole lot different from being with their adoptive family. It also helps build trust. If the birth parents know the rules in advance, they will not promise something that the adoptive parents don't allow, and will not have to go back on their word.

Birth parents show respect for a child by treating her as a valuable human being whose feelings are real. They show respect by listening to her and taking her ideas and feelings seriously. Children see through pretense easily. They can spot a phony, and they don't trust him. Birth parents need to allow their child to see them as they are, with fears and with insecurities. This doesn't mean burdening a child with their anxieties but simply being "real" when they are with the child.

ENHANCING RELATIONSHIPS WITH CHILDREN

The quality of a birth parent's relationship with a child is not directly proportionate to the amount of contact they have. Nevertheless, it's important to remember that for children, especially young children, time goes slowly. Frequent contact, if it is allowed under the terms of your open adoption agreement, helps a child remember who the birth parents are. It also establishes the birth parents in his life in a consistent way. Frequent contact needn't mean weekly visits. Postcards can be a suitable way to remind the child that the birth parents exist and are thinking about the child.

Gayle's birth parent sends cards with a two-dollar bill enclosed on holidays like Valentine's Day, St. Patrick's Day, and Halloween. Gayle has come to expect the cards and associate them with her birth mother. Kelly's birth father sends her postage stamps from other countries. Phillip was going through a phase when he was fascinated with wolves, and his birth grandmother cut out pictures of wolves and articles about wolves and sent them to him. Birth parents can also send the child audiotapes or videotapes. Maia's birth grandmother taped herself reading some of Maia's favorite stories. Kyle's birth mother sent a videotape of her new baby. These are all ways to say, "I'm thinking of you. I know your interests. I care enough to take the time." These items become treasures to a child.

A ritual can help a child remember who the birth parents are and what their relationship is. A ritual needn't be ceremonious; it can simply be a predictable event or series of events that the child comes to associate with the birth parent. For example, birth parents who write to the child can always include a new riddle or a cartoon. Birth parents who visit can develop a consistent way of greeting the child, or bring a new book to read together.

Although treasures and treats are expressions of affection and can enhance a relationship, they should not be the foundation of the relationship. Birth parents who try to be the "goody person," giving in to the child, trying to buy affection with presents, letting the child behave without any limits, or constantly entertaining the child, are not building a strong relationship. A more meaningful connection is created when birth parents and children get to know each other by doing everyday things, such as going to the birth parent's place of work, repairing the child's bike, or taking the dog for a walk.

Challenges to the Relationship

It is not always easy for birth parents and children to build relationships. Children may not have much experience with an ongoing relationship. Especially during the elementary school years, one false move can turn a best friend into someone who is shunned. Children may neglect the relationship, and sometimes adoptive parents use the child's apparent disinterest as an excuse to lessen the contact with the birth parents. Sometimes children have unreasonable expectations of a relationship, hoping to receive a reply to their letter by return mail and being disappointed and angry when it doesn't happen.

And occasionally birth parents have inadequate skills for building relationships. They neglect their shared responsibility to maintain ties or may have difficulty behaving in ways that build trust. They may be unpredictable, immature, or inconsistent, or project a false image of themselves. They may surround themselves with people who make the child feel uncomfortable. Such relationships challenge adults. They provide even greater challenges to children, whose relationship skills are still developing.

THE UNINVOLVED BIRTH PARENT

One of the greatest concerns of adoptive parents in open adoption is that the birth parents will not remain involved in the child's life and that this will compound the child's feelings of rejection. As we point out at the beginning of this chapter, birth parents have an obligation to provide their child with information, to let the child know they care and that they accept her, to let her know that she is remembered on her birthday and other special days, and to provide a link between the child and her biologic relatives. When birth parents do not live up to this obligation, it is often because they view contact with their child as a privilege rather than as a responsibility. Some may not feel they deserve this privilege. Others may view the privilege as something they can choose to take advantage of or not.

Some birth parents still have not dealt with their losses well enough to allow them contact without pain. Some don't know how to build relationships. Some have so many crises in their own lives that they do not have the energy to build and maintain relationships. T.J.'s seventeen-year-old birth father, Ted, was so devastated by the divorce of his parents that he found it difficult to maintain contact with his son. The breakup of his family of origin forced him to deal with some of the losses he had not faced when he relinquished his parenting rights to T.J., and it overwhelmed him.

Some birth parents may give in to the pressures of family members, friends, or the forces of society, all trying to convince them that they should not have contact with the child for the child's sake. These explanations are not excuses. Birth parents need to consider how the child will feel when she knows that her birth parents could have written, called, or visited, but didn't.

Adoptive parents shouldn't give up on an open adoption just because birth parents are not responsive to their overtures. There is always a possibility of contact with the birth parents in the future. Indeed, some adoptive parents have worked hard to keep in touch with the birth parents even though they did not respond for many years. While taking care not to be intrusive, these adoptive parents continued to let the birth parents know how their children were doing.

Debra wrote to her daughter's birth mother, Darcy, regularly, but rarely received a reply. Discouraged and unsure how to interpret Darcy's silence, Debra finally asked her if she'd like her to write less. Darcy's reply was immediate. The letters were important to her, even though she wasn't ready to respond as frequently. It took nearly seven years before Eileen's birth mother, Tisha, responded at all to the adoptive mother's letters. It wasn't that Tisha didn't care about Eileen; she didn't think she deserved to be involved with her. They now have the kind of relationship many people would envy.

When birth parents are not involved in a child's life, adoptive parents can ask the child why she thinks they are not involved and how she feels about it. They can explain why or hypothesize about why the birth parents are not involved, without excusing them from their responsibility to stay in touch. It can be helpful to depersonalize the situation by talking in generalities rather than specifics about the child and her birth parents. For example, rather than saying, "Your birth mother is probably too busy with her new baby to call you," the adoptive parents can say, "Sometimes when people have a new baby they are so busy and so tired that they don't have enough energy to call people they care about."

Adoptive parents should let the child know that it's all right for him to be sad or angry that his birth parents aren't involved in his life. They can say, for example, "It looks to me like you're hurt that your birth father never visits you. I'd be hurt, too. I think he's missing out on knowing a great kid." Adoptive parents can help the child feel in control of the situation. Parents can let the child know that it's okay for her to continue to write to the birth parent even though he never responds, saying, "You can write to your birth father whenever you want and ask him to write back. He hasn't responded so far, so you shouldn't get your hopes up, but you can ask." If the child reaches a point where she wants to let go of the possibility of a relationship, her adoptive parents can support her in that, too.

Sometimes birth parents are not involved in a child's life in any consistent way, but come and go depending on their life circumstances. Some birth parents connect with the adoptive family only in times of personal crisis. Others disappear during times of crisis and are only involved with the adoptive family when they are under less stress. Manuel's birth mother does a little of both. She calls during times of extremes. When she is extremely happy, she wants to share the news with the adoptive family. When she is extremely sad, she calls the adoptive family to get emotional support. Her relationship with Manuel is very unstable. He's never sure whether he'll be talking to his happy birth mother or his sad birth mother. It can be difficult for a child to realize that his birth parents are undependable, but it can also be very valuable in helping him see that it is this lack of dependability that made adoption such a responsible plan.

Although it can be painful for children when their birth parents don't stay actively involved in the open adoption, it doesn't mean that the open adoption shouldn't have been tried or even that it is a failure. Adoptive parents can try to find other birth relatives who are willing to be involved. These relatives can give the child a sense of being valued to the birth family, as well as provide important medical and social information. Through these relatives, the adoptee may also learn information about her birth parents to help her understand that their lack of involvement in her life reflects their lack of responsibility or some other problem, rather than something that is wrong with her.

Mario's paternal birth grandfather, Jorge, was the person who told him why his birth father never answered Mario's letters or came to visit him. Jorge was honest and direct, but his compassion was sincere: "You're being raised by people who are white, well educated, and who have a nice house," he told Mario. "Your birth father is Mexican, unemployed, and in a gang. He doesn't think he has anything to offer you. Someday, I hope he'll know that being your father is enough to offer you. Until then, I'll be your connection to your birth family and to your Mexican heritage."

Previous foster families, social workers who were involved with the birth parents or the child, and other significant people from the child's past, such as a special teacher, can also be valuable connections for the child to maintain.

THE UNINVOLVED CHILD

A child may appear to be uninterested in the birth parents for many reasons. Often this reflects the child's personality or a stage in her development. At age twelve, Julie is preoccupied with the social life of junior high school, so news that her birth mother, Michelle, was coming to visit with her two young sons was not welcome. The visit conflicted with plans Julie had made to go shopping with friends. "She's *my* birth mother," Julie said. "If I don't want to be here when she comes, I don't have to be." Her adoptive mother, Joanna, explained that she had a responsibility to the family to be at the house when Michelle, who was a friend of the family, came to visit. She let Julie know that she expected polite behavior from her, but she also suggested that it would be acceptable for Julie to excuse herself after a reasonable amount of time and explain that she had made previous plans. Later, Joanna explained to Michelle that it's natural for children to want more autonomy as they reach adolescence, and suggested that Michelle consult Julie personally before arranging future visits.

For many children, the value of the open adoption is simply that it is available, even if they don't choose to access it. If they have never known a confidential adoption, they may take their birth parents' presence in their lives for granted. They know they can write, call, or visit their birth parents if they need to or want to. Birth and adoptive parents can assess whether a child's attitude toward the open adoption is consistent with her approach to other relationships with extended family or friends of the family, or whether it may be unique to this situation.

Sometimes a child is dealing with other issues in her life, or with the issues raised by the adoption, and feels that contact with the birth parents would be emotionally overwhelming. For example, she may have some anger about her placement and may be afraid she wouldn't be able to control her anger if she were around her birth parents. She might worry that if she expressed her anger, she would lose her birth parents all over again. Or, a child may have received the message, perhaps from the adoptive parents or perhaps from society, that he shouldn't have contact with his birth parents. He might be worried that if he expressed an interest in his birth parents it could somehow jeopardize his relationship with his adoptive parents. If there are additional factors that make a relationship with the birth parents difficult, such as cultural differences or the fact that the birth parent is mentally retarded, the child may not know how to overcome them.

Adoptive parents can make it easier by giving their child permission to be involved in a relationship with the birth parents. They can show the child how to set boundaries and how to communicate with someone who is troubled, immature, or different from other people the child knows. The adoptive parents can also show the child how to separate a person's value as a human being from his or her actions. They can show the child that you can love someone unconditionally, even though you don't approve of the choices that person makes. Adoptive parents model this in their own relationship with the birth parents.

Although the child may not recognize her need for the birth parents today, they may become quite significant a few years down the road. The adoptive parents nurture the possibility when they maintain their relationship with the birth parents and try to help the child do so as well.

NEGATIVE REACTIONS FROM CHILDREN

Occasionally children will have negative reactions to the birth parents. They may show anxiety by acting out, regressing, biting their fingernails, or developing somatic complaints like stomachaches or headaches. Children may be picking up and expressing tensions their adoptive parents feel. Sometimes children feel insecure about their adoption, and they may be afraid a visit from the birth parents means they'll have to go home with them. This can be particularly true if the child was in foster care before the placement and sometimes did go home with the birth parents after a visit.

However, children who are feeling insecure about their place in their adoptive families do not necessarily feel safer if their birth parents don't come to visit. They may still fantasize that they will be returned to their birth parents, and repeated visits from the birth parents can be reassuring in that the children learn their fantasy is not going to happen. Often, of course, the greater understanding of adoption that comes with maturity is the best antidote for this insecurity. (A child's feelings of insecurity are addressed in more detail in Chapter 12.)

Sometimes children will have negative reactions to the birth parents because they are different from what they are used to. For example, their style of joking may seem strange. Birth parents who have chosen an adoptive family very different from them may have to be patient and wait for the child to develop enough maturity to look beyond the superficial differences.

Brandon's adoptive parents, Janice and Charles, are upper-middle-class professionals. His birth parents, Carrie and Bob, are bikers. Though there are obvious lifestyle differences between Brandon's adoptive and birth parents, the adults get along well. But when Carrie and Bob arrive for a visit dressed in leather, with a six-pack of beer strapped to the backs of their motorcycles as their contribution to a picnic, ten-year-old Brandon is noticeably embarrassed. When they leave, he begs his parents not to let them come over anymore. Janice and Charles know that Brandon's discomfort with his birth parents has more to do with what they look like than who they are, so they continue to invite Carrie and Bob to their home. They feel comfortable having them and they believe Brandon will someday understand that who his birth parents are is more important than what they look like. Moreover, they reassure Carrie and Bob by saying, "Just wait until he's a teenager. He'll love the way you dress."

CHALLENGING BIRTH PARENTS

Sometimes birth parents make promises they don't keep, or behave erratically. They may actually be mentally ill or mentally retarded. Adoptive parents should not make excuses for the birth parents or pretend their behavior is acceptable when it is not. They should ask the child why she thinks the birth parents act as they do and validate the child's perceptions and feelings. If a child is confused, the adoptive parents can provide explanations for why the birth parents may behave the way they do by putting the behavior into a context the child can understand.

For example, parents can ask their child if she has ever wanted to impress someone by embellishing the truth or telling a lie. They can ask if she has ever made promises, such as to invite people to her birthday party even though she had already invited the maximum number of guests, because she wanted to show them that she liked them. Parents can point out the other choices the birth parents had, such as, "Your birth father could have just said he wanted to take you to that football game. Why do you suppose he said he had tickets when he didn't?" These explanations place responsibility for the birth parents' actions where it belongs—with the birth parents.

Adoptive parents need to be careful, however, to not imply that because the child sometimes wants to act the way the birth parent does that she is locked into the birth parents' behavior patterns. Adoptive parents can point out to the child that she has other choices and can give examples of situations in which they have observed her making better choices, such as following through on a promise.

Sometimes the birth parents' behavior causes adoptive parents to reevaluate allowing their child to have contact with them. However, adoptive parents should consider that sometimes allowing the child to observe her birth parents' behavior directly can be an effective way to help the child understand why her birth parents could not raise a child.

In some extreme situations it may be necessary to make contact with the birth parents conditional. For instance, Jane's adoptive mother said Jane could not visit her birth mother in jail. Other adoptive parents only allow their child contact with birth parents when they are sober or if they have reported on schedule to their probation officer. In more serious situations, contact may need to take place only in a safe place or under supervision. Adoptive parents should keep in mind that *painful* is not the same as *harmful*. They may want to protect their child from a difficult truth about the birth parents, but it may be important for the child to know that fact so she can understand why it was necessary for her to be placed for adoption. Moreover, in learning how to protect themselves physically and emotionally when in a relationship with dysfunctional people, children can learn how to set boundaries. However, if the relationship is actually harming the child and the birth parents are not receptive to changing the way they interact, then the adoptive parents have a responsibility to protect their child.

Cammi's adoptive parents, Lynn and Karl, were increasingly unsure they would be able to continue in the open adoption relationship. At gatherings with the birth family, the birth relatives overwhelmed the child both physically and emotionally. Although there was nothing overtly inappropriate in their hugs and attention, Cammi began to be frightened of such occasions, telling her parents she felt she would be "swallowed up" by the birth relatives. Lynn and Karl had experienced the same attention from the birth relatives, but had good coping skills that enabled them to ignore it. They could see, however, that Cammi might not have yet developed the kind of firm boundaries she needed to handle such situations.

Following their counselor's suggestion, Lynn and Karl tried changing the nature of the gatherings from ones in which they were surrounded by birth relatives to gatherings where only a few birth relatives at a time were invited. They also arranged visits at parks and zoos where there was a lot of space and Cammi could easily move away from people when she wanted to. If they knew there would be a lot of birth relatives at a gathering, they also included a lot of other acquaintances or members of the extended adoptive family to diffuse the clinging behavior of the birth relatives.

When adoptive parents find it necessary to restrict the open adoption in some way, either by limiting contact to letters or phone calls or by making contact conditional, they need to periodically reassess the situation and allow the previous level of contact to resume when the birth parents have changed their conduct.

When Louise and David became better acquainted with their daughter Laura's birth parents, Jenna and Ben, they found that Jenna and Ben were drug users. Louise and David weren't sure they wanted to continue in the relationship under the circumstances. With the help of their support group, they realized that Laura's birth parents would be drug users whether they had contact with them or not and that this fact would have to eventually be provided to Laura if they were to explain why the birth parents made an adoption plan. They decided that by getting to know Jenna and Ben better, they might be more able to understand their behavior, and might also find good qualities about them to balance this unsettling information. But they also let the birth parents know that they were not welcome in their home as long as they were using drugs— contact would have to be limited to letters—and they educated themselves so they would know how to recognize when Jenna and Ben were in recovery.

Isaac's birth mother, Celia, made troubling statements to him, such as, "In a few years I'll have my life together and you can come and live with me if you want." The adoptive parents were understandably distraught that Celia was undermining Isaac's sense of security at the permanence of his family. In addition, they feared that as Isaac grew up, statements like this would encourage him to turn to the birth mother during times of conflict with his adoptive parents. They decided Celia could only see Isaac under supervision. When she made such comments, the adoptive parents would gently correct her, saying, "I know you wish the situation were different, but we all know that no matter how much you want that, it isn't going to happen." Later, when Isaac was not around, they would explain to Celia that they understood she wanted Isaac to know that she loved him and was not rejecting him by placing him for adoption. But they pointed out that her statements could leave Isaac feeling insecure, and Isaac might not trust her if she made promises that couldn't come true.

Reah's birth father, Martin, was arrested and convicted of armed robbery a few years after the placement. He had consistently written to Reah on her birthday and at Christmas, but when Martin's annual birthday greeting came from prison, the adoptive parents, Tracy and Paul, were in a quandary. They wondered if continuing the relationship with him implied that they approved of his behavior. They were also concerned that if they told Reah that they were discontinuing the relationship because they didn't approve of him, Reah would develop a negative view of Martin, and ultimately, of herself. Because Reah was young, Tracy and Paul decided to give her the birthday card, but not to let her know at that time that Martin was in prison. They decided to wait until she was older and could understand that people's actions are sometimes good and sometimes bad. They also decided it was important to maintain the communication with Martin, helping Reah to understand that sometimes good people make poor decisions and you can maintain a relationship with someone even though you don't approve of everything they do.

Other parents had to intervene, however, when Erin, the birth mother, who was mentally unstable, wrote abusive letters to her daughter, Robin. Erin told Robin she was crazy and predicted that Robin would turn out just like her. The adoptive parents intercepted Erin's letters, keeping them from Robin until she was a competent young adult, and then they set up a family counseling session in which Robin could read the letters in a supportive setting.

Vera Fahlberg, M.D., author of *A Child's Journey through Placement*, points out that while the amount of contact or circumstances of that contact may be influenced by a birth parent or a child's behavior, contact should never be granted as a reward or withheld as a punishment.

We can't emphasize enough the importance of communicating with each other as the child grows. Keep talking with each other about how you will handle certain circumstances and how you observe the child relating to each of you. Continue to present a united front in situations where the child may try to divide and conquer: when there is a difference of opinion, the birth parents need to back up the adoptive parents. Remember that you each have a unique, complete, and fulfilling role to play in the child's life. There's no need to feel jealous of each other or to feel threatened by each other's place in your child's heart. Just as you can love more than one person without diluting your love for each individual, the child can love each of you individually.

Children's Questions and Concerns About Adoption

A good relationship between children and their birth parents enables children to feel secure when approaching the birth parents with their questions and to trust that the answers the birth parents provide are truthful. But sometimes children can't put their questions into words. Sometimes the questions they ask are not exactly what they want to know. Children can be looking for different information each time they ask the same question. For example, an eight-year-old child who asks, "Why don't I have a picture of my birth father?" might be wondering what he looks like. A twelve-year-old might be wondering if his birth father is really a famous person. A fifteen-year-old might be wondering if the reason there are no pictures of his birth father is that his birth mother didn't know the birth father well enough to have a photograph.

Children's mental ability—the way they think—changes as they grow up, just as their physical ability changes. Not only can toddlers not tell time but they don't have the same awareness of the past and the future as an eight-year-old, a twelve-year-old, or a fifteen-year-old. Children's powers of reasoning change as they grow up. These changes inspire new questions for children as well as enable them to understand answers that were previously beyond them. But until children become adept at using new reasoning abilities, they can be frustrated by both their questions and the answers they are given, making the transition between developmental stages a particularly rocky time for parents and children alike.

It is important for you to understand what children want to know about their origins and their adoption at different ages. This will help you know how to answer their questions and when to provide information to a child even if he doesn't specifically ask about it. This chapter provides some answers to those questions, and a more thorough discussion can be found in Lois Ruskai Melina's book *Making Sense of Adoption* and in other materials listed in the Resources section at the end of this book. Though written for adoptive parents, these resources are also helpful to birth parents.

You will find it helpful not only to educate yourselves about the questions children have about adoption but to discuss with each other how you will provide the child with information as he grows up. You will need to give consistent answers to questions like, "Why didn't my birth mother keep me? Who is my birth father? Do I have any brothers or sisters? What if my birth parents want me back?" You will have to agree on when and how to tell the child information, such as criminal activity in the birth parent's past, diseases that run in the family, or the fact that the child was conceived through rape or incest.

You will also want to discuss who will provide the child with information. For example, the adoptive parents may think that providing information to the child is a parental responsibility. The adoptive parents may expect the birth parents to give them all the information, but not to provide information directly to the child. However, the birth parents may feel that since the child is asking questions about them, they should be the ones to provide the information. Or, the opposite may be true—adoptive parents may expect the birth parents to field the child's questions, whereas the birth parents may refer the child to his adoptive parents when he has questions.

Adoptive parents often want to feel in control of the flow of information to their children. They are deeply concerned that information about the child's adoption be explained in ways that leave the child feeling loved and secure. They aren't always sure that they can meet this challenge themselves; they are even less sure the birth parents can. It isn't that they don't have confidence in the birth parents personally—it's just a normal reaction for parents to assume they can meet their child's needs better than anyone else.

Adoptive parents have a responsibility to provide their children with important information, to help their children interpret personal information, and to support their children as they struggle to understand difficult information about themselves. They do not abdicate this responsibility just because there are birth parents available to provide information. At the same time, it's important to realize that some of the information adoptees need has more credibility when it comes directly from the birth parents.

Talk with each other about how you will handle this issue. Birth parents who are approached by their child can say, "It sounds like you're pretty interested in how you grew inside me. Let's wait until we get home and talk about it with your mommy, too." Birth parents who would like to be more spontaneous about responding to the child should talk with the adoptive parents a lot about how they will explain facts to the child, so that the adoptive parents can feel confident giving the birth parents permission to speak freely with the child.

As you discuss providing information to the child, keep in mind:

▪ Children have the right to know all the available information about their origins and about the circumstances that led to their adoptions.[1]

▪ Children should be given this information as they are able to understand it and are able to deal with it emotionally, not as a onetime revelation.

▪ Children should be given information by their adoptive parents or birth parents in a gentle, understanding way.

▪ Even potentially disturbing information, such as a family history of mental illness, should be shared with a child at the appropriate age. The information should be shared honestly, but in such a way that it does not damage a child's self-esteem.

▪ Children should not be knowingly deceived, either by what is said or by what is left unsaid.

▪ Information about a child's origins is private (but not secret) information that should not be shared outside the family without the child's permission.

▪ Children have the right to express their feelings about the information they are given and should be encouraged and supported as they do.

▪ Children have the right to ask questions and express their feelings without worrying that doing so might threaten their relationships with their adoptive parents or birth parents.

▪ Children are not responsible for other people's feelings about each other or about the adoption.

▪ Parents should not wait for children to ask questions but should anticipate the child's needs and look for appropriate opportunities to share information. Sometimes by "priming the pump" with a little information, children are stimulated to ask questions. At the same time, parents should be sure that information is being given to benefit the child and is neither given nor withheld to reduce a parent's anxiety, to meet some artificial timetable, or to please another parent or family member.

---

1. Ways to anticipate children's questions and provide information, even information that may be hard to share with a child, are discussed in the rest of this chapter.

Infancy to Preschool

As we discuss in Chapter 8, the birth parents often are preoccupied with the child during his first year of life. The birth parents are still in the process of understanding what they are losing and have not yet found a way to move beyond the loss, and the baby still resembles the child they bore. At the same time, the adoptive parents are coming to terms with their change of roles. As we point out in Chapter 2, the more the baby is cared for by the adoptive parents, the more he looks to them to meet his needs.

While visiting the adoptive parents, Lois, the birth mother, was feeding the infant she had placed for adoption a few months before. After the baby had eaten, Lois attempted to burp him, using all of the standard methods without success. Finally, Lois asked Sue, the adoptive mother, what to do. "Hold him like a football," Sue said. She instructed Lois to hold the baby with his head in her hand, his body extended along the inside of her arm. Once the baby was in that somewhat unusual position, Lois was able to pat him on the back and elicit the necessary burp. While Lois was pleased to be able to relieve the baby's discomfort, she was also sad to realize that after only a few short months, Sue knew the baby better than she did. Although painful, the experience helped Lois deal with the reality of the adoption.

Around the baby's eighth month (later if the baby has not been with the adoptive parents since birth), the baby's attachment to his primary caretaker has grown to the point that he becomes upset at being separated from her (fathers are sometimes the primary caretakers, but more often mothers are). It can be disconcerting for the birth mother if the baby not only doesn't want to be held by her but screams with anguish for the adoptive mother. It is a concrete sign that the birth mother has lost her parenting role. Nevertheless, birth mothers who have wondered whether their children would feel loved in their adoptive families can look at this development as a sign that their children are developing healthy attachments to their adoptive parents.

However, sometimes these experiences are reversed. Birth mothers who have raised other children are often more experienced than first-time adoptive parents, even though circumstances may have prevented them from caring for a new baby at that time in their lives. The birth mother may give the new adoptive parents advice on child care. Although the adoptive parent may welcome the advice, having to learn parenting from the birth mother may challenge her sense of entitlement. She may feel, "Maybe I'm not meant to be this child's mother. Maybe the birth mother, with all her problems, would still be a better parent."

If the child has lived with a birth relative for even a few months, he is likely to feel attached to that person for several months after placement. It may feel threatening to the adoptive parents to see their child prefer the birth relative and to witness the child's anguish each time that relative leaves after a visit. In such cases adoptive parents need to remind themselves that it is far better for the child to have developed trust in his birth relative than to have been neglected.

We point out in Chapter 9 that after the child's first year the birth parents are often (though not always) less involved in the child's life, and the adoptive parents may want a deeper relationship with the birth parents. As the child grows, he looks less and less like the baby the birth parents gave birth to and appears more and more integrated into the adoptive family. Seeing the person the child is becoming can help the birth parents move on as they grieve for the loss of the baby they held and cared for at the time of his birth. At the same time, the child's resemblance to other members of his birth family becomes more apparent, which may be a pleasant discovery or a source of discomfort. One birth mother found it comforting that the child looked like his birth father, with whom she had enjoyed a loving relationship. However, a child's resemblance to a birth parent or to another child in the birth family may not have been anticipated. Feelings of sadness or anger may emerge as the reality of the adoption is experienced in yet another way.

WHAT TO CALL THE BIRTH PARENTS

Sally, an adoptive mother, recalled a visit from Greta, her child's birth mother, when Andrew was only two years old. Andrew was playing with a jack-in-the-box Greta had brought him and Greta wanted to wind it up again for him. "Bring mommy the box, honey," the birth mother said. Sally was taken aback. She didn't want Greta referring to herself as the *mommy*. She said nothing, but later told her husband, who said, "She'll always be her mother. You can't change that." While that was an important realization for Sally, it is not a distinction a two-year-old child can be expected to make.

A child is confused by the idea that he has two mothers because he can't understand how one person who lives with him, makes him meals, and reads him bedtime stories can be addressed the same way as someone who writes him letters twice a year, calls him on his birthday, or visits weekly. Because it is confusing to young children to have the birth parents referred to as mommy and daddy, or any of the common variations for mother and father, we recommend that these terms not be used to refer to the birth parents. This is not meant to slight the birth parents or deny them the significant role they play in the child's life. The birth parents can be referred to as birth mother and birth father, since those terms accurately describe their role and are different enough to not cause confusion—just as grandmother is sufficiently different from mother.

Unfortunately, it seems stilted to address the birth parents directly in this manner. For this reason, we recommend that the birth parents be referred to or addressed by their first names, with the explanation that these are the birth parents. In other words, the birth mother would say, "Bring Renee the box," *not* "Bring mommy the box" or "Bring Mommy Renee the box." Of course, as with grandparents and stepparents, children sometimes solve this dilemma on their own, by coming up with their own ways of referring to their birth parents.

Sometimes, in an effort to demonstrate the closeness the adoptive family feels to the birth parents, they call them aunt and uncle. However, unless this is an accurate reflection of the relationship, that is, the child has been adopted by a sibling of his birth parent, these manners of address can be confusing for a child. Although the child will eventually understand his true relationship to these people, there is no need to burden him with the additional responsibility of understanding why he was led to believe they were related to him in a different way. (Ways to address birth parents in relative adoptions, where the birth mother is both birth mother and adoptive sister, or birth father and adoptive uncle, are discussed in Chapter 15.)

There is bound to be some sadness when the adoptive parents hear the birth parents refer to themselves as the child's mother and father, or when the birth parents hear the child call the adoptive parents mommy and daddy. This experience is part of the ongoing loss experienced in adoption. But if it causes extreme discomfort, it can be a sign that you do not yet feel confident that a complete transfer of roles has taken place. You may want to reflect or meditate on this, write in your journal about it, discuss it with each other or with someone close to you, talk it over with a counselor, or bring it up at your support group.

TELLING THE ADOPTION STORY

Infants and toddlers cannot understand reproduction or complicated relationships between people, so they are unable to understand the meaning of adoption. However, the subject of adoption should be discussed whenever it seems appropriate to do so. This helps adoptive parents and birth parents rehearse what they'll say to the child later and to become more comfortable talking about it with the child. But keep in mind that these discussions hold little meaning for an infant or toddler, and you shouldn't feel that you have to go out of your way to let the child know he is adopted or that he grew inside the birth mother. The word *adoption* doesn't always need to be used—adoptive parents can simply say, "I'm so glad you're our child." Birth parents can say, "I'm so glad I gave birth to you," or "I sure picked some great parents for you." What is important during the child's first few years is that he feel loved and accepted by the people who are important to him. Appropriate times to mention the way the child joined the family is when it seems natural to do so, and when adoption is relevant to the discussion.

When the child is old enough to listen to simple stories, he is ready to hear about the way he was born and joined his family. It will go something like this (although the wording may vary slightly depending on the circumstances and whether the adoptive parents or the birth parents are telling the story):

Mommy and daddy wanted a baby very much, but we couldn't make one that would grow inside mommy. Pam and Dave were going to have a baby, but they couldn't take care of a baby born to them at that time in their lives. Pam and Dave looked around for people who would be good parents for their baby. They found mommy and daddy and asked us to be your parents. We were so excited. You grew inside Pam, and when it was time for you to be born, you were born just like every other baby. Then Pam and Dave called us to tell us we had a little boy. We went to the hospital to pick you up. Pam and Dave were sad that they couldn't raise a baby then. They cried when you left the hospital with us, but they told us they were happy to have found someone like us to raise their baby. We were sad, too, seeing how sad Pam and Dave were. But we were so excited to have you.

The important part of this story is that the child learns he was born just like every other child. In the past, adoptees did not always understand this. Since their adoptive mothers didn't give birth to them, they concluded they weren't born—that they were some kind of alien. By talking about their birth as a normal occurrence, and by having the opportunity to hear about it from their birth mothers, children in open adoption can avoid some feelings of being different.

It is important for a child to hear that his birth parents could not take care of *any* baby born to them *at that time in their lives.* This communicates that it was the birth parents' situation, and not anything about the child, that was responsible for the placement. Because children are so self-centered that they think they influence all the events around them, adoptees who hear, "Your birth parents couldn't take care of you," often grow up thinking that they did something bad to cause the placement, or that the birth parents didn't want to raise them because there was something about them that was unpleasant, difficult, or undesirable. Furthermore, adoptees who grow up hearing about their birth parents' inability to parent sometimes conclude that they, too, will be unable to parent.

Adoptive parents who have a letter from the birth mother can make her words part of the adoption story by saying something like, "And this is what your birth mother said to you when she decided we should be your parents . . . " They can also show the child a photograph of the birth parents, saying, for example, "This is a picture of Pam holding you in the hospital." Some adoptive parents keep special photo albums of the birth family for their child. Others include photos of the birth family in their own albums. Some put a framed picture of the birth mother in the child's room. How adoptive parents incorporate photographs of birth parents into the child's surroundings is a matter of individual style, influenced by the kind of relationship they have. What is important is that the child grows up knowing who he looks like and where he came from, and that his birth parents are real people to him, not fantasy figures.

It is important for a child to hear that his birth parents loved him, but it can be confusing to hear that his birth parents placed him for adoption because they loved him so much. As adults, we understand that it takes an enormous amount of love and concern for a birth parent to put the child's needs above her own desire to raise that child. But there are a lot of children who are loved who are not placed for adoption. If the birth parents have other children who hear this explanation, they might think their birth parents didn't love them as much as they loved the child they placed for adoption. And the child who was adopted might think, "If people love you, they give you away." When he hears his adoptive parents say they love him, he might worry they too will place him for adoption.

Similarly, if you tell a child that he is special because he was adopted or placed for adoption, he may misinterpret your intention and believe that he must remain special to stay in his adoptive family. When he realizes that he is a normal child, and not special, he may become anxious that he will have to leave his family. Rather than telling the child he was adopted because he is special, just show him how special he is to you. Rather than telling him he was placed because the birth parents loved him so much, the birth parents can just demonstrate their affection and concern for him. When the time comes, tell him honestly the circumstances that led the birth parents and the adoptive parents to the adoption.

Preschool Through Kindergarten

During the preschool years a child may be able to correctly identify his birth relatives or recount his adoption story, but he will not comprehend the nature of the relationship or the process of adoption. That's because children repeat what they hear, but they can't understand adoption until they can understand reproduction—around the age of five or six. Shortly after her parents adopted a new baby, a five-year-old girl said to her mother in the car, "Mommy, we adopted Peter." Her mother replied that she was correct. "And I'm adopted, too," the girl said. Her mother was excited to hear how well her daughter understood adoption. Then the girl continued, "And the car seat is adopted, and the car is adopted, and the radio is adopted . . . " Her mother realized *adoption* was still just a word to her daughter.

However, even though preschool-age children can't understand adoption, they can understand that their birth parents are special people in their lives. During the preschool years, the child becomes more social and is able to interact with the birth relatives and to develop more personal relationships with them. Although they don't understand that they are related, children this age will want to be with the birth parents and any children the birth parents are raising as long as they enjoy their company.

If children reject birth relatives, it is probably because they don't enjoy their company or for some reason they do not feel safe around them. Birth parents who are afraid the child will someday reject them or be angry with them for placing them may mistakenly assume the child's lack of interest in them is due to adoption. It is important to keep in mind that this is normal childhood behavior. (Later in this chapter we discuss children who may feel insecure about being returned to their birth parents.)

Children this age have definite opinions about things. The child in an open adoption begins to exert control over the relationships with his birth parents by expressing his desire to write, call, visit, or send pictures. Around the age of six or seven, a child may try to exclude everyone else in the family when the birth parents come to visit. "My birth mother is coming to take me to the park," said Tana to her brother. "You can't come." This is a child's awkward attempt to be in control, and the situation should be treated just as if the person coming over were a friend of the family not related to the child. Parents could say, for example, "Your birth mother is coming to visit everyone in our family. You can spend some special time together just with her, but we're all looking forward to seeing her." They can give the child the control she is seeking by allowing her to make her own arrangements with the birth mother to have some one-on-one time together.

Around this time, adoptive parents may find their sense of entitlement shaken a bit as they observe the child's relationship with his birth parents developing independently. This can be especially true if the adoptive parents are now in their forties and are experiencing some of the reevaluation commonly referred to as "midlife crisis," while the birth parents may be moving into a more stable time in their lives. Children are astute enough at this age to sense any discomfort their adoptive parents may have about their relationship with the birth parents and may try to use the open adoption relationship to manipulate their adoptive parents. It is a good time for you to talk with each other about the importance of presenting a united front when dealing with the child. For example, birth parents can make it a habit to check out any plans with the adoptive parents before discussing them with the child, including ideas suggested by the child. The child who asks the birth parents to buy him a particular toy may have already had that toy selection vetoed by his adoptive parents. On those occasions when the child manages to succeed at this ploy, the birth parents can let him know that such schemes are unacceptable.

The birth parents may notice that the adoptive parents are making decisions about the child with which they don't agree. For example, the adoptive parents may be stricter than the birth parents expected them to be or may not emphasize the importance of good manners as much as the birth parents think they should. Accepting the adoptive parents' values and style of parenting is part of the adjustment the birth parents must make. Once again, it's important that they show respect for the way the adoptive parents are raising the child so that the child doesn't sense a division.

TALKING ABOUT THE ADOPTION STORY

Around the age of four, children begin to be able to imagine time and space in new ways. While some children will progress more or less quickly, and thinking ability develops at a very individual rate, by this age most children can understand that events happen outside of their immediate existence—the birth mother has another house where she lives when she isn't visiting. She doesn't exist only when she's with the adopted child. Things happened to the child that the child can't remember. For example, even though he can't remember he had an operation when he was one year old, he now understands that it happened. This realization leads children to questions about life, death, and reproduction.

Four-year-olds ask amazing questions about the existence and daily habits of God, about afterlife, and about the origins of living things. Children understand that they were once babies and will someday be adults. This is reflected in their play, as they focus on make-believe games like "baby and mommy" and dress-up games where they impersonate adults. It's only natural that their awareness that they were once babies leads them to imagine there was a time when they weren't born yet. This leads them to ask, "Did I grow inside you, mommy?" And the stage is set for their first real understanding of having been adopted.

Remember that the child probably is not asking if he is adopted. All children eventually ask their mothers if they grew inside them. So be sure to answer the question the child is asking—that he grew inside his birth mother, just like all children grow inside a woman, and that he was born just like other children. But use the opportunity to also explain that after the child was born, his birth mother made a plan for the adoptive parents to raise him. Be sure to mention the birth father's existence and role in the child's creation, even though he may not be involved in the open adoption. If you don't, the child may conclude that his adoptive father is his birth father.

Children may ask, "Did you breastfeed me? Were you sad that you couldn't keep me? What was my name before I was adopted?" Don't be offended or surprised if the child doesn't react to news that he was adopted by telling the adoptive parents, "I'm so glad you're my mommy and daddy," or by telling the birth parents, "I wish I could have stayed with you." Some ask questions by making statements, such as "I lived somewhere else before I lived here," or "You weren't always my mommy." Some may say they remember when they were with the birth mother, even though they've been with the adoptive parents since infancy. Some may insist they grew inside their adoptive mothers even though they clearly know otherwise. They may also say they wish they had never been adopted. What they mean is they wish they'd been born to their adoptive parents. These are not rejections of the birth parents, but expressions of the desire children have to be as close as possible to the people who are raising them. Some children may cry or even cover their ears with their hands. They may be reflecting the feelings of their adoptive parents or birth parents, or may be unusually sensitive individuals. In general, however, children are going to be fairly accepting of their family situation. They will probably think everyone was adopted.

Because the question, "Did I grow inside you, mommy?" is universal, other children in your family are likely to ask this question during the preschool years. This situation may lead to questions about who else in the family grew inside mommy and why the birth mother placed one child but not another. Answer questions honestly using concrete images. For example, instead of saying, "Your birth mother was too poor to take care of another baby just then," you could say, "Your birth mother already had two children to take care of. She was having a hard time finding enough money to buy them food and pay for heat. She was afraid that she wouldn't be able to feed all of you." (See also Chapter 13.)

The Middle Childhood Years (Ages Seven to Eleven)

The elementary school years is a time when children's level of curiosity increases and they actively seek information. The child who is adopted will want to know as much as possible about his birth families. During this period children become more interested in the father's role in reproduction. The child may want a lot of information about his birth father. He may want to know what the relationship was between birth parents and whether he has any biologic brothers or sisters. Particularly around the age of seven or eight, children become increasingly agile problem solvers, and mystery stories and riddles help them develop this skill further. Adopted children often use this ability to try to figure out why they were placed for adoption. Children are also learning about rules and fairness through team sports and clubs, which raises questions for them about who made decisions about their future and whether those decisions were made fairly.

Children are still thinking in concrete terms and need explicit explanations and tangible evidence whenever possible. However, they are beginning to be able to categorize and see relationships in more and more complicated ways. It isn't coincidental that children begin to develop collections at this age, such as baseball cards, shells, and insects. Their fascination with their new ability to group objects according to common characteristics can be seen as they some days group their baseball cards by team, and other days by the player's position. This same ability will help them understand the relationships in their adoptive family and birth family.

TALKING ABOUT THE ADOPTION PLAN

During the elementary school years the child attempts to understand what it means to have been placed for adoption and why it happened to him. This struggle starts earlier than you may expect—often around seven or eight years old, but sometimes even earlier. It is then that children go to school and become aware of how other families are formed. They learn that most of their classmates are being raised by at least one parent to whom they are genetically related, and that some of their classmates have parents who are young, single, uneducated, or struggling to make ends meet. They wonder why their classmates' birth parents are raising them when they were told that their own birth parents were too young, too poor, or needed to finish school. Still believing they cause the events around them, they may conclude that they were placed for adoption because they weren't good enough, lovable, or worth the time or energy the birth parents would have had to commit.

According to psychologist David Brodzinsky, Ph.D., coauthor of *Being Adopted* and *The Psychology of Adoption,* during the elementary school years, children in confidential adoptions are sometimes distracted from normal childhood interactions by questions about why they were placed for adoption, who their birth parents are, and what their birth parents are like. He believes this may be the cause of some adopted children having mild problems in school or with friends. However, the child in open adoption may feel less different from his classmates since so many children have noncustodial parents through divorce. He can join in when they talk about getting a letter from their "real" dad, and not feel out of place when two sets of parents show up at his school play. Of course, that doesn't lessen his need to understand why his birth parents couldn't raise him.

As we've already stressed, open adoption is based on the idea that if birth parents remain involved in a child's life, the child will feel less abandoned or rejected than a child in a confidential adoption. The child can know the worth he has in the birth parents' eyes and witness the love they still have for him. Moreover, open adoption provides a child with the opportunity to hear and see why his birth parents were unable to raise a child at that time in their lives.

Eight-year-old Jason, the child of a confidential adoption, used his adoption to manipulate his adoptive mother. "You're not my real mother. I want to be with my real mother," he would say when he got angry. His parents finally decided to have him discuss his interest in his birth mother with the social worker who had arranged the placement. She helped Jason verbalize what he thought it would be like to be with his birth mother and let him know the ways his birth mother was and was not as he imagined. After some counseling sessions, the social worker suggested that if Jason wanted to know more he should write to the birth mother and she would forward the letter to her.

For several months, Jason said nothing about his birth mother. It had been enough to hear from someone impartial (not his adoptive parents) what his birth mother was like. But after a while, he again asked about his birth mother. "Have you written to her?" his adoptive parents replied. By being able to offer Jason access to the information he wanted, the adoptive parents kept the issue of the birth mother from being one the boy could use to manipulate them. It was a year before he finally wrote to his birth mother, who immediately replied, explaining why she placed him for adoption and affirming her love for him. In the year since then, whenever Jason has had questions about his birth mother, he's written to her and received the answers.

When her previously confidential adoption became fully disclosed, seven-year-old Donna, who had been having difficulty learning to read and was prone to daydreaming, became able to focus and learn better. While some people might credit maturity, Donna's adoptive mother believes opening her adoption made the difference. We cite these situations in which confidential adoptions became semiopen or fully disclosed, because it allowed the adoptive parents to witness the concrete changes in their children's behavior and attitudes. When children grow up in open adoptions, it is difficult for them and for their parents to know how the experience might have been different. Ten-year-old Cara came home from soccer practice one day having learned that a friend was adopted. This friend, she told her mother with amazement, didn't know anything about her birth parents. "I feel so sorry for her that she can't know," Cara said.

Open adoption doesn't guarantee that a child will have better grades or that his struggle to understand his adoption will be easy. Children in the elementary school years are not sophisticated enough to understand the complicated situation the birth parents were in. Because children are still concrete thinkers during these years, provide the child with specific information. One adoptive mother said her daughter Liza did not have much difficulty understanding why her birth mother didn't raise her, because as Liza grew up, her birth mother graphically described the run-down trailer she was living in, the kinds of meals she could afford to eat, and the difficulty she had getting to the grocery store and the doctor's office without a car.

Social worker Deborah Silverstein, L.C.S.W., of Newport Beach, California, suggests that parents use the child's emerging love of problem solving to help him arrive at the answers to his questions himself. For example, parents can ask the child why he thinks he was placed for adoption or what kind of skills or qualities are needed to raise a child and whether his birth parents had these. By asking the child what he thinks, parents can discover whether their child is feeling inadequate or shameful about having been placed for adoption, and can help him look at the situation differently. Furthermore, when children reason out answers to their own questions, the conclusions are often more credible.

FEELINGS OF INSECURITY

Because children under the age of eleven can't understand the legal system that makes adoption permanent, the middle childhood years have been marked by feelings of insecurity among adoptees. They come to understand during this time that children can lose their parents. They struggle to understand what circumstances led to that event and wonder whether it will happen again. Their developing mental ability allows them to verbally express feelings about past experiences. As children understand that they have had a significant loss, they feel vulnerable to future, similar losses. If the loss they have experienced is the loss of a parental relationship, they may feel more vulnerable to losing their parents in other ways. Children who feel insecure about their place in their families may try to "bargain" to stay in their adoptive families by being exceptionally well behaved. Some act out to test their limits, trying to see how far they can go in misbehaving before their adoptive parents will return them to their birth parents. Some are fearful of being separated from their adoptive parents, even for a short time, such as when their parents travel without them.

Children who are feeling a little insecure may use their developing analytical skills to ponder what might happen to them. "What if you die—will I live with my birth parents? What if my birth parents want me to live with them? If my birth parents get married, will I go to live with them?" Sometimes children express their insecurities in paradoxical ways. For example, if a child says, "I want to live with my birth parents," he may not really want to leave his adoptive parents (except temporarily when he is angry at them), but may simply want to know if that is an option. He wants the reassurance of being told that his parents are not interchangeable—that he is part of the adoptive family and he belongs with them.

Eight-year-old Tessa surprised her mother one day by saying, "I'm adopted. I really don't belong with my birth family, but I really don't belong here either." Tessa could have been told that even though she was not born into the family, she belonged there, but it might have been more meaningful for her to reason the problem through to that conclusion herself, with the help of her parents if necessary.

It may help to show some adopted children the court documents finalizing their adoption. Even though they won't understand the legal process that makes adoption permanent, when something is written down it can be more believable.

Open adoption does not necessarily relieve children of the anxiety of possibly being returned to the birth parents. After all, the birth parents are available and perhaps are now mature or secure enough to parent. But although they may not be able to put it into words, children who have contact with their birth parents sense that they have separate lives and aren't looking to change the adoption plan.

Nevertheless, if the child seems to feel insecure about his place in the family or expresses concern about being separated from his adoptive parents, even to the point of not wanting to go on excursions with birth parents with whom he has previously had a good relationship, understand that this is a normal part of his development. Talk to him about his feelings and validate his concerns rather than trying to talk him out of them, possibly saying, "Sometimes it is scary to be away from people we care about." But especially stress that the child's placement was planned and that the plan continues to be for the child to remain in the adoptive family.

FEELINGS OF GRIEF

Even though the child may fear being returned to the birth parents, he grieves not being with them. He realizes being born to people entitles him to a place in a family. Even though he might not want to lose his adoptive family to regain the birth family, he understands he has lost his place in that family. Open adoption allows children to stay in contact with their birth parents, but the child realizes during the middle childhood years that the relationship he has with his birth parents is not the same as the relationship he would have if he were living with them. This realization is similar to the birth parents' awareness that their relationship with the child is not a parent–child relationship and the adoptive parents' awareness that they have lost something by not giving birth to this child.

Eleven-year-old Marion wrote her birth mother that she was sad that she couldn't be with her. Marion showed the letter to her adoptive mother, who had not realized the depth of her daughter's feelings. Another girl, who was the only child in her adoptive family, said she was sad that she couldn't have her birth mother's new son live with her. In open adoption, the birth parents can let the child know that they are sad, too, that they are not together, but that they are glad the child is with the adoptive parents. They are giving the child permission to be happy in her adoptive family without having to let go of any feelings of sadness she might have about not being with her birth family. They are letting the child know that they, too, have conflicting feelings about the adoption and that the child doesn't have to choose between the birth and adoptive parents.

Sadness is not the only reaction children have to being adopted. Anger is one of the stages of grief, and it is not at all unusual for an adoptee to feel angry at having been placed for adoption. After all, if that hadn't happened, life would be much simpler. The child wouldn't have to deal with the possibility that he had been rejected or that he might lose his adoptive parents the way he lost his birth parents. He wouldn't have birth siblings he isn't living with. Sometimes this anger is directed at the birth parents, but more often it is directed at the adoptive parents, because the adoptee generally feels more secure in his relationship with his adoptive parents, and we tend to express our anger with people only when we feel that our relationship is secure enough to weather such outbursts.

The child may not feel as secure about his relationship with his birth parents as he does about his relationship with his adoptive parents. In his mind, the birth parents left him once. Maybe they'll leave him again if he gets mad at them. Signs that a child is dealing with anger include rage—uncontrollable anger that appears to be greater than warranted by the situation, destructive behavior, psychosomatic illness, acting out, or regressive behavior. Miriam is always on her best behavior on her annual visit with Kate, the birth mother. Miriam has never asked Kate why she was placed for adoption or expressed any anger or sadness at the placement, because she is afraid to risk the relationship. She would rather have Kate around, even if it means not having the kind of relationship that would enable her to ask questions and express her feelings. In time, Miriam may feel secure enough to have both.

Ten-year-old Simon found that his feelings about being placed for adoption erupted when his birth sister, Sheila, who was six years older than he was, became pregnant and decided to parent the child herself. As Simon faced Sheila's decision and felt his discomfort with it, he came to realize that he did not think bringing a baby into his birth mother's household where Sheila lived was a responsible decision. He also found himself angry that because of the choices his birth mother made about her lifestyle—many of which were understandable given her upbringing—he was denied the opportunity to grow up in his birth family. He expressed this in anger toward his birth sister, but ultimately felt more at peace about his own placement.

The child who is angry or sad at having been adopted or placed for adoption is expressing an emotional reaction that has little to do with the actual feelings he has for his birth parents or his adoptive parents. You, too, wish that the world were ideal and that the birth parents hadn't been in a position where placing their child for adoption was the best alternative for them, and that the adoptive parents hadn't been in a position where they could only have a child through adoption. This regret doesn't mean the birth parents wish they hadn't placed this child, or that the adoptive parents wish they hadn't adopted this child. It means you wish you hadn't had to experience loss. The same is true for the child who is adopted. In adoption, what you have gained would not have happened without your initial loss, but you can have separate feelings about each event. Children shouldn't feel that they have to choose between their birth parents and their adoptive parents. They need to be allowed to express their anger and their grief, as long as they do so in appropriate ways.

Adults can help children move through their grief by helping them identify the feelings they are experiencing and giving them permission to express them. For example, the birth parent can say, "It sounds like you're angry that I didn't come to your birthday party. I wonder if you're thinking that your birthday wasn't important to me." Their feelings should also be taken seriously. Children who have experienced significant losses may feel other losses more deeply than another child might, and their pain shouldn't be minimized. A child who seems to be grieving out of proportion to the current loss may also be grieving for other losses. And don't forget that whatever has been gained as a result of the adoption doesn't cancel the loss.

Making family trees, writing autobiographies, and other activities that cause a child to focus on his family and his origins can help a child identify the questions he has and express his feelings about the answers to those questions. Some of the same resources you have used to work through your grief and adoption issues can also be useful for children: writing in a journal; attending a group with other children in open adoption; meditating; praying; and talking with family members, a school counselor, or a therapist. Children can also work through their feelings through art, music, poetry, and physical activity.

FAMILY ROMANCE FANTASIES

Psychologists tell us that it is common for children in the middle childhood years to fantasize that they've been adopted. They are attempting to split their parents into good parents and bad parents. The child may think, "Dad's being mean to me. He wouldn't be mean to me if he really loved me. He must not be my 'real' dad or he'd love me and not be mean to me. I must have been adopted." In this fantasy, the birth parents are the "good parents," who would never be mean to the child, but would always allow the child to have his way. Sometimes the fantasy is reversed. The birth parents are the "bad parents" and the adoptive parents are viewed as people who rescued the child from the "evil" birth parents. The child's task in middle childhood is to understand that people can be both good and bad at the same time—to accept the limitations in his parents along with their strengths.

The adopted child has a more difficult time dealing with family romance fantasies. Thoughts that the adoptive parents are being mean to him because he was adopted are far more threatening because they could be true, and if the child views the birth parents as good and the adoptive parents as bad, it makes his grief that much harder to bear. If he views the birth parents as bad and the adoptive parents as good, he must deal with the impact that has on his self-esteem, since he is aware of the genetic connection between him and his birth parents.

The child in open adoption has additional challenges: it is more difficult to fantasize that the child was rescued by the adoptive parents from the "evil" birth parents when those birth parents are known to the child. It is more difficult to imagine the birth parents as perfect when the child knows their shortcomings. Although realism is good in the long term, it can leave the child without the psychological escape of the family romance fantasy.

Lucy had birth parents who were far stricter than her adoptive parents. They told her on more than one occasion that if she were living with them, she wouldn't have the freedom she had with her adoptive parents. When Lucy got mad at the rules her adoptive parents made, she couldn't console herself by imagining that her birth parents would treat her better. She knew her birth parents would back the adoptive parents. However, the need for this psychological escape is so great that some children in open adoption temporarily reject the reality of their birth and adoptive families and fantasize about another birth or adoptive family. This is fine as long as it is just a temporary fantasy.

Nevertheless, children in the elementary school years have active imaginations and can believe firmly in whatever they want, regardless of overwhelming evidence suggesting otherwise. Some children in open adoptions see their birth and adoptive parents in black and white terms—at least some of the time. More mature thinking will enable them to see that people can be both bad and good, and they will integrate the two sides of both their birth parents and their adoptive parents. Sometimes a child may be confused about what needs to be integrated: like children of divorce who keep trying to get their parents back together, the adopted child may want to find a way to have all the good parts of the birth parents and none of the bad parts, and all of the good parts of the adoptive parents with none of their bad qualities. Some may even fantasize about their birth family and adoptive family all living under one roof.

For instance, Lionel went to visit his birth father and his family during the week after Christmas, and when his adoptive mother asked him what they did, Lionel replied he played Christmas carols on the piano and had everyone sing, just as they did at home on Christmas Eve, and that he had bought some peanut brittle to share with his birth family on the night they watched a movie, just as they did at home. While Lionel was entirely unaware of his motives, he was clearly trying to re-create his adoptive family within his birth family. Even though life would be so much easier if he didn't have to deal with the inherent differences between his two families, Lionel will eventually realize, whether consciously or unconsciously, that such hopes are unrealistic. His adoptive parents will be there to comfort him when he does.

FEELING EMBARRASSED

As they approach preadolescence and realize their parents are not perfect, children often become judgmental. They may be less tolerant of differences between their birth families and adoptive family that they find unacceptable. For example, they may disapprove of their birth parents' smoking or of their adoptive parents' housekeeping. They may be embarrassed that their birth parents aren't professionals or that their adoptive parents are older.

This can be a difficult time for birth parents whose deepest worry in an open adoption was that their child would hate them for placing them for adoption, wouldn't like them, or would someday reject them. It can be a difficult time for adoptive parents who have been comparing themselves to the birth parents and wondering if they would ever be good enough to replace them in the child's eyes. Resist the tendency to take what the child is saying personally, and be careful not to try to bolster your relationship with him by reinforcing any negative feelings he may have about his adoptive or birth parents. This doesn't mean being unsympathetic or denying facts, but there is a difference between a birth parent saying, "I bet you do wish you could stay up later," and saying, "You're right. Your parents should let you stay up as late as you want." There's a difference between an adoptive parent saying, "Your birth father has some problems, and it hurts me, too, to see him when he's like this," and saying, "See, this is why your birth parent will never be reliable." The most important gift you can give the child at this age is to not tell him what to think or how to feel, and to help him see he can have a range of feelings about a single event or person. Give him permission to express those feelings—even the negative ones.

IDENTITY DEVELOPMENT

During the middle childhood years, the children's abilities, interests, and talents become more developed. These are influenced by both environment and heredity. Their physical appearance matures. As they approach puberty, their bodies grow and change in ways determined genetically. The child's similarity to the birth parents becomes increasingly apparent, as do his differences. It can be a source of comfort to the child who doesn't feel that he quite "fits" into his adoptive family to have the birth family available.

A birth father who had dyslexia was able to empathize with a boy with learning disabilities in a way the boy's adoptive parents could not. An athletic child with adoptive parents who had more intellectual interests found the touch football games that he longed for in family gatherings with the birth parents. Yet this is a source of sadness, too, as he realizes he has lost the possibility of having this kind of interaction on a daily basis.

Similarly, it may become evident to a child that he is making academic achievements beyond any of those in his birth family. That can be a source of pride for him, but also a discomfort as he realizes his birth parents and birth siblings might have accomplished more under other circumstances. One adoptive mother is concerned that because in the future her son is capable of earning a higher income than his birth siblings, they might look to him for financial assistance. She's trying to help him develop good boundaries by modeling ways to help his siblings without encouraging them to be dependent.

As the child's interests and abilities become more evident, as his personality and his body matures, and as he makes choices about the directions he wants to take in life, you will no doubt be aware of the genetic contributions of the birth family and the environmental contributions of the adoptive family. You may be tempted to take credit for whatever qualities in the child you like and blame each other for the qualities you don't like. However, it isn't that simple to separate heredity and environment. You can't be sure how the child might have been different had he been born to the adoptive parents or raised in the birth family. You can't be sure how he might have been different if he had more—or less—contact with his birth family. But if you love him as he is, you must acknowledge that his other parents contributed to who he is— both in his strengths and in his weaknesses.

Even though children do not always develop as their birth parents, as the child approaches puberty, the birth parents can serve an important function by providing information about how they grew and changed. No adolescent is happy about his physical appearance. His body shape, size, skin, and hair never seem to be as good as the person's at the next locker. It can be reassuring for girls to know when their birth mother began menstruating and when her breasts began to develop and how large they became. A boy, too, will be interested in knowing his birth father's height and weight and when he reached his full growth. He'll want to know when his birth father began to shave and if there is any male pattern baldness in his family.

In one family where there were two girls a year apart in age, the younger sister, Melissa, began developing breasts and pubic hair at age nine and began menstruating at eleven. Her older sister, Karen, didn't show signs of puberty until she was twelve and didn't menstruate until she was fourteen. This could have been the basis for concern between the two girls. However, because they were both in open adoptions, Melissa knew that her birth mother had developed early, and Karen knew her birth mother had developed somewhat later. The information that adoptees need at this time can be read from a file but is far more meaningful when it is accompanied by personal stories and the empathy that can come from having had similar experiences.

Adolescence

As teenagers enter adolescence they begin to develop the ability to think abstractly. They can see all sides to a question and imagine that each side is equally possible. College, the army, a job—these are all possibilities that must be considered. Every person of the opposite sex is a potential date. Every disease they hear about is something they could contract. Every theory they hear about the destruction of the world has merit. Every religion could be the "true" religion and is worth investigating. They see their parents, whose views are clearly defined, as narrow-minded because their parents don't agree that all these possibilities are equally valid. Not surprisingly, teenagers can be overwhelmed by all their thoughts.

Teenagers who are adopted can, for the first time, imagine what their lives would have been like had they remained with the birth parents. They can begin to understand the choices their birth parents had and can think about how each choice might have affected them. Teenagers who know little or nothing about their birth parents imagine all the possibilities: Their birth father raped their birth mother. Their birth mother was a prostitute. Their birth parents are dead. Their birth parents are famous. Their birth parents sold them to support their drug habit. Their birth parents are brilliant scientists. Their birth parents are living next door.

Open adoption eliminates the unknowns and allows teenagers to deal with the reality of who their birth parents are and what the circumstances were that led to their adoption. Teenagers need and want all the information available about their birth parents and their adoption, and it should be revealed to them gradually as they become cognitively and emotionally able to handle the information. As the adoptive mother of a fifteen-year-old put it: "During adolescence, adoption issues become relationship issues. My son is not trying to come to grips with being adopted; he is trying to understand what it means to have *this* birth family."

IDENTITY FORMATION

One of the tasks of adolescence is to develop a greater awareness of personal identity. Teenagers do this by comparing themselves to the people they are most like—their parents and siblings. Teenagers in open adoption have access to information about their birth families that teens in confidential adoptions do not, which makes this task a bit easier. But they still have twice the number of comparisons as the nonadopted teen.

Most adolescents aren't aware that they are making assessments about identity. They express their desire to be unique by being as different as possible from their family—even if that means being exactly like their peers. They know they are different from their friends, even if they dress the same way and wear their hair the same way. What they are unsure of is how they are different from those to whom they are most similar. As the teenager develops a sense of identity, he may temporarily reject values that he grew up with, trying on other religious or political beliefs, or pursuing a post–high school plan contrary to whatever he thinks his parents would prefer. He may try on the identity of the birth parents in an effort to imagine what he might have been like had he remained with his birth parents, especially if he thinks this is the way to best express his differences with his adoptive family.

In one family, the birth mother, Marina, who came from a dysfunctional family, frequently turned to the adoptive mother, Lydia, for advice during the thirteen years after the placement. On a recent visit to the adoptive family, Marina related her anger at her own mother for the way she favored her youngest sister. For example, the youngest sister was loaned money for a down payment on a house, while Marina was given a lecture on being responsible when she wanted to borrow money for some medical needs. Shortly after Marina's visit, Gail, the child she had placed for adoption, began complaining that Lydia favored her other daughter. Lydia wisely realized that even though it was obvious to her that Gail was identifying with Marina, Gail would not accept that explanation. She truly believed her mother favored her younger sister. Lydia's awareness helped keep her from being vulnerable to the kind of manipulation that might arise in this situation, but it wasn't until Marina had resolved her dispute with her own mother that Gail resolved hers with Lydia.

Adolescence is a time when teenagers often become interested in the idea of being part of an extended genetic family—a clan. They think about whether they are authentic members of their adoptive family clan, their birth family clan, neither, or both. They become more interested in their ancestors and in living members of the birth family with whom they have not had a lot of contact. If the birth father has not been involved, the teenager may seek him out at this time. This is especially true for boys who are looking for male role models.

Janessa hadn't known her birth grandfather very well. When he died, her birth mother didn't call to tell her. Janessa learned of her birth grandfather's death two months later when her birth mother called for routine reasons. Janessa was angry, but the incident made her realize how important it was to her to know her extended birth family and that she might not have an unlimited amount of time to do that. She made an extra effort to get to know her birth grandmother.

INDEPENDENCE

An additional task for teenagers is to become increasingly independent so that they are ready to leave home. This means putting distance between themselves and their parents. Some teenagers do this physically—hanging out with their friends as much as possible; talking to their friends on the telephone on the rare occasions that they are at home. Teenagers also establish independence by rebelling against their parents' influence—by having different beliefs, wearing their hair in ways their parents don't like, rejecting their parents' suggestions, and disobeying rules.

For a teenager, being independent often means being in control. Adolescents who are adopted feel the same loss of control that all teenagers feel as they struggle to push for their independence while being bound by legitimate rules of family, school, and society; however, adoption magnifies these feelings. Major decisions were made about their future without consulting them. These decisions left them with losses, yet they may be expected to recognize only the gains achieved through the adoption. They may want to rebel against their parents' expectations, including their responsibility to maintain a relationship with their birth parents. In exercising what control they have, such as with whom they spend time, adoptees may resist communicating with the birth parents, or may increase the amount of time spent with them.

The adolescent's struggle for control may cause your feelings of being out of control to reemerge. The careful agreement the adoptive parents negotiated with the birth parents may be ignored by the adolescent. He may not be satisfied with letters or phone calls and may take the initiative to give the birth parents his address and arrange a visit. He may want to arrange more visits with the birth parents than his adoptive parents agreed to, or may visit them at other times or places. Birth parents, too, feel a loss of control—as their child reaches adolescence and exerts more control over the relationship, their fears that they might lose their child may resurface.

All of you may be unsure how much control the adolescent should be allowed in the open adoption. Adoptive parents may wonder whether they have the right to exert any control over the teen's relationship with the birth parents. And they may be afraid that if they try to set limits on the relationship, it will backfire and push the adoptee away from them and toward the birth parents. For many, the irrational fear that their child will one day reject them in favor of the birth parents resurfaces as their child demonstrates his desire to control his relationships. Sometimes, though, adoptive parents have legitimate concerns about the kind of influence the birth parents may have on their teenager. Birth parents may also be afraid to set limits or make demands on the teenager because they, too, fear that he will reject them.

Once again, we encourage you to think about the ways this relationship is similar to other important relationships in the child's life. Adoptive parents often are reluctant to let go of control with their adolescent because they are unsure whether the attachment they've formed over the years will be strong enough to provide them with a connection once the child doesn't need day-to-day nurturing. But the more the adoptive parents fight for control, the more the teenager usually fights back, occasionally leading to the very result the adoptive parents have tried so hard to avoid. Adoptive parents have to allow their child a reasonable amount of control over her relationships, including the right to make mistakes about how much time to spend with certain people. This doesn't mean that adoptive parents can't enforce reasonable rules or set limits when necessary—but they are more effective when they are negotiated rather than imposed.

Parents have a right to know where their child is and with whom he is spending time, and they have a right to set a curfew. They are obligated to insist that their child not associate with people who are clearly undesirable, such as those who are violent or substance abusers. Adoptive parents do not have to have different rules when the undesirable influence is a birth parent than they would if the person were a classmate; however, adoptive parents may want to keep in mind that allowing the child to spend time with a birth parent who is not a positive influence may help the teenager develop a realistic view of that birth parent. Adoptive parents may want to allow their teenager more leeway in associating with a birth parent of whom they don't approve as long as it does not appear that the teenager is developing bad habits himself as a result of the contact.

If the teenager is neglecting his relationship with his birth parents, there may be little the adoptive and birth parents can do. A phone call or visit can be arranged, but a teenager who wants to be uncommunicative will be. You have an obligation to maintain your relationship with each other, recognizing that the teenager must eventually take responsibility for his relationship with his birth parents. It may be years before the adolescent is able to develop an adult relationship with his birth parents, just as it may take time for him to develop such a relationship with his adoptive parents. The teenager must, of course, respect your right to have a relationship, including your right to talk and visit each other, just as he must respect your right to have a relationship with a close friend or sibling. And you need to respect his wishes if he no longer wants his birth parents included in his birthday celebration or invited to his graduation.

Teen rebellion can become serious, such as breaking the law, using drugs, and associating with friends who are bad influences. Birth parents can sometimes be a help to both the teenager who is acting out and his adoptive parents. If they, too, had a difficult adolescence, they can let the teenager know from firsthand experience what they learned about the harmful effects of drugs, or the long-term results of a criminal record, and they may have more credibility than the teen's parents. Furthermore, the teenager may be more likely to take advice from the birth parents simply because they aren't his parents. In situations where the birth parents were reckless as teenagers but went on to become responsible adults, it can be hopeful to the adoptive parents to be reminded that the birth parents also had problems during adolescence that have since been resolved.

Growing closeness between the birth parent and troubled teen can, of course, feel threatening to the adoptive parents, who may still harbor some fear that their child will one day reject them in favor of the birth parents. Remember, the job of the teenager is to develop a sense of identity and to assert his independence from his parents, so when the teenager wants to be closer to his birth parents he is actually signaling that he doesn't look to the birth parents as parental figures. Nevertheless, the birth parents will have to continue to walk a fine line as they provide the emotional support the teenager needs without adding to any alienation he may feel from his adoptive parents.

In one family, the birth parents have consistently backed up the adoptive parents, so when Deirdre expressed her independence from her adoptive parents, she also turned away from her birth parents. When Deirdre ran away from home, her birth father, Joe, guessed the friend she was staying with, went to get her, and brought her home with a lecture as stern as she would have received from her adoptive parents. Deirdre was as angry with Joe as she was with her adoptive parents. "What right does he have to tell me what to do?" she said, demonstrating the skill with which teenagers can find their parents' deepest vulnerabilities.

In some cases of extreme conflict between the teenager and adoptive parents, the adolescent may express a desire to live with the birth parents. You should be resolute in communicating—from childhood on—that this is not an option. If you've been discussing possible situations with each other in advance, you'll be ready to present a common answer to the teenager, pointing out that this is not, never has been, and never will be part of the plan. The birth parents are not noncustodial parents, and they should not be expected to parent the child just because there is conflict in the adoptive family, any more than a close friend or family member would be expected to step in and assume a parenting role.

We recognize that in extreme situations parents sometimes do make temporary arrangements for their teenagers. If conflict in the family has escalated to the point that the teenager and the parents cannot live together, and family therapy has not solved the problem, alternative living arrangements may need to be made for the teenager. A family member, a close friend, or a residential treatment center might be options parents would consider in that situation. Depending on the situation and on your relationship, the adoptive parents might allow the teenager to live with the birth parents; however, it should be made clear to the child that this is temporary and that this doesn't represent a change in family structure or parental responsibility.

Realistically, however, when such an extreme situation occurs, parents may have already lost control of their teenager. They are faced with a choice of sending the child to a residential treatment facility or letting him decide where he will live—either with the birth parents or somewhere unknown to the adoptive parents. When faced with this choice, some adoptive parents rationalize that at least they'll know where their teenager is if he's with the birth parents. In one family, the birth mother has tried hard to build a positive relationship with the teenager by always being pleasant and agreeable. Yet the adoptive mother is not worried about being the "bad parent" to the birth mother's "good parent." "If Janelle ever feels that things are so intolerable at home that she has to go somewhere else to live, at least I know there are people who love her and would take care of her," says this mother, with more generosity than many parents could manage.

Sometimes adoptive parents agree to let their teenager live with the birth parents as a way to deromanticize them. They reason that once the birth parents function in a parental role, the teenager will see that his adoptive parents were reasonable after all and return home. And sometimes adoptive parents believe their teenager needs to experience living with their birth parents, no matter how chaotic or violent their lives might be, to settle issues brought on by the adoption.

Maureen insisted that her life would be better if she lived with her birth mother. Eventually she ran away. Her birth mother, Sasha, was a drug abuser and Maureen found herself in the position of taking care of her. Sasha also had a boyfriend who abused both of them. It was nine months before she had the courage to return to her adoptive home, but she did so with a stronger sense of belonging. And she now understands why Sasha couldn't raise her.

Meghan ran away from home to live with her birth father, and six weeks later he called the adoptive parents and told them to come and get her. The experience was painful for Meghan, who felt rejected, but she now knows she doesn't have an "escape" from her adoptive family and must work out her problems.

Would these teenagers have run away from home if they had not had the birth parents to run to? It is impossible to know the answer to this question. Certainly there have been many adolescent adoptees in confidential adoptions who have run away from home. Some experts have hypothesized that they were actually running to the birth parents, but did not know where to go, so they simply wandered about. Whatever the answer to that question, once it appears that a teen will try to leave home, a plan should be developed that will enable him to leave in such a way that he will be safe and can return home without losing face.

Ultimately, what adoptive parents fear most as they face the growing independence of their teenagers is the loss of their role as nurturers. For adoptive parents who have understood that their most precious gift to their child is their nurturing, it can be both sad and frightening to see that role concluding. Of course, parents continue to nurture their son or daughter in many ways as he or she matures, but it isn't the ongoing daily role of parent that they've had to this point. They may wonder what will tie them together as a family when their child no longer needs this ongoing nurturing. If the adoptive parents are approaching retirement age at this time, they may be starting to think about old age and wondering if their children will be there to take care of them when they need it.

Teenagers, too, wonder what their tie to their adoptive family will be once they have left home. They look for ways to establish their independence, but they are often afraid that independence means being without a family. It may be helpful for both parents and teenagers to talk about the future and how they envision interacting after the child leaves home.

TEEN PREGNANCY

During adolescence, the subject of teen pregnancy is likely to come up. A normally touchy subject, it can be particularly difficult for adoptive parents to express their values about teenage sexual activity without being judgmental toward the birth parents or implying that they think the teen's risk of pregnancy is somehow greater because her birth parents didn't avoid it. This issue can lead to tension, particularly as the teen approaches the same age as the birth parents were when they conceived her. The birth parents can discuss unplanned pregnancy with the teenager, using their own experience to explain the importance of responsible sexual behavior. Both the birth and the adoptive parents need to convey the idea that they are not sorry the child standing before them was conceived, at the same time acknowledging the pain it caused the birth parents and the child. Once again, it is important for the birth and adoptive parents to discuss how this subject will be handled so that the birth parents are reinforcing the values the adoptive parents want communicated to their teen.

ABORTION

Some people wonder if children who have been placed for adoption will feel less rejected if it is pointed out to them that their birth mothers could have had abortions, but didn't. That reasoning implies that they should feel grateful to their birth mothers for choosing adoption. There are certainly times when adoptees will feel thankful that they were not aborted, and times when they will realize that the circumstances of their lives are probably better than they would have been had they been raised by their birth parents. But you must keep in mind that being adopted has involved losses for children and they should never be expected to feel grateful that they had to experience these losses. This is true even if the losses led to new opportunities for them. Furthermore, at times when adoptees are feeling rejected because their birth parents chose not to raise them, it may be of little help to be told they could have been "rejected" prior to birth rather than afterward. Finally, of course, it is not always true that birth mothers didn't choose abortion—sometimes they did plan abortions but found they were too late in their pregnancies.

Abortion and adoption should be discussed as separate issues. Abortion is a way to resolve an untimely pregnancy whereas adoption is a way to resolve the untimely birth of a child. A woman chooses abortion in the first trimester of her pregnancy, in many cases, long before the child she is carrying is real to her. As we discuss in Chapter 6, a woman may be strongly considering adoption during her pregnancy, but the final decision is not made until after a child is born.

FAMILIAL SEXUAL ATTRACTION

Most adults can look back on adolescence and remember having a crush on a cousin. When an adolescent is sexually attracted to members of the birth family, including birth siblings, or finds birth relatives sexually attracted to her, it is often simply the result of raging hormones—especially among birth relatives who have grown up knowing each other well. However, when attraction develops between an adoptee and birth relatives who have not had contact with each other and suddenly find their adoption more open, or who see each other infrequently, there may be another explanation.

Familial sexual attraction can be the natural outgrowth of common interests, a desire for greater intimacy, or a lack of boundaries on the part of someone with a dysfunctional upbringing. Nevertheless, it's important to recognize that this phenomenon happens sometimes and should not be ignored. Parents whose alarms go off when they see the teenager interact with certain members of the birth family should not hesitate to sit both parties down and explain matter-of-factly that it is not uncommon for adoptees and members of their birth family to be sexually attracted, but this kind of behavior is not acceptable and the feelings they are having cannot be acted upon.

Most likely the teenager and his birth relative are also confused about their feelings, not knowing if what they're feeling is the intimacy of lovers or the affection of close family members. Although they may be embarrassed, and may even defiantly reject your explanation, you have an obligation to set some boundaries for this relationship, just as you would for any relationship you thought was unsuitable. Once again, a united front between the adoptive and birth parents or other members of the birth family can be enormously helpful in this situation.

Mary, who noticed flirtatious behavior when her teenage son, Brent, was around his birth sister, sat down with the two of them and explained there would be no more going out together to movies and no more sitting in Brent's bedroom listening to music. Mary had been unable to enlist the aid of the birth mother in the discussion, who insisted that Mary was misinterpreting their feelings and was afraid that bringing the topic up would result in their comfortable relationship becoming awkward. But when the birth mother saw the red color rise to both teenagers' faces when Mary confronted them, she realized Mary had been right.

Keeping Each Other Informed

It is important for adoptive parents and birth parents to discuss not only what the child might want to know but also what the child has actually asked. Sometimes, of course, a child will want his conversations to be kept private, and it is all right for the child and the adoptive parents to have conversations they don't share with the birth parents—they are a family unit and parents have an obligation to respect their child's request for confidentiality.

However, when birth parents and a child have secrets from the adoptive parents, the birth parent is in effect taking on a parenting role that she doesn't have. While children sometimes confide in people besides their parents, good friends and relatives recognize that unless there is a good reason to keep information from the child's parents, for them to form an alliance with the child is to take sides against the child's parents. Birth parents who support secrets outside the adoptive family encourage the child not to have as full a relationship with his adoptive parents as he can. Secrets also give people power, and although birth parents may be tempted by the possibility of a superior relationship with the child, it is in the child's best interests to have a solid, open relationship with his adoptive parents.

Birth parents who are faced with this issue can be explicit in telling the child that they won't keep secrets from the adoptive parents. They can say they are friends with the whole family and that they wouldn't be being a good friend to the child's parents if they had secrets from them. They can explain that they don't always share their conversations with the adoptive parents, but that they won't promise not to, and they can talk with the child about why he might be reluctant to let his adoptive parents know something, and work with the child to resolve his concerns.

When the child is young, the secret may be nothing of consequence. The child may just be exploring whether this is an effective tactic to use with the birth parents. But sometimes parents do need to know something told to another adult in confidence. Perhaps a young child has witnessed something disturbing, has been a victim of abuse, or is having problems his parents are unaware of. An older child or adolescent may have been arrested for shoplifting, may have been suspended from school, or may be dealing with an untimely pregnancy. In those situations, birth parents could say, "I'll help you tell your mother," or, "I'll give you two weeks to tell your mother yourself, and if you haven't, I'll tell her." They can talk about why secrets are harmful within a family.

Birth parents who keep secrets with the child also threaten their own relationship with the adoptive parents. The adoptive parents' biggest fear in open adoption is that they will somehow lose the child to the birth parents. When a child confides in the birth parents and not in them, it seems that the birth parents have usurped an important parenting function. The adoptive parents should be able to expect that the birth parents will not usurp their role, but will support it. When their expectations are not realized, the trust that is the foundation for the relationship may be damaged.

When Information Is Not Available

There is an assumption that children in open adoption will have full access to the information they want and need. Unfortunately, that isn't always true. Not all children in open adoptions will have access to their birth relatives, and sometimes birth parents do not want to give children information because they are ashamed. Dolly's birth mother, Cleo, has never named her birth father. She has been adamant about not discussing him in any way. The adoptive parents don't know whether Cleo doesn't know the birth father's identity, whether she's trying to protect a married man or someone in her family, or whether she's afraid the birth father would object to the adoption if he knew. As Dolly grows up and asks questions about her birth father, the adoptive parents can tell her that they don't know. They can say that only Cleo can answer those questions and that Dolly should ask her.

They can also ask Dolly for her thoughts about her birth father—what she thinks is true and why she thinks Cleo isn't giving her information. They can let Cleo know of Dolly's interest, and explain to her that without facts, Dolly will eventually imagine all the possibilities and have to work through what it would mean if each one of the possibilities were true. They can help Cleo understand that it might be easier for Dolly to deal with only one possibility, even though it may contain some disturbing information. They can also suggest that Cleo provide Dolly with at least some information, such as how old her birth father was or how well they knew each other.

The birth mother who insists on secrecy can still counter some of Dolly's curiosity by saying, "He wasn't a bad man." If Dolly is expressing some particular concerns about her birth father, the adoptive parents can say to the birth mother, "Dolly is worried that her birth father raped you. Can you at least tell her that isn't true?" They may also want to suggest that Cleo get some assistance working through whatever issues are keeping her from talking freely about the birth father.

A birth parent who is reluctant to provide the child or the adoptive parents with information may want to consider writing down the information and putting it in a safe place—in a safety deposit box at a bank or with a person whom she trusts. She can make arrangements for the information to be provided to the child after her death, and this ensures that the information will never be completely lost. If information is simply not available to a child, adoptive parents can validate their child's need to know and their anger or sadness at not having that information. They can say, "I wish I could give you those answers. It must be terrible not knowing."

Unreliable Information

Sometimes the information that is given by the birth parents is unreliable. All the facts may not add up. The birth parents may have told different stories to different people at different times. Luke's birth mother, Wendy, said she got pregnant after her high school prom. She was drunk, she said, and didn't know what she was doing. "It only happened that one time," she said. But Luke's birthday, seven months after the prom, indicates that he couldn't have been conceived then. Wendy claims Luke was premature, but his birth weight says otherwise. The adoptive parents are sure that Wendy feels ashamed of her sexual activity, and they hope that as they show her they accept her, and as Luke shows his acceptance of her, she'll feel secure enough to be honest with them.

In the meantime, they feel torn between their desire to be honest with Luke and their feelings of loyalty to his birth mother. They wonder whether they should tell Luke a story consistent with Wendy's, or present the facts as they see them. They need to trust Luke's ability to analyze Wendy's story as he grows up and sees the inconsistencies, allowing him to raise questions about her story himself. When he does, they can validate his logical reasoning and suggest he go to Wendy for validation of his conclusion. They can also ask Luke why he thinks his birth mother might not have told the full story, compassionately suggesting possible explanations, if necessary.

Sharing Difficult Information

Although some of the information may be difficult to share with children, and may even lead to some temporary crises, it is contrary to the whole philosophy of open adoption for there to be secrets. We believe even information such as a birth parent's criminal record, a family history of incest, or that the birth mother considered abortion should all be provided to the child. Naturally, parents should not provide this kind of information until they believe the child is emotionally mature enough to handle it.

However, it is important to keep in mind that at some point you will be providing the child with all the available information. When the child is young, tell stories of the adoption that will allow more details to be added as the child grows up, without contradicting earlier versions of the story. For example, if a child was conceived through rape, early versions of the adoption story could include, "We don't know much about your birth father," and "I think the reason your birth father doesn't write to you or visit you is that he didn't know your birth mother had a baby."

During the late elementary school years, when children begin to understand that people can be both bad and good, they may be ready to be given more details about their birth parents and the disturbing reasons they were placed for adoption. For example, this information may include explaining that a birth mother was addicted to drugs at the time of the child's placement, or a birth father has not acknowledged paternity. During this period a child is able to understand what social factors may have contributed to the birth parent's behavior, such as the fact that the birth parent had been abused as a child or was raised by alcoholic parents.

Information that may affect the child's self-image, such as that his conception resulted from rape or incest, may need to be delayed until the child is a little older, unless the child specifically asks. Often the information that you are most reluctant to give the child is the missing puzzle piece that makes the story of why he was placed for adoption make sense. For example, it makes sense to a child that his birth mother couldn't raise him because when he was born she was having a serious emotional crisis that required hospitalization. Sometimes a child is ready for information, but a parent isn't ready for the child to have the information—perhaps because of wanting to protect the child or fearing the child's emotional reaction to the information. If you are holding back information, make sure the reason is that it is in the child's best interest to wait.

Either the birth parents or the adoptive parents can provide a child with this kind of information, but it is important that the child be given a clear message that the circumstances surrounding his placement were the responsibility of his birth parents. It's also important that children know they have other choices if faced with similar circumstances and that they are expected to make better choices. Children may assume they have to behave the way the birth parents behaved.

Birth parents or adoptive parents who are providing children with potentially disturbing information can refer to Lois Ruskai Melina's book, *Making Sense of Adoption,* for advice. In general:

▪ Don't wait for the child to ask questions. Look for natural opportunities to provide that information, taking cues from the child that he is ready to hear the information. For example, don't wait for a child to ask if his birth father was ever in jail. If he asks whether his birth father was present when he was born, that's an opportunity to tell him that his birth father couldn't be there because he was in jail.

▪ Separate the birth parents' actions from their inherent value as human beings. Communicate that the birth parents are good people who sometimes made poor choices. Explain their actions without excusing them from the responsibility for those actions. Lead the child into a discussion of other choices the birth parents could have made and why they might not have made those choices. Reinforce your confidence in the child to make better choices in the same circumstances.

▪ Discuss the birth parent's situation in terms familiar to a child. For example, a child may not understand the panic that sometimes causes a birth father to flee or to deny paternity when faced with raising a baby, but a child can understand the panic caused by breaking a window with a baseball. Explain that like the child who runs away after breaking a window, and, when caught, pretends he didn't do it, the birth parent was afraid people would be angry with him.

When Children Don't Ask

Sometimes children do not ask questions about their origins or the reasons for their placement. Parents who are unsure whether their child is fully expressing his interest in his adoption can compare the child's approach to this topic to his approach to other topics. Does the child generally ask a lot of questions, or does he quietly go about investigating the world on his own? A child who needs a lot of preparation and information before he feels comfortable in a new setting may need more details about his adoption than a child who needs minimal information before proceeding into unknown territory. A child who is more intense about life may bring more intensity to his quest to understand his adoption than a child who is more easygoing. When a child's style of dealing with adoption is inconsistent with the way he approaches other situations, parents may want to look at whether there are other reasons for the child's apparent reluctance to talk about adoption.

As we've pointed out, unless children have developed a good relationship with their birth parents, they may not want to reveal their vulnerabilities by asking the questions that really matter. Children may wonder if asking questions will affect their relationships with their adoptive or birth parents. Children may think that if they show too much interest in their birth parents they aren't being loyal to their adoptive family. If the adoptive parents feel threatened by the birth parents and are still worried that the birth parents and the child will become closer than they want them to be, they may send the child subtle messages that deter him from asking questions.

Some children may be both eager to have their questions answered and fearful of the information they will be given. For example, a question about the identity of the birth father could lead to the revelation that the birth father raped the birth mother, that the birth father and birth mother were close relatives, or that the birth mother doesn't know who fathered her child.

Nine-year-old Keith asked his adoptive mother, April, several questions about his birth father. She told him what she knew, then suggested that he ask his birth mother, Rosa, when he went to visit her. After the visit, April asked Keith if his questions had been answered satisfactorily. He said he had been too embarrassed to ask her. This situation could be handled in a number of ways. Rosa and the adoptive parents could have discussed the fact that around the age of nine children develop more interest in their birth fathers. They could have decided how they would provide information about Keith's birth father to him. This might have been a time when the adoptive parents could have asked Rosa some of the questions they have about the birth father, so that they had the information for Keith.

April also could have responded the way another adoptive mother did in a similar situation. Bryan's adoptive mother told him that his questions needed to be answered by the birth mother. "I'll call her and let her know that you want to discuss this with her the next time you see her," his adoptive mother said. By taking responsibility for seeing to it that his questions were answered, Bryan's adoptive mother took the burden off the child of asking for information. She also gave the birth mother notice that she would have to be ready to provide this information.

Sometimes parents are advised not to give a child information until he asks. A child who doesn't ask isn't ready for the information, some people believe. However, if the child seems intellectually and emotionally mature enough for the information being provided, parents needn't be overly concerned about whether the child expresses a desire to know. Furthermore, sometimes children's reluctance to hear the information is due to their fantasies that the facts could be disturbing. They are often relieved to hear the information and know that all their horrible fantasies are not true. And even when the information is disturbing, a known fact eliminates all the other horrible possibilities.

Follow your instincts in dealing with situations in which a child seems reluctant to ask about his birth parents or his origins. But don't routinely let the child carry the burden of asking questions to get information. Be aware of what children are likely to be wondering about and provide them with the answers to their questions even before they are asked. Take natural opportunities to bring up discussions of birth relatives and the circumstances surrounding the adoption. Don't feel every piece of information needs to be provided in a formal setting. The more naturally you can discuss these topics, the more comfortable the child will feel about bringing them up. For example, while riding in the car, the birth mother could point out the school the birth father attended, saying, "This is the high school Dan, your birth father, went to. I used to come here to watch him play football. He was a center." That will naturally lead to a discussion of other qualities and abilities in the birth father.

In some cases in which a child grows up in open adoption and has a good relationship with his birth parents, the information he needs will be provided to him so naturally that you may not be able to isolate times when the child is seeking information or the birth parents are providing information. The child may get answers to his questions as part of the stories he's told about his family as he grows up—stories told by both his birth parents and his adoptive parents.

13

Brothers and Sisters
in Open Adoption

When the birth or adoptive parents have other children, the open adoption becomes more complex. From the moment they become aware of the adoption plan, and on through the interactions between the birth and adoptive families, these other children will have their own interpretations of the events going on around them as well as their own reactions to them. And any disparities between children, from how many birthday cards they receive to differences in opportunities they may have, will be analyzed by them for any hidden meaning. This is not unlike what generally happens in families where there is more than one child, but it often seems very different—and sometimes situations are unique.

Before the Adoption

If there are other children in the family, how you discuss an impending adoption with them depends on their ability to understand what is happening and how much time remains before the baby's birth. Very young children have difficulty understanding the concept of a distant future. If you say a baby is coming, they want it today. Furthermore, children under the age of six cannot really understand adoption, although they may seem to understand that a baby is growing inside someone, or that a baby might come to live with them. Nevertheless, some children need a lot of preparation for major changes, particularly if one of the changes is that a baby brother or sister is going to be entering their family. And some children will feel the tension or excitement in the family or overhear conversations and need to know what is going on. If you have a "hush-hush" attitude about the adoption plan, the child may think something bad is going to happen. When the child combines the secrecy with bits of overheard conversation, he may reach some disturbing conclusions, such as that he is being placed for adoption.

Early in the open adoption, when the plans are still tentative (even though you may feel committed to them), children in the birth and adoptive families can be told that the birth mother might ask the adoptive parents to take care of her baby after it's born while she decides if she is able to parent the child. However, as the birth approaches, adoptive parents and their other children need to begin to make the transition to being a bigger family. They can tell their children they are getting the nursery ready because they hope the baby will become part of their family, at the same time acknowledging that it may not turn out that way.

After Placement

If the birth parents follow through with their plan and place the child for adoption, the awareness of the change in the birth family needs to be acknowledged. Although it may be tempting to try to shield other children in the birth family from the adoption plan, if they are old enough to be aware of the birth mother's pregnancy, they deserve to know what happened to the baby. The birth parent should tell her other children that the baby was born, whether it was a boy or a girl, what the baby's name is, where the baby will be, and what kind of contact they can expect to have with the baby. Being able to see the baby, saying good-bye to him, meeting the adoptive parents, and participating in an entrustment ceremony are all concrete ways to help children understand what has happened.

Birth parents may be reluctant to discuss the adoption plan with other children in the family because they are concerned about what their reactions might be. But it is better to discuss what has happened and give the children an outlet for their feelings about the event than to risk the kinds of shameful feelings and anxious fantasies that often result when children are left to piece together explanations on their own.

Children who are old enough to understand the adoption may worry that they will be placed for adoption, too. They may feel insecure and may not want to spend the night at grandma's house, fearing that like the new baby, they won't come home again. Parents can explain that they made a plan for the child who was placed for adoption so that she could be cared for in ways that the parents could not care for her, but that the other children in the family aren't going anywhere. Birth parents can put the situation into terms the child can understand by explaining how a child might be able to meet the responsibilities of caring for one or two pets, but not have the time or energy to care for a third. It doesn't mean they are no longer able to care for the pets they have, or that they don't like pets anymore, but that they've assessed their capabilities and found that they can't handle more responsibility at this time in their lives.

They can also say that the children might not understand why this had to happen, but that parents make decisions that they believe is best for *all* their children, and that they believe it is best for the children at home to stay at home, but best for the other child to be placed for adoption. Sometimes it's useful for birth parents to ask the other children in the family why they think the child was placed for adoption. Children are often very astute and may surprise you with their understanding of the situation.

Children who are old enough to understand the adoption may grieve for the loss of the brother or sister they will not be living with. Seven- to eleven-year-old girls in particular are often devastated to know their sibling has been placed outside the family. Children who have been longing for a younger brother or sister also may have a difficult time adjusting to the loss.

Older children and teenagers may feel guilty that they are staying in the family while the baby is being placed. They may think, "A baby needs a mother. I'm the one who should've gone." Some may think they should have dropped out of school to get a job to help support the family or to care for the baby.

Children's feelings are real, and parents should respect them and allow them to be expressed, rather than distracting children or minimizing their feelings. Children grieve in similar ways to adults, by first feeling numb and denying the loss, by believing they caused the loss and trying to recover it through some "bargain," by feeling angry and sad, and ultimately moving beyond the loss. Children who are grieving will not be comforted by ideas like, "You haven't lost a brother—you've gained two sisters" (i.e., the adoptive siblings of the child placed for adoption), any more than the birth parent might be comforted by that thought. They won't be comforted by the thought that their birth mother will have more time for them, or that little babies are fussy and are not much fun anyway. They are more likely to be comforted in the same way the birth parents are—by being allowed to express their feelings; by writing to the baby or seeing him and knowing that he's all right; by being held and rocked.

During times of stress in a family, and especially during times when the parents are so stressed that they may not be fully available to meet their children's needs, children may need counseling. The best choice is a therapist with experience in adoption issues or grief issues. Your adoption facilitator may be able to recommend someone. However, don't overlook your local school psychologist, who may have groups for children who have experienced loss.

It can be helpful for children to have planned responses to potentially troubling questions, so it is important for birth parents to discuss with their children how they can respond when someone asks them what happened to the baby their mother had. For example, they can say, "Some other parents are going to raise the baby, but we get to see him sometimes."

Explaining the Adoption Plan Later

Children raised by the birth parents who were too young at the time of the placement to be aware of the adoption, as well as those born after the placement, will eventually want to know why a sibling is being raised by other parents. They will need the same kinds of explanations at the same ages as the child who was adopted, as well as reassurance that their parents won't suddenly place them for adoption (see Chapter 12).

When Mercedes, a birth mother, went to the hospital for surgery, she left her seven-year-old son, Kyle, in the care of the couple who had adopted her daughter three years earlier. Kyle, who had been well behaved on other visits to the adoptive parents' home, was out of control on this visit. Eventually Kyle revealed he was afraid his mother wouldn't come back for him. Although the adoptive parents worried that they were letting Mercedes down by not taking care of Kyle as they had promised, they felt the best situation for the frightened child was for him to be in his own home. They arranged for his grandmother to stay with him until Mercedes had recovered.

One couple with two children were having marital problems at the time Marcie, the wife, discovered she was pregnant. Her husband left her a few months before she was due to give birth. Feeling unable to take care of another child, Marcie decided to make an adoption plan, but insisted on an open adoption—because she was already a mother, she knew she would be unable to go through life without ever having contact with one of her children. Two years after the child had gone home with the adoptive parents, the birth parents reconciled. Before they decided to have another child, they needed to figure out how they would explain to the child who was placed for adoption why they raised other children before and after her.

You can explain why one child was placed for adoption while another child was not by describing in concrete terms the difference in circumstances that the birth parents experienced. For example, a birth parent who was raising one child at the time of the placement could say, "When Mason was born, I didn't know what it would be like to raise a child. I thought it would be easy. But it was hard for me to be a good mother to Mason. I had to go to work because I didn't have anyone to help me. When I got home at night it was difficult for me to be patient with him. But I tried real hard. When I found out I was pregnant with you, I knew that I didn't have enough energy for both of you. Mason and I were already used to being together. It would have been harder for him to leave me because he already knew me as his mother. I thought that if I found new parents for you right away, you might not miss me as much."

Sometimes it helps to explain this situation using an experience a child is familiar with. Although the situations are not completely comparable, parents can ask a child to recall a situation in which he wanted very badly to do something, but it turned out to be too difficult. Although it may seem obvious to you, it also helps children to understand that what happened was not by chance. It was planned very carefully by you. This helps them feel that people they know and trust have some control over events that affect them.

Although the concept of a plan seems a bit uncertain, it is all that you can promise to any child. Your children have already learned that sometimes children leave their parents to live elsewhere; you can't promise that will never happen again: you could become seriously ill; you could die. Consequently, you can't be convincing if you try to promise that your child will be where he is permanently. Your child will feel more secure with a limited, but sincere, assurance that you plan to be together because his place is with you, and that if you are ever prevented from caring for him by unforeseen circumstances, someone else will take care of him.

Sometimes a child being raised by his birth parents will express a desire to live with a sibling's adoptive parents. She may have no siblings in her family of birth and she knows that she would in the adoptive family. She may think her life would be better if she lived with the adoptive family, and in some cases, her perception would be correct. Serena found it difficult to explain to the children she was raising why Matt, whom she had placed for adoption, had nicer things than they had. It hurt her when it was time to leave the adoptive parents' home and her children said they wanted to stay with the adoptive parents, too. This is one of those situations when telling children the truth, that life isn't fair, is the only answer, albeit an unsatisfactory one. Serena will have to trust that if she is meeting her children's emotional and physical needs that they will not regret their upbringing.

Sometimes the child who was adopted wants her birth siblings to come and live with her. Erica, who had the same genetic disease as her birth sister, Nina, became aware that her community offered far more resources for children with her disabilities than the community where the birth family lived. She wanted Nina to live with her, or at least for the birth family to move nearby, so that Nina could have more opportunities. Erica's parents carefully but firmly explained to her that her birth parents were responsible for making decisions about Nina and that she had to respect their decisions. Understanding that Erica felt naturally protective of her birth sister, though, they encouraged her to write to Nina often and to let her know what she was learning about her disease so that Nina could benefit from the information.

Naturally a child placed for adoption whose birth parent raised other children will need these same kinds of explanations as she struggles to understand why she experienced a loss that her birth siblings did not. After Aaron's birth mother and the two children she was raising visited, Aaron remarked to his adoptive mother, "Aren't I part of the set if we have the same birth mother?" His adoptive mother replied, "You belong here, with us." The boy then asked, "But isn't she sad that I'm not part of the set?" His adoptive mother replied that his birth mother was probably sad and encouraged him to ask his birth mother that question himself. When he did, the birth mother explained her reasons for making an adoption plan, said that she was sad that Aaron wasn't "part of the set," but that he belonged with his adoptive parents and she was happy that they had made a good home for him. She also said she was happy that she could sometimes see him together with his birth brothers.

When Adoptions Become More Open

If you are changing the level of openness in your adoption, you will have to prepare not only the child who will be having more contact with his birth parents but other children in the birth and adoptive families. As we point out in Chapter 10, this transition means major changes for the whole family. Some of the effect on the children is simply that of any change. Children can sense your tension and preoccupation and may become demanding or act out to recapture your attention. Being aware of this, you can try to normalize family life as much as possible, making a special effort so no one feels ignored. At the same time, acknowledge the change and validate the child's perception that mom and dad are behaving differently.

The change in openness may release some old feelings. Adoptive parents may be fearful the birth parents will physically or emotionally abduct the child and may become more protective of all their children as a result, or may seek more affection from them to reassure themselves. Monitor your behavior so that you don't expect your other children to make up for what you fear you might lose as the adoption becomes more open.

Your children may have a complex range of fears or other emotional reactions as they sort out what the increased openness in the adoption means. Adoptive siblings may be jealous of the attention the adoptee is getting, and if they are in confidential or semiopen adoptions themselves, they may envy the increased openness she is having with her birth family. They may be worried that she will go back to live with her birth parents and that they will lose her. They may be worried that their own birth parents will come to see them—or that they won't. Birth siblings may be worried that their parents' affection will be diluted, much the way siblings worry about how their position in the family will be affected when a new baby joins the family. Be alert to signs that other children in the family have concerns that need to be addressed, and be prepared to offer them extra support and reassurance at this stressful time. Keep children informed about the changes that are unfolding and check their perceptions about what is going on as well as their feelings about the events as they progress.

Relationships Between Siblings

Siblings are children who share the experience of growing up together. While they probably squabble, and may even declare deep animosity toward each other from time to time, there is a closeness that comes from being the only people who know what it was like to grow up in their families. This sense of shared memories and shared experience often keeps siblings close long into adulthood. For this reason, the children who grow up together in an adoptive family feel like brothers and sisters even though they may not be genetically related. The relationship they have with their biologic brothers and sisters who are being raised by their birth parents or by other adoptive parents may also be special, especially if they have the opportunity to get to know each other well. But just as the birth parents in an open adoption feel more like special friends or aunt and uncle to the child, the relationship between biologic siblings who do not grow up together usually is closer to that between cousins.

Preschoolers tend to enjoy playing with other children regardless of how well they know each other. Give them a sandbox or a box of action figures and they're happy. As children get older, however, they increasingly want control over the choice of their playmates. Compatibility becomes more important, both in personality and in interests. By the time children reach junior high, they may not make much of an effort to interact with another child unless they already have a longstanding relationship and enjoy each other's company.

The more opportunities children have to interact with each other as they grow up, the more likely they are to feel close. Not surprisingly, siblings who see each other often will probably feel closer to each other than those who must build their relationship through an occasional long-distance phone call. Close relationships between birth siblings raised apart are also more common when a child the birth parent is raising is old enough to remember the placement of a younger sibling, or when the siblings are the only children in their families. Timothy was fifteen months old when his mother placed his birth sister, Ruth, for adoption. Eight years later, his mother gave birth to another child she chose to parent. Despite the fact that he now had a sibling at home, Timothy felt closer to Ruth, who was closer to him in age and with whom he had a longer relationship. His feelings may be different years from now, after he and his baby sister are grown and their age difference matters less.

WHAT TO CALL EACH OTHER

Children will not be able to understand their relationship to their birth siblings (or other birth relatives) until they can understand both reproduction and relationships. Furthermore, preschoolers can't understand how one word can be used to describe two different relationships. They will have difficulty understanding how the word *sister* can be used to describe the other child in her family, with whom she lives, eats breakfast, and shares a bedroom, and to describe a child in another family, whom she may never see or may see only occasionally. Even when the children in the two families get together frequently, it isn't the same as living with a sibling. One little girl was complaining at preschool about her little brother's annoying habit of playing with her toys. A five-year-old girl in open adoption responded, "I get to have my baby brother only when I want to. Then he goes home and my things are my things." Although she was correctly using the word *brother* to describe her birth sibling, she was not describing a sibling relationship. If she had a younger brother at home with her, that would have been clear.

If a child's birth mother is expecting a baby, it is confusing to tell the child, "You're going to have a new baby brother or sister," since from her perspective, she isn't, because the baby brother or sister will not be living with her. It is probably best to simply refer to "the baby." After the birth, the baby can be referred to by name or as "the baby Christine gave birth to."

For similar reasons, references to the birth parent's other children can be by name or by their relationship to the birth mother. For example, if the child placed for adoption receives an invitation to her birth sibling's birthday and doesn't remember who Evan is, her mother can say, "Evan is your birth mother Amy's little boy." That is much clearer to a child than, "Evan is your birth brother."

As children reach elementary school they can understand not just reproduction but more complex relationships. The preoccupation children have with collections (shells, rocks, toy cars) around the age of seven is evidence of their growing ability to categorize and see how things are both alike and different. At this time, they will make the connection that they are related to other children born to the same birth parent whether or not they live in different households. As they become aware of this connection, they need to be clear about what people's names and roles are.

It may require even more maturity for them to make the necessary distinction if they closely resemble their birth siblings. For example, an African-American child placed in a family with European-American children and European-American parents will see that he is physically similar to his African-American birth siblings but shares cultural experiences with his adoptive siblings, and his relationship with each family group will be affected (and complicated) by these distinctions.

Some older children claim their birth relatives as siblings whereas others do not. They may want to count the child as a sibling when asked how many brothers or sisters they have and they may not. This may have to do with how close their relationship is, whether they feel different or embarrassed when they talk about the adoption, whether they enjoy the dramatic effect of revealing a sibling who's living elsewhere, or whether they feel jealous of the sibling. Again, parents can talk with them about the ways they might want to answer questions like how many brothers and sisters they have. Sometimes it is appropriate for a child to respond, "I have two sisters, but only one lives with me," and sometimes she will feel more comfortable saying, "I have one sister," just as the birth parent might acknowledge the child placed for adoption in some situations and not in others.

Conflicting Parenting Styles

Parents may find it difficult to have their children together if they think the other child is a bad influence on their own. This may simply result from different parenting styles—you may have different ways of disciplining your children, or may value behavior differently. Perhaps one parent feels strongly that children should never use swear words, whereas the other parent believes in ignoring such language; or one child runs through the house breaking objects and teasing the dog without his parent setting limits. Visits like these may leave you exhausted and upset, particularly if your child tries some of the words she's heard or has difficulty unwinding after being around the other child.

You may be tempted to limit the contact the children have with each other, believing less contact is in your child's best interests. However, it's important to remember that your child's most important influence is you, and as long as your example and the rules you set are firm and consistent, your child will most likely pass over the other child's possibly negative influences. Furthermore, remember that you can't isolate your child. You can't ensure that he will only have contact with well-behaved children. You can, however, help your child learn how to maintain the values you are trying to teach him in the face of other influences.

There is value in your child knowing her birth relatives, including her birth siblings. These are people who would have grown up together had circumstances been different. Their relationship would have been closer than their relationship with any other person, with the possible exception of the birth parents. Look for ways to solve the problem you are facing rather than removing the problem.

Think about how you would respond if the child visiting was the child of a relative or close friend. Rather than exclude the child, you might want to arrange visits outside your home where there is a lot of space. You might want to choose more structured activities that give the other child less opportunity to act out, such as bowling, or you may want to make arrangements that will allow you to always supervise the children when they are together.

One summer an adoptive family planned a visit to another state where many of their twelve-year-old daughter Sunni's birth relatives lived. After a visit with Sunni's birth aunt, which went well, Sunni was asked to stay overnight. Later her parents learned that the fourteen-year-old boy in the family had dropped out of school, and the fifteen-year-old girl was dating a twenty-four-year-old man. They used the opportunity to discuss the choices her cousins had made, and to reinforce their own values. They were encouraged to learn that Sunni was as uncomfortable with her birth cousins' lifestyle as they were. However, they recognized that it might be asking too much of Sunni to put her in a situation in which she might be pressured to go out with older boys herself, so they limited subsequent visits to daytime only.

When Children Have Joined the Family in Different Ways

Some adoptive families have had children by both birth and adoption. Some have different levels of contact with the birth families of the children they have adopted. When circumstances are not the same among the children in the family, parents sometimes feel anxious or guilty. They are concerned that the inequality between the children will result in tension within the family, or that the adopted child will feel like less than a full member of the family if there are also children by birth. They worry that the child who does not hear from his birth parents will feel deprived of something his sibling has.

Parents have to remember that circumstances are never completely equal for siblings, even if they're both born into the family. One child may be invited to more birthday parties than the other, one may have more success in athletics or academics than the other, and one may be healthier. Parents shouldn't try to equalize these circumstances, since to do so usually involves depriving one child of what he has, or diminishing what makes the two children individuals. For example, parents might refuse to allow a child to attend a birthday party unless her sibling is also invited, or they may try to minimize the achievements of one sibling to make it appear that the two are more alike than they really are.

Sometimes parents try to build up the other sibling with false praise or by pushing her to achieve in the same ways as her sibling. Children recognize these attempts to equalize their circumstances for what they are and resent them. Parents must allow each child to develop to her full potential and should rejoice in that development, no matter what the particular strengths and weaknesses. A sign of a healthy family is its ability to celebrate each individual's unique qualities.

When differences create discomfort, parents can be sincere in the support they give each child, and can recognize their responsibility to comfort a child when she feels sad or angry. Parents must also realize that treating children fairly doesn't necessarily mean treating them equally. The child who has the potential to get all A's at school and comes home with all C's may have privileges taken away until she pulls up her grades, whereas the child with the potential for all C's who achieves all C's may be rewarded. Children may not see this as fair for many years, but it is.

In an adoptive family, the differences between the children need to be acknowledged and respected, and each child should be able to express her feelings about the way she joined the family or the circumstances of her adoption. Sometimes it is the adoptive parents who feel the greatest responsibility to equalize or compensate for any differences between their children. They might be aware that because of adoption, their children have experienced profound losses and are different in ways that cannot be changed. Although their intentions are good, they are really treating their children as victims of adoption who need to be protected from further wounds. They will serve their children far better if they help them learn to manage life's inequalities.

CHILDREN BY ADOPTION AND BIRTH

During the elementary school years, children try to evaluate their places in their families. If there are children by both birth and adoption in the family, they all will try to determine whether their places in their families are affected by the ways in which they joined them. Like all siblings, they will look for signs that one or the other is more privileged, gets more recognition, or gets more love. Furthermore, children are aware that parents can be vulnerable to accusations that they are not behaving fairly toward each child and will try to see if making such accusations results in better treatment. Parents can respond to complaints that they treat their children unfairly by pointing out that there are three ways to join a family: by birth, by adoption, and by marriage. They can say, "How you joined the family is not the issue. No matter how you joined the family, once you are in it, you are a member and you are treated like everyone else."

Sometimes parents do relate better to one child in the family—their personalities or interests may be more in sync with each other. However, sometimes the parent–child duo in the family with the most conflict are the people who are most alike in temperament. Unfortunately, on occasion, parents who have not resolved the losses of infertility and adoption may feel closer to the children they are related to by birth than to those who were adopted. Parents should monitor themselves to see if their behavior or attitude indicates real unfairness. If this is the case, counseling may be necessary for the family.

Birth parents should be aware that children may use complaints about unfair treatment in their adoptive families as ways to manipulate them through the divide-and-conquer tactic. Children know their birth parents may feel guilty if they think they placed their child in a family where she is not loved as much as the other children. They may try to see what advantages they can gain from suggesting this is the case. Birth parents with the opportunity to observe the adoptive family may be able to evaluate the reality of the situation and provide important feedback to the child and the adoptive parents.

Sometimes the adoptive parents' biologic child feels left out because the child in open adoption gets attention and presents from the birth family. Alex, who was born into his family, was jealous of the annual trips his siblings got to make to gatherings of their birth families. Other children have been jealous of the fact that their adoptive siblings received presents from their birth relatives.

As we've pointed out, the birth family develops a relationship with the entire adoptive family, not just with their child. While birth relatives may not be able to include every child in the family in every gathering, it is important to remember to include other children in the family whenever possible. They can buy a special gift for the child related to them by birth, but can also include thoughtful gifts for other children in the family. This is true whether the other children in the family were added by birth or by adoption, and whether the adopted children have contact with their own birth relatives or not. (For more on gift giving and celebrating holidays, see Chapter 8.)

DIFFERENT LEVELS OF OPENNESS

Sometimes one child in the family has a fully disclosed adoption while another child has a confidential adoption, or one child's birth parents are very involved with the adoptive family while another child has little contact with his birth relatives. Children who do not have the opportunity to have contact with their birth relatives as often as a sibling may feel jealous, angry, and sad. It is a loss to them that they do not have this contact. But this does not mean that parents should deprive another child of contact with her birth family. There can be benefits to the child in confidential or semiopen adoption to seeing her sibling's relationship with her birth family. A sibling's birth parents may be the child's only contact with birth parents. Even though they are not their birth parents and all birth parents are not alike, they give the child an idea of what birth parents are like, which can help counter the stereotypes of birth parents.

Furthermore, although being accepted by a sibling's birth parents is not the same as being accepted by one's own birth parents, it can be helpful to a child who is feeling rejected. For instance, Jared's birth father, Rich, was actively involved in his life. Jared's adoptive brother had contact with his birth mother, but not his birth father. Rich included the older child in their activities, wanting to counteract the stereotype of the birth father who doesn't care. Another way for adoptive parents to deal with this issue is for them to find a special friend for their child—what one adoptive parent calls a "cookie person"—who could take the child who feels left out on excursions and bring him special treats.

At some point, though, parents have to deal with the child's specific feelings about not having as much contact with her birth parents as she would like to have. Although it may be hard for parents to know their child is hurting, the feelings the child has about not having contact with her birth family are probably there anyway. Her sibling's contact with her birth family only brings the emotions to the surface—just as open adoption often brings parents' feelings out. Parents can help their child express her emotions, even though they may feel powerless to change the situation. It may be important for the child to be given control in this situation. Like the boy mentioned in Chapter 11, encouraging a child to contact the adoption facilitator to express her need for information and encouraging her to write a letter or make a phone call to the birth parents expressing her feelings are two strategies that respect her feelings while giving her something active to do.

Parents can also allow the child to fantasize aloud about what a letter, phone call, or visit from his birth parents would be like. What would he say to them? What would they look like? What would they do together? The child can be encouraged to write letters or draw pictures that can be saved in case contact is ever established. When eight-year-old Mindy was allowed to fantasize like this, the image of her birth mother she described was precisely that of her adoptive mother. For the adoptive mother, who had been the target of Mindy's anger as she tried to deal with her birth mother's unwillingness to communicate with her, knowing that Mindy's fantasy mother was just like her was the best gift she could have been given.

COMPARING BIRTH PARENTS

When there is more than one open adoption in a family, children see that not all birth parents are like theirs. For example, while theirs may be young and unmarried, their sibling's birth parents may be older and married. This helps give children a broader perspective on the reasons birth parents place children for adoption. However, it can also lead to jealousy or sadness. A child who wishes her birth parents were different—more educated, wealthier, or more refined, for example—may envy her sibling's birth parents. When children are old enough to think abstractly, parents can talk with their child about how her life might be different if her birth parents were the way she wants them to be. By playing out her fantasy, she is freer to accept reality. They can commiserate with her if they share her wish that her birth parents were different—more organized or more stable, for example. They can give her permission to spend time with her sibling's birth parents, too, if she enjoys their company.

In some families, especially those into which older children from the foster-care system have been adopted, children play a different version of "My dad's stronger than your dad." They try to outdo each other with tales of their birth parents' misdeeds. "My dad held up a grocery store," one might say, to which the other child might respond, "Yeah, well, my dad robbed a stereo store." Their bravado probably hides their true feelings about their birth parents and is only an attempt to get an edge on a sibling, however undesirable.

A New Baby

A pregnancy by the birth mother or the adoptive mother can have many implications for children and adults in both families. The birth mother who is pregnant again and planning to raise the new baby may want to show the adoptive parents not only that she is more capable than she was at the time of the placement but that she is as good as the adoptive parents. This situation can lead to feelings of competition between them that may not have been present before. The birth mother may resent advice on child care from the adoptive parents, even if they have had a kind of parent–child relationship with the birth mother in the past.

Adoptive parents should be aware of this possibility and should be sensitive to the birth mother's need to demonstrate her capability as a parent.

The child who was adopted may feel jealous of her birth mother's new baby. Shirley said, "I don't like that she has another baby. She doesn't need another baby. She has me." Her feelings that she will be displaced by the new baby are similar to those older siblings have when a new baby joins the family—even though the baby is joining the birth mother's family and not the adoptee's family. Parents need to respond the way they would if the sibling were being added to the adoptive family. Shirley's birth mother probably will have less time for her once she has the baby, and the child needs to be prepared for that. But she also needs to know that the new baby will not take her place in her birth mother's heart or dilute her birth mother's affection for her. The birth mother needs to be aware that Shirley may feel rejected, and also needs to remember that she continues to have a responsibility to Shirley even though she may not have as much time for her as she has had in the past.

Extended family members, too, need to treat the new baby as an additional child in the family and not as a replacement child. After Amy's birth mother, Amanda, gave birth to a child she would be raising, Amy's adoptive mother, Judy, was hurt to hear Amy's birth grandmother refer with excitement to her "first grandchild." Judy and her husband had supported the birth grandparents in their role, regularly sent photographs and videotapes of Amy, and included them in Amy's birthday parties. Judy worried that Amy would be ignored. Since the adoptive parents valued the participation of the birth grandparents in Amy's life, Judy explained her feelings to the birth grandmother and continued to send her photographs and videos and invite her to birthday parties.

If the birth mother is making an adoption plan for the new baby, she may ask the adoptive parents to adopt this child, also, to keep her children together. There are some good reasons for birth siblings being placed together: It ensures that they will know each other. It gives both children someone in their own families to whom they are biologically related. They may feel less different than they would in separate adoptive families. Competition between them based on the amount of involvement by their birth parents would likely be reduced. And as they reach adolescence and focus on their identity, some of their tasks may be eased by having a biologic relative in the next room. From a practical standpoint, it makes it easier for both the birth mother and the adoptive parents to arrange visits, and since they already know each other, they have hopefully developed a level of trust and understanding.

However, birth parents should not assume the adoptive parents will be able or willing to adopt another child. The adoptive family has changed since the birth parents and adoptive parents first met. The adoptive parents may not be ready to add another child or they may have already made a commitment to work with another birth mother. There may be stresses in the family that would be increased by the addition of another child—for instance, the adoptive parents may not have saved enough money for another adoption. And if the child has a different birth father, the adoptive parents will need information about him before deciding whether to adopt the child. Adoptive parents who decide against adopting the biologic sibling of a child they have already adopted should at least keep in touch with the other adoptive family so that the siblings can know each other.

Margaret was a single mother when she adopted the child of a European-American mother and African-American father. When the birth mother approached Margaret about adopting her second child, Margaret was torn, since this child would not be biracial. Margaret had hoped to adopt another child of mixed racial heritage so that her child would grow up with someone with a similar ethnic identity. However, knowing how difficult it was for a single mother to adopt, Margaret decided it was as important for her child to be raised with a biologically related sibling as with a sibling of the same race.

Adoptive parents should not assume, however, that the birth parents will select them a second time. Perhaps the birth mother wants this child to live closer to her. Or she might want this child to go to a family with a different makeup, such as a family without any children. Sometimes a birth mother whose open adoption experience has not lived up to her expectations will choose other parents in the hope of having the kind of relationship she wants. However, although the birth mother may have valid reasons for choosing new adoptive parents for a subsequent child, it can send a powerful message to the first child that the birth mother doesn't support his adoptive parents. The child will have a difficult time feeling good about her placement and her family if her birth mother indicates she regrets her choice of parents. That doesn't mean the birth mother should place with parents she doesn't trust—it is, however, another good reason for the birth parents and the adoptive parents to work through whatever differences they may have or renegotiate their open adoption agreement.

Natalie placed her first child, Hope, in a semiopen adoption in which she and the adoptive parents agreed to write to each other anonymously and send the letters through an intermediary. After the adoption was finalized, the adoptive parents stopped writing, even though Natalie kept inquiring about Hope and requesting pictures that had been promised. Given this disappointing experience, with her second child, Natalie chose a fully disclosed adoption. She wrote to the first adoptive parents and told them of the second adoption, including the names of the new parents, Roy and Marti, and expressing her hope that the two sisters could get to know each other. However, they have not responded. It is a source of sadness to Natalie and to Roy and Marti that the birth sisters do not know each other. Roy and Marti haven't stopped trying to make contact, though, writing to the first adoptive parents through the intermediary. They hope the other adoptive parents will feel less threatened by them than they may be by Natalie and someday will allow the girls to know each other.

Abortion

If the birth mother chooses abortion as a solution to a subsequent untimely pregnancy, the effect on the child placed for adoption can be powerful. Naturally, you will not want to share this private information with a young child, but you may choose to tell an adolescent. Most people feel strongly one way or the other about abortion and teenagers are no exception. Being adopted provides them with a different outlook on abortion, however. They are aware that abortion was an option their birth mother could have chosen for them, and when their birth mother chooses to terminate a subsequent pregnancy, it may strike too close to home for them to feel comfortable with it (see Chapter 12). Those in open adoption may feel that by choosing abortion their birth mother has deprived them of a biologic sibling. They may feel a great loss and may express anger. The birth mother can talk to the teenager about her circumstances and explain why she chose abortion and not adoption this time. While the adoptee needs to understand that this was an adult decision, her grief should nonetheless be understood and respected.

A Child's Right to Privacy

When there are children in the birth family or adoptive family who are older than the adopted child, there is a tendency to give them information suitable for their level of maturity. Although this is often appropriate, sometimes parents give their older children information about the younger child that should not be given to other people before it is provided to the child. Children can be angry when they learn that their parents kept information from them while sharing it with their older siblings. Furthermore, you can't control what a child will do with information. He may deliberately or unwittingly give the information to the younger child before she is ready to hear it. Giving older siblings information with the admonishment to keep it a secret lets them know that they have something powerful in their control, and all but assures that they will reveal the information at an inappropriate time.

Helping Children Feel Comfortable

Look for ways to help children "map" their families, be creative about developing such images for your children to use, or encourage them to come up with their own ways of picturing the relationships in their lives. For example, psychologist Joyce Maguire Pavao, Ed.D., suggests replacing the standard "family tree" with a "family orchard," in which some "trees" (family members) are closer to the child's "tree" than others, but all share some common ground. One child put together a family album with a separate page for each member of her birth and adoptive families, describing not only each person but each person's relationship to her or to a significant person in her life. Mobiles could be used to depict individual family units and a giant mobile could be made from the smaller ones to show the interrelatedness of the family units. An updated version of the old television show "This Is Your Life" could be done with a camcorder. Asking each relative in the birth and adoptive family to contribute to the video might spark involvement from any relatives who have been reluctant to participate in the open adoption.

Families today are formed in many different ways, and though each method is unique, with its own set of challenges, they have much in common. If you feel isolated because your situation seems so different from other families, try to find the similarities between your family and some of the "blended" families formed through divorce and remarriage. Though literature written for them or contact with them may not address all your issues, you will surely find many families in which children have a variety of stepsiblings and half-siblings in their lives, not all of whom live with them.

part six

Special
Situations

14

When the Birth Parent
Decides to Raise
the Baby

When a birth mother decides to raise her child herself and cancels the adoption plans, she leaves a great deal of turmoil in her wake, whether or not her decision was predictable or even understandable. The adoptive parents will have a painful loss to confront. And the birth parents who had assumed they would be relinquishing their parental authority are suddenly faced with complete responsibility for this child.

At the time the decision is made, it may appear to some people that the birth mother is not acting in the child's best interest. But no one has a crystal ball, and no one knows for sure who will make the best parents. Just as some marriages at high risk for failure turn out to be long-term, loving unions, sometimes a birth mother who didn't appear to be ready to parent suddenly matures and reaches within herself to find the skills she needs.

Reasons that Plans Change

As we point out in Chapter 6, birth parents may not know how they will relate to a child who looks like them or like someone they know until after they see that child. They may have underestimated their parenting ability or their ability to separate from the child. It is important for them to reevaluate their adoption plan after the baby is born so they can look back on the decision with the knowledge that they gave it every consideration, or so they can make another decision.

Sometimes, however, the birth mother doesn't reevaluate her decision before the baby leaves the hospital. Sometimes she has the idea that she'd like to parent the child, but she feels obligated to the adoptive parents, doesn't want to be responsible for the emotional disturbance that will result if she changes her plan, or isn't sure whether her second thoughts are due to grief or to a real desire to parent. After a few weeks or even months, she may have a clearer idea about what she was feeling after the birth and may decide to reclaim the baby.

However, in many cases where the birth mother has reclaimed her parenting role, she has done so because her situation has changed since the birth. Perhaps people who were unaware of the birth and adoption plan learn about it and provide her with unexpected support. Perhaps the baby had a difficult birth or was at risk after birth and the birth mother's concern for the child and desire to continue to care for him has not abated. Perhaps the birth mother has found stability in her life that she didn't expect—a new boyfriend, reconciliation with her family, or a new job. Perhaps she and the birth father have renewed their relationship. Often the birth mother finds that she simply is not able to get on with her life as she expected to.

Sometimes there is conflict between the birth mother and the adoptive parents and the birth mother thinks her needs aren't being understood. The birth mother may have interpreted some of their actions (correctly or incorrectly) as signs that they didn't intend to stay in contact with her. Openness may have been a "bargain" for a birth mother who was not completely committed to adoption. She may have convinced herself that she could go through with the adoption because she wouldn't really be losing her child, only to discover that she was losing more than she thought.

Sometimes the adoptive parents' situation has changed and the birth mother is concerned about the child. The birth mother may have learned something about the adoptive parents that affects her desire to have her baby placed with them, such as the adoptive mother is pregnant or the adoptive mother has returned to work. Or she may have seen a different side of them during the birth or after the placement than they showed her during the pregnancy.

When something about the baby is unexpected, such as having medical problems or an unexpected racial makeup, the birth mother may later start to worry about whether the adoptive parents were sincere in wanting to adopt the child. In some situations the birth mother may be sensing some natural ambivalence on the part of the adoptive parents as they adjust to the new information, or she may be sensing that the adoptive parents really are disappointed.

On occasion, a birth mother who has made an adoption plan in the past that was unsatisfactory will make an adoption plan for a second child and reclaim him as a way of reenacting the first placement and doing what she wishes she had done at that time.

Adoption facilitators are generally reluctant to encourage a birth mother to maintain an adoption plan if the birth mother is expressing a desire to keep or reclaim the baby. Not only is the adoption invalid if the birth mother's consent has been coerced but it isn't ethical for a child to be adopted against his birth mother's wishes unless that birth mother has been shown to be unfit. And no one wants the birth mother to make a decision that she'll regret forever.

Making the Decision

The birth mother who is thinking about changing the plan and raising the baby will want to give this new idea the same careful consideration that she gave to her plan to place the child. This doesn't mean giving it six months of thought, but it does mean she should systematically review her options in light of her current perspectives. As soon as she begins to seriously consider changing her mind, she should call in her counselor and review with him the reasons she originally decided to make an adoption plan and chose the family she did. She can explore what might have changed since that time and examine how much of her desire to keep her baby is due to grief, the intense connection she feels to the baby that was perhaps unexpected, or lack of trust in the adoptive parents. They can also discuss how her decision will affect other people in her life, such as her extended family, the birth father, and the adoptive parents. In particular, they should discuss how she will meet her child's needs.

A birth mother who is considering reclaiming a child already placed with the adoptive parents must be aware that even though she has a valid legal and biological claim to the child, once that child has been placed with the adoptive parents a family has been created. The family may have no legal standing; nor is it a family by virtue of shared genetic heritage. But it is a psychological family. The decision to disrupt that family cannot be made capriciously, but must be given careful thought, especially with regard to the effect on the child.

The child has begun to consider the adoptive parents to be his parents, and the longer the child has been with them, the more attached to them he is. He will experience disruption if he is moved to another family, even if it is his birth family. (For more information about the effect of such a move, see Chapter 7.) This is not to suggest that babies who are moved from one caretaker to another during the first year will be unable to adjust. Certainly research has shown that infants who have learned to trust one caretaker can transfer that trust to others. (And the experience of many adoptive parents will back that up.) But a birth mother should not mislead herself into thinking that the baby will be unaffected by the move, or that it will be easy to care for a child who is grieving for the parents he has known.

While birth parents may be afraid of the reaction the adoptive parents will have to the news—reluctant to risk losing the goodwill they have enjoyed—they have a responsibility to discuss the possible change of plans with the adoptive parents. The adoptive parents need to prepare for the possibility of such a painful loss, and if the birth mother is reconsidering her plan at the hospital, the adoptive parents should certainly not take the baby home without knowing how tenuous this placement may be.

If the birth mother is still at the hospital, the person who has been designated as the birth mother's advocate in the hospital also needs to be aware of the possible change of plans so that she can help the birth mother establish and enforce boundaries that will enable her to discuss her decision only with the appropriate people. Sometimes, when a birth mother is wavering in her decision, people who want to influence her decision will descend upon her with arguments for their preferred outcome. The birth mother has the right to choose the people with whom she'll discuss her options, and even the adoptive parents must respect the boundaries the birth mother sets for how often and under what circumstances she will discuss her decision with them.

Adoptive parents who learn that the birth parents are considering changing their plans respond in different ways. Some become belligerent, reminding the birth parents of their promise and of how much they have done for them. Some plead with the birth parents, asking them to keep in mind their needs and the emotional turmoil they will experience, and others remind the birth parents how much more they can offer the child. We hope most are sensitive enough to realize the birth parents have the right to make this choice and no one owes anyone a child, no matter what their needs or how nice they have been. Adoptive parents should step back and allow a professional counselor to explore with the birth parents the advantages and disadvantages of the different options facing them. Of course, adoptive parents are only human and they cannot be expected to meet the possibility of such disappointment with complete composure. When a birth mother told one adoptive father she wanted to think about taking the baby home from the hospital, he responded angrily, "You should have thought about that a long time ago." But after recovering from his initial shock, he apologized for his outburst and told her, "Of course you'll want to think about this. Take all the time you need."

Birth parents may be surprised by the adoptive parents' response. They may seem different than the agreeable people the birth parents got to know during the pregnancy. Birth parents sometimes wonder if the friendly, good-natured image the adoptive parents projected was sincere or merely manipulative. They are concerned that the angry, "self-centered" side they are now seeing is their true personality, and it may become the final factor in the birth parents deciding to raise their baby themselves.

Birth parents need to make their decision based on their own ability to raise the child, the needs of the child, as well as what they've learned about the adoptive parents over time, rather than on the reaction of the adoptive parents under stress. The news that the birth parents might keep the baby raises in the adoptive parents their deepest fear—that they will lose this child. Their willingness to fight for the child they think of as theirs may not be sensitive to the birth parents or reflect what they know about the adoption process, but it is still a normal response for parents. Birth parents should not take the adoptive parents' response personally, but should recognize it as a reaction to their fear of loss and should be generous in their ability to forgive the adoptive parents. The adoptive parents would have been expected to forgive the behavior of the birth parents while they were grieving.

Because you may be unsure how to act around each other now that you may not be assuming the roles you thought you would, you should take some time to talk with each other about how you will function during the decision-making time. If the birth mother and baby are still at the hospital, will the adoptive parents continue to visit them? If the child is with the adoptive parents, can the birth parents continue to call or visit? Will you discuss the birth parents' options with each other or leave that discussion for a counselor? How will the birth parents communicate their decision to the adoptive parents?

Blocking the Reclaiming

Adoptive parents nearly always want to keep the birth parents from reclaiming the child, and those who have been raising a child may go to court to prevent the child's return to the birth parents. Our purpose here is not to discuss the legal standing of adoptive parents who want to prevent the birth mother from reclaiming. Much depends on state laws, the length of time the child has been with the adoptive parents, what kind of documents the birth parents signed, and whether any fraud or coercion of the birth parents was involved. But we do want to provide adoptive parents who are considering that course of action with some points to ponder:

- Keep in mind how you will explain to the child why you kept his birth mother from reclaiming him. Whereas you may see this as a demonstration of your love for the child (and it is), your child may be angry and blame you for his losses (see Chapter 11).
- If you are going to fight, fight fair. Don't use legal ploys to drag out the court case until several years have passed, then claim that the child belongs with you because she has lived with you for so long. Don't allow your finances to give you an unfair advantage over the birth mother. Let the case be decided on its merits, not on the basis of who could afford to fight longer. Furthermore, keep in mind that if the case drags on for many years and then the court finds in favor of the birth mother, your pain will be much deeper, and the disruption to the child will be great.
- Make sure you are making a decision in the best interests of the child. Although it is disruptive for children to be moved from one caretaker to another, they do adjust. Adjustment is easier if they have received loving care from the first caretaker and continue to receive loving care from the next caretaker, if the number of moves is minimal, and if care is taken to make the transition gentle. But if you believe the child will be physically or emotionally harmed, not just because she is being moved but because you have reason to believe the birth mother cannot meet the child's needs consistently, then fighting to keep the child may be in the child's best interests.

Sometimes a birth mother with no legal basis for reclaiming her child will pursue that action knowing she will lose. She may not want to reclaim the child, but may be bowing to pressure from her family or the birth father to try to reclaim. Birth mothers should realize that such action seriously jeopardizes their relationship with the adoptive parents. They are likely to have a difficult time trusting a birth mother who has tried to reclaim a child and has been prevented from doing so. Birth mothers should therefore try to reclaim only when they truly want to do so, when they believe it is in the child's best interest, and when they have a legal basis for the action.

Adoptive parents who win the battle over a child may not have the blessings from the birth parents that often enhance their sense of entitlement and will have to work hard to overcome any feeling that they weren't meant to be the child's parents. Furthermore, if it isn't completely clear why it was in the child's best interests for the adoptive parents to raise him, they may have difficulty explaining their decision to him. Although they were motivated by their attachment to their child, their child may, at times, see only that his adoptive parents kept him from being with his birth parents and he may be angry. Because this has the potential to be a no-win situation for everyone involved, when the adoptive parents fight for the child and win, every effort needs to be made for the adoptive and birth parents to mend their relationship.

The Transition

Once the birth parents have made a decision to keep the baby, all the plans that have been made shift. The adoption facilitator's job is to help the birth parents prepare physically, emotionally, psychologically, intellectually, and materially for their roles as mother and father. The facilitator should also help prepare the birth parents to inform the adoptive parents. The birth parents might like the facilitator to let the adoptive parents know what is about to transpire, and the facilitator might want to undertake that role, perhaps to ensure that the news is given as gently as possible or to avoid a confrontation between the birth and adoptive parents.

Nevertheless, it is the birth parent's responsibility to inform the adoptive parents. And although difficult, this direct communication can help everyone heal. Birth parents need to remember that they invited the adoptive parents into their lives. The adoptive parents have been completely vulnerable in the relationship, taking emotional and financial risks. Adoptive parents who have been open, caring, and trusting throughout the pregnancy deserve an explanation and answers to their questions. If the birth parents cannot inform the adoptive parents directly because the facilitator has been serving as an intermediary all along, the birth parents can still write a letter explaining their decision and can have the facilitator give the letter to the adoptive parents.

Whether the baby is still in the hospital or has already been placed, the adoptive parents deserve time alone with him to say good-bye, just as birth parents do when they are relinquishing their parenting roles. Adoptive parents shouldn't be asked to hide their sadness from the birth parents, but they ought to communicate to the birth parents their good wishes. While they may have reservations about the parenting ability of the birth parents, they do want a good life for the child and the parents. Even though they are grieving, the adoptive parents shouldn't rob the birth parents of their joy at becoming parents; they would expect the same consideration had the baby been placed with them.

Because there is so much pain involved when a baby is reclaimed, there is a tendency when a birth mother appears likely to reclaim for everyone involved to want to hurry the process along. Once she has decided to be the child's parent, the birth mother understandably wants to undertake that role immediately. The adoptive parents want to hold onto the child, but if they know they will have to return the child to the birth mother, having the child with them may become unbearable. The adoptive parents may withdraw emotionally from the child due to their own depression.

There is also a tendency for everyone to avoid each other. The birth mother feels guilty and sometimes ashamed that she is putting the adoptive parents through what she knows is a difficult time. The adoption facilitator doesn't want to be around people in turmoil, even though that's his job. The adoptive parents are angry and don't want to see the people they believe have betrayed them.

You need to resist the temptation to undertake the reclaiming process hastily and plan for a gentle transition for the child. The reclaiming needs to be done as deliberately as the original placement—indeed, it is as much a transfer of parental roles and rights as the original placement was.

The older the child is, the more important it is that the transition maintain familiar foods, sounds, smells, and routines. If possible, the birth parents should go to the adoptive parents' house and have the adoptive parents show them the child's routine. By beginning a task, such as feeding or bathing, and allowing the birth parents to finish the task, the adoptive parents not only demonstrate how the baby is used to being cared for but give the child permission to receive care from the birth parents. However, the adoptive parents can also write out the child's preferences and schedule to be given to the birth parents.

Just as it is important to have an entrustment ceremony when the birth mother placed the child with the adoptive parents, it is helpful for the adoptive parents to transfer the parental roles back to the mother through a ritual. Though this may be exceedingly difficult, remember that rituals do more than celebrate—they mark transitions and help people understand how relationships have changed.

The Emotional Reactions of Adoptive Parents

When told that the birth parents have decided to keep the baby or are strongly considering that option, adoptive parents often feel sadness, fear, and anger. When adoptive parents lose the child before taking him home, they experience the loss of expectations—loss of the dreams they had, not for some baby, but for this baby. As they got to know the birth parents, they began to imagine the baby's coloring, abilities, and mannerisms as a composite of the birth parents' genetic contribution and their own environmental contributions, just as expectant parents imagine their child to be a combination of the father's and mother's genetic and environmental gifts. They visualized themselves being parents—rocking and feeding the baby and taking him to the park. In realizing their dream is canceled, they are experiencing the same feelings of loss that the birth parents were anticipating up to the point at which they changed their plans.

In addition, the adoptive parents are experiencing the practical loss of time and financial resources. By putting their energy into developing the open adoption relationship with these birth parents, they may have passed over other opportunities to adopt, or they may wonder if they missed other opportunities by being taken out of the adoption facilitator's pool of prospective adoptive parents. Having already spent many years trying to conceive and trying to adopt, a setback of even a few months in their quest to become parents seems like an eternity. The adoptive parents are no doubt also thinking about the money they have invested in this adoption.

Even though their financial relationship with the birth mother has not been as simple as that of a consumer and a supplier, there was the expectation that they were paying for the prenatal care of their baby. And even the most giving adoptive parents have a limit to their financial resources. They may not have enough money left to pursue another adoption.

In many ways, this feels like the same loss they experienced so many times through infertility, only now there is a human factor involved. When they experienced the loss of a potential pregnancy or child through infertility, the cause of their loss wasn't clear. They blamed their bodies, society's expectations about sexual freedom or women's careers, or their own fate. Often, the uncertainty of what caused the infertility added to the frustration of the loss itself. However, the cause of this current loss seems clear: the birth parent.

All the old feelings adoptive parents may have had about being infertile may revisit them at this time—feelings that they aren't good enough, that they aren't meant to be parents, that they're being punished for some known or unknown misconduct. While they were coming to terms with infertility, they could rationalize that infertility was a medical condition and not some kind of personal retribution. Now, they may wonder if they did something to cause the birth mother to not like them or to want to hurt them, or if she saw in them some qualities that made her fear for the well-being of her child.

In an attempt to gain control of the loss to ensure that it won't happen again, adoptive parents may want the birth mother to tell them what it was about them that caused her to change her plans. In some cases, birth parents decide to parent their child because they have lost confidence in the adoptive parents for some reason. More often, though, the birth parents' decision has nothing to do with the adoptive parents, even if they will sometimes try to justify their decision by finding fault with the adoptive parents.

If the baby has lived with them for even a short time, the adoptive parents' grief will be tantamount to that of parents whose child has died. They will have many of the same feelings of the adoptive parents who expected a baby only to have the birth mother change her mind prior to placement, but their grief will be even greater because they actually had the baby in their family and were functioning as the parents. They are very likely to blame the birth mother for the loss of their child, even though intellectually they may recognize her right to reclaim and may support her decision to exercise that claim.

Is their grief, having had the child in their home for several weeks or months, greater than that of the birth mother, who had the baby as part of her body for nine months and gave birth to him, but never expected to parent him? That's an unanswerable question. Surely many adoptive parents feel their grief is greater, while many birth parents believe their grief is greater. But it is important to remember that this isn't a game in which the answer to "Who gets the baby?" is determined by who can demonstrate the most grief. Both the birth parents and the adoptive parents have significant claims to this child. But both cannot be the parents. The adoptive parents may not think the situation is fair. After all, they were asked by the birth parents to be the child's parents. The birth mother placed the child with them voluntarily. They've been caring for the child—dealing with colic, late-night feedings, and the general disruption a new baby brings to a family. And nagging at them, also, may be the legacy of infertility—the birth mother can have another baby and they can't. It isn't fair. But any child the birth parents have later will not replace this child. Nor is it fair to expect birth parents to be sure of their plan for their child's future within a few hours of his birth. Absent some kind of futuristic device that would demonstrate clearly who would be the better parents for the child, the birth parents can only make the decision they think is best. Whatever they decide, someone is going to be deeply hurt. (See Chapter 2 and the Resources section at the end of this book for more information about grieving.)

DEALING WITH ANGER

Anger is a natural expression of grief, and even adoptive parents who understand the birth mother's decision or recognize her right to change her mind will feel angry. Adoptive parents may feel betrayed, especially if the birth mother expressed certainty about her adoption plan. Adoptive parents can ask themselves if they could give up their child just because they had promised to do so. Perhaps at this time, with their intense pain, they may think the birth parents should have kept their obligation no matter what, but on another level they know they could not have a close, honest relationship with a child that they had not been given freely.

The fact that the birth mother seemed to have all the control in the relationship may leave the adoptive parents feeling powerless. They may have been willing to endure this lack of control if it meant getting a baby, but after putting a lot of energy into the relationship only to end up with empty arms, their anger at their lack of power may seem overwhelming.

Adoptive parents may feel they've been emotionally and financially manipulated. They wonder if the birth parents ever intended to place their child for adoption or if they were trying to get financial assistance with the pregnancy or were enjoying the emotional power they had over others. Unfortunately, this is sometimes true, but it is not often the case. When it is, adoptive parents sometimes suspect quite early on, or the adoption facilitator may suspect and alert the adoptive parents to the possibility. They then have the option of choosing whether to take the risk.

Adoptive parents who knowingly risk becoming involved with birth parents who appear to be manipulative have to take responsibility for that decision. When it becomes clear that their suspicions were justified, the anger the adoptive parents often feel is at themselves for allowing the manipulation. If the birth parents were so skilled at deception that neither the adoptive parents nor the adoption facilitator caught on, the adoptive parents shouldn't blame themselves for believing the best about fellow human beings.

Most of the time, birth parents have been as honest with the adoptive parents and the adoption facilitator as they've been with themselves about their plans for the baby's future. Often they haven't allowed themselves to thoroughly explore the option of parenting the baby, perhaps because they have been pressured by other people into the adoption. And sometimes birth parents who have shown maturity and responsibility in making an adoption plan realize at the time of the baby's birth that they are ready to take on parental obligations as well. Often these women are in their thirties and had never viewed themselves as maternal. One such birth mother, who had become pregnant as a result of an affair with a married man, changed her mind when she saw that the baby resembled her family and not the birth father. She had been capable all along of parenting a child; she just was not emotionally prepared for what she thought would be a constant reminder of her mistake.

Although it still hurts when responsible, capable birth parents decide to raise their baby, their decision is often easier for adoptive parents to accept than when the birth parents' ability to parent is in question due to their immaturity, history of substance abuse, or erratic behavior. When that happens, adoptive parents, who have already begun to think of this baby as theirs, are not only grieving for their own loss of the child but are grieving as parents for the neglect, abuse, or inadequate care they fear the child will now receive. There is no greater anguish for parents than to believe their child may suffer.

Adoptive parents have the right to feel angry and sad as they grieve for the loss of the baby, but they need to express their feelings in appropriate ways. (See Chapter 5 along with Resources listed at the end of this book.) They know they have begun to recover, says psychologist Randolph W. Severson, Ph.D., of Hope Cottage in Texas, when they can say that despite their pain, they have learned something about themselves—about being human.

The adoptive mother and father may react differently to this loss. Sometimes the adoptive father represses his grief and concentrates on protecting or taking care of his wife. He has had a loss, too, and needs to allow himself to grieve. Adoptive parents should be aware of the stress it places on the marital relationship to lose a child, especially if they have had the child for a time. They are both hurting and aren't available to help each other. The adoptive couple might blame each other for the loss, especially if one partner was more enthusiastic than the other about the decision to become involved with the birth mother. Generally, loss is beyond one's control. At the same time, adoptive parents have to remind each other that they were aware of the risks and they voluntarily agreed to those risks—even if one was less enthusiastic about doing so than his or her partner. Adoptive parents need to work hard to maintain their relationship as they grieve.

Keep in mind that one of the normal reactions to loss is the desire to withdraw. Adoptive parents may feel that no one understands their pain—indeed their friends and family may not fully understand the depth of their loss. This is especially true when the birth mother changes her mind at the hospital. Friends may think that since they never actually had the baby, they aren't suffering. People who have experienced a miscarriage or stillbirth sometimes experience a similar lack of empathy.

Friends and relatives cannot overestimate the depth of the anguish the adoptive parents are experiencing at the loss of the baby they thought of as theirs. The adoptive parents will need their support at this time, and for many months to come.

The Role of Openness

Some adoptive parents blame openness for the birth mother's decision to keep or reclaim the baby. They think she wouldn't have made that decision in a confidential adoption, or they wouldn't hurt as much if they weren't so exposed. However, openness doesn't cause birth parents to keep a baby they originally intended to place for adoption. Much of the time, if birth parents are undecided about adoption, the knowledge that they will be able to choose where the child will be and to keep in touch with the child actually enables them to choose adoption.

Of course, in some cases, birth parents who make an adoption plan reluctantly or with little preparation will use openness as a bargaining chip in their internal conflict. "I won't really be placing my child for adoption because I'll be able to see him whenever I want," they think. When they realize that even with openness they have a significant loss, they keep the baby or reclaim. Even in those situations, it isn't the system of open adoption that upsets the plan but the birth parent's unrealistic expectations.

The only way the adoptive parents can be spared the hurt is to be spared the awareness that they have been chosen as parents until all the consents have been signed. But the cost is that adoptive parents do not get to prepare themselves; they do not get a chance to know the birth parents and perhaps to participate in the incredible joy of their child's birth.

When babies were placed in foster families until the parental rights were terminated, and adoptive parents were not even notified that they were to become parents until a child was legally free for adoption, birth parents could reclaim their children without hurting the adoptive parents. Adoptive parents take the risk of having a child reclaimed not when they become involved in open adoption but when they become involved in an adoption system that places children with their adoptive parents before the children are legally free for adoption—a process that includes confidential adoptions as well as open adoptions.

They take the risk because it is best for a child to be placed as soon as possible with the parents who will be raising her. The very attachment to the child that makes it so difficult for adoptive parents to separate from her came about because she learned to trust her parents because they put her needs above their own. It is the most important lesson of infancy, and adoptive parents shouldn't minimize the important contribution they have made to that child.

The Birth Parents' Feelings

Birth parents who decide to keep their baby or reclaim their parenting role are often afraid that people will be angry with·them. They are frightened of the reaction of the adoptive parents, the adoption facilitator, and perhaps their own family members or friends. They often look for reasons to be angry at the adoptive parents or adoption facilitator to justify their decision not to place their baby for adoption or not to place with these adoptive parents. Their counselor can help them examine their true feelings about the adoptive parents and their reasons for changing their plans.

Birth parents may feel sad knowing the pain the adoptive parents are experiencing, and they may feel guilty for causing them that pain. They may feel they failed by not providing the adoptive parents with a child. Birth parents who have not always acted responsibly in the past may have received a lot of positive reinforcement for making an adoption plan. They may now feel that they have let people down once again. If birth parents are thinking that parenting their child represents a failure, they are not getting a good start as parents. Their counselor will want to explore this issue with them.

If the birth parents are afraid of the facilitator's response, or are worried that the facilitator will try to talk them out of their decision, they will often withdraw and will refuse to discuss their new plan. They may think that since they are no longer planning an adoption, they don't need a counselor, or the facilitator will no longer be willing to provide them with services. Birth parents sometimes attempt to use hospital personnel to shield them from the people they don't want to talk to. The adoptive parents and a facilitator may suddenly find that the hospital won't put their calls through or allow them to visit.

Naturally, if the adoptive parents or adoption facilitator are being threatening or abusive, the birth parents have a right to protect themselves, and withdrawal can be an appropriate way for people to take care of themselves at an emotionally difficult time. But birth parents need to balance their need to protect themselves with the legitimate needs of others who have been involved in the adoption plan. The adoptive parents deserve to be treated with the same respect that the birth parents would have wanted shown toward them if they were the ones grieving their loss. It will be difficult for the birth parents to witness the pain the adoptive parents are in, but that is all part of the experience.

The birth parents may be afraid the adoptive parents will feel so attached to the child that they'll try to kidnap him, just as the adoptive parents might have felt threatened by the birth parents spending time alone with the baby they were going to adopt. These fears are understandable, but usually groundless. You need to be able to trust each other and to take reasonable risks in your relationship. If the adoptive parents have been behaving irrationally, discreet precautions can be taken to ensure the child's safety while still allowing the adoptive parents the time they need with the child.

The Next Step

Once the birth parents have decided to keep the baby, both the birth parents and the adoptive parents need to notify their friends and family members of the change in plans and begin to prepare for the changes in their lives.

THE BIRTH PARENTS' PREPARATIONS

Since they were not planning to parent, the birth parents may not have spent much time learning about caring for a baby. The birth parents may want to arrange for visits from a community health nurse to discuss other aspects of caring for their infant, sign up for a new parent class, or read one of the many books available about the physical and emotional needs of newborns. The birth mother who will raise the child as a single parent will need to consider what role the birth father and his family will play in the child's life. If the birth mother is employed, she will have to make a decision about when and if to return to work, and if necessary, make arrangements for a leave of absence. If she is in school, she will want to investigate the options available for continuing her education, and either way she will have to look into day care for the child while she is away. Some high schools and colleges have day-care centers on campus. The birth parents should also make arrangements for health insurance for the baby and should investigate any public assistance programs for which they are eligible.

Obviously a lot needs to be done in a short amount of time. It is not unreasonable for birth parents to feel frightened of the responsibility they are undertaking, especially since they probably have not prepared for it. They may feel overwhelmed. This is a common feeling for even the most prepared new parents. However, birth parents may feel that they aren't entitled to make any mistakes in parenting this child. They may feel they have to prove their ability to those people who have been telling them that adoption would have been better for the child. Birth parents will need help, especially since the birth mother is recovering from the delivery and is focusing her energy on getting to know her baby and learning how to meet his needs. The birth parents need to identify people they can depend on for support and let them know specifically how they can help at this time.

If it is within their means, birth parents can make arrangements to repay the adoptive parents for the expenses they incurred during the pregnancy. While no amount of money can make up for the loss of the child for the adoptive parents, even a token payment of ten dollars a month can be an important way for the birth parents to let the adoptive parents know they did not intend to hurt them.

THE ADOPTIVE PARENTS' PREPARATIONS

Adoptive parents will have to prepare to grieve and to fill up the days they expected would be filled with the care of a child. They, too, can send a simple printed announcement, something like this:

> Dear Friends,
>   The baby we had been waiting for finally arrived on July 11.
> However, our joy was interrupted when the birth mother decided to parent the baby herself. We need your comfort and support as much as if we had lost a child born to us, for that is how we feel.
>
> (Signed)

If the adoptive parents have received baby gifts, the announcement could also acknowledge those gifts and indicate the adoptive parents' plans to return them, keep them for the next child, or give them to the birth parents.

Adoptive parents who have arranged their lives to accommodate the arrival of a baby may feel lost. Perhaps one of them has quit a job or they have taken leaves of absence from work. First, adoptive parents need to give themselves permission to not be prepared for what has happened, even though they knew the risks. They could not prepare simultaneously for both the joy of the arrival of a child and the grief of the loss of a child.

Next, they need to realize that their reaction to this turn of events is grief at the loss of a child. They should ask themselves what they would do if their child had died. They would probably take some time off from work or from other routine responsibilities. They would want to remind themselves not to make any major changes in their lives for a while. Some would want family and friends around them for support, whereas others would want privacy. Adoptive parents should resist the temptation to get rid of the child's belongings or nursery items quickly, or to have friends do the job for them. However, they might want to close the door to the nursery and later ask a friend to help them pack it up and put the painful reminders away. Adoptive parents should save pictures of the child and other memorabilia. That child will always be part of their family story, just as though the child were born into the family and died. They also might want to have some kind of memorial service.

As we discuss in Chapter 6, rituals are effective ways to deal with change, especially sudden change. They help crystallize our feelings and bring them to the surface. They bring together people who can help us during a difficult time of transition. In this way, they help us heal. Just as the entrustment ceremony described in Chapter 6 helps birth parents face their loss, a memorial service can help adoptive parents put closure to this experience. Such a ritual could incorporate symbols of the child, such as the outfit the adoptive parents bought for the child to wear home, and could include comforting prayers, readings, songs, or the planting of a tree in memory. (For more on rituals, see the Resources section at the end of this book.)

Finally, adoptive parents should give themselves adequate time to grieve (See Chapter 2), especially before resuming attempts to become parents. Grief experts believe that a child added to the family before parents have adequately grieved for the loss of an earlier child becomes a replacement child rather than being loved and accepted for himself. Furthermore, adopting or resuming infertility treatments represents a major decision and one that should not be made while in the midst of grief. And the adoptive parents may not be ready emotionally to get close to another child.

Adoptive parents often say they will not allow themselves to again be as vulnerable as they were. Adoptive parents who attempt to pursue another adoption too soon sometimes sabotage their efforts by being suspicious of birth mothers or taking out their anger at the birth mother who reclaimed on the next birth mother they meet. Some insist on a confidential adoption, unfairly blaming openness for their pain. All adoption carries some risk. It takes time and a lot of work to be willing to take the risks of adoption again. Adoptive parents who are selected for another placement within a few months after an expected child doesn't arrive need to explore with a counselor whether they are ready to welcome another child at this time.

An experience like this sometimes adds to the desperation adoptive parents can feel about their quest for a child. Adoptive parents need to take special care of themselves during their grieving so that their self-esteem remains intact—those adoptive parents who feel good about themselves will emerge from this experience confident that they will make good parents and that other birth parents will see this and choose them for their child. Adoptive parents can and do move beyond the loss of a child they expected to raise. But, like infertility, it is a significant experience that affects them for life.

THE ROLE OF THE BIRTH FAMILY

Like the birth parents and the adoptive parents, the extended family members have been preparing for different roles and feelings than they will now have. The birth family will no longer have to experience the grief they had been expecting; they must now prepare to accept a new child into their family and begin to think about the many ways their family will change. If they viewed the adoption plan with relief after the crisis of the pregnancy, this new development may feel as though they are being thrust into a new crisis. Once again, they may be feeling that they are out of control of a decision that will affect them intimately. But the birth parents will need help at this time, and birth families should let the birth parents know that even if they don't agree with their decision, they do respect their choice and will support them emotionally. Providing emotional support means being willing to listen, giving advice when it is solicited, and accepting the child as a full member of the family.

Even if the birth families agree with the birth parents' decision, they need to discuss expectations and plans. Otherwise, members of the birth families may make assumptions that aren't shared by everyone. For example, a birth mother who moved to a different state to be near the adoptive parents may decide to remain there, while her family may expect her to return home. If they haven't discussed this before, birth families need to let the birth parents know in what specific ways they will assist them if they decide to parent the baby themselves. Can the birth parents come home with the baby temporarily? Can they come home permanently? Will members of the birth family babysit while the birth parents attend school or go to work? What kind of financial assistance will be available?

If the birth parents are young and will be returning home with the child, the birth family and the birth parents may want to discuss with a counselor what their roles will be. The birth grandmother, for example, may have a difficult time allowing her teenage daughter to make decisions about her child's welfare. The birth grandmother may be accustomed to making the parenting decisions in the family and may have difficulty seeing her daughter as a parent and not as a child. The birth father may feel that if he has assumed responsibilities as a father to the child, he is also entitled to greater independence within the family.

THE EXTENDED ADOPTIVE FAMILY

The extended families of the adoptive parents will also experience grief at the loss of the child. In addition, they will be saddened that a loved one has had a significant loss. They, too, may feel out of control and wonder what they could have done to protect the adoptive parents from this hurt. They should remember that the adoptive parents made a decision to become involved with the birth parents knowing the risks, and they were willing to take those risks because it offered them hope of having a child.

The adoptive parents' mourning of the loss of a child is intense and deep; it will last a long time, and that is normal. Extended family can ask the adoptive parents how they can be of help, whether they want company or prefer privacy, and if they want the extended family members to participate in a memorial service or ritual. Sensitive people will also understand that the adoptive parents do not need to be second-guessed on whether it was prudent for them to pursue this adoption. Whatever reservations family members and friends might have had about the adoption, this is not the time to state them. Their unconditional support is far more productive.

Extended family members can offer the adoptive parents tickets to the theater, a gift certificate to a restaurant, or some other activity. The purpose is not to keep the adoptive parents busy so that they can't think about the baby, or try to fill up the time they'd set aside for caring for a newborn, but to help them do something nice for themselves. Family members can use as guidelines the cultural and familial traditions for comforting family members in times of grief, such as bringing food to the house. And it is always appropriate for people to ask those who are grieving whether the gestures of support they are thinking of offering are welcome, or whether another offering would be preferred.

It may be difficult for the adoptive parents and extended family members to help each other during this time because they are all feeling such grief that they aren't emotionally available to each other. They need to communicate with each other about ways they can be of help. At the same time, they may need to look beyond each other for support, such as to friends, a minister, or a counselor.

Staying in Touch

You may believe your relationship with each other is over now that you aren't going to have an open adoption. However, the change in plans for the child needn't require that you terminate all contact. Just a short time ago you were planning to stay in touch with each other forever. You had this plan in part because you shared an interest in a child. Adoptive parents often remain interested in that child even if they never take him home. They wonder what he looks like and how he is growing—if he is developing the way they imagined he would.

Birth parents should offer to let the adoptive parents know how the baby is doing and to send them pictures. At first, the adoptive parents may say they don't want to know about the baby. They may think it won't hurt as much that way—just as some people still think birth parents will hurt less after placing a baby for adoption if they don't think about him, see him, or hear about him. It may not be easy for the adoptive parents to hear about the baby or see pictures, but the pain may help the adoptive parents face their loss. And knowing that the baby is thriving may be comforting as well. Adoptive parents who are concerned about the ability of the birth parents to raise a baby can also remain a resource for the birth parents, being available to them if they have questions about how to care for the baby.

If you have developed a relationship with each other that went beyond your common interest in the baby, you are likely to remain interested in each other, too. For example, adoptive parents will want to know whether the birth mother went back to school, if the birth father ever acknowledged his child, or whether the birth grandparents allowed the birth mother to return home. Birth parents, who cared enough about the adoptive parents to consider letting them raise their child, often want to know how the adoptive parents are doing, especially if they got another baby.

After the birth mother had informed them at the hospital of her plan to keep the baby, one adoptive couple told her that they wished her success with the child and wanted to know if there was anything they could do to help her and the baby get off to a good start. She told them it would help if they could pay the hospital bill so that she wouldn't be starting out in debt. They did so as a gift to her and her child. Although this is an extreme example, it does point out the depth of caring that develops in some relationships.

When Lina, a birth mother, decided to parent her child herself three weeks after the placement, Neil and Pat, the adoptive parents, continued to express their genuine caring for her. They congratulated her, brought the baby a gift, and grieved in front of her, but saved their intense feelings for their counselor's office where they sat with arms around each other, rocking back and forth as they wept. Neil said he never believed he could hurt as much as he was hurting, but he finally understood what it would cost a birth mother to place a child. Eight weeks later, Lina decided the responsibilities of parenting were more than she could meet. She called Neil and Pat and placed the baby with them. She felt free to call them only because they hadn't become angry with her or accused her of being insincere or insensitive to their feelings.

We do not want to suggest that adoptive parents be nice to birth parents who are keeping the baby in the hope that they'll change their plans again and place the baby with them. Nor are we suggesting that the outcome might have been different for those adoptive parents who have expressed their anger. We are stressing that the adoptive parents be understanding because it is the appropriate response and it is what they would have expected the birth parents to do despite their grief had the situation been reversed. Nevertheless, the reality is that some birth parents will find that parenting is more difficult than they imagined, and some need to try it to prove to themselves that it is as difficult as they thought. If the connection between them and the adoptive parents has been severed, or if the adoptive parents have tried to plead their case by pointing out the birth parents' deficiencies, birth parents who are feeling overwhelmed by their parenting responsibilities will not feel they can turn to the adoptive parents. They will probably keep the child despite their own reservations

Adoptive parents may be reluctant to become involved again with the birth parent who can't seem to stick to a plan, but sometimes even after a temporary reclaim, an adoption proceeds smoothly. Once again, by working through your feelings, perhaps with professional help, you may be able to proceed with a relationship that has been severely tested, because it is what is best for the child.

Taylor made an adoption plan at the urging of the birth father. While she was a capable woman, she knew the birth father was immature and could not be relied on as a parent or partner. Nor did she have the support of her family, from whom she had distanced herself because of their dysfunctional behavior. Taylor was honest with the adoptive parents when she selected them, telling them she was not at all sure of the adoption plan, but that if she chose adoption, she would place with them. When she decided to raise the baby herself, the adoptive parents were gentle and understanding in their response. They told her they knew she had not always had a good relationship with her family and that they cared about her and the baby and would help her in whatever way they could. They took her home with them when she was released from the hospital. When it came time for her to move to another state, the adoptive father drove her. The adoptive parents look upon Taylor's child as a kind of niece. Their relationship is much like the relationship between birth mothers and adoptive parents in open adoption, with the exception that in this family, the birth mother kept the child.

15

Open Adoptions Within Families, with Older Child Placements, and in Other Situations

Jill was in and out of foster care for many years, returning for brief periods of time to her birth mother, LuAnn. When Jill was eleven, her foster mother approached the county social service agency about adopting her. LuAnn said she would only agree to adoption if she could continue to see Jill. Jill's adoptive mother believes that without open adoption, Jill would have resisted forming an attachment to her, because she would have felt that she was abandoning her birth mother. With open adoption Jill realizes she doesn't have to stop loving one to love the other.

When fourteen-year-old Rayanne told her parents she was pregnant, there was no question in their minds that Rayanne was too young to raise a child. But they couldn't face giving away their own "flesh and blood." Although Rayanne considered open adoption, the family knew the adoptive parents didn't have to live up to their agreement. They considered letting Rayanne bring the child home and helping her raise him, but they felt it would lead to too many conflicts. They felt the child needed one set of parents, and Rayanne wasn't mature enough to be a parent, so they decided to offer to adopt the child themselves.

Linda and Christine had been life partners for three years when they decided they wanted to be parents. After considering their options, they approached their friend Tom and asked if he would provide sperm to be used for a donor insemination of Christine. Tom agreed, with the understanding that the child would always know that he was the father and that he would be allowed to develop a relationship with him. Linda and Christine did not want to share parenting with Tom, but they recognized their child's need to know his biologic origins. After much discussion, they all understood that Tom could have a special relationship with the child without intruding on Linda and Christine's parenting roles.

Much of the discussion in this book assumes that open adoption involves the placement of an infant with an infertile couple unknown to the birth parents prior to their making an adoption plan. But not all open adoptions fit this mold. Many adoptions are open because a child is placed within the family. Some are open because a child is adopted by her foster parents who have had contact with the birth parents all along, or the child is old enough at the time of placement to know her birth parents' names and how to contact them. However, an increasing number of older child adoptions are open because professionals are recognizing the importance of allowing children to remain in contact with birth relatives with whom they have had a lifelong relationship, even though the birth parents may be dysfunctional or violent.

There is also a growing awareness that donor insemination, surrogacy, and technology-assisted reproduction, such as in vitro fertilization with a donor egg or gestational surrogate, create families who share many of the same issues as those in traditional adoption—even though there may be no legal proceeding necessary, as is the case with donor insemination. Although open adoptions are not as common in these families, children can realize the same benefits when they have contact with their birth relatives. Furthermore, open adoption has allowed children adopted transracially or internationally to maintain family ties that have given them important racial and cultural experiences.

Older Child Placements

Occasionally parents make adoption plans for their children even though they have lived together for several months or several years. They may be doing the best they can raising their children but realize they are not meeting their children's needs as well as they should. However, this scenario is rare. More commonly children are adopted at an older age because there is a history of trauma. At best, they have been shuffled in and out of foster families, sometimes returning to their birth relatives in between foster-care placements. More often they also have experienced some degree of physical, sexual, or emotional abuse, or neglect. Their birth parents may be mentally retarded, mentally ill, substance abusers, violent, or extremely irresponsible. Generally child protective services and the courts have intervened to remove the child from the birth parents. Often, though not always, parental rights have been involuntarily terminated.

Children who have experienced neglect or abuse have diminished trust that adults will protect or provide for them, and consequently may never have formed a healthy attachment to a caretaker. Not only have they not had their basic needs met but they often aren't capable of identifying what these needs are—and probably wouldn't expect gratification even if they could articulate them. At one time it was believed that children from circumstances like these needed only the love and attention of emotionally healthy parents who could meet their needs. It is now widely understood that children who learned during their early years that adults were untrustworthy do not change their attitude easily. Consequently, these children can present serious challenges to parents who adopt them.

It is beyond the scope of this book to describe those challenges or all the ways to deal with them. Suggested resources for parents raising children adopted at an older age are given at the end of this book. However, we do want to address some false assumptions about open adoptions with older child placements. Some people believe children who have been abused or neglected by their birth parents should never have contact with them again. They believe these birth parents do not deserve to continue the relationship, and that the children themselves don't want to be exposed to people who have hurt them. It is often feared that children may be hurt again through contact with troubled birth parents, and that adoptive parents who take on the challenges of older child placements should not also have to deal with difficult or perhaps dangerous birth parents. However, many families are finding that they can develop a relationship with troubled birth parents, that children feel a strong attachment to their birth parents despite the trauma they may have experienced, and that many of the benefits of open adoption seen in infant adoptions are also seen in older child adoptions. Ultimately, they are finding the challenges of open adoption with older children to be outweighed by the benefits.

BENEFITS OF OPEN ADOPTION WITH OLDER CHILD PLACEMENTS

Children who are older at the time of placement can derive the same benefits as other children from open adoption, although these benefits may be long-term and may be occasionally obscured by the crises that can arise from complex and difficult family interactions. In open adoption older children gain access to reliable information about their birth families and why they were placed for adoption. This information can be a relief, as children learn that their siblings are all right, or that, for example, their adoption was due to a birth parent's unstable lifestyle rather than to a serious mental illness that the child had been worried was hereditary.

Even when the facts they learn about their birth families are harsh, and confronting them is not easy, children benefit long-term from dealing with truth rather than fantasy. They can compare their birth families to their adoptive families and see why adults determined they would be better off being adopted. They can also see the problem that led to their placement was their birth parents' and not theirs. This frees them to believe they deserve better treatment than they received from the birth parents and allows them to accept it from the adoptive parents, which is an important step toward attachment.

LaDonna's adoption, when she was nine years old, was initially confidential, since LaDonna's birth father was violent and physically abused her. LaDonna's exact memories of the abuse faded quickly, although the effects of the trauma didn't. She had difficulty expressing anger except through violent tantrums, and she frequently told her adoptive parents she wanted to go back to her birth parents. "It wasn't as bad there as it is here," she told them. As a compromise, when she was twelve, LaDonna's adoptive parents agreed to let her have contact with her birth family. Over the next few years, LaDonna's seventeen-year-old birth brother was killed in a gang fight. Her fourteen-year-old sister became pregnant and her father beat her up when he found out. Witnessing all this, LaDonna has had to face what her life might have been like had she remained with her birth family. She fears for her birth siblings, but she knows she can't do anything for them, and she now realizes her uncontrollable anger is related to the violence she suffered and the fact that she didn't have the kind of upbringing she had a right to expect. Although it is difficult, she is now starting to deal with her anger and her feelings of powerlessness.

For some children, having contact with their birth parents forces them to confront extremely painful events they experienced at their birth family's hands. However, by facing the issues, they can grieve for them and eventually move on. Some are able to then deal from a position of strength with the people who hurt them. Frank, who has attention deficit hyperactivity disorder (ADHD), was sometimes tied to a chair or locked in a closet by his birth mother. After his adoption, Frank told people his birth mother was in the army and traveled around a lot, even though he had been told she was mentally retarded. It wasn't until he was able to have contact with her that he accepted the truth. Someday he may also realize that her method of dealing with his hyperactivity was the best she was able to do, although it wasn't an acceptable way.

Once they are removed from a dangerous situation and begin to heal from the trauma they suffered, children can also forgive their birth parents and see that they also had good qualities. They learn they can love them without approving of all their actions. By having contact with their birth parents, children are able to see the ways they are different from their birth parents and perhaps the changes they have experienced since being adopted. When they see that their behavior is different than it used to be, or different than their birth parents' or birth siblings' behavior, they believe that they have choices and their destiny isn't completely genetically determined.

Children adopted at an older age sometimes resist forming an attachment to their adoptive parents because they feel they must be loyal to their birth parents. Open adoption enables them to stay connected to their birth parents so that they don't have to "choose" one set of parents over the other. For example, Rikki's birth mother, Zena, was a good parent—when she was out of jail. Most of the time, however, Zena was in jail for various crimes or probation violations. Dealing with Zena is a challenge for Rikki's adoptive mother—Zena often ignores the rules they negotiated, and several times the adoptive mother has been tempted to terminate contact. But when she sees Rikki and Zena together, she knows her efforts are worthwhile. There is genuine affection between the two, and most of the visit is spent discussing what Rikki's other birth relatives are doing. Furthermore, Rikki's adoptive mother believes Rikki has been able to accept her as a mother because she knows she does not have to give up Zena to do so.

For some children, the greatest advantage of open adoption is that it enables them to be adopted into a permanent home. Some birth parents are able to delay action that would terminate their parental rights without their consent. When the birth parents are offered the opportunity to stay in contact with their children through open adoption, some of them agree, giving their children the opportunity for permanency that they might otherwise not have known. Cecile, who had a long history of mental illness, had placed a child for adoption fifteen years before her second child was born. Her negative experience with that adoption, which was confidential, kept her from considering adoption for her second child. However, when she tried to parent the child, her mental illness resulted in a chaotic life for the child. She agreed to adoption only when she learned she could meet the adoptive parents and continue to have contact with her child.

There are also advantages for the parents. In Chapter 2 we discuss the potential open adoption has for helping birth parents grieve and move on with their lives. This is also true when the child placed for adoption is older at the time of the placement. Birth parents who might have had a particularly difficult time accepting the placement because their rights were involuntarily terminated can be helped to face the finality of the decision when they see the child in his adoptive family.

And birth parents may benefit from having the adoptive parents act as positive role models in their lives, as well as from having ongoing contact with the social service system. Cheryl Reber, L.S.W., who facilitated semi-open adoptions for the Hamilton County (Ohio) Department of Human Services for five years, says the contact birth parents maintained with social services so that they could see their children after adoption sometimes led to birth parents seeking help for themselves.

Adoptive parents, too, benefit from having access to information about their children's pasts. Even when the facts are grim, parents can better know how to meet their children's needs and have more realistic expectations when they have accurate information about prior abuse, drug exposure, or inheritable conditions. Adoptive parents also benefit from open adoptions because their children benefit—when their children can face the reality of their past, grieve for it, and move beyond it to accept a new future, parenting is more fulfilling.

Children adopted at an older age also benefit when they maintain contact with their previous foster families, especially if they developed attachments there or spent a significant amount of time with them. They not only maintain ties to their past but they can learn why their foster parents didn't adopt them, reducing possible feelings of rejection.

RISKS OF OPEN ADOPTION WITH OLDER CHILD PLACEMENTS

In an older child adoption, adoptive parents must develop a relationship with people who may be unpredictable, untrustworthy, or perhaps violent. Having seen the damage these people have caused their children in the past, they may be concerned that future contact with the birth parents will only harm their children more. If the birth parents have not agreed to the adoption, but have had their rights involuntarily terminated, adoptive parents may worry that the birth parents will try to abduct the children. Furthermore, they are concerned that if birth parents know their identities or whereabouts, they may be placing their whole family at risk.

Throughout this book we have given examples of ways adoptive parents can set and maintain boundaries with dysfunctional birth parents. These can range from only allowing contact when birth parents follow specified rules to having contact only through an intermediary in supervised settings. Some families have specific contracts outlining the type and frequency of contact. For example, Malcolm's birth mother is not allowed to call the adoptive family at home; she must call the adoptive parents at work. If she violates this rule, the adoptive parents can deny her visitation, which is always held under the supervision of her social worker. Malcolm is hurt when his visits with his birth mother are canceled, but his adoptive parents try to help him understand that it is his birth mother's actions that lead to the cancellation.

Some families choose semiopen adoption when they believe a fully disclosed adoption will put them at personal risk. They exchange letters, and sometimes audiotapes or videotapes, through an intermediary. Others have one-sided openness, in which the adoptive parents know how to contact the birth parents, but the birth parents do not know how to contact the adoptive parents except through an intermediary.

Jayne and Pete arrange meetings with their daughter's birth father, who is extremely violent, through their social worker. They meet at a public place—often a park. For these meetings they hire a bodyguard who keeps an eye on the situation, ready to intervene if necessary, but who otherwise maintains an unobtrusive presence.

Of course, semiopen adoptions can become fully disclosed through error. Bonnie's birth father was mistakenly sent copies of court documents with the adoptive family's name and address on them. He began hanging around the school grounds to talk to Bonnie, despite warnings from the adoptive parents and the local police. Eventually, he actually abducted

Bonnie, and FBI assistance was required to find the girl, who was scared, but otherwise unharmed. But even after such a frightening experience, Bonnie's adoptive mother says that overall the unexpected openness has been beneficial. As a result, Bonnie has a clear idea of what her life might have been like with her birth parents, and she has established a warm relationship with a birth grandmother. For more on ways to interact with dysfunctional birth parents, see Chapter 9.

Since it can be difficult for adoptive parents and a child adopted at an older age to build a strong parent–child attachment, and since children want more independence as they get older, children who continue to have contact with their birth parents may have a harder time building a strong attachment to the new adoptive parents. Adoptive parents may feel more competition with the birth parents under these circumstances and therefore may have a more difficult time setting limits with the child, which is essential if they are to have a successful parent–child relationship. However, it may also be true that older children who are able to maintain their relationship with their birth parents will be less resistant to forming an attachment to their adoptive parents because they will not feel disloyal, especially if they have the blessings of the birth parent. And as we discuss in Chapter 2, this blessing can help adoptive parents feel a greater sense of entitlement, which helps them set limits and be effective parents. Given how complicated attachment is with older child placements, we really don't know yet how openness will affect it.

Birth parents in older child adoptions see many of the same risks in open adoption as birth parents who are placing infants. They know there are no guarantees that they will be able to stay in contact with their children, and birth parents who have had contact with the child welfare system may have a particular lack of confidence in open adoption. They may have a difficult time trusting the professionals who tell them they can continue to have contact with their children, since these are often the same professionals who took their children away from them in the first place. Birth parents may have difficulty trusting the adoptive parents, as well, especially if they view them as part of the system. They may resent the adoptive parents even more if they view them as privileged.

The lack of trust on both sides, along with the birth parents' resistance to the adoption itself, makes it more difficult to build a relationship. Furthermore, because birth parents in older child adoptions are not always allowed to select the parents for their children, there may not be the chemistry between them that can help a relationship get off the ground. You may have to work hard at building trust with each other and have reasonable expectations of what you hope to achieve. You may never be as close or as comfortable with each other as you'd like, but at least the child will have opportunities to maintain connections with her past. Social worker Cheryl Reber, L.S.W., points out that while there are many reasons for adoptions in older child placements to be less than fully open, there is rarely a reason for them to be completely confidential.

Of course, not all birth parents approach the adoption belligerently. Some birth parents feel shame that their children have been taken away from them, and are reluctant to participate in the open adoption because they don't believe they deserve to have contact, or because they believe they have nothing to offer. Adoptive parents need to let them know they are welcome in their lives and that their relationship with the child is both needed and valued.

Sometimes adoptive parents who believe an open adoption could be beneficial for their child must locate the birth family on their own, either because the birth parents have abandoned the child or have not maintained contact with the social service system or because the agency does not practice open adoptions with older child placements. This can be scary, especially when little is known about the birth parents, but it may be worth the risk for the child. In this situation, adoptive parents may want to begin with a semiopen or one-sided open adoption until they can assess the situation more fully.

CHANGING NAMES

Adoptive parents are generally advised to change the last name of an older child being adopted immediately to symbolize new family membership, although if the adoption is to be open, the child can keep her previous family name as a middle name to symbolize the connection she still has to her birth family. Some children may want to maintain this connection, whereas others may be embarrassed by their family of origin and may not want others to know of their connection. Some may not want to have to explain their unusual middle name or why they have more than one middle name. Adoptive parents and their children can talk about this option, discussing both the advantages and the disadvantages.

Although a child's last name is usually not changed legally until the adoption is finalized, there are advantages to calling a child by her new last name immediately. It lets her know that she is a full member of the family. It also eliminates the need for her to explain why her last name is different from other members of her family, although with as many blended families as there are today, it is not that unusual for children to have different last names from their siblings or parents. However, parents should be aware that schools may not be willing to recognize the child's new name until it is legal, and it can draw more, rather than less, attention to a child if she must explain why she is going by a name that is different from the one on her records. Again, parents and children should discuss the choices they have. Whatever they decide should be discussed with the schools so that situations that might be embarrassing for the child can be avoided.

Adoptive parents are generally advised not to change the first name of a child old enough to recognize her name—an awareness that is believed to come before the child's first birthday, perhaps even by six months. A child's identity is closely associated with her first name, and when it is changed, a child can think that she herself has changed in some way. If the child is young enough that she still thinks in black and white extremes, she may conclude that one name was her "bad self" and her other name is her "good self."

Sometimes families want to rename a child because it is a symbol of parenthood (see Chapter 6). Though naming is one way parents claim a child, the giving of a family name can be sufficient. Parents may want to change a child's name because they don't like the child's name, they want to give the child a name that is consistent with family tradition, or they may already have a child with that name. However, even those are not necessarily compelling reasons to change a child's name if she wants to keep it. Jack was adopted at age fourteen into a family who already had a boy named Jack. Understandably, both wanted to keep their names. The family accommodated their wishes even though it sometimes was confusing, and eventually the boys became known as "Big Jack" and "Little Jack."

Children adopted at an older age sometimes want to change their first names. Doing so often symbolizes the end to the life they have known to that point and the start of a new life. But as we've pointed out, there is no clean break in adoption, and this is particularly true in an older child adoption. The child adopted at an older age not only has a genetic connection to the birth parents but has been influenced by the environment of the birth family, and although she may no longer be living with parents who are abusive or alcoholic, for example, she remains a child shaped by her experiences with these parents. She cannot change who she is by changing her name, and she needs to be helped to understand that. As long as this is clear to the child, a new first name or a new method of address, such as by her initials or middle name, can be fine. Parents can, however, suggest other ways to mark the important change in her life, such as a ritual.

RITUAL OF CHANGE

Many adoption professionals recommend that an older child be moved gradually into her new adoptive family. Brief visits lead to longer visits, then overnight stays, then extended stays. This gives the parents and the child a chance to adjust to each other and makes the changes the child is experiencing less abrupt. Because older children from the child welfare system often have significant behavior problems, finalization of their adoption is not always done at the earliest possible time, but may be delayed until the parents are confident the child is going to fit into their family and form an attachment to them, or until the parents feel comfortable taking the risks that come with the child. Adoption does not involve any change in residence or routine for the child who is adopted by foster parents, but it is still a significant event.

While a gradual transition is key in a successful older child placement, it is also important to mark the significant change that is occurring. An entrustment ceremony, like the ones described in Chapter 6, is helpful, but it is not always possible, especially when the birth parents' rights are being terminated involuntarily. Nevertheless, at least one agency works with birth parents to help them understand the importance of communicating to the child that they are letting go of their parenting roles and giving her their blessings to love her adoptive parents and be happy. These messages are videotaped and given to the children.

The adoptive family can also design a ritual to celebrate the child's joining the adoptive family. It is important for the child being adopted to participate in the planning of this ceremony. It could involve the child selecting symbols of her past that she wants to leave behind, which could be burned or buried, along with symbols of her past that she wants to bring with her. Other members of the adoptive family, including siblings and extended family members, could also select symbols of welcoming. For example, to the only boy in the adoptive family, the adoption of a new boy may mean giving up his place in the family and perhaps having his own room, but it could also mean someone with whom to play catch. He might choose to give his new brother a baseball or mitt. This ritual not only marks change but actually helps the transition take place. The child may feel more like a member of the family—to the child and to other members of the family—after the ceremony.

Kinship or Relative Adoption

In many cultures, the benefits of a child remaining within the family are seen as so great that every effort is made for children to be adopted by relatives if they cannot be cared for by their birth parents. This often makes sense, for the adoption of a child by a relative offers that child certain advantages. The child does not have to lose her connection to her birth relatives, and can grow up in her family of origin with a sense of truly "belonging." She doesn't have to wonder why nobody in her family wanted her, and she can be raised within her own racial or ethnic culture. If her birth parents are dysfunctional, she can get to know birth relatives who are not. She can often have closer relationships with her birth siblings than she might in an open adoption outside the family. Indeed, her contact with her birth relatives is likely to be more "normal" because she is within the birth family. Photo albums are easily accessible; family stories are shared routinely; visits from the birth parents may be handled more casually. It is easier to explain the adoption plan.

When the birth parents and adoptive parents are related, they already have a relationship and don't have to wonder if they want to be involved with each other for life. They may already know each other well enough to know whether they can trust each other or whether they are likely to get along with each other. And they have already developed strategies for handling conflict when it arises. They know that they probably will have an easier time finding each other should they lose touch. They share some family history and the adoptive parents may be less fearful of "unknown" factors in the child's genetic background.

However, if you are part of the same immediate family—parents and children or brothers and sisters—you may face some unique challenges that are often overlooked in kinship adoption. In an in-family adoption, everyone has two relationships to the child. The child's birth relatives are also her adoptive relatives. Adoption within a nuclear family may have strings attached that reflect underlying issues in the family. Furthermore, there is no guarantee that even adoption between close relatives will reflect openness and honesty—sometimes a child is placed within the family to keep the true nature of the relationships in the family a secret.

DUAL RELATIONSHIPS

When a child is adopted by immediate relatives, everyone has a dual relationship to the child. For example, when the birth grandparents adopt the child, they become her adoptive parents as well as her birth grandparents. Her birth mother becomes her adoptive sister. Her birth mother's other children—her birth siblings—become her nieces and nephews.

Young children can't understand how the same person can be both her birth mother and her adoptive sister. This awareness requires an understanding of reproduction, which children generally develop around the age of six, and the ability to categorize and see relationships, which develops a little later. Children adopted within their families should call their birth relatives by the name that corresponds with their new role, which may not be the same as their genetic relationship. Grandparents who adopt a grandchild should be called whatever forms of mother and father are used in that family. Even birth relatives should be called by the familial relationship that has been created by the adoption. The child who is adopted by her aunt and uncle would call them mother and father and would call her birth mother aunt, or by her first name if that is appropriate.

This doesn't mean that families should hide or ignore the birth relative's biologic relationship to the child. That information should be revealed to the child at the same time and in the same way as it would be in any adoptive family. For example, when the adoptive parents are telling the child the story of how she joined the family, they can say, "You grew inside Aunt Claire. But Aunt Claire couldn't take care of any child born to her at that time in her life, so after you were born, Aunt Claire asked us to be your parents." It isn't necessary to use the term *birth mother* to refer to Aunt Claire until the child is old enough to understand how the same person could be both her birth mother and her aunt. It is sufficient for the child to understand that she shares a history with Aunt Claire that she doesn't share with her adoptive mother—or with any others in the family.

Sometimes it is difficult for adults to keep their roles distinct. When Claudine became pregnant, she decided to place her child with her brother Keenan and his wife, who were infertile and had been waiting for nearly two years to adopt. Claudine's parents agreed with her decision to place the child for adoption and were pleased that by solving her problem, she could also solve Keenan's. None of them anticipated how emotionally complicated the birth and placement of the child would be. When it came time for the baby to go home with his adoptive parents, Claudine's parents were torn between their desire to comfort their daughter in her grief and their desire to rejoice with their son. Claudine felt that her family would have understood her grief better if she had placed her child outside the family. No one else in the family lost a significant relationship to the child. Her parents remained the child's grandparents. Keenan and his wife took on a more significant role. She felt alone.

Keenan, however, felt that his parents held back their joy at the arrival of their child because they didn't want to hurt Claudine. And he missed sharing his joy with Claudine, who could cope only with her pain at that time. He felt that if he and his wife had adopted from outside the family, his parents and sister would have been happier for him. None of them regret the in-family placement, but they wish they had been better prepared for the reactions they would have. A "vision matching" session, like that described in Chapter 5, is helpful in kinship adoption, so that families have a chance to express their expectations in advance.

Sometimes families are so concerned about the dual relationship between birth parents and the child that they require the birth parents give up their adoptive relationship altogether. The birth parents are expected to function as if they were unrelated to the family. After Valerie's parents adopted her baby, they told her she could no longer drop by the house without calling first. Other birth parents have had to move out of the home they shared with their parents when their parents adopted their babies. When this happens, the birth parent not only loses the child but loses her place in her family.

Birth parents should not have to put distance between themselves and their families simply because they have placed a child with a close relative. Even when a birth parent is living at home, the child is not going to be confused about who her parents are as long as the adults are not confused and function in ways consistent with their adoptive relationship to the child. For example, when grandparents adopt a child and then expect the birth parent living at home to assume a major share of the responsibility of raising the child, the child may be confused or develop a closer attachment to her birth parent/sibling than to her grandparent/adoptive parent. But she will build a parent–child attachment to her grandparents/adoptive parents if they are her primary caretakers and meet her needs the way parents do. And she will have a sibling relationship with her birth parent if that person acts toward her as a brother or sister would.

Finally, because everyone has dual relationships to the child in a relative adoption, an entrustment ceremony like that described in Chapter 6 is highly conducive to helping people make the transition to new relationships and roles.

FAMILY ISSUES

When an in-family adoption is arranged, families should look at the roles each person plays in the family and how those roles may be affected by the adoption plan. There are sometimes underlying family issues that family members think may be solved by the adoption or that families are unaware of until a child is placed for adoption within the family.

Families should ask themselves how the birth parent is viewed in the family and how that role may be affected by the placement. Is he the "troublemaker" who is always being bailed out by his parents? Will the adoption of his birth child by the grandparents cement his negative role in the family and make it more difficult for him to someday be viewed with respect?

If the birth mother has felt that her parents always favored her brother, how will things change if she lets that same brother, who is experiencing infertility, adopt her child? Is she trying to improve her parent's opinion of her by giving her brother the child he wants and the child her parents have been wanting for him? For example, Toni had always been the "black sheep" in the family. Her sister could do no wrong in her parents' eyes. When Toni got pregnant, she placed her child with her sister, who was infertile. Unconsciously, she expected that this sacrifice would gain her respect she had never had from her parents. Her counselor helped her identify her feelings about her family and helped her see that she could not "buy" respect with a baby. Nonetheless, the placement forced Toni's family to look at her anew and see that she was more mature and sensitive than they realized.

Sometimes a mother whose children are nearly grown will adopt a grandchild to extend her nurturing role. Unless she has planned for other ways to feel useful, she may unconsciously be afraid that she will not have an identity once she is not raising children. Or a couple may adopt a grandchild because they are worried that once they no longer have the distractions of children they will find that they've grown apart. When people adopt a child to fill a void in their lives, they are being unfair to themselves and to the child. They need to make sure they feel worthy as individuals and stable as a couple before taking on the responsibility of a child. Otherwise, they may blame the child for not "fixing" a problem that was beyond the child's ability to solve.

However, some grandparents view the adoption of a grandchild as a second chance—to benefit from what they've learned raising their other children and to do better with this new child.

When birth parents who are irresponsible or otherwise make poor choices make an adoption plan, family members must ask themselves whether they can accept the child as a unique individual or whether they already assume the child will have the same weaknesses as the birth parents. They must also be prepared to explain the birth parents' problems compassionately. This doesn't mean that they excuse the birth parents from responsibility for their actions but that they separate these actions from the birth parents' value as human beings, so that the child can feel good about being connected to these people (see Chapter 12).

While all adoptive parents have this same responsibility, when the birth parent is a family member, the situation can be more complicated. For example, it can be easier for a nonrelative to speak compassionately about a birth parent who is an alcoholic than for a family member who has experienced firsthand the birth parent's violence when drunk, and the person's refusal to seek help.

FEELINGS OF LOSS IN KINSHIP ADOPTION

Because the child is remaining in the family, it may be assumed that the losses usually associated with adoption will not be felt, especially if the adopting parents are not infertile. However, the birth parents still lose their parenting roles, and the adopting parents still lose the sense of connection that comes from creating and giving birth to a child. Families may also discover that they have experienced unexpected losses. For example, Marshall and Mary Elizabeth had looked forward to the day when their youngest child would leave home and they would be able to travel more frequently. They lost that dream when, at the age of forty-two, they adopted their grandchild.

Other families find that, like Claudine and her brother who were described earlier, they have lost the full emotional support of their families because relatives feel their loyalties are being torn between the birth parents and the adoptive parents. Family members may discover that some of their feelings conflict with each other, which is only natural. Doreen's daughter, Gloria, placed her child with her older sister, Tricia. One Sunday afternoon when the family had gathered for dinner, the baby was crying and Gloria was trying unsuccessfully to comfort him. "Oh, you want your mommy, don't you," she said, as she sought out Tricia. Doreen was both sad for Gloria who had lost her parenting role and happy for Tricia whose baby had made a secure attachment to her. Neither of these responses are wrong, nor should they be suppressed.

FAMILY SECRETS

Despite the potential for full disclosure of everyone's biologic relationship to the child, in-family adoptions are not always fully open. The child may be told she is adopted, but may not know her biologic relationship to the members of her family. Because most adoptions in the recent past have been confidential, families may assume that they should be close-mouthed about the identity of the child's birth parents. If Uncle Adam is attentive when he comes over to visit, his attention can honestly be explained as that of an interested uncle. Furthermore, the adoptive parents may keep the identity of the birth parents from the child so that they don't have to "compete" with them for the child's love and loyalty. Adoptive parents in relative adoptions are not immune to the fear that their child will love their birth parents more if they know their relationship to them.

Sometimes families are secretive about the adoption because they are ashamed to have had an untimely pregnancy in their family. Indeed, sometimes grandparents adopt the child of their son or daughter primarily to keep the pregnancy hidden. Their attitude is that this is a family problem that doesn't need to be taken outside the family. However, the child who grows up in a family in which her conception or adoption is viewed with shame or embarrassment receives a negative message about herself. She has the right to grow up in a family that can express their joy at her creation and entry into the family.

When an adoption is within the family, both the family and the professionals may feel education and counseling are not necessary. Furthermore, when adoptions are handled within the family, professionals may not become involved with the placement except to provide the court with a home study—an evaluation that may be less thorough than it would be in a nonrelative adoption. But a counselor can help families uncover underlying issues, identify and grieve for their losses, express feelings about the dual relationships they will have with the child, or anticipate how relationships in the family might be affected by the placement. Among the issues a counselor should explore with a family is what will happen to relationships in the family if the birth parent changes her mind and decides to raise the baby herself, or if the prospective adoptive parents change their minds once the baby is born.

Stepparent Adoption

Like other birth parents, a noncustodial parent sometimes allows his parental rights to be terminated because he believes he has less to offer a child than her stepparent who wants to adopt her. Families in which the parents never married or later got a divorce need to acknowledge that even though a noncustodial parent may not be able or willing to assume his responsibilities as a parent, there are other important roles he can play in a child's life. Unfortunately, the adoption of a child by a stepparent is often open technically, but not in practice. Usually a stepparent adopts a child because the birth parent seldom has any contact with the child.

Although parents may understand that children are curious about their biologic origins, they may have issues themselves that keep them from acknowledging the importance of the birth parent to the child or keep them from encouraging contact between them. They may feel the birth parent made a choice not to be involved with the child and to encourage the child's interest in the birth parent would only lead to further rejection.

The parent may also feel it is an insult to her spouse, who has taken on the responsibility of raising her children, if she treats the children's birth parent as though he were significant. The stepparent may not only agree with that attitude but he may fear that he would lose the children's love to the birth parent if the children knew him. Indeed, since the birth parent is also the spouse's former lover, the stepparent may not only worry about losing the child's love but competing for his spouse's love as well.

Sometimes one of the most difficult challenges for the parent and stepparent is presenting the birth parent positively, so that the child can feel good about having a genetic connection to him, especially if they have had bad experiences with the birth parent in the past or are angry at him for abandoning the child. Part of the solution is grieving for the losses that have occurred and may be contributing to the parent or stepparent's anger or resentment, such as the loss of the relationship. In addition, the parent can remember that there was, in most cases, once an attraction that led to the child's conception. Although eventually those qualities may not have been sufficient to maintain the relationship, they nonetheless are part of the birth parent. Furthermore, they may also be part of the child. The parent and stepparent may want to discount any contribution to the child from the birth parent, but if they are honest they must acknowledge that in addition to their own ongoing influence, the child they love so much has qualities that came from the birth parent.

Of course, often the breakup of the birth parents' relationship was due to animosity between them or resulted in bitterness or resentment. The parent raising the child doesn't want the child to have contact with the birth parent because it creates stress for her. Although it's easy to suggest that the birth parents should work through their differences for the sake of the child, the birth parents have a long history of being unable to work through their differences, often even with the help of professionals.

Nevertheless, as we've seen, it is important for children to be able to have information about both of their birth parents, to know that they are cared about by both of them, and to feel good about being related to both of them. It is also important for them to understand why their birth parents decided not to parent them and why they relinquished their parenting rights, especially in families where the birth parent raised the child for a time. They may need contact to understand that the problem that led to their birth parent leaving or relinquishing his parenting role had to do with the birth parent and not with them. Furthermore, as with any adoption, children who do not have contact with their birth parents will fantasize about them, usually imagining them as an extreme of goodness or badness. Contact with the birth parent gives them a realistic image rather than one filtered through their own imaginations or the bitter memories of the parent who is raising them.

Ideally, a birth parent should remain in contact with his children to provide them with information about their full heritage, to show that he cares, to answer questions, and to help the children overcome any feelings of rejection or abandonment. This is true whether or not the birth parent retains his parental rights. It is an obligation that comes with bringing life onto the planet; it is not a privilege that comes from providing economic support or daily nurturing to the child. You should remember that this contact is necessary for the child's psychological well-being; it is not a reward given to the noncustodial birth parent or transferred to the step-parent when he takes over the financial and emotional responsibilities of raising the child.

The child's birth parent and custodial parents should make an effort to resolve whatever differences they have had and to grieve for the losses they have experienced through their relationship, so that they can put the child's interests ahead of their own. When this is done, the need to termi-nate the noncustodial birth parent's parental rights may seem far less criti-cal. The stepparent can become the child's legal guardian. Although the noncustodial birth parent must be given notice of this action and an opportunity to object to it, legal guardianship does not require termination of parental rights. The stepparent can also be given authorization to make medical decisions for the child and to obtain school records.

Of course, sometimes the birth parent was violent, and any redeeming qualities may be obscured by those memories. In those situations, contact with other birth relatives may let both the parent and the child know that there are good qualities in the child's family of origin. Maggie was raped and beaten by her husband during their brief marriage. After she gave birth, she fled the marriage to protect her child from his violent temper. She does not want to have contact with her ex-husband, but has managed to stay in contact with his parents so that her child can know that side of her family and see that her father's violence is not a "family trait."

In less extreme situations, the parents and birth parent should keep in mind that although they or the birth parent may not want involvement in each other's lives now, the child may want more contact in the future. In addition, as we discuss in other chapters, the birth parent's extended family may want to continue to be involved with the adoption. The child has a right to those relationships and the parent and stepparent need to make the necessary accommodations to include those relatives in the child's life. (For information about how to explain a birth parent's lack of involvement in a child's life, see Chapter 11.)

Medically or Developmentally Challenged Children

Sometimes parents make an adoption plan for a child who is developmentally delayed or has medical challenges. As we explain in Chapter 12, children should not feel that they caused their losses—the adoption plan should be explained in a way that places the responsibility for the decision on the adults. In the case of children with special needs, children need to understand that some parents feel more capable than others to deal with physical or developmental disabilities. Once again, open adoption gives birth parents the opportunity to let their children know they were not abandoned or rejected because of their special needs. They can not only stay in contact with the child but they can come to the hospital when the child is sick or receiving treatments, participate in advocacy efforts on behalf of the child if the adoptive parents want their help, and even help care for the child.

As they remain involved in the child's life in these ways, and see that they have a role even though they won't be the child's day-to-day parents, birth parents often feel less guilty for making an adoption plan for a child with medical or developmental disabilities when they probably would not have made one for a healthy child. Furthermore, other children in the family are less prone to worrying about the child. Siblings may feel guilty because they are relieved their sister is no longer in the home; ongoing contact with her may make them feel better.

When Todd and Jeanne learned that their son, Gavin, had Down's syndrome, they were determined to keep him at home with them. But after seven years they decided they could not meet his needs while still meeting the needs of their other three children. They placed Gavin with adoptive parents with the understanding that they would not only visit Gavin but would give the adoptive parents one weekend each month of respite care and would be available at other times if the adoptive parents needed their help.

Transracial Adoption

When a child is adopted transracially, the physical differences between the child and the adoptive parents may be obvious, so it may be easier for the adoptive parents to acknowledge the child's connection to the birth parents. And, for the child in a transracial adoption, open adoption offers the chance to know and maintain her racial or cultural heritage within her family of origin. Moreover, the child's need to know her birth parents and understand the reasons her birth parents made an adoption plan takes on added importance when she is faced with stereotypes of minority birth parents as promiscuous or addicted to drugs.

If the child is of mixed racial heritage, families may want to discount part of the child's parentage that is racially different from them, but doing so denies full acceptance. Open adoption can offer children of mixed racial heritage opportunities for enriching cultural experiences. Adoptive parents should take care that they are making an effort to develop relationships with both the child's birth parents and their families and not just the birth parent who is racially like them.

For adoptive parents, a relationship with the birth parents may be their first experience being in a close relationship with people of another color or culture. Birth parents, too, may feel awkward developing a relationship described as "familial" with adoptive parents of another race, especially if there is a big difference in educational background or socioeconomic status. You will need to get beyond superficial differences and get to know each other to feel comfortable in the relationship. That should happen during the time you spend with each other before the child's placement. But you may not have had the opportunity to get to know each other well or even to meet prior to the placement. Or you may find that you get along with each other, but there are members of each other's extended families with whom you feel awkward. The more common ground you can find with each other, the more at ease you will feel and the easier it will be for the child to feel proud of being a person who has the racial culture of his birth family and the social culture of his adoptive family.

If one of the factors leading to the adoption plan was that the child was of mixed racial heritage and one birth family couldn't accept a child of another race, it may take time before that birth family is able to see beyond the racial differences to similarities that will enable them to claim the child. As you get to know each other you may find that some of the conflicts you are having are due to cultural differences. Darnell's birth mother was always several hours late bringing Darnell home from a visit. Each time she was late, Darnell's adoptive mother feared the worst—that the birth mother had abducted Darnell. None of her efforts to get the birth mother to honor Darnell's curfew were successful. It was Darnell who finally explained to his adoptive mother that his birth family treated time differently than they did in the adoptive family. In the birth family's culture, nine o'clock meant any time between nine o'clock and twelve o'clock. His birth mother couldn't bring him home *on time* because being on time was not one of her cultural values.

RACIAL HERITAGE

The responsibility to acquaint a child adopted transracially with her racial and cultural heritage is shared by the birth and adoptive parents. Birth parents can provide information ranging from how to care for a child's hair or apply makeup, to a sense of pride at being a part of a racial group with a rich history and cultural legacy. But this doesn't relieve adoptive parents of their responsibilities as parents, which include helping a child develop a full identity—an identity that includes her racial or cultural heritage. It is not difficult for adoptive parents to help children develop a sense of their racial heritage by introducing them to foods, customs, and folk tales of their racial group. But knowing the history and cultural practices of a racial group is only part of what it takes to feel like a full member of that group. Adoptive parents of a Hispanic child can make tamales and thoroughly enjoy them, but it is different from feeling that it wouldn't be Christmas Eve without tamales. That's a feeling the child would only get if the adoptive family celebrated Christmas Eve with their child's birth family.

Furthermore, being a person of color in the United States and other countries settled by Europeans often means experiencing bigotry or discrimination. Adoptive parents may not be able to understand what this means and may not know how to prepare their child for it. They may feel guilty that they do not know how to help their child deal with racial incidents and may unconsciously minimize them. Or they may be so outraged that they overreact, leaving their child feeling embarrassed.

The birth parents can act as resources for the adoptive parents as they try to help their child interpret experiences. Mick's adoptive parents joined an African Baptist church like the one Mick's birth mother attended. It gave Mick a valuable cultural experience, but it also gave his birth and adoptive parents some common ground. Dion was ten before he was able to visit his Native American grandfather on the reservation. There he participated in a ritual celebrating the death of a tribal leader. The experience gave him a sense of his origins that he had not had before. Mona learns what it is like to be African-American just being around her birth mother. She fixes Mona's hair in ways her adoptive mother doesn't. She talks about routine incidents—experiences she doesn't even realize are unique to being African-American. She doesn't set out to give Mona a cultural lesson, but she tells stories and sings songs that her mother told her and sang to her, which contain rich strains of the African-American experience.

But even an adopted child's birth parent of the same race can't completely understand what it is like to live straddling two cultures. Keana's adoptive parents are a liberal, upper-middle-class European-American couple. They understood why Keana, who is African-American, was angry when she noticed that she was followed by a security guard at a department store when she shopped alone, but not when she shopped with her mother. However, they couldn't relate to the experience on a personal level. Keana's African-American birth mother was so accustomed to being scrutinized by the security guard at the mall that she didn't realize this was an experience Keana might have to be prepared for, or helped to understand. She couldn't put what it meant to be African-American into words. Moreover, she is so resigned to discrimination that she hardly notices the less hateful incidents.

When sixteen-year-old Luis, who is Hispanic, was babysitting his younger brother, who had been born to his European-American adoptive parents, he had to drag him screaming away from the playground when it was time to go home. The police were called to investigate a child snatching. Luis's parents were outraged, but they could not feel his humiliation. His birth mother couldn't understand his shame, either. She thought it was a good joke on the police, who had hassled her many times. Luis's adoptive parents realized their son's humiliation was related in part to his upbringing in a middle-class, suburban family that saw arrest as shameful.

Mylana's African-American birth father is angry about the injustices done to people of color. In fact, Mylana's adoptive parents think he is so accustomed to experiencing bigotry that he sees it in even harmless inter-actions. When they try to discuss this with him, he accuses them of not understanding the African-American experience. They acknowledge that he could be right, but they don't know for sure.

Douglas's birth father is Native American, but his birth family doesn't maintain any cultural ties to the tribe. He is frustrated at not being able to have his questions about Native Americans answered, but someday he will understand that he wouldn't have learned much about his heritage if he had grown up in his birth family. His loss of heritage was unrelated to his adoption losses.

Kelsey's birth mother, who is Filipino, brings native foods when she comes to visit, sends Kelsey presents that reflect her ethnic heritage, and tells her how things would be different for her in a Filipino household. Kelsey would prefer that she didn't. "I don't like that kind of stuff," she tells her adoptive mother. Kelsey is going through a time when she wants to be like her peers, and wants to minimize any differences between them. Some day she will probably feel differently and will want to know more about her Filipino heritage. Her adoptive mother treats the situation as she would if an immigrant grandparent were insisting on an ethnic awareness that a grandchild didn't want to have. To Kelsey she says, "Your birth mother is bringing you a gift. Accept it graciously. When she leaves, you can put it away." She shrugs when the birth mother asks why Kelsey doesn't like *lumpia,* saying: "Your *lumpia* is wonderful. Kelsey just prefers hamburgers right now. Someday she'll wish she knew how to make *lumpia.*"

Talk with each other about the child's need for racial and ethnic awareness and cultural experiences, and how the birth family can help provide those. Adoptive parents can help birth parents know how they can share their experiences and their insight with their children. Birth parents can share what it is like to be a person of color by just being with the child and sharing the everyday experiences of their lives— many of which are colored by race or ethnicity. They can help the child learn ways to cope with discrimination, but no one person can expose a child to all the methods of coping. The more opportunities the child has to know people who share his racial background, including mem-bers of his extended birth family, the more diverse resources he will have on which to draw.

International Adoption

Despite the stereotype that children in other countries are available for adoption solely due to abandonment, there are many adoptive families who have contact with their children's birth parents. International adoptions that are open give children the same benefits as other open adoptions. Furthermore, like children adopted transracially who have contact with their birth families, children adopted internationally gain a better awareness of their ethnic background by having close contact with their birth families. They may also gain information about their country of origin that can be useful in countering negative stereotypes portrayed in the news media, such as that Colombia is full of drug dealers or Thailand is full of prostitutes.

Children also learn that some of the stereotypes about why children in developing countries are placed for adoption are false. While it is often presumed that birth parents in other countries place children for adoption due to poverty, sometimes adoption plans are made because middle-class women will be disowned by their families if they bring home a child born out of wedlock. And while adoptive parents may have this information, because their own circumstances and practices are different, they may unconsciously convey a judgmental attitude toward the birth parents' actions when they try to explain them. Children in open adoptions have the opportunity to hear this information from the birth parents themselves, who can explain the circumstances in their cultural context. They can also learn about circumstances, cultural practices, or beliefs that may have led to the need to place the child overseas. This can be a great help to children who are feeling not only that they were rejected by their birth parents but that no one in their entire country of origin wanted them.

Adoptive parents who remain fearful that open adoption carries the risk that the birth parents will physically abduct the child often feel more secure when the birth parents live in another country. However, communication by letter can pose unexpected difficulties. The birth parents may be illiterate, and often the birth parents and adoptive parents may have no shared language in which to correspond.

Vickie had to learn about the cultural practices of communicating with her daughter's birth mother in Korea. From accommodating people in her community she learned that you can't just jump right in and talk about what the child did that week. First you must talk about something neutral, like the weather. It is also polite to inquire about all the family members.

People who know each other only through letters—correspondence that may be affected by cultural differences or the limitations of translations—may find it difficult to maintain communication. Nancy found it increasingly difficult to write to her son's birth mother in Mexico. Every letter sounded the same as she related his academic progress and extracurricular activities. The suggestions given in Chapter 9 for getting to know each other through correspondence can be useful for families involved in international open adoptions.

Becky and Jon found the challenges of communicating with their child's birth mother in Peru personally satisfying, in addition to the benefits they saw for their child. Becky had not had much opportunity to use her Spanish since she was an exchange student in high school. Her desire to communicate with the birth mother was just the motivation she needed to brush up on her language skills and to develop a better understanding of the history and culture of Peru.

Even if contact with the birth parents of a child from another country is not possible, adoptive parents can maintain connections with the child's origins by corresponding with staff at the orphanage or with the child's foster parents. In addition, adoptive parents who learn the language of their child's country of origin may be able to help the child preserve his language skills or at least develop a fuller awareness of his origins. By visiting the child's country of origin, adoptive families can gain important insight into the child's culture.

SETTING BOUNDARIES

Sometimes birth parents are in extreme poverty, and adoptive parents want to help them. This is not an attempt to pay back the birth parents but simply what many people in better circumstances would do to help someone close to them. However, helping requires that adoptive parents be able to set good boundaries, and they should be prepared to deny a request that is not in their family's best interests. They need to be certain they are acting out of concern for the birth family and not out of guilt. They also must realize the limitations of what they can do to make a difference.

Paco's adoptive parents considered their family complete when they adopted their third child. They regularly wrote to Cristina, the birth mother, who was still raising five other children, and kept Paco's ties to his siblings alive. Several years later, they were distraught to hear that Cristina had developed a terminal illness. Cristina asked Paco's adoptive parents to adopt her five other children after her death. It was a request they felt they had to consider, since they worried about the fate of the children if they did not adopt them. They were concerned that Paco would lose touch with them, and they felt guilty saying that they did not have the financial resources to raise eight children, when the reduced standard of living they would experience would still be so much more than the children would otherwise have. After much prayer, they decided they could not adopt the children. However, they discussed alternatives with Cristina and were satisfied that the children would receive true affection from an aunt, if not a high standard of living. They could also send gifts, clothing, or school supplies to the siblings; establish a scholarship fund that the children could draw on for their education; and invite the children for regular visits.

Angela's birth mother offered to be a maid in the adoptive family's household if Angela's adoptive parents would bring her to the United States. They, too, said no. They didn't think they could make their child's birth mother a servant, even though it would have meant a better life for her.

Some people are able to be remarkably generous with the birth family, flying them to the United States for visits or supporting them financially. Corinne sends money each month to her daughter's birth mother and sister, who are living in a developing country. Corinne said the money isn't repayment or given out of guilt. "These are my daughter's relatives who are living in abject poverty. I want to help them," she said. Sometimes families who do not have open adoptions sponsor a child or make contributions to the orphanage as a way to try to share their good fortune with others.

When her birth family is poor, the child who was adopted may feel guilty that she did not have to suffer while other members of her birth family did. She needs to have a blessing from her birth family to enjoy the privileges she has achieved. She also needs to be allowed to express the sadness that adoptees feel at having lost the opportunity to grow up in their family of origin, even though she would have had far fewer advantages, or perhaps been in life-threatening circumstances due to poverty or disease. As we explain in Chapter 12, the advantages the child has gained do not eliminate her feelings about what she has lost.

Surrogacy, Donor Insemination, and Technology-Assisted Conceptions

Surrogacy, donor insemination, and technology-assisted conceptions,[1] in which one or both legal parents are not the same as the genetic parents, all constitute forms of adoption, even though a legal process is not always required. Before choosing to proceed with surrogacy, donor insemination, or technology-assisted conception, we urge you to investigate the program and the physician you will be working with. Make sure you have the opportunity to receive education or counseling, so that you understand the ways these types of reproduction are different from a typical adoption and giving birth.

Some people mistakenly think they will not have feelings of loss usually associated with adoption if the child is biologically related to one parent who will be raising her, and may be unprepared for feelings of jealousy, inadequacy, or sadness that may arise due to one partner's infertility. Take some time to work through infertility issues, just as you would in any adoption. Make sure the other parents are also receiving education and counseling. Find out the program's policy toward allowing the biologic and adoptive parents to have contact with each other and their experience in facilitating open adoption relationships. Learn what kind of postadoption resources are available. If these are not available through the program or facilitator, find out what other resources in the community can be used. Have a "vision matching" session like that described in Chapter 5, so that everyone is clear about his or her expectations.

---

1. Surrogacy is when a woman agrees to be artificially inseminated by the husband of the couple that will adopt the baby. The surrogate mother carries the child, then places the child for adoption with the couple. The legal process is similar to that of a traditional adoption. Donor insemination is the artificial insemination of a woman by a known or unknown sperm donor, using either live or frozen sperm. No legal adoption is necessary since in most states a child is legally the child of the woman who gives birth and her husband. Technology-assisted conception includes those procedures in which an egg is removed from a woman's body, fertilized in a laboratory, and then implanted in the uterus of a woman. When the egg or sperm are donated by someone other than the people who will be the child's legal parents, the process constitutes adoption, although no legal process is necessary if the woman who carries the child is the same one who will be raising the child. However, if the embryo is implanted into a surrogate mother (a "donor womb" or "gestational surrogate"), a legal proceeding is required—even when the embryo is biologically related to both the adoptive mother and the adoptive father.

Because there are so many possibilities today for technology-assisted conception, some with the donors serving as the child's parents, it is difficult to generalize, or to find language suitable for every instance. Nevertheless, the issues raised in this section can provide you with some idea of the complex world you are entering with these types of adoption.

Children who come into their families through surrogacy, donor insemination, and technology-assisted conception have the same need to know their full identity and have a connection to their biologic relatives as children in other adoptions. But this need is not always recognized. Because the biologic parent's contribution was made in a doctor's office, and because the child was always intended for the legal parents, the connection between the biologic parent and the child may seem clinical rather than emotional, especially in the case of donor insemination. Even in surrogacy, regardless of whether the surrogate is the birth mother through donor insemination or a gestational surrogate through in vitro fertilization, the emotional bond between the mother and child is often treated as less intense even though it may not be.

Psychologist Hillary Hanafin, Ph.D., of the Center for Surrogate Parenting in Los Angeles, says some surrogates expect to feel less emotion than they do when their child is born and placed for adoption, whereas others expect to feel more of a connection. However, the fact that the birth parents did not have an emotional relationship leading to the conception, or that they planned the conception with the adoption in mind, does not change the child's need for information about her genetic background or the actual connection that exists whenever a woman carries and gives birth to a child.

Nevertheless, open adoption in surrogacy, donor insemination, and technology-assisted conceptions can have fewer complications than more typical adoptions. For instance, in the open adoptions we describe in this book, the birth parents and adoptive parents must make a decision quickly about whether they want to be involved with each other. The birth mother is in crisis and feels a pressing need to select adoptive parents. In surrogacy, donor insemination, or technology-assisted conceptions, the biologic parents and the adoptive parents have as much time as they want to get to know each other and establish a relationship. Often, the biologic parents are more mature and more functional than those in a crisis pregnancy. They may be a family member (see the section in this chapter on kinship adoption), a close friend, or someone motivated by the desire to help an infertile couple. The relationship is often healthier because the biologic parent is not in emotional turmoil and the adoptive parents feel more control.

Because the biologic parents are involved voluntarily, both adoptive parents and biologic parents feel less vulnerable. Adoptive parents have a greater sense of trust and biologic parents feel less exploited. Even in surrogacy, adoptive parents worry less that the biologic parent will choose to raise the child because the whole focus of the conception is on creating a child for the adoptive parents. The biologic parents may have less guilt in placing the child with the adoptive parents because the child was always intended for the adoptive parents and may be biologically related to one or both. For the same reasons, the adoptive parents feel less guilt taking the child. If one or both adoptive parents are also donors, they have some legal standing in the rare cases when the biologic parent changes her mind and wants to parent the child herself.

There is often less confusion over the transfer of parenting role because the biologic parent never intended to have one. For example, a surrogate mother is less likely to want to name the child, believing that is the adoptive parents' role. For the child, there may be less wondering why her biologic parents didn't raise her, since the plan was always for her to be adopted. And, of course, often one biologic parent is actually raising her.

Nevertheless, there are unique issues in surrogacy, donor insemination, or technology-assisted conception. An adoption arising out of an untimely pregnancy is often thought of as a process that has benefits for everyone (in addition to losses for everyone). When the biologic parent is participating in the creation of the child solely to help the infertile couple, the adoptive parents may feel a greater sense of indebtedness. This is particularly true in surrogacy, in which the woman carrying the child experiences all the physical discomforts of pregnancy, labor, and delivery, and risks complications that could be life-threatening or could affect her ability to bear future children. Although she may be compensated for taking these risks, freely chooses to take them, and often does so in part because she is someone who enjoys pregnancy, there is still a sense that the relationship is imbalanced by her sacrifice. This is something you will want to discuss before proceeding with this kind of adoption.

In addition, you should discuss the plan should the child have mental or physical disabilities. If these are diagnosed prior to birth, would abortion be an option? If not diagnosed until after the birth, or if abortion is not an option, will the adoptive parents still adopt the child? In situations in which the conception was planned for the adoptive parents, they may feel a greater responsibility to proceed with the adoption under these circumstances. The biologic parent, too, may feel that the adoptive parents have this obligation.

Getting Help

Although each type of adoption mentioned has its unique challenges, don't forget the issues common to all types of adoption. Look for a support system that understands your particular situation, but don't limit yourself to groups for surrogate mothers, donor insemination fathers, or parents of autistic children, for example. Even when it seems like 90 percent of what you are dealing with has to do with race or with your child's particular medical problem, you will also benefit from acquainting yourself with information about adoption, for even when adoption seems less significant than other issues, it is still important to you and to the child.

Afterword

In 1950, when Mary Martin Mason was two years old, her mother died, and her father placed her and her two older brothers in an orphanage temporarily. A couple who had known her father took Mary home for visits occasionally and offered several times to adopt her. After Mary became seriously ill, her father agreed, with the stipulation that she remain in contact with him and her brothers. Open adoption was uncommon at the time, but Mary's birth father and adoptive parents didn't know that, and they just made an arrangement that seemed natural to them. Mary, now grown and the author of *The Miracle Seekers*, experienced aspects of both secrecy and openness in adoption.

As she grew up, Mary occasionally visited her birth father and brothers, who eventually returned to live with their birth father, and remains in contact with them today. However, Mary knew nothing of her birth mother. Her grief-stricken birth father never talked of her, and all her photographs mysteriously disappeared. Nor did she have any contact with her birth mother's family, as a result of a rift that occurred when her birth father placed Mary for adoption rather than calling on her maternal grandparents to help raise her.

Mary's birth father was emotionally distant, even from the children who lived with him, and rarely initiated contact with Mary. Most of his letters contained religious messages rather than personal communication. Her birth father never told her she looked exactly like her birth mother. When they saw each other, they never discussed the circumstances of Mary's adoption or their feelings about it. Mary struggled on her own to understand why she was placed for adoption and not her brothers. But, at the same time, she was comforted by the knowledge that it was important for her birth father to remain in contact with her and to choose parents that he trusted. And he validated Mary's adoptive parents as her parents and as good people. From her adoptive parents she learned that however imperfect her birth father might be, he was a good man.

But her birth mother was a taboo subject—in addition to her birth father's secrecy, her adoptive mother felt threatened by any talk of her. When she was in her twenties, Mary became consumed by the desire for information about her birth mother, searched for her maternal birth family, and saw a photograph of her birth mother for the first time. As a result of her research, she learned that the secrecy surrounding her birth mother was not there to hide any unpleasant truths, as she had imagined growing up.

Mary always considered her adoptive parents and brother to be her family. Her birth father seemed like a distant relative, and even though her adoptive brother was grown and had left home by the time she joined the family, she considered him more her sibling than her two birth brothers. "The family you're with, and the pictures you see on the wall—that's family to you," she says. Nevertheless, Mary believes that even a less than satisfactory relationship with her birth father was better than the void she felt where her birth mother was concerned.

It wasn't until Mary and her husband, Doug, discovered their infertility and began looking into adoption that Mary realized how unusual her adoption was for its time. In keeping with the agency's practice, when their son was born, Mary and Doug met his birth mother, but exchanged no identifying information. They communicated anonymously through the adoption agency for five years. During this time, Mary increasingly felt her son should know his birth mother. None of the reasons she heard for keeping adoptees and birth parents apart was consistent with her experience, although Doug had many of the same reservations as others who hear about open adoption for the first time. Mary and her husband discussed the advantages and disadvantages of fully disclosed adoption and eventually decided to meet and have direct contact with their son's birth mother. They now have a close, comfortable relationship with her, although their son's birth father has not been willing to meet them.

Mary Mason's adoption was not typical nor was it ideal. But it reminds us that all adoptions are unique, and none are perfect. They are imperfect because they involve relationships between people, who are, by nature, imperfect. They are complex because people are complex. For this reason, there can be as much variability among open adoptions as there is in any other kind of relationship. If we have not addressed a situation you are facing in your open adoption, it is because open adoptions are as individual as all human relationships.

When confronting a unique or challenging circumstance in your open adoption relationship, look at how you have been able to approach other, perhaps similar, situations in other relationships. Draw on your basic belief system and the wealth of literature available on problem solving and healthy relationships. Believe that while adoption colors your relationship, the feelings and behaviors you are encountering in yourself and others are common to many human experiences. Although sometimes you may have to reach deep within yourself to find the strength, you do have the ability to work out whatever you may encounter. When it's hard, remember that you are making the effort for your child, and that parenthood often means putting aside your own needs or desires to serve your children. Finally, have faith that when you meet the challenges of open adoption with love, hope, and respect for each other, you will realize tremendous personal and family growth.

Resources

General Adoption

Adopted Child newsletter, by Lois Ruskai Melina (P.O. Box 9362, Moscow, ID 83843).

Adoption: An Annotated Bibliography, by Lois Ruskai Melina (New York: Garland Publishing, 1987).

Ours magazine (Adoptive Families of America, 3333 Hwy. 100 North, Minneapolis, MN 55422, 612/535-4829).

Raising Adopted Children, by Lois Ruskai Melina (New York: Harper and Row, 1986).

Roots and Wings magazine (P.O. Box 638, Chester, NJ 07930).

Open Adoption

Adoption: A Handful of Hope, by Suzanne Arms (Celestial Arts, P.O. Box 7327, Berkeley, CA 94707, 1990).

Adoption Without Fear, Ed. by James Gritter (Corona Publishing Co., 1037 S. Alamo, San Antonio, TX 78210, 1989).

AdoptNet magazine (P.O. Box 50514, Palo Alto, CA 94303-0514).

Birthparents Today newsletter (3423 Blue Rock, Cincinnati, OH 45239).

Children of Open Adoption, by Kathleen Silber and Patricia Martinez Dorner (Corona Publishing Co., 1037 S. Alamo, San Antonio, TX 78210, 1990).

Cooperative Adoption, by Mary Jo Rillera and Sharon Kaplan (Triadoption Publications, P.O. Box 638, Westminster, CA 92684, 1985).

Dear Birthfather, by Randolph W. Severson (House of Tomorrow Productions, 4209 McKinney Ave. Suite 200, Dallas, TX 75205, 1991).

Dear Birthmother, by Kathleen Silber and Phylis Speedlin (Corona Publishing Co., 1037 S. Alamo, San Antonio, TX 78210, 1991).

Eyes That Shine: Essays on Open Adoption, by Randolph W. Severson (House of Tomorrow Productions, 4209 McKinney Ave. Suite 200, Dallas, TX 75205, n.d.).

A Letter to Adoptive Parents on Open Adoption, by Randolph W. Severson (House of Tomorrow Productions, 4209 McKinney Ave., Suite 200, Dallas, TX 75205, n.d.).

An Open Adoption, by Lincoln Caplan (New York: Farrar, Straus and Giroux, 1990).

The Open Adoption Book, by Bruce M. Rappaport (New York: Macmillan Publishing Co., 1992).

Open Adoption: A Caring Option, by Jeanne Warren Lindsay (Morning Glory Press Inc., 6595 San Haraldo Way, Buena Park, CA 90620, 1987).

Open Adoption: The Experts Speak Out, video produced by Carol Land and Sharon Kaplan (Parenting Resources, 250 El Camino Real, Suite 216, Tustin, CA 92680, 714/669-8100).

Openness in Adoption: New Practices, New Issues, by Ruth G. McRoy, Harold D. Grotevant, and Kerry L. White (Praeger Publishers, One Madison Ave., New York, NY 10010, 1988).

To Keera With Love, by Kayla M. Becker with Connie K. Heckert (Sheed and Ward, 115 E. Armour Blvd., Kansas City, MO 64141-0281, 1987).

Readiness to Adopt: Birth and Adoptive Parents

Adopting After Infertility, by Patricia Irwin Johnston (Perspectives Press, P.O. Box 90318, Indianapolis, IN 46290-0318, 1992).

Adoption Is Not Second Best, audiotape by Lois Ruskai Melina (P.O. Box 9362, Moscow, ID 83843).

Dear Barbara, Dear Lynne, by Barbara Shulgold and Lynne Sipiora (Reading, MA: Addison-Wesley, 1991).

The Joys and Challenges of Raising Adopted Children, audiotape by Lois Ruskai Melina (P.O. Box 9362, Moscow, ID 83843).

Pregnant Too Soon: Adoption Is an Option, by Jeanne Warren Lindsay (Morning Glory Press, 6595 San Heraldo Way, Buena Park, CA 90620, 1988).

While You Wait to Adopt, audiotape by Lois Ruskai Melina (P.O. Box 9362, Moscow, ID 83843).

Winning at Adoption, videotapes and audiotapes produced by Carol Land and Sharon Kaplan (The Family Network, P.O. Box 1995, Studio City, CA 91614-0995, 800/456-4056).

About the Adoptee

The Adopted Child in Middle Childhood (Ages 7–11), audiotape by Lois Ruskai Melina (P.O. Box 9362, Moscow, ID 83843).

The Adoption Life Cycle: The Children and Their Families Through the Years, by Elinor B. Rosenberg (New York: The Free Press, 1992).

Being Adopted: The Lifelong Search for Self, by David M. Brodzinsky, Ph.D., Marshall D. Schechter, M.D., and Robin Marantz Henig (New York: Doubleday, 1992).

Journey of the Adopted Self: A Quest for Wholeness, by Betty Jean Lifton (New York: Basic Books, forthcoming 1994).

Answering Your Child's Questions About Adoption

Answering Your Child's Questions About Adoption, audiotape by Lois Ruskai Melina (P.O. Box 9362, Moscow, ID 83843).

Communicating with the Adopted Child, by Miriam Komar, D.S.W. (Walker and Co., 720 Fifth Ave., New York, NY 10019, 1991).

Making Sense of Adoption, by Lois Ruskai Melina (New York: Harper and Row, 1989).

Grief Resolution

The Courage to Grieve: Creative Living, Recovery, and Growth Through Grief, by Judy Tatelbaum (New York: Harper and Row, 1984).

The Grief Recovery Handbook: A Step-by-Step Program for Moving Beyond Loss, by John W. James and Frank Cherry (New York: Harper and Row, 1989).

Helping Children Cope with Separation and Loss, by Claudia L. Jewett (The Harvard Common Press, The Common, Harvard, MA 01451, 1982).

Learned Optimism: The Skill to Conquer Life's Obstacles, Large and Small, by Martin Seligman, Ph.D. (New York: Random House, 1990).

Necessary Losses, by Judith Viorst (New York: Fawcett Books, 1987).

Saying Goodbye to a Baby: Volume I: The Birthparent's Guide to Loss and Grief in Adoption, by Patricia Roles (Washington, DC: Child Welfare League of America, 1989).

When Bad Things Happen to Good People, by Harold S. Kushner (Schocken Books, 201 E. 50th St., New York, NY 10022, 1989).

Conflict Resolution

The Adoption Mediation Training Manual, by Jeanne Etter, M.S., and John Chally, J.D. (Adoption Mediation Seminars, 239 E. 14th Ave., Eugene, OR 97401, 1988).

The Angry Book, by Theodore Isaac Rubin, M.D. (New York: Macmillan, 1970).

The Art of Negotiating, by Gerard I. Nierenberg (New York: Pocket Books, 1989).

The Dance of Anger, by Harriet Goldhor Lerner, Ph.D. (New York: Harper and Row, 1986).

Dr. Weisinger's Anger Workout Book, by Hendrie D. Weisinger, Ed. by Pat Golbitz (New York: Morrow, 1985).

Don't Say Yes When You Want to Say No, by Herbert Fensterheim, Ph.D., and Jean Baer (New York: Dell, 1975).

Getting Together, by Roger Fisher and Scott Brown (New York: Viking Penguin, 1989).

That's Not What I Meant, by Debra Tannen, Ph.D. (New York: Ballantine Books, 1992).

When I Say No, I Feel Guilty, by Manuel J. Smith, Ph.D. (New York: Bantam Books, 1985).

Winning, by David Viscott, M.D. (New York: Pocket Books, 1972).

The Win–Win Negotiator, by Ross R. Reck, Ph.D., and Brian Long, Ph.D. (New York: Pocket Books, 1989).

Relationship Building

Conscious Loving, by Gay Hendricks, Ph.D., and Kathlyn Hendricks, Ph.D. (New York: Bantam Books, 1992).

The Dance of Intimacy, by Harriet Goldhor Lerner, Ph.D. (New York: Harper and Row, 1989).

Love Is a Decision, by Gary Smalley and John Trent, Ph.D., Ed. by Denise Silvestro (Pocket Books, 1993).

Risking, by David Viscott, M.D. (New York: Pocket Books, 1977).
Struggle for Intimacy, by Janet G. Woititz (Health Communications, 3201 S.W. 15th St., Deerfield Beach, FL 33442-8142, 1985).

For information on how a dysfunctional upbringing can interfere with one's ability to build a relationship, consult some of the many excellent resources on recovery, adult children of alcoholics, healing from sexual abuse, etc., available at your local bookstore or library.

Child Development

The Secret Life of the Unborn Child, by Thomas Verny, M.D., and John Kelly (New York: Delacorte, 1982).
Touchpoints: Your Child's Emotional and Behavioral Development, by T. B. Brazelton, M.D. (Reading, MA: Addison-Wesley, 1992).
You and Your Adolescent: A Parents Guide for Ages 10–20, by Laurence Steinberg, Ph.D., and Ann Levine (New York: Harper and Row, 1990).
Your   -Year-Old, by Louis Bates Ames; Ames and Frances Ilg; Ames and Carol C. Haber. This is a series of books that provide readable discussions of each year of a child's growth and development (New York: Delacorte, various years).

Extended Family

Introduction to Adoption for Family and Friends, audiotape by Lois Ruskai Melina (P.O. Box 9362, Moscow, ID 83843).
Parents, Pregnant Teens and the Adoption Option, by Jeanne Warren Lindsay (Morning Glory Press, 6595 San Haraldo Way, Buena Park, CA 90620, 1989).
Supporting an Adoption, by Pat Holmes (Our Child Press, 800 Maple Glen Lane, Wayne, PA 19087-4797, 800/356-9315, 1984).
Understanding: A Guide to Impaired Fertility for Family and Friends, by Patricia Irwin Johnston (Perspectives Press, P.O. Box 90318, Indianapolis, IN 46290-0318, 1983).

Rituals

Adoption: Charms and Rituals for Healing, by Randolph W. Severson (House of Tomorrow Productions, 4209 McKinney Ave., Dallas, TX 75205, 1991).

Bittersweet. . . . Hellogoodbye: A Resource in Planning Farewell Rituals When a Baby Dies, by Sr. Jane Marie Lamb, OSF (Charis Communications, P.O. Box 8351, Belleville, IL 62222, 1989).

A Circle Is Cast: Rounds, Chants, and Songs for Celebration and Ritual, audiotape by Libana (Libana, Inc., P.O. Box 530, Cambridge, MA 02140, 1986).

New Traditions: Redefining Celebrations for Today's Family, by Susan Abel Lieberman (New York: Farrar, Straus, and Giroux, 1991).

Rituals for Our Times, by Evan Imber-Black, Ph.D., and Janine Roberts, Ed.D. (New York: HarperCollins 1992).

Older Child Placements

A Child's Journey Through Placement, by Vera I. Fahlberg, M.D. (Perspectives Press, P.O. Box 90318, Indianapolis, IN 46290-0318, 1991).

from we to just me, by Kristapher Ryan (Freedom to Be Me Seminars, P.O. Box 52057, Winnipeg, Manitoba, R2M 5P9, Canada, 1990).

High Risk: Children Without a Conscience, by Ken Magid and Carole A. McKelvey (New York: Bantam, 1989).

Holding Time, by Martha Welch (New York: Simon and Schuster, 1988).

Parenting With Love and Logic, by Foster Cline, M.D., and Jim Fay (Piñon Press, P.O. Box 35007, Colorado Springs, CO 80935, 1990).

Residential Treatment: A Tapestry of Many Therapies, by Vera I. Fahlberg, M.D. (Perspectives Press, P.O. Box 90318, Indianapolis, IN 46290-0318, 1990).

Who's the Boss, by Gerald Nelson, M.D., and Richard Lewark (Shambhala Press, 6867 Soledad Canyon Rd., Acton, CA 93510, 1985).

Prenatal Drug and Alcohol Exposure

The Broken Cord, by Michael Dorris (New York: Harper and Row, 1989).

Fetal Alcohol Education Program, Boston University School of Medicine, 7 Kent St., Brookline, MA 02146.

National Association for Perinatal Addiction, Research and Education (NAPARE), 200 N. Michigan, 3rd floor, Chicago, IL 60601. 312/541-1272.

Perinatal Wellness Program, 333 E. Superior, Room 400, Chicago, IL 60611. 312/908-0867.

International or Transracial Adoption

Adopting a Child of a Different Race or Ethnic Background, audiotape by Lois Ruskai Melina (P.O. Box 9362, Moscow, ID 83843).

"Are Those Kids Yours?" by Cheri Register (New York: Free Press, 1990).

Donor Insemination, Surrogacy, and Technology-Assisted Conception

Having Your Baby by Donor Insemination, by Elizabeth Noble (Boston: Houghton-Mifflin, 1987).

Lethal Secrets: The Shocking Consequenses and Unsolved Problems of Artificial Insemination, by Annette Baran and Rueben Pannor (New York: Warner Books, 1989).

Children's Literature

Adoption Literature for Children and Young Adults: An Annotated Bibliography, by Susan G. Miles (Greenwood Press, 88 Post Rd. W., Westport, CT 06881, 1991).

"Mommy, Did I Grow in Your Tummy?": Where Some Babies Come From, by Elaine R. Gordon, Ph.D. (E. M. Greenburg Press, 1460 7th St., Santa Monica, CA 90401, 1992).

Tell Me a Real Adoption Story, by Betty Jean Lifton (New York: Knopf, forthcoming 1994).

Several booklets by The Rosen Publishing Group may be helpful to children and adolescents trying to understand a difficult situation with their birth parents. Among the titles are: *Everything You Need to Know When a Parent Doesn't Speak English; Everything You Need to Know When a Parent Is in Jail,* by Stephanie St. Pierre; *Everything You Need to Know About a Drug-Abusing Parent,* by Frances Shuker-Haines. For a complete catalog write: 29 E. 21st St., New York, NY 10010.

Organizations and Referrals

Adoptive Families of America advocates for adoptive families and can refer families to adoption support groups (3333 Hwy. 100 North, Minneapolis, MN 55422, 612/535-4829).

ALMA provides information for adoptees (P.O. Box 154, Washington Bridge Station, New York, NY 10033, 212/581-1568).

American Adoption Congress offers services to adoptees, adoptive parents, and birth parents (P.O. Box 44040, L'Enfant Plaza Station, Washington, DC 20026).

American Association of Open Adoption Agencies can refer families to agencies who practice open adoption (616/947-8110).

Attachment Center at Evergreen is a treatment center for children with attachment disorders (P.O. Box 2764, Evergreen, CO 80439, 303/674-1910).

Attachment Disorder Parents Network is a support group for families of children with attachment disorders (P.O. Box 18475, Boulder, CO 80308, 303/443-1446).

Birthparents Support provides peer support for birth families who are considering an adoption plan or who have placed a child for adoption (3423 Blue Rock, Cincinnati, OH 45239).

Center for Surrogate Parenting facilitates surrogate parenting arrangements, but also provides information about surrogacy (8383 Wilshire Blvd., Suite 750, Beverly Hills, CA 90211, 213/655-1974).

International Concerns Committee for Children has information about international adoption (911 Cypress Dr., Boulder, CO 80303, 303/494-8333).

National Adoption Information Clearinghouse has pamphlets available on specific topics in adoption and can refer families to therapists and other professionals (11426 Rockville Pike, Suite 410, Rockville, MD 20852, 301/231-6512).

National Federation for Open Adoption Education can refer families to facilitators who have completed special training in open adoption (391 Taylor Blvd., Suite 100, Pleasant Hill, CA 94523, 510/827-2229).

References

Introduction

Cooperative Adoption: A Handbook, by Mary Jo Rillera and Sharon Kaplan (Triadoptions Publications, P.O. Box 638, Westminster, CA 92684, 1985).

Preliminary findings of their ongoing study of open adoptions were presented in the talk: "The Research on Open Adoption," by Harold Grotevant and Ruth McRoy, Adoptive Families of America, Inc., Los Angeles, CA, June 26–28, 1992.

Chapter 1

Information on the history of adoption in the United States and other parts of the world was obtained from: *The Adoption Triangle: Sealed or Open Records: How They Affect Adoptees, Birthparents, and Adoptive Parents,* by Arthur D. Sorosky, Annette Baran, and Reuben Pannor (Corona Publishing Co., 1037 S. Alamo, San Antonio, TX 78210, 1989); *Adoption in America Coming of Age,* by Hal Aigner (Paradigm Press, 127 Greenbrae Boardwalk, Greenbrae, CA 94904, 1986); *Not in Our Genes,* by R. C. Lewontin, Steven Rose, and Leon J. Kamin (Pantheon Books, 201 E. 50th Ave., New York, NY 10022, 1984); "Secrecy in Adoption: Its History and Implications for Open Adoption," by Harriet E. Gross, American Sociological Association, Cincinnati, OH, August 27, 1991; *Transactions in Kinship: Adoption and Fosterage in Oceania,* Ed. by Ivan Brady (Honolulu: The University Press of Hawaii, 1976); "Adoption on Kosrae Island: Solidarity and Sterility," by Philip L. Ritter, *Ethnology* 20 (January 1981):45–61.

More about the stages of grief can be found in *Attachment and Loss,* by John Bowlby (New York: Basic Books, 1969, 1973, 1980), and in many of the books by Elisabeth Kübler-Ross, while the subject of grieving for infertility is discussed in *Infertility: A Guide for the Childless Couple,* by Barbara Eck Menning (New York: Prentice Hall, 1988), *The Long-Awaited Stork: Parenting After Infertility,* by Ellen Glazer (Lexington Books, D. C. Heath and Co., 125 Spring St., Lexington, MA 02173, 1990), and *Adopting After*

Infertility, by Patricia Irwin Johnston (Perspectives Press, P.O. Box 90318, Indianapolis, IN 46290-0318, 1992).

There have been many studies of the psychological effects of adoption on birth parents and adoptees. Many of the key studies are included in *The Psychology of Adoption,* by David M. Brodzinsky and Marshall D. Schechter (New York: Oxford University Press, 1990). (For a more complete listing, see Lois Ruskai Melina's *Adoption: An Annotated Bibliography and Guide* [Garland Publishing, 1987]). *Being Adopted: The Lifelong Search for Self,* by David Brodzinsky, Marshall Schechter, and Robin Marantz Henig (New York: Doubleday, 1992), is a highly readable discussion of the issues faced by adoptees—especially those in confidential adoptions. Suzanne Arms's important book, *To Love and Let Go* (New York: Alfred A. Knopf, 1983), describes the effect of adoption on birth mothers. David Kirk's classic reference, *Shared Fate* (Ben Simon Publications, P.O. Box 318, Brentwood Bay, B.C., Canada V0S 1A0, 1983), and Jerome Smith and Franklin I. Miroff's book, *You're Our Child: A Social/Psychological Approach to Adoption* (Madison Books, 4720 Boston Way, Lanhan, MD 20706, 1987), does the same for adoptive parents.

Orphan Voyage, by Jean Paton (New York: Vantage, 1968).

The Search for Anna Fisher, by Florence Fisher (New York: Arthur Fields, 1973).

Dear Birthmother, by Kathleen Silber and Phylis Speedlin (Corona Publishing Co., 1037 S. Alamo, San Antonio, TX 78210, 1983).

Children of Open Adoption, by Kathleen Silber and Patricia Martinez Dorner (Corona Publishing Co., 1037 S. Alamo, San Antonio, TX 78210, 1989).

Chapter 2

Studies of open adoption consulted include: "Research on Open Adoption," a presentation by Marianne Berry on the California Long-Range Adoption Study by Marianne Berry and Richard P. Barth, National Federation for Open Adoption Education, San Antonio, TX, November 1991; *A Study of Open Adoption Placements,* by Mary Iwanek, 14 Emerson St., Petone, New Zealand, 1987; "Levels of Cooperation and Satisfaction in 56 Open Adoptions," by Jeanne Etter, Adoption Teamwork, 85444 Teague Loop, Eugene, OR 97405, unpublished paper (a summary of this can be found in *Child Welfare,* June–July, 1993); "Use of Mediated Agreements in

Adoptions," by Jeanne Etter, Ed. by J. A. Lemmon, *Techniques and Results in Family Mediation, Mediation Quarterly*, No. 22, Winter 1988, pages 83–89; "Open Adoption of Infants: Adoptive Parents' Perceptions of Advantages and Disadvantages," by Deborah H. Siegel, *Social Work* 38 (issue 1, January 1993):15–23; preliminary findings of their ongoing study into open adoptions were presented in the talk: "The Research on Open Adoption," by Harold Grotevant and Ruth McRoy, Adoptive Families of America, Inc., Los Angeles, CA, June 26–28, 1992.

The effect of open adoption on birth mothers' grief is discussed in: "The Relation of Learned Helplessness, Social Support, and Avoidance of Grief and Depression in Women Who Have Placed an Infant for Adoption," by Anne Brodzinsky, unpublished dissertation, New York University, 1992; "Biological Mothers' Grief: The Postadoptive Experience in Open Versus Confidential Adoption," by Terril L. Blanton and Jeanne Deschner, *Child Welfare* LXIX (issue 6, November–December):525–535, 1990.

The advantages and disadvantages of open adoption are discussed in: "Open Adoption: Allowing Adopted Children to 'Stay in Touch' with Blood Relatives," by Carol Amadio and Stuart L. Deutsch, *The Journal of Family Law* 22:59–93, 1983–84; "Adolescent Mothers' Beliefs About Open Adoption," by Richard P. Barth, *Social Casework: The Journal of Contemporary Social Work*, June 1987, pp. 323–331; "The Case for Confidential Adoption," by A. Dean Byrd, *Public Welfare,* Fall 1988, pp. 20–23; "Meeting the Needs of the Adoption Triangle Through Open Adoption: The Adoptive Parent," by Cathy Chapman, O.P., M.A., Patricia Dorner, M.A., Kathy Silber, M.S.W., and Terry S. Winterberg, M.S.W., *Child and Adolescent Social Work* 4 (issue 1, Spring 1987):3–12; "Meeting the Needs of the Adoption Triangle Through Open Adoption: The Adoptee," by Cathy Chapman, O.P., M.A., Patricia Dorner, M.A., Kathy Silber, M.S.W., and Terry S. Winterberg, M.S.W., *Child and Adolescent Social Work* 4 (issue 2, Summer 1987):78–91; "The Debate Over Open Adoption: How People Feel About Open Adoption Seems to Depend on Their Point of View," by Deborah Churchman, *Public Welfare,* Spring 1986, pp. 11–14; "Open Adoption: A Psychodynamic Analysis," unpublished paper by Deborah Silverstein (Focus Counseling, 186½ Hampshire St., Cambridge, MA 02139, 1990); "Attitudes of Prospective Adoptive Parents Towards Agency Adoption Practices, Particularly Open Adoption: Preliminary Empirical Findings," unpublished paper by Jerome Smith, Ph.D., Indiana University School of Social Work; "The Case for Open Adoption," by Kenneth W. Watson, *Public Welfare,* Fall 1988, pp. 24–28.

When Bonding Fails: Clinical Assessment of High-Risk Families, by Frank Bolton, Jr. (Beverly Hills, CA: Sage Publications, 1983).

The concept of "boundaries" is discussed by Pia Mellody in her tapes (P.O. Box 1739, Wickenburg, AZ 85358, 800/626-6779).

Chapter 4

James Gritter, personal communication, 1992.

"Levels of Cooperation and Satisfaction in 56 Open Adoptions," by Jeanne Etter, Adoption Teamwork, 85444 Teague Loop, Eugene, OR 97405, unpublished paper.

Chapter 5

"Use of Mediated Agreements in Adoptions," by Jeanne Etter, Ed. by J. A. Lemmon, *Techniques and Results in Family Mediation, Mediation Quarterly,* No. 22, Winter 1988, pp. 83–89.

Chapter 6

Marshall Schechter was quoted in "Child Needs to Know Birth Story," by Lois R. Melina, *Adopted Child* newsletter, P.O. Box 9362, Moscow, ID 83843, September 1982.

Information about adoptive mothers who breastfeed was obtained from: "Breastfeeding: Goal Is Emotional Not Nutritional Benefit," by Lois Ruskai Melina, *Adopted Child* newsletter, March 1983. "Induced Lactation: A Study of Adoptive Nursing by 240 Women," by Kathleen G. Auerbach and Jimmie Lynne Avery, *American Journal of Diseases of Children* 135 (April 1981):340–343. *Nursing Your Adopted Baby,* by Kathryn Anderson (LaLeche League International, 9616 Minneapolis Ave., Franklin Park, IL 60131, 1983). "Protein Values of Milk Samples from Mothers Without Biologic Pregnancies," by Ronald Kleinman, Linda Jacobson, Elizabeth Hormann, and W. Allan Walker, *Journal of Pediatrics* 97 (October 1980):612–615.

Kathleen Silber, personal communication, 1992.

Information about rituals was obtained from *Rituals for Our Times,* by Evan Imber-Black, Ph.D., and Janine Roberts, Ed.D. (New York: HarperCollins, 1992). *Rituals in Psychotherapy: Transition and Continuity,* by Onno van der Hart, trans. Angie Pleit-Kuiper (Irving Publishers, Inc., 551 Fifth Ave., New York, NY 10017, 1983). *The Rites of Passage,* by A. van Gennep, English edition (London: Routledge and Kegan Paul, 1960). *Rituals in Families and Family Therapy,* ed. by Evan Imber-Black (New York: W. W. Norton, 1988). More material on rituals can be found in the list of Resources.

Chapter 7

"Helping Children Cope with Change," by Justin Call, *Early Child Development and Care* 3 (January 1974):229–247.

Chapter 8

"Adopting Children Affected by Drugs, Alcohol," by Lois R. Melina, *Adopted Child* newsletter, P.O. Box 9362, Moscow, ID 83843, November 1988.

The concept of "entitlement" was first developed in *How They Fared in Adoption: A Follow-up Study,* by Benson Jaffee and David Fanshel (New York: Columbia University Press, 1970). Jerome Smith and Franklin I. Miroff also discuss the issue of entitlement in their book, *You're Our Child: A Social/Psychological Approach to Adoption* (Madison Books, 4720 Boston Way, Lanhan, MD 20706, 1987). Ellen Roseman-Curtis has promoted a distinction between entitlement and ownership in her presentations at adoption conferences.

"Authenticity and Disclosure of the Information Preserve: The Case of Adoptive Parenthood," by Charlene E. Miall, *Qualitative Sociology,* Fall 1989, pp. 279–302.

Chapter 9

"Intervention Techniques for Difficult Open Adoption Cases," by Leslie Foge, Gail Mosconi, and Susan Dupuis. National Federation for Open Adoption Education, November 5–6, 1992, in San Francisco, CA.

Chapter 10

Randolph W. Severson, personal communication, 1993.

Chapter 11

"Lifelong Responsibilities of Birthparents, Adoptive Parents, and Adoptees," by Reuben Pannor and Annette Baran, unpublished paper.

Vera Fahlberg, M.D., Workshop presentation, March 26-27, 1993, Seattle, WA.

Chapter 12

Making Sense of Adoption, by Lois R. Melina (New York: Harper and Row, 1989).

Being Adopted: The Lifelong Search for Self, by David M. Brodzinsky, Ph.D., Marshall Schechter, M.D., and Robin Marantz Henig (New York: Doubleday, 1992).

Helping Children Cope with Separation and Loss, by Claudia L. Jewett (Harvard, MA: Harvard Common Press, 1982).

Mary Martin Mason contributed significantly to our understanding of the ways that interactions between adoptive parents, birth parents, and adoptees can be influenced by the developmental passages adults experience. Mason, who has experienced open adoption both as an adoptee and as an adoptive parent and has lectured extensively on infertility and adoption, presented a workshop, "Life Passages for Triad Members in Open Adoption: Examining the Long-Term Picture," National Federation for Open Adoption Education, November 5–6, 1992, San Francisco, CA.

Deborah Silverstein (Newport Beach, California), personal communication, 1992.

"The Family Romance Fantasies of Adopted Children," by Herbert Weider, *Psychoanalytic Quarterly* 46 (April 1977), pp. 185–200.

"Adoption Predicts Psychiatric Treatment Resistances in Hospitalized Adolescents," by Carol S. Fullerton, M.A., Wells Goodrich, M.D., and Linda Beth Berman. *Journal of the American Academy of Child Psychiatry* 25(4):542–551, 1986.

"Observations on Adopted Children," by Marshall Schechter, *Archives of General Psychiatry* 3:21–32, 1960.

"Thoughts Regarding the Etiology of Psychological Difficulties in Adopted Children," by P. W. Toussieng, *Child Welfare* 41:59–71, 1962.

Chapter 13

Joyce Maguire Pavao has discussed the concept of the "family orchard" at several conferences.

Chapter 14

Randolph W. Severson, personal communication, 1993.

Chapter 15

Cheryl Reber, L.S.W., personal communication, 1993.

Hillary Hanafin, Ph.D., personal communication, 1992.

Index

388 : Index

Postadoption blues, 150
Power struggle, 20, 124, 170–72
Preadoption agreement, 90–91, 210–12
Preadoption counseling, 139
Preparation
    adoptive parents, 95–99, 126–28,
        321–23
    anticipated feelings, 92
    birth parents, 112, 320–21
    last-minute adoptions, 138
    significance of, 211
Preplacement period, 223
Preschool through kindergarten age
    adoption story, 251–52
    information for, 249–51
Privacy rights, 300
Problem-solving skills, 32
Protest, in grief process, 28–29

Readiness
    adoptive parents, 42–43, 61–62
    birth parents, 41–42, 62–63,
        99–101
    caution signs, 61–63
    See also Preparation
Reber, Cheryl, L.S.W., 333, 336
Reclaiming
    adoptive parents, response to,
        308–9, 326
    birth family, role of, 323–24
    birth parents' feelings, 319–20
    blocking, 310–11
    consideration of, 169, 307–10
    emotional reactions, adoptive
        parents, 313–17
    extended adopted family and,
        324–25
    fears regarding, 150
    influences on, 172
    last-minute adoptions and, 139–40
    legal action for, 91
    openness, role of, 318
    preparations, 320–25
    staying in touch, 325–27
    transition and, 311–13

Reconsideration, 52, 58
Recovery, 30
Rejection
    dealing with, 6, 8
    fear of, 120, 268, 271
    reduction of, 333
Relationship(s)
    between adoptive and birth fathers,
        71–72
    between adoptive and birth mothers,
        65–66, 68
    between adoptive mother and birth
        grandmother, 73
    building, 229
    challenges, 231–40
    child and birth parents, 226–30
    close, 197
    compatible but distant, 186–88
    conflictual, 191–93
    difficult, 75–81
    dissolution of, 58–59, 61, 74, 88–89
    enhancing, 230
    enmeshed, 195
    evaluation of, 88–89
    familiarity in, 195–97
    formation of. See Relationship
        formation
    maintaining, 193, 226
    uncomfortable, 188–91
    unhealthy, 193–95
Relationship formation
    gradual, 18
    learning about each other, 59–61
    starting point, 48
    strategies for, 30–32
    uniqueness of, 20
Relative adoption
    adoption plan and, 342–43
    benefits of, 52, 339
    dual relationships, 340–42
    family secrets, 344–45
    loss, feelings of, 343–44
Relocation, 209
Resentment, 123, 170
Resolution, in grief process, 30
Resolve, Inc., 7–8